The Chosen Few

THE PRINCETON ECONOMIC HISTORY
OF THE WESTERN WORLD

Joel Mokyr, Series Editor

A list of titles in this series appears at the back of the book

The Chosen Few

How Education Shaped Jewish History, 70–1492

Maristella Botticini and Zvi Eckstein

PRINCETON UNIVERSITY PRESS

PRINCETON AND OXFORD

Copyright © 2012 by Princeton University Press

Published by Princeton University Press, 41 William Street, Princeton, New Jersey 08540
In the United Kingdom: Princeton University Press, 6 Oxford Street, Woodstock,
Oxfordshire OX20 1TW

press.princeton.edu

Jacket Art: Detail of *Passover*, Arthur Szyk (1894–1951). Tempera and ink on paper. New
Canaan, Connecticut, 1948. Collection of Yeshiva University Museum (1970.006). Gift of
Charles Frost.

Fifth printing, and first paperback printing, 2014

Paperback ISBN 978-0-691-16351-2

The Library of Congress has cataloged the cloth edition of this book as follows

Botticini, Maristella.
    The chosen few : how education shaped Jewish history, 70-1492 / Maristella Botticini
and Zvi Eckstein.
        p. cm. — (The Princeton economic history of the Western world)
    Includes bibliographical references and index.
    ISBN 978-0-691-14487-0 (alk. paper)
    1. Jews—History—To 1500. 2. Judaism—History—To 1500. 3. Jews—Economic
conditions—To 1500. I. Eckstein, Zvi. II. Title.
    DS117.B68 2012
    909'.04924—dc23   2012001314

British Library Cataloging-in-Publication Data is available

Publication of this book has been aided by

This book has been composed in Verdigris MVB Pro Text

Printed on acid-free paper. ∞

Printed in the United States of America

10 9 8 7 6 5

Contents

Illustrations

Tables

Preface

IMAGINE TWO ECONOMISTS TRAVELING BACK IN TIME AND ARRIVING IN the town of Sepphoris, in the Galilee, in the year 200. Upon entering the synagogue, they see a nine-year-old Jewish boy—the son of a farmer—reading a portion of the Torah in front of the local community. The economists, who know some stylized facts about the occupational structure and demography of the Jewish people today, wonder whether there might be a connection between what they saw in their journey back in time and the subsequent economic and demographic history of the Jews.

This research project has been a twelve-year long journey of studying and learning that began one day over a lunch conversation in the cafeteria of Boston University, during which we put ourselves in the shoes of the economist time travelers. We never imagined that what we thought was an interesting question for an article would develop into more than a decade of work that involved sifting through an immense body of literature, meeting with scholars and experts on Judaism and Jewish history, visiting ancient synagogues in the Galilee, thinking about and discussing how to interpret the key facts and puzzles of the history of the Jewish people through the lens of economic theory, and ultimately writing a book. The book relies on two pillars of scholarship: the remarkable body of literature that generations of historians and scholars of Judaism have produced and the thinking that economists adopt when studying a wide array of topics, including the choice of occupation, the decision to invest in education, the impact a social norm may have on the way individuals make choices and communities organize themselves, and the choice of a religion.

During this journey of learning, we accumulated many debts of gratitude to colleagues, scholars, and institutions. Joel Mokyr, at Northwestern University, is the person to whom we owe the most. Since the very beginning, he encouraged us with his boundless enthusiasm and provided valuable suggestions and deeply thoughtful comments. Joel was extremely generous in reading our manuscript several times and contributing in a major way to shaping the book. He was also pivotal in organizing a conference at Tel Aviv University in December 2010 in which a group of scholars from various fields read our manuscript and provided us with invaluable feedback.

At various stages of this project, our research and manuscript greatly benefited from the generous help and very useful suggestions of Mark

Cohen, Moshe Gil, Claudia Goldin, Rachel McCleary, Aharon Oppenheimer, Peter Temin, and Michael Toch. In particular, Michael Toch's forthcoming book on the economic history of the Jews in medieval Europe is an important companion to the arguments we put forth in chapters 2, 7, and 8.

For their insightful comments, we are extremely grateful to a long list of scholars, including Ran Abramitsky, Robert Barro, Albert Baumgarten, Menahem Ben-Sasson, Benni Bental, Eli Berman, Batsheva Bonné-Tamir, Robert Brody, Barry Chiswick, Carmel Chiswick, Sergio DellaPergola, Mauricio Drelichman, Jonathan Eaton, Stanley Engerman, Stefano Fenoaltea, Israel Finkelstein, Simha Goldin, Avner Greif, Nachum Gross, Elhanan Helpman, Philip Hoffman, Edi Karni, Aryeh Kasher, Steven Katz, Ephraim Kleiman, Timur Kuran, Larry Iannaccone, Kevin Lang, Uzi Leibner, Bernard Lewis, Ora Limor, Erzo Luttmer, Michael Manove, Robert Margo, Jacob Metzer, Jacob Neusner, Roberto Perotti, Yossef Rapoport, Zeev Safrai, Kenneth Sokoloff, Yannay Spitzer, Nathan Sussman, Manuel Trajtenberg, Yoram Weiss, and Jeffrey Williamson. We also thank many colleagues who provided us with helpful suggestions when we presented our research at seminars and conferences.

We worked very hard to sift through the enormous body of literature related to the topic of our book in order to make sure that we incorporated the most relevant works. Despite our lengthy bibliography, it was impossible to cite all the books and articles written on the fifteen centuries of Jewish history covered in our book. Of the hundreds of scholarly books and articles we read, the works of two scholars—Salo Baron, for the breadth of his scholarship, and Shelomo Dov Goitein, for his masterly work on the Cairo Geniza documents—served as our polar stars in this project. In surveying the enormous body of historical literature, Dalit Engelhardt, Dan Goldenberg, Polina Kroik, Eliezer Moav, Claudia Rei, and Maria Cecilia Vieira da Silva provided us with outstanding research assistance.

We owe a huge debt of gratitude to several institutions and organizations that provided financial support to our research over the years. In particular, we thank the National Science Foundation (Grant 0318364), the Israel Science Foundation (Grant 815-04), Boston University (seed grant), the Collegio Carlo Alberto in Torino (seed grant), Bocconi University (funding for copyediting the manuscript), and, for Botticini, a John M. Olin Junior Faculty fellowship and an Alfred P. Sloan research fellowship. The data presented, the statements made, and the views expressed in this book are our own responsibility.

We also gratefully acknowledge the logistic support and hospitality of the economics departments of Bocconi University, Boston University, Tel Aviv University, the University of Minnesota, and the University of

Torino, as well as the Bank of Israel, the Collegio Carlo Alberto, and the Minneapolis Federal Reserve. We are extremely grateful to the Pinhas Sapir Center for Development at Tel Aviv University for funding and hosting the conference organized by Joel Mokyr in December 2010.

At Princeton University Press, we cannot thank Peter Dougherty and Seth Ditchik enough for being truly wonderful and supportive editors and for their patience in waiting for our manuscript through all these years. We thank Janie Y. Chan, Kathleen Cioffi, and Dimitri Karetnikov for their outstanding help in the production stage. We also thank three anonymous referees for their very insightful comments and constructive criticism.

We are immensely grateful to Barbara Karni, who provided us with editorial advice and help well beyond the standard copyediting task. Barbara offered an endless list of deep and substantial suggestions on the entire manuscript, helped us shape it in a much better way, and improved our prose. We are also extremely indebted to Molan Goldstein for her thoughtful and painstaking editing of the manuscript. By checking an enormous number of details and offering plenty of excellent suggestions, Molan greatly helped in making the manuscript accurate and polished. We thank Richard Comfort for his superb help in preparing the index.

This long list of debts ends with the personal ones. In the twelve years during which we worked so hard writing the book, our spouses, Massimo and Dassie, patiently listened to the two of us arguing and discussing for hours and hours during our many meetings in Israel, Italy, and the United States. They have been the major supporters of this book, in ways both visible and invisible. We cannot thank them enough.

Milan and Tel Aviv, April 2012

Introduction

THIS BOOK IS A JOURNEY BACK IN TIME, EMBARKED UPON IN ORDER TO uncover why the Jews became the people they did. The journey begins in Jerusalem in Judea and in Sepphoris and Tiberias in Galilee during the first and second centuries. It takes us to Babylon in Mesopotamia in the fifth and sixth centuries; to Baghdad, Cairo, Córdoba, and Palermo, the new urban centers of the Middle East and the Mediterranean, in the ninth and tenth centuries; to Tudela in Spain and Mangalore in India in the late twelfth century; and back to Baghdad in the 1250s before ending in Seville in 1492.

The purpose of this passage through 1,500 years of Jewish history is to ask and answer a variety of questions. Why are there so few Jewish farmers? Why are the Jews an urban population of traders, entrepreneurs, bankers, financiers, lawyers, physicians, and scholars? When and why did these occupational and residential patterns become the distinctive features of the Jews? Why did the Jewish population shrink from 5–5.5 million at the time of Jesus to 1–1.2 million in the days of Muhammad? Why did the number of Jews reach its lowest level (less than 1 million) on the eve of the mass expulsion from the Iberian Peninsula in 1492–97? Why have the Jewish people experienced one of the most scattered diasporas in world history, living as a minority in cities and towns around the globe for millennia? When, how, and why did the Jews become "the chosen few"?[1]

Most people think they know the answers to these questions. Asked to explain these phenomena, an Israeli Jew would respond: "We are not farmers because our ancestors in the Middle Ages were prohibited from owning land. We were a diaspora population for almost 2,000 years after the destruction of the Second Temple in Jerusalem.[2] We were persecuted in and expelled from our country and many others. Our numbers dwindled through the centuries because our ancestors were repeatedly massacred."

A European would argue that in medieval Europe, Christians were banned from lending money at interest, and Jews were excluded from

---

[1] Some of these questions have also attracted the interest of leading social scientists, including Karl Marx ([1844] 2007), Werner Sombart ([1911] 1913), Max Weber ([1917] 1952), Thorstein Veblen (1919), and Simon Kuznets (1960, 1972).

[2] Chapters 1 and 3 explain the meaning of "First Temple," "Second Temple," "Written Torah," "Oral Torah," and other main terms used in Judaism.

membership in craft and merchant guilds. Given these restrictions, over time the Jews became a population of moneylenders, bankers, and financiers. Like the Israeli respondent, the European would argue that persecutions, expulsions, and massacres accounted for the Jews' dispersal and declining number.

An economist would maintain that like other religious and ethnic minorities, the Jews were repeatedly persecuted, reducing their incentive to invest in physical capital (e.g., land). As a result, since mobility had a high value for them, they invested in human capital, which is easily portable and not subject to the risk of expropriation. The Jews' transition into urban and skilled occupations was the outcome of this sequence of events, set in motion by their status as a persecuted religious minority.

The answers from the three groups of people are remarkably similar. They are also consistent with most of the explanations in the literature. But are they correct?

Analyzed from the point of view of an economist, the historical record suggests that none of these long-held views is valid. The true explanation, we suggest, lies elsewhere. As we show in the chapters that follow, these distinctive characteristics of the Jewish people were the outcome of a profound transformation of the Jewish religion after the destruction of the Second Temple in 70 CE.[3] This change shifted the religious leadership within the Jewish community and transformed Judaism from a cult based on ritual sacrifices in the temple to a religion whose main norm required every Jewish man to read and to study the Torah in Hebrew and to send his sons from the age of six or seven to primary school or synagogue to learn to do so.

The implementation of this new religious norm during the Talmud era (third to sixth century), coupled with the development of institutions fostering contract enforcement, determined three major patterns in Jewish history:

- the growth and spread of literacy among the predominantly rural Jewish population, as well as a slow but significant process of conversion out of Judaism, which caused a significant drop in the Jewish population during the first half of the first millennium
- a comparative advantage in urban skilled occupations (e.g., crafts, trade, and moneylending), which literate Jews chose to enter when urbanization and the development of a commercial economy provided them with the opportunity to earn pecuniary returns on their investment in literacy and education

[3]Throughout the book, we use BCE after all dates before the year 1. We use CE only for dates in the first century. Thus, for example, "the tenth century" means "the tenth century CE."

- the voluntary diaspora of the Jews in search of worldwide opportunities in crafts, trade, commerce, moneylending, banking, finance, and medicine

The book is organized as follows.[4] We start our journey in chapter 1 by describing how many Jews there were, where they lived, and how they earned their living from the time of the destruction of the Second Temple to the mass expulsion of the Jews from the Iberian Peninsula. We consider three subperiods, each marked by a "historical accident" (that is, an exogenous event):

- the destruction of the Second Temple by the Roman army during the Great Jewish Revolt in 66–70 CE
- the establishment of the Muslim Empire under the Umayyad and Abbasid caliphates during the seventh and eighth centuries, with the concomitant urbanization and growth of a commercial economy over a vast territory
- the Mongol invasions that ravaged Mesopotamia and Persia and contributed to the demise of the urban and commercial Abbasid Empire during the thirteenth century

These exogenous events interacted with the internal dynamics of the Jewish religion to determine the unique demographic and economic traits of the Jews before 1500.

During the six centuries between the time of Jesus and the time of Muhammad, the number of Jews declined precipitously, from 5–5.5 million in the early first century to 1–1.2 million in the early seventh century. War-related massacres and general population decline account for only about half of this drop. During the first century, the largest Jewish community (about 2.5 million people) dwelled in the Land of Israel (*Eretz Israel* in Hebrew, as mentioned in biblical sources).[5] Six centuries later, the

---

[4]To avoid repetition, we do not add footnotes with detailed references in this introductory chapter, as we supply them in the chapters that follow.

[5]Geographically speaking, the Land of Israel refers roughly to the area bounded by the Mediterranean Sea, the Jordan River, the Arabian Desert, and the Red Sea. Throughout the book, the term "Land of Israel" does *not* refer to the current State of Israel, which was established in 1948. Rather, it designates the land that, according to the Bible, was promised as an inheritance to the Israelite tribes. Different passages in the Bible refer to a variety of geographical boundaries when referring to Eretz Israel. By the end of the Second Temple period (first century BCE–first century CE), the term became fixed and its usage widespread among the Jewish people. The name "Palestine" referring to the same region was originally an adjective derived from Philistia. The Greek historian Herodotus first mentioned it as "the Philistine Syria." After crushing the Bar Kokhba revolt in 135, the Roman emperor Hadrian applied the term "Syria Palaestina" to the area, with the goal of eradicating the name Judea—the southern region in the Land of Israel. From Byzantine times, Palestine became the name of Eretz Israel in non-Jewish languages. See Brawer (2007) for a detailed discussion of the biblical meaning and historical origins of the term "Eretz Israel."

center of Jewish life had moved to Mesopotamia (and, to a lesser extent, Persia), where roughly 75 percent of world Jewry lived. Throughout these six centuries, farming was the occupation of the vast majority of the world population. Like almost everyone else, most Jews earned their living from agriculture, as farmers, sharecroppers, fixed-rent tenants, or wage laborers.

In the two centuries after the death of Muhammad in 632, the Muslim Umayyad and, later, Abbasid caliphs conquered many lands and established a vast empire stretching from the Iberian Peninsula to India, with a common language (Arabic), religion (Islam), laws, and institutions. Concomitant with the ascent of this empire, agricultural productivity grew, new industries developed as the outcome of technological progress in a variety of sectors, local trade and long-distance commerce greatly expanded, and new cities and towns developed in Mesopotamia and Persia and, later, in North Africa, Syria, the Iberian Peninsula, and Sicily. These changes vastly increased the demand for skilled occupations in the newly established urban centers and opened new destinations of trade and commerce from the Iberian Peninsula to India.

How did these events affect world Jewry? Between 750 and 900, almost all the Jews in Mesopotamia and Persia—nearly 75 percent of world Jewry—left agriculture, moved to the cities and towns of the newly established Abbasid Empire, and entered myriad skilled occupations. Having abandoned agriculture as their main occupation, many of these Jews began migrating to Yemen, Syria, Egypt, and the Maghreb. The migrations of Jews in search of business opportunities also reached Christian Europe. Migrations of Jews within and from the lands of the Byzantine Empire, which included southern Italy, may have set the foundations, via Italy, for much of European Jewry. Similarly, Jews from Egypt and the Maghreb settled in the Iberian Peninsula and, later, in Sicily and parts of southern Italy.

By the mid-twelfth century, when the Jewish traveler Benjamin of Tudela ventured on his long journey from the Iberian Peninsula to the Middle East and recorded the Jewish communities he visited or heard of, Jews could be found in almost all locations from Tudela in Spain to Mangalore in India. By then, their transition into urban skilled occupations was complete. Their specialization into these occupations remains their distinctive feature until today.

Beginning in 1219, the Mongols invaded northern Persia and Armenia, bringing devastation. Their conquest of Persia and Mesopotamia continued in the next three decades, causing urban centers and trade to collapse and taking a heavy toll on the population. The final blow to the Abbasid Empire came in 1258 when the Mongol army demolished Baghdad. In the aftermath of the Mongol Conquest, the economy in Mesopotamia and Persia returned to a subsistence farming and nomadic pastoral stage.

Throughout the two centuries following the Mongol shock, the number of Jews fell to its lowest level since the first century. By 1450 more than half of the world's 1 million Jews lived in Christian Europe. During the Middle Ages, the Jews in the Iberian Peninsula, Sicily, and southern Italy remained engaged in a wide variety of urban occupations. In contrast, the Jews in England, France, Germany, and northern and central Italy became specialized in moneylending. While the Jews in the Middle East were facing the consequences of the Mongol invasions, European Jews were facing increasing restrictions and persecutions, which culminated in the mass expulsions of the Jews from England (1290), France (1306, 1321–22, 1394), Spain (1492), Sicily (1492–93), and Portugal (1496–97) and smaller ones in parts of Italy and localities in the Holy Roman Empire.

In chapter 2 we examine the arguments set forth to explain why the Jews became a population of skilled craftsmen, traders, bankers, and physicians and why they created a worldwide urban diaspora. These arguments are grouped into two main categories: ones that highlight exogenous factors (discrimination, restrictions, persecutions, massacres) and ones that emphasize endogenous choices (voluntary self-segregation in order to maintain religious rites, voluntary migration to cities to preserve group identity). By relying on the facts presented in chapter 1, we show that these theories are not consistent with the historical evidence: none of these arguments can explain why the Jews voluntarily left farming or voluntarily became a diaspora population.

We then present our thesis, that in a world populated by illiterate people—as the world of the first millennium was—the ability to read and write contracts, business letters, and account books using a common alphabet gave the Jews a comparative advantage over other people. The Jews also developed a uniform code of law (the Talmud) and a set of institutions (rabbinic courts, the responsa) that fostered contract enforcement, networking, and arbitrage across distant locations. High levels of literacy and the existence of contract-enforcement institutions became the levers of the Jewish people.

Why did the Jews become more literate and educated than the rest of the population during the first millennium? In chapter 3 we describe the well-documented shift of the religious norm that transformed the Jews into the People of the Book. During the first millennium BCE, the Temple in Jerusalem and the Written Torah were the two pillars of Judaism. Temple service and ritual sacrifices performed by an elite of high priests were common features of all religions. Judaism was the only monotheistic faith based on a written text.

During the first century BCE, some Jewish scholars and religious leaders promoted the establishment of free secondary schools. A century later, they issued a religious ordinance requiring all Jewish fathers to send their sons from the age of six or seven to primary school to learn to read and study the Torah in Hebrew. Throughout the first millennium, no people other than the Jews had a norm requiring fathers to educate their sons.

With the destruction of the Second Temple, the Jewish religion permanently lost one of its two pillars (the Temple) and set out on a unique trajectory. Scholars and rabbis, the new religious leaders in the aftermath of the first Jewish-Roman war, replaced temple service and ritual sacrifices with the study of the Torah in the synagogue, the new focal institution of Judaism. Its core function was to provide religious instruction to both children and adults. Being a devout Jew became identified with reading and studying the Torah and sending one's children to school to learn to do so. During the next century, the rabbis and scholars in the academies in the Galilee interpreted the Written Torah, discussed religious norms as well as social and economic matters pertaining to daily life, and organized the body of Oral Law accumulated through the centuries. In about 200, Rabbi Judah haNasi completed this work by redacting the six volumes of the Mishna, which with its subsequent development, the Talmud, became the canon of law for the whole of world Jewry. Under the leadership of the scholars in the academies, illiterate people came to be considered outcasts.

The implementation of the religious norm centered on reading and studying the Torah generated potential benefits and costs for the Jews living at the time of Rabbi Judah haNasi and his fellow scholars. What are the implications of the implementation of the new religious norm for the behavior of Jews during the first half of the first millennium? To answer this question, in chapter 4 we present an economic theory that describes the choices regarding religious affiliation and the investment in children's literacy and education in a world populated by Jewish and non-Jewish farmers, like the Land of Israel at the beginning of the first millennium. To explain the rationale behind our theory, we put ourselves in the shoes of the Jewish farmers living at that time in order to understand their economic and religious choices under the new religious norm imposed by rabbinic Judaism.

Our theory yields two main implications. First, because individuals differ in religious preferences, skills, costs of education, and earnings, some Jewish farmers invest in their children's religious literacy whereas others do not. Second, Jewish farmers who find it too costly to obey the norms of Judaism, including the costly norm requiring them to send their sons to school, convert to other religions. If the economy remains mainly agrarian, literate people cannot find urban and skilled occupations in which their investment in literacy and education yields positive economic returns. As a result, the Jewish population keeps shrinking and becoming more literate. In the long run, Judaism cannot survive in a subsistence farming economy because of the process of conversions.

In chapter 5 we show that these implications of our theory are consistent with what happened to the Jewish people during the five centuries following the destruction of the Second Temple. It is during the Talmud era that the Jews became the "chosen few"—a small population of literate people.

An impressive body of evidence from both the Talmud and archaeological discoveries indicates that during the Talmudic period, Jews in the Land of Israel and Mesopotamia—the two main centers of Jewish life—began obeying the religious obligation to educate their sons. A larger and larger proportion of Jewish farmers sent their sons to the primary schools located in or near synagogues. Words such as "teacher's salary," "duties of teachers," "pupils," "length of the school day," "schools," "books," and "education tax" filled pages and pages of debates and rulings contained in the Talmud. No other ancient civilization had a similar body of discussions related to the communal organization of a primary education system. The Jews who decided not to obey the religious norm regarding children's literacy and education became outcasts within Jewish communities.

As for conversions, a variety of literary and archaeological sources document that many Jewish farmers in the Land of Israel, Mesopotamia, Egypt, Syria, Asia Minor, the Balkans, and western Europe converted to Christianity during the Talmud era. By embracing Christianity, Jews who converted still maintained their core belief in the existence of one God and the pillar of the Written Torah but were no longer obliged to obey the religious laws and tenets of Judaism, including the costly norm requiring fathers to educate their sons. This wave of voluntary conversions during the Talmudic period, together with war-related massacres and general population decline, caused the near disappearance of the Jewish populations of the Land of Israel, Egypt, Syria, Asia Minor, the Balkans, and western Europe by 600. The only Jewish community that survived and almost maintained its size was the one in Mesopotamia, which became the new religious and economic center of world Jewry.

One could argue that if, after the implementation of the religious norm requiring fathers to send their sons to primary school, children became more expensive, some families might have decided to have fewer children in order to be able to obey the religious norm. To the best of our knowledge, there is no historical evidence showing that Jewish households reduced their fertility rates following the transformation of Judaism into a literate religion.

Although sending children to school to learn to read and study the Torah was a sacrifice with no economic returns in the agrarian economies in which the Jews lived, during the Talmud era a proportion of Jewish farmers did not convert, obeyed this norm of their religion, and invested in their children's literacy. Over time, what happened to the literate Jewish farmers? In chapter 6 we show that they abandoned farming and became small, urban populations of skilled craftsmen, shopkeepers, traders, money changers, moneylenders, scholars, and physicians. The establishment of the Muslim caliphates during the seventh and eighth centuries, and the concomitant vast urbanization and growth of manufacture and trade in the Middle East, acted as a catalyst for the massive transition of the Jews from farming to crafts and trade.

The literacy of the Jewish people, coupled with a set of contract-enforcement institutions developed during the five centuries after the destruction of the Second Temple, gave the Jews a comparative advantage in occupations such as crafts, trade, and moneylending—occupations that benefited from literacy, contract-enforcement mechanisms, and networking. Once the Jews were engaged in these occupations, they rarely converted, which is consistent with the fact that the Jewish population grew slightly from the seventh to the twelfth century.

In chapter 7 we show that once the Jews became literate, urban, and engaged in skilled occupations, they began migrating within the vast territory under Muslim rule, stretching from the Iberian Peninsula to India during the eighth through the twelfth century, and from the Byzantine Empire to western Europe via Italy and within western Europe in the ninth through the thirteenth century. In early medieval Europe, the revival of trade concomitant with the Commercial Revolution and the growth of an urban and commercial economy paralleled the vast urbanization and the growth of trade that had occurred in the Umayyad and Abbasid caliphates four to five centuries earlier. The Jewish Diaspora during the early Middle Ages was mainly the outcome of literate Jewish craftsmen, shopkeepers, traders, scholars, teachers, physicians, and moneylenders migrating in search of business opportunities to reap returns on their investment in literacy and education.

Already during the twelfth and thirteenth centuries, moneylending was the occupation par excellence of the Jews in England, France, and Germany and one of the main professions of the Jews in the Iberian Peninsula, Italy, and other locations in western Europe. Why? A popular view contends that both their exclusion from craft and merchant guilds and usury bans on Christians segregated European Jews into moneylending during the Middle Ages. In chapter 8 we show that this argument is untenable. Based on the historical information and the economic theory we present in earlier chapters, we advance an alternative explanation that is consistent with the salient features that mark the history of the Jews: the Jews in medieval Europe voluntarily entered and later specialized in moneylending because they had the key assets for being successful players in credit markets: capital, networking, literacy and numeracy, and contract-enforcement institutions.

Given the comparative advantages of the Jews relative to the local populations in high-earning professions, why did the size of the world's Jewish population reach its nadir by the end of the fifteenth century? Suppose, as a thought experiment, that a negative shock (e.g., a war or a plague) destroys the urban and commercial economy, returning it to a rural and pastoral stage, in which literacy has little value. What would happen to the Jews and Judaism in the long run? Our theory predicts that in a subsistence farming society, some Jews find it too costly to obey the norms of their religion, including the high cost of investing in children's literacy and education, and hence they would convert. Eventually, Judaism might disappear.

In chapter 9 we show that the Mongol invasion of Persia and Mesopotamia, beginning in 1219 and culminating in the razing of Baghdad in 1258, contributed to the demise of the urban and commercial economy of the Abbasid Empire and brought the economies of Mesopotamia and Persia back to an agrarian and pastoral stage for a long period. As a consequence, a certain proportion of Persian, Mesopotamian, and then Egyptian, and Syrian Jewry abandoned Judaism—whose religious norms, especially the one requiring fathers to educate their sons, had once again become a heavy burden with no economic return—and converted to Islam. This process of conversions of Jews in the Middle East and North Africa, as well as episodes of persecutions, massacres, and plagues (e.g., the Black Death of 1348) in these regions and in western Europe, explain why world Jewry reached its lowest level by the end of the fifteenth century.

In chapter 10 we end our voyage back in time by highlighting some puzzles that punctuate Jewish history, from the mass expulsion of the Jews from the Iberian Peninsula in 1492–97 to today. Addressing these puzzles will be the task of our next journey, which we will take in our next book.

In recent years, economists and economic historians have highlighted and analyzed the numerous interactions between cultural values, social norms, and economic outcomes.[6] The issues studied range from explaining the successful performance of the Maghrebi traders in the Mediterranean in the early Middle Ages to elucidating the emergence of the spirit of capitalism in early modern Europe, the spectacular technological change that sparked the Industrial Revolution in eighteenth-century Britain, the economic ascendancy and decline of the Muslim Empire, the increase in female labor force participation in the United States in the twentieth century, the ways in which ethnic fragmentation affects economic behavior, and the two-way interaction between trust and economic performance over time and across countries. To this literature our book adds the insight that the cultural values and social norms that Judaism fostered two

---

[6]See, e.g., Greif (1989, 1993, 1994, 2006); Mokyr (1990, 2002, 2005, 2008, 2009); Temin (1997); Alesina and La Ferrara (2000, 2002); Kuran (2004, 2010a, 2010b); Fernández, Fogli, and Olivetti (2004); Fernández and Fogli (2006, 2009); Guiso, Sapienza, and Zingales (2006); Botticini and Eckstein (2005, 2007, 2008, 2011); Doepke and Zilibotti (2008); Tabellini (2008, 2010); Mokyr and Voth (2010).

millennia ago shaped the demographic and economic history of the Jewish people through today.

A growing number of scholars have been studying the long-term impact of institutions by illustrating that some contemporary economic patterns have been influenced by institutions that emerged centuries ago.[7] Economic and political institutions, legal systems and codes of law, and contract-enforcement mechanisms have played an important role in shaping the paths of the economic performance of groups that held a prominent role in trade during the Middle Ages, the economic ascendancy of the Atlantic states in western Europe after 1500, the economic setback of the Muslim Middle East after centuries of economic and intellectual splendor, the engines of scientific and technological creativity that led to the Industrial Revolution, the intriguing features of the Israeli kibbutz, and the economic success or failure of various regions of the world throughout history. We contribute to this literature by showing that the transition of the Jews from farming into crafts, trade, finance, and other high-skill occupations has also been the outcome of the availability of contract-enforcement institutions shaped by the unique features of the Jewish religion.

Social scientists have always been fascinated by the study of religion and by the influence religious values and norms may have on human behavior. In the past two decades, economists have become increasingly intrigued by the nexus between religion and economic outcomes.[8] The issues studied span from analyzing the nexus between Protestantism and human capital accumulation in modern Europe to studying the religious foundations of extremism and terrorism, the long-lasting economic legacy of Judaism, the ways in which religions behave as clubs, and the two-way relationship between religious values and economic outcomes in a cross section of countries in the world. We contribute to this growing literature by linking the key features of Judaism to the unique demographic and economic traits that have shaped the history of the Jews in the past two millennia.

[7]See, e.g., Greif (1989, 1993, 1994, 2006); Mokyr (1990, 2002, 2005, 2008, 2009); North (1990); Acemoglu, Johnson, and Robinson (2001, 2002, 2005); Acemoglu and Johnson (2005); Abramitsky (2008, 2011a, 2011b); Tabellini (2008, 2010); Kuran (2010a, 2010b, 2010c); Mokyr and Voth (2010).

[8]See, e.g., B. Chiswick (1988, 2010); Iannaccone (1992, 1998); Iannaccone, Stark, and Finke (1998); C. Chiswick (1999, 2006); Berman (2000, 2009); Carlton and Weiss (2001); Guiso, Sapienza, and Zingales (2003); McCleary and Barro (2003, 2006); Barro and McCleary (2005, 2006); Botticini and Eckstein (2005, 2007, 2008, 2011); Rapoport and Weiss (2007); Becker and Woessmann (2009); Cantoni (2010); Acemoglu, Hassan, and Robinson (2011). See McCleary (2011) for a very recent collection of works on the economics of religion.

CHAPTER 1

70 CE–1492

HOW MANY JEWS WERE THERE, AND WHERE
AND HOW DID THEY LIVE?

> Ours is not a maritime country; neither commerce nor the
> intercourse which it promotes with the outside world has
> any attraction for us. Our cities are built inland, remote from
> the sea, and we devote ourselves to the cultivation of the
> productive country.
>
> —*Flavius Josephus, c. 96 CE*

> The Route of the Jewish Rādhānite merchants, who speak
> Arabic and Persian and Rūmī (Greek), and Ifranjī (Latin)
> and Andalusī (Spanish) and Slavic. They travel from [the] east
> to [the] west and from the west to the east, by land and by
> sea. . . . They transport from China. . . . sometimes they turn to
> Constantinople with their merchandise . . . ; sometimes they
> travel with it to the king of Firanja (Frankish Kingdom) and
> sell it there. And if they wish, they transport their goods from
> Firanja . . . to Baghdad, and from there . . . to Sind and to Hind
> and to China.
>
> —*Ibn Khordadbeh, c. 850*

SPIN A GLOBE, WAIT FOR IT TO STOP, THEN PUT YOUR FINGER ON THE
first place you see. A Jewish community is likely to have lived there, in the
ancient past or in recent times. Jews have lived in so many places, in such
vastly diverse political, economic, and religious environments, that their history is difficult to summarize in multiple volumes, much less a single chapter. Familiarity with the basic facts of Jewish history from the destruction
of the Second Temple in Jerusalem to the mass expulsion of the Jews from
the Iberian Peninsula is critical, however, to understanding why the Jewish
people came to share certain characteristics. In this chapter, we therefore
illustrate and examine Jewish population and occupational trends.

For centuries, Jews lived in Judea, Samaria, and the Galilee—the three
main regions in the Land of Israel. The center of Jewish religious practice

was the Temple in Jerusalem, erected during the tenth or ninth century BCE. In 586 BCE, the Babylonian army demolished it under the leadership of King Nebuchadnezzar II during the military campaign to expand his empire and deported a number of Jews from Judea to Mesopotamia, particularly to its capital, Babylon (map 1.1). This marked the end of the First Temple period.[1]

The Babylonian exile brought a number of pivotal changes, including the emergence of the central role of the Torah in Jewish life and the rise of scribes and sages as Jewish leaders. The Written Torah consisted of the Five Books of Moses (Genesis, Exodus, Leviticus, Numbers, and Deuteronomy).[2] In 538 BCE, the Persian emperor Cyrus, who had conquered Mesopotamia, issued an edict permitting the Jews to return to Judea and rebuild the Temple in Jerusalem. Nearly 40,000 Jews returned to the Land of Israel in subsequent waves of migrations. A large number of Jews, though, remained in Mesopotamia, which in the following centuries hosted one of the largest and most prominent Jewish communities in the Diaspora—that is, outside the Land of Israel.

The reconstruction of the Temple took about twenty years; its dedication in 515 BCE initiated the period of the Second Temple.[3] In the following four centuries, the Land of Israel fell under the control of the Hellenistic ruler Alexander the Great, the Ptolemaic dynasty ruling over Egypt, and the Hellenistic Seleucid dynasty. During this era, especially in the later part, generations of prophets, scholars, and high priests studied, clarified, and supplemented the Written Torah. Their discussions, judgments, and rulings are called the Oral Torah, which together with the Written Torah would form the backbone for the entire body of Jewish law (halakha) in the subsequent centuries. The halakha sanctioned what a Jew could and could not do, as well as what a Jew should and should not do, in every aspect of daily life—from the observance of religious and ritualistic duties to marital relations, from behavior within the community to civil and criminal law.

The Greeks granted the Jews a kind of communal autonomy as well as religious freedom, which was interrupted by a persecution around 167 BCE, which in turn precipitated a Jewish revolt. From 140 BCE, Judea enjoyed a period of freedom for almost a century under the Hasmonaean

---

[1] See Tadmor (1976) for a summary of Jewish history during the First Temple era.

[2] Traditionally ascribed to Moses, the Torah was most likely redacted by various unknown authors in subsequent centuries and canonized in either the seventh or the sixth century BCE. The three subdivisions of Torah, Prophets, and Scriptures form the Tanakh (the Hebrew name of the Bible). See chapter 3 for more details on the historical development of the Bible.

[3] See M. Stern (1976) for a summary of the Second Temple period, including the Hasmonaean kingdom.

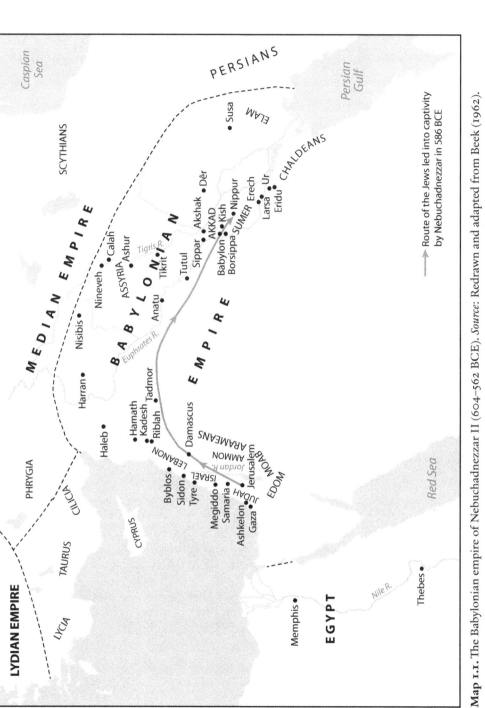

Map 1.1. The Babylonian empire of Nebuchadnezzar II (604–562 BCE). *Source:* Redrawn and adapted from Beek (1962).

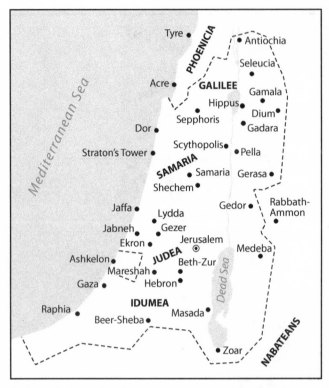

Map 1.2. The Land of Israel in the first century BCE. *Source*: Redrawn and adapted from Aharoni et al. (2002). *Note*: The dashed line shows the borders of the Hasmonaean kingdom of Alexander Yannai (103–76 BCE), who ruled over the Land of Israel during the first century BCE.

dynasty (map 1.2).[4] In 63 BCE, Roman influence and then dominion over the region began. Rome, however, granted the Jews religious autonomy and bestowed on them some judicial and legislative rights through the Sanhedrin in Jerusalem, which functioned as a parliament, a high court, and an academy (yeshiva).

The Second Temple period came to a traumatic end in 70 CE. This is when our book starts. The focus is on three periods, each marked by a "historical accident": the destruction of the Second Temple by the Roman

[4]The Hasmonaeans were a priestly family headed by the Jewish priest Mattathias. His sons—Jonathan, Simon, and Judah known by the nickname Maccabee—led the revolt against the Hellenistic Seleucid rulers and freed Judea, setting the foundations for the establishment of an independent Jewish state.

army during the first Jewish-Roman war (also known as the Great Revolt); the rise of Islam during the seventh century, with the subsequent establishment of one of the largest, most urban, and most commercial empires in history; and the Mongol conquest of Mesopotamia and Persia during the early and mid-thirteenth century, which contributed to the collapse of the urban and commercial economy of the Abbasid caliphate. These exogenous events interacted with the internal dynamics of the Jewish religion to shape the unique demographic and economic traits that characterize the history of the Jews before 1500.

FROM JESUS TO MUHAMMAD (1 CE–622): A WORLD OF FARMERS

Who was a Jew during the Second Temple period?[5] Up to the destruction of the Second Temple, the daily lives of the Jews were similar to those of non-Jews: they dressed alike, spoke the same local languages (Aramaic, Hebrew, or Greek), and earned their living from the same occupations (mainly farming). As in other religions, including pagan cults, the central feature of Jewish religious life consisted of temple service and ritual sacrifices performed by a small elite of high priests.

Jews differed from pagans in three major ways: they believed in one God; their religious, social, and economic life was shaped by the Torah; and they practiced male circumcision, ate kosher food, and observed the Sabbath.[6] During the later part of the Second Temple era (300 BCE–65 CE), Judaism witnessed the emergence of a variety of sects (Sadducees, Pharisees, Essenes, Samaritans, Zealots, Sicarii), increasingly differentiated by their religious norms. Christianity also grew within Judaism in the early decades of the first century. All of these Jewish sects shared the three features that distinguished them from pagan cults. Hence, up to 70 CE, all of these people are considered to be Jews. Later, especially after 200, the answer to "who is a Jew" changed drastically (see chapters 3 and 5).

Jewish Demographic Collapse

Estimates of the Jewish population in ancient times are at best crude approximations. Salo Baron, one of the most eminent scholars of Jewish

[5] For an overview of this complex issue see Schiffman (1985); S. Cohen (1999); Grintz and Posner (2007); Hertzberg and Skolnik (2007). The definition of Jewish identity in both the past and the present is complex. It has changed through the ages. The most enduring definition of Jewish identity has been that of the halakha, but it was not the first definition and is not the only one. According to the halakha, a Jew is either someone who is born to a Jewish mother or converts to Judaism.

[6] Cahill (1998) summarizes the historical development of Judaism in antiquity.

history, puts the number at about 8 million on the eve of the first Jewish-Roman war, in 65 CE. Sergio DellaPergola, one of the leading scholars of Jewish demography, estimates the Jewish population in the first century BCE at 4.5 million and in the first century CE at a number between 4 and 5 million (table 1.1). Other prominent scholars, such as Magen Broshi, Gildas Hamel, and Seth Schwartz, have proposed even lower estimates, arguing that world Jewry in the early first century CE amounted to no more than 2–2.5 million. We agree with DellaPergola's estimates, and for 65 CE, we propose an estimate of 5–5.5 million Jews—about 9–10 percent of the population of the Persian Empire in the East and the entire Roman Empire.[7]

How were these 5–5.5 million Jews distributed geographically on the eve of the first Jewish-Roman war? The largest Jewish population was the one in the Land of Israel, where about 2.5 million Jews, including 300,000 Samaritans, lived. Two types of communities coexisted side by side. The coastal areas hosted Hellenistic towns, in which Greek was the main spoken language; the Galilee (in the north), the Jordan Valley, and South Judea hosted Jewish communities that spoke mainly Aramaic. A relatively peaceful political situation and good economic conditions during the Hasmonaean period (140–63 BCE), as well as a wave of conversions of pagans to Judaism in the 200 years before the destruction of the Second Temple, likely contributed to the growth of the Jewish population in the Land of Israel, which by 65 CE was larger than it had ever been before.

The other major Jewish population centers were North Africa under Roman rule and Mesopotamia under Parthian dominion. About 1 million Hellenistic Jews lived in North Africa (mainly in Egypt) in the early decades of the first century CE. In the same period, roughly 1 million Aramaic-speaking Jews lived in the Parthian Empire, which ruled Mesopotamia and Persia.

Jews also dwelled all over the vast Roman Empire. Circa 65 CE, the region corresponding to Syria and Lebanon likely hosted 200,000–400,000 Jews. Similarly, Asia Minor (the area corresponding roughly to modern-day Turkey) and the Balkans (Albania, Bulgaria, Greece, and the former Yugoslavia) was home to 200,000–400,000 Jews. Another 100,000–200,000 Jews likely lived in western Europe (especially central and southern Italy, France, and the Iberian Peninsula). Cities with large

[7] Baron (1971b); Broshi (1979, 1982, 2001); Hamel (1990); DellaPergola (1992, 2001); S. Schwartz (2001, pp. 10–11; 2006, pp. 23, 36). The appendix explains why the Jewish population estimates for the first century CE diverge. It also describes the references and sources of information on the size of the Jewish population presented in this section.

TABLE I.I. Jewish and Total Population, 65 CE–650, by Region (millions, except where otherwise indicated)

Region	Jewish population						Total population					
	c. 65 CE	c. 100	c. 150	c. 300	c. 550	c. 650	c. 65 CE	c. 100	c. 150	c. 300	c. 550	c. 650
Land of Israel	2.5	1.8	1.2	0.5	0.2	0.1	3	2.3	1.8	1.1	1.5	1–1.5
Mesopotamia and Persia[a]	1	1	1–1.2	1–1.2	0.8–1	0.7–0.9	7	7.3	7.5	8.8	10.5	11.8
North Africa (mainly Egypt)	1	0.8–1	0.5	—	—	0.004	8.2	8.4	8.8	8.2	6.2	7.8
Syria and Lebanon	0.2–0.4	—	—	—	—	0.005	2.3	2.3	2.3	2	1.5	2
Asia Minor and the Balkans	0.2–0.4	—	—	—	—	0.040	10.3	11	11.5	11	8.5	8.9
Western Europe	0.1–0.2	—	—	—	—	0.001	21.1	22.6	23	22	17	17
Eastern Europe	...	...	...	...	...	...	3.1	3.3	3.3	3.3	2.7	3
All locations	5–5.5	—	—	—	—	1–1.2	55	57.2	58.2	56.4	47.9	51.5–52
Jewish population as percentage of total population	9–10	—	—	—	—	1.9–2.3						

Source: Authors' estimates, explained in appendix.

Notes: Asia Minor is the historical term for the area that corresponds to modern-day Turkey. The Balkans include Albania, Bulgaria, Greece, and the former Yugoslavia. Eastern Europe includes Hungary, Romania, Poland, and the former Czechoslovakia. Western Europe includes Italy, the Iberian Peninsula, France, Belgium, the Netherlands, Germany, Austria, and Britain, all of which were under Roman rule for most of the first four centuries.

... Negligible.

— Not available.

[a] Figures include the Arabian Peninsula.

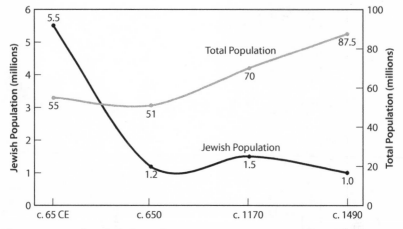

Figure 1.1. Jewish and total population, c. 65 CE, 650, 1170, and 1490 (millions). *Source*: Authors' estimates, explained in appendix. *Note*: The estimates of the Jewish and total population refer to the following geographical areas: the Land of Israel, Syria, Lebanon, Mesopotamia, Persia, the Arabian Peninsula, North Africa, Asia Minor (the historical term for the area that corresponds to modern-day Turkey), the Balkans (Albania, Bulgaria, Greece, and the former Yugoslavia), eastern Europe (Hungary, Romania, Poland, and the former Czechoslovakia), and western Europe (Italy, the Iberian Peninsula, France, Belgium, the Netherlands, Austria, Germany, and Britain).

Jewish communities included Rome, Corinth, Ephesus, Antioch, and Damascus.

However many Jews there were on the eve of the first Jewish-Roman war, *all* scholars concur that the Jewish population was beginning a steep decline.[8] By the time of Muhammad, in the early seventh century, world Jewry added up to no more than 1–1.2 million people, 1.9–2.3 percent of the total population in the regions in which they lived (figure 1.1).

Jewish communities in the Land of Israel, North Africa, Syria, Lebanon, Asia Minor, the Balkans, and western Europe had shrunk to no more than a few thousand people. The only Jewish community that remained fairly stable was in Mesopotamia (and to a lesser extent Persia), which, by the time of Muhammad, had become the center of Judaism and home to nearly 75 percent of world Jewry.

[8] Baron (1971b); Broshi (1979, 1982, 2001); Avi-Yonah (1984); Hamel (1990); Herr and Oppenheimer (1990); DellaPergola (1992, 2001); Stemberger (2000); S. Schwartz (2001, 2006); Schiffman (2003); Goodblatt (2006c).

What accounts for the staggering drop of world Jewry over these six centuries? Did war-related massacres and a general dwindling of the population make the Jewish population decline? Or did something else cause the number of Jews in the world to fall by nearly 80 percent?

THE LAND OF ISRAEL

The Jewish population of Judea waged two major rebellions against the Roman Empire in the first and second centuries. The first Jewish-Roman war was sparked by a combination of religious tension and economic motives at the time that Judea became a Roman province, at the very beginning of the first century. Abuses in tax collection and the establishment of the Roman census in Judea, the theft of a large amount of money from the Temple treasury by the Roman procurator Gessius Florus, and interference with religious matters (such as the appointment of the high priest or the imperative to build statues of the Roman emperor Caligula in temples throughout the empire) all helped increase the popularity of the sect of the Zealots, who incited their fellow Jews to revolt in order to attain political and religious independence.[9]

The revolt began in 66 CE in the town of Caesarea, apparently provoked by the failure of the Roman garrison stationed there to intercede to stop Greeks from sacrificing birds in front of a local synagogue. During the initial stages of the war, the rebels defeated the Romans.

The rebels' fortunes changed when Emperor Nero appointed General Vespasian as head of Roman forces in the Land of Israel. In 67 CE, with nearly 60,000 professional soldiers under his command, Vespasian crushed the rebellion in the Galilee by conquering Jewish strongholds such as Gamla and Jotapata, where Flavius Josephus (henceforth Josephus), the military commander of the Jewish army, was taken prisoner.[10] Vespasian then headed toward Jerusalem, to which the leaders of the revolt

---

[9]The information in this section comes from several historical surveys of the Jewish-Roman wars, e.g., Applebaum (1976a); Avi-Yonah (1976); M. Stern (1976); S. Safrai (1976b); Zeitlin (1978); Griffin (1984); Goodman (1987, 2008); S. Schwartz (1990, 2001); Fuchs and Sevener (1995); Morgan (2006).

[10]Joseph ben Matitiahu was born to an aristocratic priestly family in Jerusalem in 37 CE. Drawn unwillingly into the revolt against Rome, he was appointed military commander of Galilee and fell prisoner. Led in chains before Vespasian, he predicted that the general would soon become the Roman emperor. When, in 69 CE, Vespasian was proclaimed emperor, Josephus regained his freedom and joined the Romans, acting as intermediary with the Jewish rebels. Unable to convince the Jews to surrender, he ended up watching the siege of Jerusalem and the destruction of the Temple. Josephus adopted Vespasian's family name (Flavius) and settled in Rome, where he devoted the rest of his life to writing. Archaeological evidence has confirmed many details of the events described in his works, making Josephus one of the most authoritative sources on first century Judaism and early Christianity.

had fled and where they began preparing for the siege. While these events were unfolding, Nero's death, in 68 CE, prompted Vespasian to return to Rome, where the political situation was precipitating a civil war. With the death of Otho and Galba and the subsequent defeat of Vitellius, Vespasian was proclaimed emperor on December 21, 69 CE, in what became known as the "Year of the Four Emperors."

To put down the revolt in Judea, Vespasian sent his son Titus, who led the final siege and assault. Titus's decision was to quickly give the final blow to Jerusalem instead of waiting and starving the population out. Internal fights among the Zealots and the Sicarii, who wanted to keep fighting, and Jews, including many Pharisees, who wanted to surrender to the Romans, contributed to seal the fate of Jerusalem. The war ended when Titus's Roman legions entered and destroyed Jerusalem, looted and then burned the Temple, and massacred a large part of the Jewish population.[11] Even if one does not take at face value the report of the Roman historian Tacitus, who reported that at least 600,000 Jews died during the first Jewish-Roman war, the number of casualties was certainly very high.[12] Although some Jews were taken to Rome as slaves (as depicted on the Arch of Titus), there is no evidence of mass deportations or forced migrations of the Jewish population to Rome after the Great Revolt.[13]

The first Jewish-Roman war profoundly altered the balance of power among the various Jewish religious groups. The Sadducees, the wealthy elite that dominated the Temple cult, lost their source of wealth and power. The Zealots and the Sicarii, the major instigators and supporters of the rebellion, were exterminated during the sieges of Jerusalem and of the fortress of Masada three years later. In contrast, the sect of the Pharisees to which leading scholars and sages in the academies in Jerusalem belonged, did not participate in the war. They survived the massacres and emerged as religious and political leaders. One of the key figures was Rabbi Johanan ben Zakkai, who received permission from the Romans to reconstitute the Sanhedrin in the coastal town of Jabneh, which became the most important center of Jewish learning until 135. The new Jewish leadership consisting of teachers, scholars, and rabbis replaced temple service and ritual sacrifices with learning and the study of the Scriptures.[14]

The conclusion of the first Jewish-Roman war reinforced Roman dominion over Judea and other areas along the Mediterranean and in

---

[11] The Jewish holiday Tisha B'Av commemorates the destruction of the Second Temple.

[12] Recent scholarship (e.g., S. Schwartz [2006, pp. 23, 36]) questions whether the number of Jewish casualties during both the Great Revolt, and later, the Bar Kokhba revolt was this high.

[13] Baron (1971b); DellaPergola (2001).

[14] S. Safrai (1976b, pp. 317–22).

the Middle East. Emperor Trajan increased the pressure on the Jews, which precipitated the Diaspora revolt in 115 that was put down in 117.[15] The second Jewish-Roman war in the Land of Israel—also known as the Bar Kokhba revolt, after the name of its leader, Simon bar Kokhba— broke out in 132 upon the departure for Greece of the Roman emperor Hadrian, who had spent three years in the Land of Israel.[16] The Roman historian Cassius Dio—the main source of information about this event—maintains that the rebellion was fueled by several repressive edicts, including one against circumcision. According to him, the spark that ignited the revolt was Hadrian's decision to construct a new city in Jerusalem, called Aelia Capitolina (after his own name, Aelius), in which a temple in honor of Jupiter Capitolinus was to be erected. Unlike the Great Revolt, which the Pharisees opposed, the second Jewish-Roman war was led by the Pharisees, including the head of the Sanhedrin, Rabbi Akiva, who proclaimed Bar Kokhba the Jewish Messiah.

The first phase of the revolt was successful. The Jews seized towns, which they fortified, and inflicted severe losses on the Romans, decimating an entire legion (*Legio XXII Deiotariana*). Emperor Hadrian reacted to this debacle by sending several legions under the command of one of his most capable generals, Julius Severus, who arrived from Britain. Severus surrounded the Jewish fortresses and defeated the rebels, following a three-and-a-half-year war. Cassius Dio reports that the Romans demolished fifty fortresses, destroyed hundreds of villages, and killed about 580,000 people. Although his estimate of the number of people killed is likely a vast exaggeration, the massacre was a major one. The Talmud (Tanit 4:5) notes that the Romans killed so many Jews "that the blood reached their horses' noses." Rabbi Akiva and other Jewish religious leaders were executed.

Judea ceased to exist as an independent state, becoming the Roman province of Syria Palestina. The Jewish center of gravity moved north to the Galilee, as did the hub of Jewish learning. The academy of Jabneh moved to Usha, then to Shefaram, Bet Shearim, Sepphoris, Caeasarea, and Tiberias. It is in these academies that the Tannaim and, later, the Amoraim, codified the two fundamental texts of Jewish law: the Mishna (c. 200) and the Talmud of the Land of Israel (350–400), also known as Jerusalem Talmud or Talmud Yerushalmi.[17] Both the Tannaim and the

---

[15] Goodman (2004).

[16] S. Safrai (1976b), pp. 332–38); Oppenheimer (2005).

[17] S. Safrai (1976b, pp. 335–42). Rabbi Judah haNasi (c. 135–219), the most eminent scholar of the last generation of the Tannaim, compiled the Mishna. The Amoraim commented and clarified many rulings in the Mishna; their commentaries are known as the Gemara. The Mishna and the Gemara form the Talmud. Chapter 3 outlines the historical developments of the Mishna and the Talmud.

Amoraim considered the uprising against Rome a terrible mistake by the Jewish leadership. The list of religious holidays sanctioned in the Mishna includes no commemoration of the Bar Kokhba revolt.

The crushing of the rebellion did not affect the Samaritans, who sided with the Romans, exacerbating hostility between the Samaritans and the Jews. The various Jewish-Christian sects, which began appearing during the first and second centuries, participated in neither the Great Revolt (they left Jerusalem during the siege) nor the Bar Kokhba revolt. The significance of these events for the internal dynamics of Judaism and Jewish demography will become evident later.

The accounts of Josephus, Tacitus, and Cassius Dio, as well as archaeological excavations, document the extent of the disappearance of villages and towns and the consequent shrinking in size of Jewish communities in the Land of Israel. According to the estimates of the ancient historians, more than 1 million Jews died in the Jewish-Roman wars.[18] Hence, war-related deaths would account for nearly 40 percent of the decrease in the Jewish population in the Land of Israel during the first and second centuries (table 1.2). As a consequence of both wars, some Jews were brought as captives to Rome, but the numbers were not large. Because the economy of the Land of Israel started deteriorating during the third century, some Jews migrated to Mesopotamia.[19] Rabbis and religious leaders tried but failed to prevent these migrations.

This reasoning would not change if, as Broshi, Hamel, and Schwartz have suggested, one started with lower estimates of the Jewish population circa 65 CE and assumed that the number of war-related deaths of Jews during the Jewish-Roman wars in the first and second centuries was much lower than reported by Josephus, Tacitus, and Cassius Dio.[20] Hence, nearly half of the Jewish demographic decline in the Land of Israel from the early first to the early seventh century remains to be explained. Neither wars nor migrations can fully account for the roughly 96 percent total drop in the number of Jews at a time when the non-Jewish population doubled or tripled in size from nearly 500,000 Greeks, pagans, and some Christians in the first century to about 0.9–1.4 million people, mainly Christians, in the early seventh century.

[18] Baron (1971b); Herr and Oppenheimer (1990, p. 109).

[19] There is no clear explanation for the well-documented economic decline of the Land of Israel during the third century. The weakening of the Roman Empire, heavy taxation, droughts, and cyclical economic conditions are all mentioned as possible factors. For discussions of this issue, see Avi-Yonah (1984); Z. Safrai (1994); Bar (2001, 2002, 2003b); Leibner (2006, 2009); Gil (2008, pp. 164–65).

[20] Broshi (1979, 1982, 2001); Hamel (1990); S. Schwartz (2001, 2006).

EGYPT AND NORTH AFRICA

At the birth of Islam, in the mid-seventh century, Egyptian Jewry—one of the largest and most prosperous communities in the days of Jesus, numbering about 1 million—consisted of only a few thousand people. What explains this astonishing drop?

In 115, Emperor Trajan launched a major campaign against the Parthian Empire to secure the eastern borders of the Roman Empire. During this campaign, Mesopotamian Jews revolted against Rome in support of the Persian rulers. This revolt was relentlessly suppressed by Lucius Quietus, who was rewarded by being appointed governor of Judea and Galilee.

The revolt quickly spread to the Land of Israel and, to a much larger extent, the Diaspora. The massacre of Roman and Greek citizens by armed Jewish mobs in Cyprus, Alexandria, and Cyrene on the northern coast of Africa, as well as the destruction of pagan temples, prompted brutal retaliation by Trajan. In 117, after almost a year of fighting, Trajan's general, Marcius Turbo, put down the rebellion. Destruction was extensive in many locations. The Jewish community in Cyprus was exterminated and Jews were forbidden to settle there. The Jews in Cyrenaica and Libya also suffered greatly. Jewish communities in many rural areas in Egypt were massacred. In Alexandria the great synagogue and library were destroyed. A large proportion of Alexandria's 150,000–200,000 Jews was massacred. Some Egyptian Jews fled to Mesopotamia (especially to Babylon), as Jews in the Land of Israel had done after the two Jewish-Roman wars.[21]

During the six centuries from 65 CE to 650, Egyptian Jewry virtually vanished. The Jewish-Roman war in 115–17 accounts for roughly 25 percent of the decline (table 1.2). The migrations of Egyptian Jews to Mesopotamia also took a toll. But what accounts for the 60–70 percent decrease that neither massacres nor migrations can explain? The near disappearance of the Jewish community in North Africa is particularly surprising because the size of the non-Jewish population grew by roughly 8.3 percent between the first and early seventh centuries.

SYRIA, LEBANON, ASIA MINOR, THE BALKANS, AND WESTERN EUROPE

Tables 1.1 and 1.2 reveal a stunning demographic decline in the sizes of the large Jewish communities living in other areas of the Roman Empire (Syria, Lebanon, Asia Minor, the Balkans, and western Europe). Thousands of Jews lived in the Roman Empire in the first century CE. In the centuries that followed, western European Jewry almost disappeared,

[21] See Baron (1937, vol. 1; 1971b); Tchericover (1945); Applebaum (1976b); S. Safrai (1976b, pp. 330–31, 370–73); Alon (1980–84); Smallwood (1981, pp. 389–427); Kasher (1985, pp. 26–29); and Goodman (2004) for historical surveys on Egyptian Jewry during the Roman period.

TABLE 1.2. Effect of Wars on Jewish Population, 65 CE–650, by Region (millions, except where otherwise indicated)

Region	Jewish population				Non-Jewish population		
	c. 65 CE	c. 650	Change caused by wars (%)	Total change (%)[b]	c. 65 CE	c. 650	Total change (%)[b]
Land of Israel	2.5	0.1	-40	-96	0.5	0.9-1.4	+130.0
Mesopotamia and Persia[a]	1	0.7-0.9	-10	-20	6.0	11.0	+83.4
North Africa (mainly Egypt)	1	0.004	-25	-99	7.2	7.8	+8.3
Syria and Lebanon	0.2-0.4	0.005	-10	-98	2.0	2.0	...
Asia Minor and the Balkans	0.2-0.4	0.040	-10	-87	9.8	8.4	-14.3
Western Europe	0.1-0.2	0.001	-10	-99	20.9	16.9	-19.1
Eastern Europe	...	...	—	—	3.1	3.0	-3.2
All locations	5-5.5	1-1.2	—	-79	55	51.5-52	-6.9

Source: Authors' estimates, explained in appendix.

Notes: Asia Minor is the historical term for the area that corresponds to modern-day Turkey. The Balkans includes Albania, Bulgaria, Greece, and the former Yugoslavia. Eastern Europe includes Hungary, Romania, Poland, and the former Czechoslovakia. Western Europe includes Italy, the Iberian Peninsula, France, Belgium, the Netherlands, Germany, Austria, and Britain, all of which were under Roman rule for most of the first four centuries.

... Negligible.

— Not available.

[a] Figures include the Arabian Peninsula.

[b] When the population estimates are ranges of values (e.g., 5–5.5 million), the percentage changes in this column have been computed by taking the midpoint (e.g., 5.25 million).

as suggested by the scarcity of information on Jewish communities in Europe during the seventh and eighth centuries.[22] The very large Jewish communities in first-century Lebanon, Syria, Asia Minor, and the Balkans also dwindled in size. What explains this demographic collapse?

Persecutions and forced conversions of Jews—in, for example, Visigoth Spain during the sixth and early seventh centuries—contributed to the shrinking of the Jewish communities in these locations, although it is not possible to ascertain to what extent. Horrific as they were, these episodes did not annihilate the Jews of Europe. Assuming that Jews and non-Jews had the same life expectancies during the first millennium, the general population decline in Asia Minor and the Balkans (14.3 percent) and western Europe (19.1 percent) during the first six centuries likely affected the Jews living there (table 1.2). Like the rest of the population, the Jewish population suffered the consequences of the plague of Justinian. The pandemic probably arrived from Egypt via Central Asia. It broke out in Constantinople in 541, during the reign of Emperor Justinian, before spreading to Syria, Lebanon, the Land of Israel, North Africa, Asia Minor, the Balkans, and western Europe as far north as Denmark, Britain, and Ireland. The 22–23 percent decline in the population of Asia Minor and the Balkans, as well as of western Europe, between 300 and 550 (table 1.1) is consistent with the notion that the Justinian pandemic took a heavy toll.

During this period, there was a geographical dispersion of Jews within the Byzantine Empire, but there is no record of mass migrations, voluntary or forced, of Jews from Syria, Lebanon, Asia Minor, the Balkans, or western Europe toward Mesopotamia from the first to the seventh century.[23] Something else must explain the staggering demographic decline of the Jewish population in these locations.

MESOPOTAMIA AND PERSIA

The Roman Empire, embracing a vast territory that stretched from Britain to Persia, was one of two powerful empires in the first century. The other was the Parthian Empire, which extended from Armenia to Afghanistan. On the eve of the first Jewish-Roman war in the first century, Mesopotamia (and to a smaller extent Persia) under Parthian rule hosted one of the largest Jewish communities in the world, with almost 1 million people living in rural villages as well as in cities such as Babylon, Edessa, Nehardea, Nisibis, Pumbedita, Seleucia on the Tigris, and Sura.[24]

---

[22] Schwarzfuchs (1966a, p. 125); Toch (2005, p. 548; 2012).

[23] Toch (2005, p. 549; 2012).

[24] Neusner (1965–70, vols. 1 and 2); Baron (1971b); Applebaum (1976b); DellaPergola (2001).

Mesopotamian Jewry remained fairly stable and continued to thrive after the Parthians ceased ruling the region in 224 and the Sassanid Persian dynasty took over and vastly expanded the empire.[25] During the four centuries of Sassanid rule (224–651), Jews in Mesopotamia and Persia underwent a smaller demographic decline than the Jewish communities in the Land of Israel and Egypt (tables 1.1 and 1.2), so that by the early seventh century, nearly 75 percent of world Jewry lived in Mesopotamia and Persia.

During this period, the center of Jewish learning, previously located in Judea and the Galilee, relocated to the academies in Mesopotamia (the most famous being the ones in Sura, Pumbedita, and Nehardea), where the Amoraim produced the vast compilation of commentaries known as the Babylonian Talmud (or Talmud Bavli). This Talmud would eventually overshadow the Talmud of the Land of Israel and become recognized by most Jewish communities as the ultimate source of Jewish legal and religious authority.

Despite the absence of mass massacres, significant general population growth (table 1.1), and migrations of Jews from the Land of Israel and Egypt to Mesopotamia, by the early seventh century the Jewish population in Mesopotamia and Persia was almost 20 percent smaller than it had been in the first century. Given these circumstances, why did the number of Jews fall?

A World of Farmers

In the first century, most Jews everywhere earned their living from agriculture (table 1.3). The overwhelming majority of Jews in the Land of Israel were farmers.[26] Both the writings of Josephus and the New Testament clearly depict the predominantly rural character of the Land of Israel.

These accounts are consistent with the portrayal that emerges from the reading of the Mishna, the canon of Jewish law redacted by Rabbi Judah haNasi at the turn of the third century.[27] Each *seder*, one of the six volumes of the Mishna, contains smaller tractates, totaling sixty-three books, which cover agriculture, festivals, family law, civil law, ritual purity, and sacrifices. Even the volumes not specifically devoted to agriculture include

---

[25] The Sassanid Empire encompassed all of modern-day Syria; Iraq; Iran; Afghanistan; the Caucasus (Armenia, Georgia, Azerbaijan, and Dagestan); and southwestern Central Asia; part of Turkey, certain coastal parts of the Arabian Peninsula; the Persian Gulf area; and areas of southwestern Pakistan.

[26] See the appendix for the references and sources that describe the occupational structure of the Jews in the Land of Israel, Egypt, and Mesopotamia covered in this section.

[27] Neusner (1998).

Table 1.3. Percentage of Jewish Labor Force Engaged in Farming and Skilled Occupations, 1 CE–650, by Region

Region	1 CE–400		400–650	
	Farming[a]	Crafts, trade, moneylending[a]	Farming[a]	Crafts, trade, moneylending[a]
Land of Israel	85–90	10–15	80–85	15–20
Mesopotamia and Persia[b]	85–90	10–15	70–80	20–30
North Africa (mainly Egypt)	70–80	20–30	—	—
Syria and Lebanon	85–90	10–15	—	—
Asia Minor and the Balkans	40–50	50–60	30–40	60–70
Western Europe	70–80	20–30	—	—
Eastern Europe	—	—	—	—

Source: Authors' estimates, explained in appendix.

Notes: Asia Minor is the historical term for the area that corresponds to modern-day Turkey. The Balkans includes Albania, Bulgaria, Greece, and the former Yugoslavia. Eastern Europe includes Hungary, Romania, Poland, and the former Czechoslovakia. Western Europe includes Italy, the Iberian Peninsula, France, Belgium, the Netherlands, Germany, Austria, and Britain, all of which were under Roman rule for most of the first four centuries.

— Not available.

[a] The following taxonomy of occupations is used to group hundreds of occupations into a few categories that can be displayed in a table. "Farming" includes all occupations related to agriculture, herding, cattle rearing, and fishing, as well as unskilled workers unrelated to farming. "Crafts" includes a large number of artisans and skilled workers, such as tailors, dyers, blacksmiths, armorers, glass manufacturers, stone engravers, goldsmiths, makers of scientific instruments, carpenters, and locksmiths. "Trade" includes shopkeepers, local merchants, and long-distance traders, who typically bought and sold goods produced by artisans and craftsmen. "Moneylending" includes minters, money changers, moneylenders, bankers, and tax collectors, as well as all other highly educated professionals, such as scribes, notaries, teachers, scholars, and physicians.

[b] Figures include the Arabian Peninsula.

discussions of and rulings on farming and pastoral activities. Many of the damages discussed in the volume of that name (*Nezikim*), for example, refer to agricultural damages. Numerous debates and rulings on festivals in the volume *Moed* ("appointed season") deal with feasts, fasts, and holy days occurring at specific times during the agricultural season. Among the thirty-nine categories of activities prohibited on the Sabbath, eleven refer to specific agricultural tasks, such as plowing, reaping, binding sheaves, threshing, winnowing, selecting, grinding, and sifting.

The amount of space devoted to agricultural matters in *Zeraim* ("seeds"), the first volume of the Mishna, probably best demonstrates the extent to which Judaism emerged out of an agriculturally based society. The rabbis and sages during the Second Temple period, and subsequently the Tannaim during the first and second centuries, did not devote time and attention to philosophical discussions. They ruled on practical questions, such as regulations concerning the commandment to leave the corner of one's field for the poor; the forbidden mixtures in agriculture, clothing, and breeding; the laws of Shemitah during the sabbatical year, when farming was prohibited; the categories of forbidden agricultural work; and the prohibition on eating from trees that were younger than three years.[28]

Similar attention to farming and pastoral activities appears in the discussions and rulings of the Tannaim's successors, the Amoraim, the scholars in the academies in the Galilee from the early third to the late fifth century. The outcome of this process is that the Talmud of the Land of Israel is full of discussions, rulings, and norms on farming and agricultural matters.

The wealth of archaeological excavations further corroborates the picture of a rural Land of Israel in the first half of the first millennium. The archaeological record shows that the bulk of the Jewish population lived in rural villages and engaged in farming; most towns, typically located on the coast, were populated by Greeks, who engaged in crafts and trade.[29]

Was this occupational distribution similar in the other two major centers of Jewish life—North Africa (mainly Egypt) and Mesopotamia—where the Jews, though numerous, represented a minority of the local populations? Egypt was a prosperous Roman province in which agriculture accounted for most of its wealth. Trade with central Africa, the Arabian Peninsula, and India flourished along the Nile, desert routes, and sea routes from the Red Sea. Rome's revenues from Egypt were much higher than those from Judea. Alexandria, with its great library and community of writers, philosophers, and scientists known throughout the ancient world, was the economic and cultural hub of Egypt.

First-century Jews in North Africa thrived in the wealthy Roman province, as the literary accounts of the Jewish philosopher Philo and the

---

[28] The laws of tithing are another example that shows how the Mishna dealt with practical matters. The obligation to tithe was derived from a series of biblical passages. The Mishna transforms the biblical requirement into a precise set of laws and defines precisely the various tithes: (a) *Terumah*: a gift to the Kohanim of 1/60–1/40 of one's crop; (b) *Ma'aser rishon*: a gift to the Levites of 1/10 of the crop that remains after the *Terumah* has been separated; the Levite, in turn, gives the Kohen 1/10 of this gift; (c) *Ma'aser sheni*: during the first, second, fourth, and fifth years of the seven-year cycle, 1/10 of the remaining produce is set aside to be brought to Jerusalem and eaten there by the owner; (d) *Ma'aser oni*: during the third and sixth years of the seven-year cycle, a tithe for the poor replaces the *Ma'aser sheni*. Oppenheimer (2007).

[29] Sperber (1978); Z. Safrai (1989, p. 9; 1994); J. Schwartz (2006, pp. 431–56).

wealth of evidence from papyri indicate.[30] Like Jews in the Land of Israel, most first-century Egyptian Jews earned their living from agriculture (table 1.3). In Alexandria, though, the Jews were also involved in a variety of crafts, trade, and moneylending, like the rest of the local population. The Jewish community had shrunk to a few thousand people in the centuries following the Jewish-Roman war in 115. Little is known about the occupational structure of the Jews in North Africa from the late second to the early seventh century.

During the first half of the first millennium, most Jews in Mesopotamia and Persia also earned their living from agriculture, like the rest of the population. The region was blessed by the natural fertility of the soil, and the Parthian and later the Sassanid rulers invested heavily in the irrigation system, which allowed cultivation of a vast area.

The Jews had been farming in Mesopotamia since the times of their captivity, in the sixth century BCE. Passages from the writings of the prophets Jeremiah, Ezra, and Nehemiah indicate that the Jewish exiles were not banned from owning land and did engage in farming. Josephus maintains that when the Jewish exiles were permitted to return to Judea, many decided to stay, not wanting to abandon their landed estates. The predominance of agriculture seems to have continued in subsequent centuries, as illustrated in a letter written by the Hellenistic Seleucid king Antiochus III (between 210 and 205 BCE) to one of his officials, Zeuxis, in which Antiochus notes that the Jews in Mesopotamia had long been farmers.[31]

The myriad rabbinic debates in the Babylonian Talmud mention many villages and rural locations. They refer to Jews earning their living from agriculture, as landowners, sharecroppers (arisim), fixed-rent tenants (hokerim), or wage laborers (kablanim). Even the scholars in the Mesopotamian academies, the Amoraim, were landowners. Some worked their own land; others hired workers. Their interest in agriculture is indicated by their discussions and rulings in the Talmud on matters such as the proper cultivation of the land to make it as profitable as possible, permission to

[30] Connected to the Herodian dynasty in the Land of Israel, Philo Judaeus (20 BCE–50 CE) belonged to the noblest family of Alexandrian Jewry (his brother Alexander was a rich banker; his nephew Tiberius Julius Alexander was the Roman governor of Judea and Egypt and one of the commanders of the Roman army during the siege of Jerusalem). Two of Philo's books (written in Greek) portray events that he witnessed. *Flaccus* depicts the Jewish pogroms in Alexandria in 38 CE; *On the Embassy to Gaius* describes Philo's mission to Rome in 40 CE to protest the erection of statues of Emperor Caligula in Alexandrian synagogues and the Jerusalem Temple.

[31] The two references are in Josephus's *The Antiquities of the Jews* (bk. 11, chap. 1, sec. 3, and bk. 12, chap. 3, sec. 4) edited and translated in Flavius Josephus (1998).

purchase land from Gentiles, and competition for land created by population pressure.

In addition to owning land and engaging in farming, many Amoraim traded in wine and sesame oil. A few seem to have been engaged in moneylending. Although some Amoraim noted the advantage of commerce over agriculture at this time, there is no direct evidence that during the first three centuries, the Jews in Mesopotamia were heavily engaged in crafts or trade.[32]

This occupational pattern began changing during the late Talmud era, especially in Mesopotamia (table 1.3). During the fifth and sixth centuries, some Jews abandoned agriculture, moved to towns, and became small shopkeepers and artisans in the tanning, linen, silk, dyeing, and glassware industries. The Amoraim in the academies were the first to enter the most skilled occupations, becoming traders and merchants.[33]

Summary

The history of the Jews from the time of Jesus to the time of Muhammad is punctuated by three key facts. First, the number of Jews in the world declined by about 4 million people—from 5–5.5 million in the early first century to only 1–1.2 million in the early seventh century. War-related massacres and the general decline in the population accounted for about half of this loss. Chapter 5 explains how and why the other Jews disappeared.

Second, the center of Jewish life shifted from the Land of Israel to Mesopotamia (and, to a lesser extent, Persia), where nearly 75 percent of world Jewry lived at the onset of Islam. Chapter 5 examines whether this shift was the outcome of voluntary choices prompted by economic incentives or the result of persecutions.

Third, almost all Jews worked in agriculture during the six centuries between Jesus and Muhammad. In cities such as Alexandria, Babylon, Jerusalem, and Rome, Jews were also engaged in a wide variety of crafts and trade, but most Jews and non-Jews everywhere earned their living as farmers, sharecroppers, tenants, or agricultural laborers. Today the overwhelming majority of the world's Jews earn their living from trade, banking, finance, high-tech industries, medicine, law, and a wide array of other skilled and high-income professions. The next section explains when and how their occupational structure changed.

[32] Baron (1937, vol. 2; 1952, vols. 1 and 2); Beer (1974); Baron, Kahan, and Gross (1975).
[33] Newman (1932); Baron (1937, vol. 2); Neusner (1965–70, vol. 5, p. 134); Beer (1974); Baron, Kahan, and Gross (1975); S. Safrai (1976b); L. Jacobs (1990).

From Muhammad to Hulagu Khan (622–1258): Farmers to Merchants

The destruction of the Second Temple was the first "historical accident" in the centuries of Jewish history surveyed here. The second was the rise of Islam and the establishment of one of the largest, most urban, and most commercial empires in history. This exogenous event interacted with the internal dynamics of Judaism to lead to an unprecedented and long-lasting change in the occupational and residential structure of world Jewry.

The Rise of the Muslim Caliphates

How did Europe, North Africa, and the Middle East look when Muhammad appeared on the stage of history in the early seventh century? In the five centuries following the fall of Rome in 476 and subsequent invasions of Germanic populations from central and northern Europe, western Europe became largely a subsistence agrarian economy, fragmented into many rival kingdoms.

In contrast, the eastern half of the Roman Empire continued as the Byzantine Empire, which remained a bastion of Christianity for centuries. At the apex of its expansion, during Justinian's reign (527–65), the empire embraced a territory that included southern Spain, most of Italy, the Balkans, Asia Minor, North Africa, Lebanon, Syria, and the Land of Israel. Its capital, Constantinople, was a city of nearly 1 million people. Heir to the civilization of the Hellenistic era, the Byzantine Empire was a commercial and urban economy. Constantinople dominated the trade routes between Europe and Asia, providing a stable gold currency for the Mediterranean region and acting as a vibrant cultural center.[34]

The Byzantine Empire's primary enemy was the Sassanid Empire ruling over Mesopotamia, Persia, the Caucasus, and parts of Central Asia between 224 and 651. Constantinople lost some of its territories to the Persian power, but during Emperor Heraclius's reign (610–41), it managed to inflict a fatal defeat on the Sassanid Empire. The consequent vulnerability of the once powerful Sassanid Empire facilitated the invasion of the Middle East by the Arab tribes united under the newly established religion of Islam.

After Muhammad's death in 632, the Muslim caliphs belonging to the Umayyad dynasty conquered Syria, Mesopotamia, the Land of Israel, Egypt, Libya, Cyprus, Persia, Tunisia, Cappadocia and Cilicia in modern Turkey, Algeria, and Morocco. After taking control of southern Spain

[34]Louth (2005).

in 711–12, the Muslims crossed the Pyrenees and captured Narbonne, Autun, and Bordeaux and started the siege of Tours in 732. They were defeated that year by the Frankish forces led by Charles Martel at the battle of Poitiers near Tours, just 100 years after the death of Muhammad. The outcome of the battle was a decisive point in history, as the Arab conquest of Europe north of the Pyrenees came to an end.

In 750 the Abbasid dynasty took power. Over the next 200 years, it extended the empire's conquests to Sicily and parts of southern Italy, all of Persia, Afghanistan, and a large part of India. At the height of its expansion, the Abbasid caliphate embraced a vast territory, stretching from the Iberian Peninsula to India, within which it was relatively easy to move and to migrate. Muslim rule, which imposed a common language (Arabic) and a uniform set of institutions and laws based on the principles established in the Koran, greatly favored manufacture, trade, and commerce.

The ascent of the Muslim caliphates brought about many technological advancements in agriculture and manufacturing, as well as the blossoming of local commerce and long-distance trade over a vast area. Economic growth went hand in hand with a spectacular level of urbanization (see chapter 6).[35] New cities were founded in Mesopotamia. The Umayyad dynasty, which had its capital in Damascus, established Basra and Kufa as main centers in 638; the Abbasid caliphs developed Baghdad in 762 and Samarra in 836. The population in these four cities reached astonishing levels for the time, ranging from 400,000 in Kufa to almost 1 million people in Baghdad (table 1.4). Cities also grew in Persia, with several, such as Isfahan, home to more than 100,000 people.[36] Urbanization in the Abbasid caliphate during the eighth and ninth centuries is even more impressive when one compares it with that of Europe. Circa 1050, none of the eight largest cities in Europe—Córdoba, Palermo, Seville, Salerno, Venice, Regensburg, Toledo, and Rome—had a population of more than 150,000 people.[37]

From an economic point of view, the major consequence of the urbanization in the Middle East and the growth of new industries and trade over a vast area was that the demand for skilled occupations in the newly established urban centers greatly increased. How did these events affect the Jews living under Muslim rule?

[35] Lewis (1976, 1984); Mokyr (1990, chap. 6); Stillman (1995).
[36] Lapidus (1981, p. 203); Watson (1981, p. 56 n. 45).
[37] DeLong and Shleifer (1993, table 1). Half of these large cities in Europe were under Muslim rule.

TABLE 1.4. Urbanization in the Middle East, North Africa, and Europe, 850–1050 (thousands)

City	Total population
Largest cities in Mesopotamia, Persia, Egypt, and Tunisia, c. 850	
Baghdad	600–1,000
Samarra	500+
Basra	200–600
Kufa	400
Cairo	300
Nishapur	100–500
Isfahan	100
Qayrawan	100
Largest cities in Europe, c. 1050	
Córdoba	150
Palermo	115
Seville	90
Salerno	50
Venice	45
Regensburg	40
Toledo	37
Rome	35

Sources: For cities in Mesopotamia and Persia, Ashtor (1976, p. 254), Lapidus (1981, p. 203), and Watson (1981, p. 56, n. 45). For Cairo and Qayrawan, Ashtor (1976, p. 89). For European cities, DeLong and Shleifer (1993, table 1).

The Jewish Occupational Transition (750–900)

The transition from agriculture to crafts and trade, which started in the late Talmud era (fifth to sixth century), mainly in Mesopotamia, culminated with the establishment of the Abbasid caliphate.

From the mid-eighth century, the Jews in Mesopotamia and Persia left the rural villages and moved to the newly established towns and urban centers. This movement was so overwhelming that by the late ninth century, the Jewish population in the Middle East was almost entirely urban.[38] The migration to the cities coincided with the fact that agriculture was no longer the main occupation and source of income of the Jews in the Middle East (table 1.5). Urban Jews were engaged in a wide range of crafts, trade, moneylending, tax collection, state bureaucracy, and medicine.

[38] Baron (1952, vol. 4, chap. 22); H. Ben-Sasson (1976, pp. 393–400); M. Ben-Sasson (1992); Gil (2004, pp. 491–92, 597–600).

TABLE 1.5. Percentage of Jewish Labor Force Engaged in Farming and Skilled Occupations, 400–1250, by Region

Region	400–650		650–1250	
	Farming	Crafts, trade, moneylending	Farming	Crafts, trade, moneylending
Land of Israel	80–85	15–20	20–30	70–80
Mesopotamia and Persia[a]	70–80	20–30	10–20	80–90
North Africa (mainly Egypt)	—	—	10–20	80–90
Syria and Lebanon	—	—	10–20	80–90
Asia Minor and the Balkans	30–40	60–70	10–20	80–90
Western Europe	—	—	1–5	95–99
Eastern Europe	—	—	1–5	95–99

Source: Authors' estimates, explained in appendix.

Notes: Asia Minor is the historical term for the area that corresponds to modern-day Turkey. The Balkans includes Albania, Bulgaria, Greece, and the former Yugoslavia. Eastern Europe includes Hungary, Romania, Poland, and the former Czechoslovakia. Western Europe includes Italy, the Iberian Peninsula, France, Belgium, the Netherlands, Germany, Austria, and Britain. See table 1.3 for the taxonomy of occupations.

— Not available.

[a] Figures include the Arabian Peninsula.

The Jews' residential and occupational transition took about 150 years; by 900, most Jews in Mesopotamia, Persia, Syria, Lebanon, and North Africa had transitioned out of farming. They were wine sellers, corn and cattle dealers, builders, clothiers, booksellers, agents and brokers, makers of water clocks, dealers in houses, innkeepers, tanners, manufacturers of silk and purple cloth, glass manufacturers, artisans, shipowners, pearl dealers, shopkeepers, goldsmiths, coin minters, money changers, financiers, court bankers, pharmacists, physicians, local merchants, and long-distance traders.[39]

The main primary sources describing the occupational transition of the Jews in the Muslim Middle East and North Africa are the documents of the Cairo Geniza, the Gaonic responsa, and the diaries and reports of writers, geographers, and travelers. The Cairo Geniza was a repository of thousands of contracts (sales, marriage deeds, loans, business partnerships), wills, letters, account books, and court records.[40] Very few

[39] Baron (1952, vol. 4, chap. 22); Ashtor (1959b, pp. 147–54); H. Ben-Sasson (1976, pp. 388–400); Gil (2004, pp. 603–62).

[40] See Reif (2000) and M. R. Cohen (2006) for detailed descriptions of the history of the Cairo Geniza. *Geniza* in Hebrew means "burying" and, by extension, "burial place." The Cairo Geniza is the most famous of all *genizot*. It contains about a third of a million manuscript pages, discovered in the nineteenth century in the Ben Ezra synagogue in Old

of these documents concern Jewish farmers, tenants, sharecroppers, or agricultural laborers. Instead, they portray the Jews in the countries of the Mediterranean (mainly Egypt, the Maghreb, Sicily, and the Iberian Peninsula) as engaged in about 450 occupations, including shopkeeping, trade, crafts, medicine, teaching, money changing, and moneylending. The same occupational structure emerges from the documents of the Cairo Geniza pertaining to the large Jewish communities in Mesopotamia and Persia.[41]

It is possible that as farmers and rural households rarely left written records—either because they were illiterate or because the nature of their business did not require writing contracts, letters, or deeds—the documents of the Cairo Geniza overrepresent urban households, giving a distorted image of the occupational structure of the Jews. The other main primary source, the Gaonic responsa, does not suffer from this potential source of selection bias.[42] The Gaonic responsa are the thousands of written opinions and rulings that the Geonim (the heads of the Jewish academies in Mesopotamia from the sixth to the late eleventh century) sent in response to the letters they received from Jews living in rural and urban locations all over the vast territory under Muslim rule.

Two key pieces of information come from these documents. First, in 787 the Geonim of the two leading academies abrogated a Talmudic law when they decreed that debts from orphans and women's dowries could be exacted from movable property (until their ruling, creditors could claim only landed property). This ruling was dispatched to all Jewish communities in the Diaspora. A few decades later, in the early ninth century, Rabbi Moses Gaon explained that "the current situation in which most

---

Cairo (then Fustat). The synagogue was attended by Jews who had migrated from Mesopotamia to Cairo and followed the religious and intellectual tradition of the Talmud of the Land of Israel. Most pages found in the Geniza come from literary works, such as medieval Hebrew poetry, halakhic literature, midrashic texts, philosophical works, magical texts, and prayerbooks. The other documents in the Geniza date mostly from the eleventh to thirteenth century and comprise correspondence—business letters, communal letters, and personal letters—court records, marriage contracts, deeds of divorce, wills, accounts, lists of recipients of charity and of gifts for charitable purposes, and official documents, such as petitions to be submitted to the Muslim authorities. Although many are in Hebrew or Aramaic, most were written in Judaeo-Arabic—Arabic in Hebrew characters and displaying grammatical and syntactic features differentiating it from the language of the Koran and other medieval classical Arabic writings. Administrative documents addressed to Muslim authorities are in Arabic script. The Geniza contains fragments from Islamic books in Arabic script as well as pages of the Koran in Hebrew transcription. Chapter 6 describes these documents in more detail.

[41] Goitein (1967–88, vol. 1); Gil (2004, pp. 597–662).

[42] Gil (2004, pp. 603).

Jewish people here do not own land estates" motivated the ruling by the earlier Geonim.[43]

Second, the responsa also deal with a number of questions posed by farmers, indicating that some proportion of Jews in the vast territory under Muslim rule were still engaged in agriculture. The documents represent a small percentage of the total number of responsa, however, suggesting that crafts, trade, moneylending, and medicine were much more common occupations of the Jews in the Muslim Middle East.

The occupational issues raised during the Mishna and the Talmud period tended to concern agriculture. In contrast, the issues raised in the Gaonic responsa concerned crafts and trade. Moreover, during the first half of the millennium, questions were posed largely by farmers; by the second half of the millennium, most questions came from skilled workers, craftsmen, shopkeepers, and traders in urban areas. The occupational structure of the Jews in the vast Abbasid caliphate was no longer that described by Josephus or Philo at the beginning of the millennium.

Migrations within the Muslim Empire (800–1200)

The Umayyad and Abbasid caliphs created a vast kingdom with common institutions, laws, and language, making migration within its territories relatively easy. In search of business opportunities, beginning in the ninth century, Jews freely moved from Mesopotamia and Persia to Yemen, Syria, Lebanon, and the Land of Israel. These Jewish immigrants played an important role in trade all over the Mediterranean. Egypt and the Maghreb also became attractive destinations for many Jewish traders from Mesopotamia, who were also learned scholars.[44]

In the aftermath of the Umayyad conquest of southern Spain in 711–12, a sizable number of Jews settled there.[45] When the Umayyad kingdom of Córdoba was established in 756, the city was the largest in Europe, with a population of about 100,000 people. Two centuries later, Córdoba hosted a population of nearly half a million people, thousands of shops, and many libraries (the one of the caliph alone contained 400,000 volumes), and it belonged to a trading network that connected Constantinople, Alexandria, Baghdad, and Damascus with India and China.[46]

The Jews who settled in the Iberian Peninsula were engaged in a large set of crafts and skilled occupations, held dominant roles in local

[43] Mann (1917–21, p. 311); Brody (1998, chap. 4); Gil (2004, p. 600).

[44] Goitein (1967–88); M. Ben-Sasson (1992; 1996, pp. 54–60); Gil (2004, pp. 676–721).

[45] Toch (2005). No data on the exact number of Jews who settled in the Iberian Peninsula during and after the Muslim Conquest are available.

[46] In 1031 the Córdoba caliphate was split into several kingdoms; for two centuries it was under the Almoravidi (Berber) rulers. It fell into Christian hands in 1236, ending Muslim rule.

trade, and gained a near monopoly in international trade. Some of them migrated to the bustling cities and towns of Egypt and the Maghreb, creating a trading connection between southern Europe and North Africa. The Jewish Diaspora within the vast territory under Muslim rule also created a web of intellectual and cultural exchanges, as documented by the correspondence between the Geonim in the academies in Mesopotamia and the rabbis and scholars in the towns hosting sizable Jewish communities, such as Qayrawan in Tunisia and Barcelona, Granada, Lucena, and Tarragona in Spain.[47]

From the ninth century onward, Sicily and parts of southern Italy conquered by the Arabs also became favorite destinations of Jewish emigrants from Egypt, the Maghreb, and the Iberian Peninsula. The Jews in Sicily and southern Italy developed into one of the wealthiest and also intellectually prominent communities in this period.[48]

Byzantine Jewry between East and West (600–1200)

The history of the Jews in the lands of the Byzantine Empire[49] from the reign of Heraclius I (610–641) to the end of the Fourth Crusade in 1204 overlaps with the history of the Jewish population in the vast territory under Muslim rule and the history of the Jewish communities in medieval Christian Europe. On the one hand, Byzantine Jews had continuous economic connections and cultural interactions with their co-religionaries in the Muslim world, especially those in North Africa and the Mediterranean basin. On the other hand, through migrations to southern Italy from the ninth century onward, Byzantine Jews established a permanent link with Europe.[50]

In the early seventh century, the Jews living in the lands under Byzantine dominion were no longer the large community that had dwelled in

[47]Goitein (1967–88); H. Ben-Sasson (1976, pp. 393–400); M. Ben-Sasson (1992, 1996).

[48]Goitein (1967–88); M. Ben-Sasson (1991, 1992, 1996); Simonsohn (1997–2010, 2011); Abulafia (2000); Gil (2004, pp. 535–93).

[49]Until 650, the Byzantine Empire included the Land of Israel, Syria, Lebanon, Egypt, Asia Minor, the Balkans, and, during Justinian I's reign (527–65), Italy, a small area in southern Spain, and some regions in North Africa. After 650, the Byzantine Empire included mainly Asia Minor, Greece, and, until the early ninth century, southern and parts of central Italy.

[50]Unlike the Jews in the Umayyad, Abbasid, and Fatimid Muslim caliphates or the Jews in the regions of medieval Christian Europe, which an enormous body of literature has described, Byzantine Jewry has received a comparatively smaller attention. This trend has been recently reversed, with a growing number of studies on the cultural, demographic, economic, and social history of the Jews in the Byzantine Empire; see, e.g., Holo (2009); Jacoby (2011); Bonfil, Irshai, Stroumsa, and Talgam (2011); and the many references therein. The overview on Byzantine Jewry in this section is based on these recent works.

Asia Minor, the Balkans, and southern Italy during the first century CE (see table 1.1). They were a tiny religious minority whose legal status partly continued the one they had during the Roman period.

During the six centuries from the reign of Heraclius I onward, most Byzantine Jews lived in towns and urban centers. Few were engaged in what were the backbones of the Byzantine economy—agriculture, the army, and imperial administration. The overwhelming majority of Byzantine Jews were engaged in a variety of crafts, local trade, and long-distance commerce. In some sectors, such as the textile industry and trade, they were disproportionately overrepresented with respect to the rest of the population. Their prominent role in local trade and long-distance commerce grew even further concomitant with the rise of Pisa, Genoa, and Venice as commercial centers and powers during the twelfth and thirteenth centuries and the subsequent growth of commerce all over the Mediterranean. Interestingly, at this time Byzantine Jews neither specialized nor became prominent in moneylending.

From the eighth to the late tenth century, migrations of Jews within and from the Byzantine Empire reached the northern and southern shores of the Mediterranean. This trend was reversed in the subsequent three centuries, and Constantinople and other urban centers under its rule became attractive destinations for Jewish craftsmen, traders, and scholars from Egypt and the Maghreb (see chapter 7).

Migrations to and within Christian Europe (850–1250)

The migrations of Jews in search of business opportunities also reached Europe.[51] On the one hand, as Michael Toch documents, migrations of Jews within and from the lands of the Byzantine Empire, which included southern Italy, may have set the foundations, via Italy, for much of European Jewry. On the other hand, during the eighth and ninth centuries, Jews from the Maghreb and Egypt settled in the Iberian Peninsula, and later in Sicily. Beginning in the late ninth and especially during the tenth and eleventh centuries, Jewish communities of varying size appeared in southern and then central and northern France.

The growth of Jewish communities in northern France occurred parallel to a similar development in Germany, where Jews, probably from France and Italy, began settling and establishing communities from the tenth century onward. Jewish traders from France began migrating to England starting from the late eleventh century, setting the foundations for medieval Anglo Jewry. Similarly, the migrations of Jews from the

---

[51] Toch (2005, 2012) describes in detail the timing and characteristics of the Jewish communities in various countries in early medieval Europe.

Byzantine Empire and Germany to eastern Europe established the basis for the rise of the Ashkenazi Jewish communities in these areas in subsequent centuries.

Whereas in the Muslim caliphates Jews could freely move within what was a single commonwealth, their movements in Christian Europe were regulated by the rulers of rival kingdoms. Like other foreign craftsmen, merchants, and moneylenders, Jews who intended to dwell and to start a business in a town needed special permission, the details of which were spelled out in bilateral charters between them and the local rulers (chapter 7).

The Jews who settled in western and then central Europe during the early Middle Ages—even those who owned land—almost exclusively engaged in nonagricultural occupations.[52] They held prominent positions in highly technical specialized branches, such as dyeing, silk weaving, and tanning. Many were craftsmen—smiths, sculptors, armorers, stone engravers, makers of scientific instruments, tailors, goldsmiths, glaziers, grinders, bookbinders—but a large number were local and long-distance merchants, moneylenders, tax collectors, court bankers, royal treasurers, coiners, vintners, spice importers, scholars, scribes, astronomers, physicians, and booksellers. Starting in the eleventh and twelfth centuries, the Jews in France, England, Germany, and northern and central Italy increasingly specialized in moneylending, to the point of becoming identified with this highly skilled and profitable profession (chapter 8).[53]

The specialization of European Jews during the early Middle Ages in crafts, commerce, and moneylending by no means suggests that they alone worked in these occupations. Non-Jews also worked as artisans, merchants, traders, and moneylenders. What is peculiar about the Jews is that almost all of them worked in these professions at a time when most of the population in medieval Europe consisted mainly of illiterate peasants, sharecroppers, and agricultural laborers.

Jewish Demography

At the time of Muhammad, nearly 75 percent of world Jewry was located in the Middle East, mainly in Mesopotamia and Persia (table 1.6). The Jewish communities in the Land of Israel, Syria, Lebanon, Asia Minor, the Balkans, and North Africa, once among the largest, consisted of fewer than 4,000 to no more than 100,000 people each. Compared with the thousands of Jews who lived in the western half of the Roman Empire during the first century, European Jewry had almost disappeared, as witnessed by

[52]Toch (2005, 2011, 2012).
[53]Baron (1952, vol. 4, pp. 205–7); Toch (2005, 2012); Sapir Abulafia (2011).

TABLE 1.6. Jewish and Total Population, c. 650 and c. 1170, by Region (millions, except where indicated otherwise)

Region	Jewish population		Total population	
	c. 650	c. 1170	c. 650	c. 1170
Land of Israel	0.1	0.006	1–1.5	0.5
Mesopotamia and Persia[a]	0.7–0.9	0.8–1	11.8	10.8
North Africa (mainly Egypt)	0.004	0.07	7.8	8.5
Syria and Lebanon	0.005	0.055	2	1.5
Asia Minor and the Balkans	0.04	0.04	8.9	11
Western Europe	0.001	0.103	17	32.4
Eastern Europe	...	0.007	3	5.3
All locations	1–1.2	1.2–1.5[b]	51.5–52	70
Jewish population as percentage of total population	1.9–2.3	1.7–2.1		

Source: Authors' estimates, explained in appendix.

Notes: Asia Minor is the historical term for the area that corresponds to modern-day Turkey. The Balkans includes Albania, Bulgaria, Greece, and the former Yugoslavia. Eastern Europe includes Hungary, Romania, Poland, and the former Czechoslovakia. Western Europe includes Italy, the Iberian Peninsula, France, Belgium, the Netherlands, Germany, Austria, and Britain.

... Negligible.

[a] Figures include the Arabian Peninsula.

[b] The figure includes about 157,000 Jews in Central Asia, India, and East Asia.

the paucity of information on Jewish communities in Europe during the seventh and eighth centuries.[54] World Jewry in the mid-seventh century amounted to no more than 1–1.2 million people.

Five centuries later, Benjamin of Tudela, one of the most famous travelers of all time, undertook an eight-year journey (c. 1165–73) that started in the Iberian Peninsula and brought him to France, Italy, Greece, Asia Minor, Lebanon, the Land of Israel, Syria, Mesopotamia, Egypt, and through Sicily back to Europe. In his travel itinerary, he describes the size and occupational structure of the communities he saw or heard of during his trip (map 1.3 and appendix, table A.2).[55] His "census," as well as other contemporary sources, documents that the geographical distribution of world Jewry circa 1170 was similar to what it had been five centuries earlier. The largest Jewish community circa 650—consisting of 700,000–900,000

[54] Roth (1966a, p. 13); Toch (2005, 2012).

[55] See the appendix for a discussion of how we and other scholars have interpreted Benjamin of Tudela's numbers. The appendix also explains why Benjamin's Jewish population estimates for Yemen and the Arabian Peninsula need to be significantly revised and corrected.

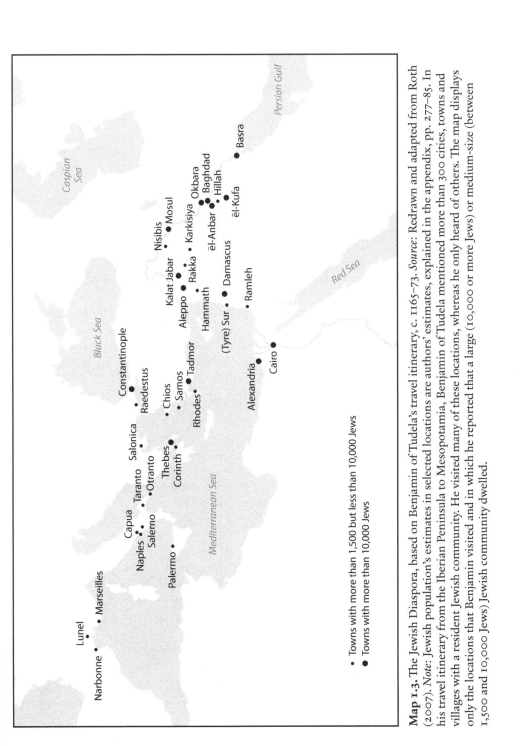

Map 1.3. The Jewish Diaspora, based on Benjamin of Tudela's travel itinerary, c. 1165–73. *Source:* Redrawn and adapted from Roth (2007). *Note:* Jewish population's estimates in selected locations are authors' estimates, explained in the appendix, pp. 277–85. In his travel itinerary from the Iberian Peninsula to Mesopotamia, Benjamin of Tudela mentioned more than 300 cities, towns and villages with a resident Jewish community. He visited many of these locations, whereas he only heard of others. The map displays only the locations that Benjamin visited and in which he reported that a large (10,000 or more Jews) or medium-size (between 1,500 and 10,000 Jews) Jewish community dwelled.

Legend:
- Towns with more than 1,500 but less than 10,000 Jews
- Towns with more than 10,000 Jews

Labels on map: Narbonne, Lunel, Marseilles, Naples, Capua, Taranto, Salerno, Otranto, Palermo, Salonica, Thebes, Corinth, Constantinople, Raedestus, Chios, Samos, Rhodes, Tadmor, Alexandria, Cairo, Ramleh, (Tyre) Sur, Damascus, Hammath, Aleppo, Rakka, Kalat Jabar, Nisibis, Mosul, Karkisiya, Okbara, Baghdad, ēl-Anbar, Hillāh, ēl-Kufa, Basra

Seas: Mediterranean Sea, Black Sea, Caspian Sea, Red Sea, Persian Gulf

Jews in Mesopotamia and Persia—was still the largest community circa 1170 (table 1.6 and appendix, table A.1). At this time, a numerous and wealthy Jewish community (probably numbering 100,000 to 120,000 people) also dwelled in Yemen and other regions of the Arabian Peninsula; Aden, Sana'a, and other cities were commercial hubs for Jewish and non-Jewish traders from the Mediterranean all the way to the Indian Ocean.

By 1170, however, the Jewish population in the Land of Israel had shrunk to a mere 6,000 people. About 70,000 Jews lived in Egypt and the Maghreb, about 55,000 in Syria and Lebanon, roughly 40,000 in Asia Minor and the Balkans, and roughly 103,000 lived in western Europe. Overall, world Jewry in the late twelfth century had grown in absolute terms with respect to the early seventh century, reaching about 1.2–1.5 million people (1.7–2.1 percent of the total population).[56] The overwhelming majority of Jews at the time of Benjamin of Tudela's journey earned their living from a variety of crafts, local commerce, long-distance trade, moneylending, tax collection, medicine, and teaching.

While world Jewry was undergoing these changes, the total population grew about 37 percent, from nearly 51 million to almost 70 million. Most of this growth occurred in western Europe at the turn of the millennium, concomitant with expanding urbanization and the rebirth of a commercial economy. The Jewish population grew as the outcome of both the general trend and its own high standard of living. This growth was partly halted by the deaths caused by the waves of intolerance that swept through Visigoth Spain, Merovingian France, and Lombard Italy in the seventh century and, later, by the bloodbath of the Crusades, which significantly shrank some of the Jewish communities in Germany in the decades after 1096.

Circa 1170—five centuries after the rise of Islam—world Jewry was scattered across three separate centers: (a) Mesopotamia, Persia, and the Arabian Peninsula (mainly Yemen) under Muslim rule, which hosted about 70 percent of world Jewry; (b) the Iberian Peninsula (under partly Muslim and partly Christian rule), in which wealthy communities lived in hundreds of cities and towns; and (c) Christian France, England, Germany, and Italy where small (ranging from a handful to a few hundred households) but prominent communities existed in hundreds of locations. Small Jewish communities existed in myriad locations in Bohemia, Poland, the Balkans, the regions located between the Black and Caspian Seas, Asia Minor, Lebanon, Syria, the Land of Israel, Egypt, and the Maghreb all the way to Central Asia, China, and India.[57]

---

[56] Ashtor (1967, 1968, 1973–84, 1976); Baron (1971b); DellaPergola (1992, 2001).

[57] Information on Jews in Asia is scant. Hence, we do not consider these communities, except in chapter 7 when we describe commerce in the Indian Ocean during the eleventh to thirteenth century in which Jewish traders actively participated. In chapter 10, note 5, we

Summary

From the point of view of demographic strength, economic achievements, and intellectual prominence, the centuries from 800 to 1200 mark the so-called golden age of Jewish history. The large Jewish communities in the Muslim Middle East and North Africa, Iberian Jews under Christian and Muslim rule, and the myriad Jewish communities in Christian Europe all achieved high standards of living and left a permanent intellectual legacy to Judaism.

The golden age of Jewish history is marked by three key changes, which raise several questions answered in this book. First, from 750 to 900, most Jews in Mesopotamia and Persia (nearly 75 percent of world Jewry) left agriculture and moved to the cities and towns of the newly established Abbasid caliphate. Why did the Jews undergo such a spectacular occupational transition, transforming themselves from a population of farmers to a population of skilled artisans, local merchants, long-distance traders, moneylenders, scholars, and physicians? More puzzling still, why were they the only people to do so?

Second, once they abandoned agriculture, many Mesopotamian and Persian Jews moved within the lands of the Muslim caliphates, in particular to Yemen, Syria, Lebanon, Egypt, and the Maghreb. Jews from North Africa settled in the Iberian Peninsula and, later, Sicily. Jews from the Byzantine Empire settled in southern Italy. These Jewish migrations created a worldwide diaspora of small urban communities. A map of the world on which red pins indicate places with a resident Jewish community in 1170 would be covered with red from England and the Iberian Peninsula to India and China. The golden age of Jewish history coincides with the zenith of their Diaspora.

Why did the Jews migrate everywhere? Why, instead of remaining in Mesopotamia as one large and homogenous community of farmers as they had been for centuries, did they migrate? Why was world Jewry at the time of Benjamin of Tudela's journey a worldwide diaspora of urban dwellers who worked in the most profitable occupations from the Middle East to Europe?

Third, the number of Jews in the world grew slightly between 650 and 1170, and roughly 70 percent of all Jews still lived in Mesopotamia and Persia. Migrations of Jews from North Africa to the Iberian Peninsula and Sicily and from the Byzantine Empire to Europe via Italy, as well as natural growth, made western European Jewry grow substantially from the ninth to the late twelfth century. Jewish intellectual and religious leadership also

---

refer very briefly to the history of the Jews in the kingdom of Kuzaria, located between the Black and Caspian Seas.

moved from the Middle East to the West. Why did world Jewry grow during this period, after declining sharply in the six centuries between Jesus
and Muhammad? Why did the center of Jewish life and Judaism move
from Mesopotamia to the West?

From Hulagu Khan to Tomás de Torquemada (1258–1492): The End of the Golden Age

The Mongol conquest of the Middle East is the third "historical accident"
in Jewish history surveyed here. It was one of the most traumatic shocks,
with major consequences on the demography and economy of a vast territory. This exogenous event interacted with the internal dynamics of Judaism to bring major changes to the Jewish communities in Mesopotamia,
Persia, North Africa, Syria, and Lebanon. Surprisingly, most scholars of
Jewish history, with the exception of Eliyahu Ashtor and Salo Baron, have
ignored it.

While the Jews in the Middle East were facing the consequences of the
Mongol invasions, European Jewry was encountering increasing restrictions, prohibitions, confiscations of property, persecutions, forced conversions, and massacres. These changes culminated with the mass expulsions
of the Jews from England (1290), France (1306, 1321–22, 1394), Spain
(1492), Sicily (1492–93), and Portugal (1496–97).

The Mongol Shock in the Middle East

During the twelfth and early thirteenth centuries, the Abbasid caliphate
was undergoing a period of political weakness and turmoil. To this situation of growing internal weakness of the Abbasid dynasty, the arrival of
a formidable external threat in the early thirteenth century—the Mongol
invasions—helped deliver the fatal blow to the empire.[58]

After conquering most of Central Asia, in 1219 Genghis Khan invaded
northern Persia and Armenia. In the aftermath of the Mongol Conquest,
urban centers collapsed, agricultural production fell sharply, and the population of the conquered area fell dramatically, as a result of massacres,
epidemics, and famines.[59]

At the death of Genghis Khan in 1227, his son Ogedei continued the
Mongol invasion of Persia, reaching as far east as Russia and eastern
Europe. In 1252 Mongke Khan, a grandson of Genghis Khan, put his
brother Hulagu in command of the army, with the task of conquering the

[58] Lewis (1984, 2002).
[59] Ashtor (1939, 1976); Gil (2004, pp. 431–33).

Middle East and gaining full control of the entire territory under Muslim rule. After the Abbasid caliph al-Mustasim refused the ultimatum to surrender, in 1258 the Mongols demolished Baghdad, one of the largest cities in the world and the leading center of Islamic learning. The defeat ended nearly five centuries of Abbasid rule in the Middle East. From Baghdad, the Mongol army quickly conquered the main cities in Mesopotamia and Syria and then headed toward Egypt. In Egypt, though, they were held back by the Mamluks, who defeated them in 1260 in the battle of Ain Jalut in the eastern Galilee. This victory marked a watershed, as it ended the Mongol expansion in North Africa and the Levant.

The Mongol Conquest was a turning point in the demographic history of the Middle East (table 1.7). While the population in western Europe grew by roughly 47 percent from 1170 to 1490, the population in Mesopotamia, Persia, and the Arabian Peninsula declined by about 35 percent. The Mongol ravages, famines, and epidemics (e.g., the Black Death of 1348) all contributed to this staggering drop in the total population. Circa 1170, 800,000 to 1 million Jews (nearly 70 percent of world Jewry) lived in Mesopotamia, Persia, and the Arabian Peninsula (mainly Yemen). Three centuries later, the Jewish population there had fallen to just 250,000–350,000 (a two-thirds decline).[60]

The economic consequences of the Mongol Conquest were also devastating. The urban and commercial economy that had flourished under the Umayyad and Abbasid caliphates collapsed. Farming and especially nomadic pastoral activities became the source of income of most households. The ravages of the invasions, the destruction of the irrigation system, and harsh taxation left many farmers at subsistence levels. Eighty years after the Mongol invasions, tax revenues in Baghdad were only 10 percent what they had been before the invasion. In Mesopotamia as a whole, tax revenues dropped by 80 percent.[61]

The carnage that hit the Muslim population during the Mongol Conquest largely spared Mesopotamian and Persian Jews. Neither Jewish nor non-Jewish primary sources (travelers' reports, letters, responsa, and the wealth of documents from the Cairo Geniza) report massacres of Jews under the Mongol rulers.[62] Epidemics and famines took a toll on the Jewish population, as they did on the rest of the population. But there is no reason to think that the Jews suffered from famines and epidemic diseases more than Muslims or other minorities did.

During and after the Mongol Conquest, some Jews fled to Egypt and Syria, both ruled by the Mamluks. However, as table 1.7 shows, the

[60] Baron (1952, vol. 17, pp. 150–51); Ashtor (1976, pp. 251–57).
[61] Petrushevsky (1968, pp. 497–504); Bausani (1971, pp. 101–23); Lambton (1988).
[62] Ashtor (1939); Gil (2004, pp. 431–33).

TABLE 1.7. Jewish and Total Population, 1170–1490, by Region (millions, except where indicated otherwise)

Region	Jewish population				Total population			
	c. 1170	c. 1300	c. 1400	c. 1490	c. 1170	c. 1300	c. 1400	c. 1490
Land of Israel	0.006	...	...	...	0.5	0.5	0.5	0.5
Mesopotamia and Persia[a]	0.8–1	—	—	0.25–0.35	10.8	—	—	7
Egypt	0.040	—	—	0.005	4	5	3.5	4
North Africa (except Egypt)	0.030	...	...	...	4–5	5.2	4	4
Syria and Lebanon	0.055	—	—	0.007	1.5	1.8	1.3	1.5
Asia Minor, the Balkans, Eastern Europe	0.047	0.065	—	0.090	16.3	23.3	18.3	22.8
Western Europe	0.103	0.385	0.3	0.510	32.4	49.6	34.9	47.7
All locations	1.2–1.5[b]	—	—	0.8–1	70	—	—	87.5
Jewish population as percentage of total population	1.7–2.1	—	—	0.9–1.1				

Source: Authors' estimates, explained in appendix.

Notes: Asia Minor is the historical term for the area that corresponds to modern-day Turkey. The Balkans includes Albania, Bulgaria, Greece, and the former Yugoslavia. Eastern Europe includes Hungary, Romania, Poland, and the former Czechoslovakia. Western Europe includes Italy, the Iberian Peninsula, France, Belgium, the Netherlands, Germany, Austria, and Britain.

... Negligible.

— Not available.

[a] Figures include the Arabian Peninsula.

[b] The figure includes about 157,000 Jews in Central Asia, India, and East Asia.

numbers of Egyptian and Syrian Jews also dwindled, even though there is no evidence of mass expulsions or mass forced conversions of Jews there.[63]

Some Jews who left North Africa migrated to Europe. However, unlike the ample documentation of mass migrations of Iberian Jews after the expulsions of the 1490s, neither Jewish nor non-Jewish sources contain a single reference of mass migrations of Jews from the Middle East in the aftermath of the Mongol Conquest. As described earlier, Jews from the Muslim caliphates could not freely migrate to and settle in the countries of Christian Europe, where kings, princes, bishops, and local town governments regulated the settlement and economic activities of Jewish immigrants through charters and special privileges. The Jewish communities themselves strictly regulated the arrival of fellow Jews, who were potential competitors.

There are also no records pointing to mass migrations of Jews from Mesopotamia, Persia, Armenia, and Khazaria to eastern Europe during or after the Mongol Conquest. The Jews of northern Persia and Khazaria were under Mongol rule from 1220; their fate was similar to that of the Jewish population of the rest of Persia and Mesopotamia. Hence one cannot connect the decline of the Jewish community in the Middle East in the aftermath of the Mongol invasions to the growth of eastern European Jewry centuries later (see chapters 9 and 10).

According to the accounts of Jewish travelers on their way from Italy to Jerusalem in the 1480s, most Jews in Egypt, Syria, and the Land of Israel were skilled artisans, merchants, traders, physicians, moneylenders, and scholars. Jewish communities were still centered on the synagogues, under the religious and intellectual leadership of rabbis and scholars. Yet the overall impression from these late medieval travel itineraries and letters is of smaller and poorer communities, an impression that is consistent with the population data presented in table 1.7. If these communities were small and other locales failed to absorb the Jews who lived in pre–Mongol conquest Mesopotamia and Persia, where did hundreds of thousands Jews go?

Jews in Late Medieval Europe

From 1250 to 1492, the Jews in the Iberian Peninsula, Sicily, southern Italy, and the Balkans remained engaged in a wide variety of urban occupations such as crafts, commerce, long-distance trade, moneylending, tax collection, medicine, and teaching. By about 1100, lending money

---

[63] The small surviving Jewish communities in Egypt and Syria consisted mostly of poverty-stricken people (Baron 1952, vol. 17, pp. 160–66, 219; Ashtor 1959a, pp. 65–68; 1967; 1968).

at interest was *the* occupation par excellence of the Jews in England and continued to remain so until their expulsion in 1290 (chapter 8). At this time, moneylending was also a very important occupation of French Jews; their specialization and prominence in moneylending grew in the following century and remained such until their expulsion in 1394. In the two centuries beginning about 1300, almost all Jews in Germany and northern and central Italy were engaged in moneylending.[64]

Since about 1250, the history of European Jewry has been punctuated by episodes of persecutions and forced conversions to Christianity, as well as by the constant threat of temporary banishments and permanent expulsions. The expulsion from England in 1290 was the first mass expulsion of Jews in medieval Europe. It presents some striking features that corroborate our interpretation of the key facts and puzzles of Jewish history presented later in the book. In 1275, the English king, Edward I, issued a decree forbidding Jews from lending money at interest, while permitting them to engage in trade and crafts and even to lease farms. In response to the Jews' apparent refusal (or inability) to engage in farming, crafts, or trade, in 1290 the king issued an edict for the banishment of the Jews from England. England's nearly 15,000 Jews preferred to leave the country and to migrate to Flanders, France, Italy, Germany, the Iberian Peninsula, and, in small numbers, to the Maghreb and Egypt, rather than give up moneylending and become farmers or artisans.[65]

In France, starting in 1182 under the reign of King Philip Augustus, the Jews became subjected to edicts of banishment, many of which were later revoked. Philip Augustus himself readmitted the Jews to France in 1198; Louis X called the Jews back in 1315, just nine years after the decree of banishment issued by his predecessor, Philip the Fair. The last expulsion of French Jews came in 1394, under the reign of Charles VI, after which they were not permitted to return to France for more than two centuries.[66]

The chronology of the banishments in Germany is more complicated, because Jews expelled from one town or principality were often invited to settle in another autonomous town or princedom, which issued them charters or privileges. As in other parts of Europe, major banishments occurred in the wake of the Black Death of 1348 and also in 1394. But the numerous decrees of banishment of the Jews from German towns during the fifteenth and sixteenth centuries indicate that the Jews never left Germany for a long period, as was the case in England.[67]

---

[64] Baron (1952, vol. 4, chaps. 20 and 22); Stein (2007).
[65] Elman (1937); Roth (1964); Singer (1964); Ovrut (1977); Mundill (1991, 2010). The Jews were not officially permitted to return to England until the second half of the seventeenth century.
[66] Benbassa (1999).
[67] H. Ben-Sasson (1976, pp. 561–66); Toch (2005, 2008, 2012); Chazan (2006).

Jewish migrations from Germany to Bohemia, Moravia, and Poland occurred during the fourteenth and fifteenth centuries. These migrations contributed to the initial growth of the Jewish communities in eastern Europe, which would reach almost 5 million people circa 1880.[68]

The worst expulsion of European Jews occurred in the late-fifteenth-century Iberian Peninsula. A large Jewish community scattered in many locations had dwelled there since the Arab Conquest in 711. Iberian Jewry thrived, and the Iberian Peninsula became one of the three leading centers of Jewish economic and intellectual life during the early Middle Ages. Episodes of violence against Jews in some towns—such as the massacre that took place in Granada in 1066, in which as many as 4,000 Jews may have been killed in a single day—broke out in the seven and a half centuries following the Arab Conquest. Despite these episodes, the Jewish community in the Iberian Peninsula remained numerous, wealthy, and culturally prominent.[69]

Attitudes toward the Jews in Spain began hardening during the fourteenth and fifteenth centuries. They deteriorated dramatically when King Ferdinand II of Aragon married Queen Isabella of Castile in 1469 and joined the two realms, creating the united Kingdom of Spain. On March 31, 1492, the two monarchs, with the support of Tomás de Torquemada, the Inquisitor General of Spain, issued the Alhambra decree, ordering that Jews either convert to Christianity or be permanently expelled from the Kingdom of Spain and its territories within three months. As a consequence, some Jews remained in Spain as *conversos* or crypto-Jews, but the majority migrated to the Maghreb, Italy, and the lands of the Ottoman Empire (today Turkey and the Balkans), where they formed flourishing communities. Many Spanish Jews migrated to Portugal. When, in 1496, King Manuel I of Portugal issued an edict of expulsion, some Jews converted and remained there, but many Portuguese Jews emigrated to Italy, the Low Countries, the Muslim Middle East, and the Ottoman Empire. The Diaspora from the Iberian Peninsula grew in subsequent decades, as many Jews who had decided to remain as crypto-Jews reverted to Judaism and abandoned the Iberian Peninsula, migrating to Amsterdam, England, the Ottoman Empire, Italy, Egypt, the Maghreb, and the New World.[70]

By 1500, the number of Jews in the world had fallen to no more than 1 million, scattered mostly in western and eastern Europe, the Balkans,

---

[68] H. Ben-Sasson (1976, p. 571); DellaPergola (1992; 2001, table 2).

[69] Baer (1961); Ashtor (1973–84); Beinart (2007b).

[70] Baer (1961); Baron (1971b); H. Ben-Sasson (1976, p. 570); Gampel (1989, 1998); Beinart (1992–93, 1998); T. Glick (1998).

North Africa, and the Middle East. They represented about 1 percent of the total populations in these areas—the smallest percentage in 1,500 years.[71]

Of the world's 1 million Jews, about half adhered to the Sephardic religious tradition centered on the Spanish academies' interpretation of the halakha. They lived mainly in Greece and the Balkans under Ottoman rule, Egypt, the Maghreb, the Middle East, parts of Italy, and Flanders, as well as in the Iberian Peninsula as crypto-Jews. They were urban dwellers, specializing in the same skilled occupations (crafts, commerce, moneylending, and medicine) in which Mesopotamian and Persian Jews had specialized under the Abbasid caliphate. The remaining half consisted of Ashkenazi Jews, who followed the religious and cultural tradition centered on the French and German academies' interpretation of the halakha. They lived mainly in Germany, Austria, northern and central Italy, and eastern Europe, where they specialized in moneylending and finance.[72]

Summary

The Mongol conquest of the Middle East during the 1220s to 1250s caused a demographic and economic collapse that brought the economy back to a subsistence farming stage. The Jewish population in Mesopotamia, Persia, Syria, and Egypt shrank greatly following the conquest, with the Jews who remained living largely in cities.

From the late thirteenth through the fifteenth century, most Jews lived in Europe. The Jews in the Iberian Peninsula, Sicily, southern Italy, and the Balkans remained engaged in a wide variety of crafts and urban skilled occupations including commerce and trade. In contrast, the Jews of England, France, Germany, and northern and central Italy became increasingly specialized in moneylending.

In late medieval Europe, Jews faced tighter restrictions, persecutions, forced conversions, and banishments, culminating with their mass expulsion from the Iberian Peninsula in 1492–97. With these events, the golden age of Jewish history came to a disastrous end.

[71] Baron (1971b); DellaPergola (1992, 2001).
[72] The word Sephardi comes from *Sepharad*, a Biblical location not exactly identified. "Sepharad" was identified by later Jews as the Iberian Peninsula. A Sephardic Jew is a Jew who follows the religious and cultural traditions adopted by Jews who lived in the Iberian Peninsula before their expulsion in the 1490s. Ashkenazi Jews are Jews who descend from the medieval Jewish communities along the Rhine in Germany. *Ashkenaz* is the medieval Hebrew name for Germany. Thus, Ashkenazi Jews are literally "German Jews." Later, Jews from western and central Europe came to be called Ashkenaz. Chapters 7, 8, and 10 describe the demographic, economic, and intellectual history of the Sephardic and Ashkenazi Jewish communities during the Middle Ages.

JEWISH HISTORY, 70 CE–1492: PUZZLES

This gallop across the many centuries of Jewish history raises some intriguing questions. This book answers them—with a novel interpretation of the history of the Jews.

The first set of questions concerns the unique occupational structure of the Jews. Why did almost all the Jews in Mesopotamia and Persia under Muslim rule during the eighth and ninth centuries (that is, nearly 75 percent of world Jewry) leave agriculture and become craftsmen, shopkeepers, local merchants, long-distance traders, physicians, money changers, moneylenders, and court bankers? Why have Jews almost everywhere continued to work in these occupations since then? Why did almost all the Jews in England, France, Germany, and northern and central Italy specialize in moneylending during the Middle Ages?

The second set of questions concerns why the Jews migrated within the vast territory under Muslim rule, within the Byzantine Empire and the Mediterranean, and to and within Christian Europe starting in the mid-ninth century. Why did the Jews create a worldwide diaspora of small urban communities from England all the way to India? Are these patterns somehow related to their occupational specialization into skilled occupations?

The third set of questions relates to the demographic history of the Jewish people. What accounts for the stunning demographic decline that hit world Jewry from the early first to the early seventh century? What happened to the Jews whose disappearance cannot be explained by wars, massacres, famine, epidemics, or the general decline in population? Why did the number of Jews slightly increase from 650 to 1250? What happened to the Mesopotamian, Persian, Egyptian, and Syrian Jews after the Mongol invasions of the Middle East in the early and mid-thirteenth century? Is their apparent disappearance somehow connected to the occupational structure of world Jewry in those centuries? We address these questions, one by one, in the chapters that follow.

CHAPTER 2

Were the Jews a Persecuted Minority?

> The Jew was driven by the unfortunate circumstances of his
> history to be predominantly a townsman. He had to seek an
> outlet, despairingly, in every branch of the urban economy.
> —*Cecil Roth, 1938*

> Why are there few Jews in farming? . . . Reuben Kessel offered
> an attractive explanation: since Jews have been persecuted
> so often and forced to flee to other countries, they have not
> invested in immobile land, but in mobile human capital. . . . Of
> course, someone might counter with the more basic query: but
> why are they Jews and not Christians or Moslems?
> —*George J. Stigler and Gary S. Becker, 1977*

DO LEGAL STRICTURES OR DISCRIMINATORY MEASURES LIMITING THE
economic activities of the Jews throughout much of their history explain
their occupational structure? Did their religious customs lead them to
specialize in certain professions? Or did the Jews perhaps choose to invest
in human rather than physical capital because of the precariousness of
their situation as persecuted minorities, leading them to leave farming
and enter urban skilled occupations such as crafts, trade, medicine, and
moneylending?

RESTRICTIONS ON JEWISH ECONOMIC ACTIVITIES

During the medieval and early modern period, monarchs, religious
authorities, and local rulers subjected Jews in Europe to a variety of economic regulations. Based on this observation, nineteenth- and twentieth-
century scholars contended that the Jews specialized in trade and
moneylending because of such constraints and prohibitions.[1] Although

---

[1] Scholars like Israel Abrahams and Cecil Roth lived at a time when Jews were savagely
persecuted in Europe and the Zionist movement that eventually created the State of Israel
was rising. Their apologetic views of the history of the Jews should be understood in the context of this cultural and political milieu.

recent historiography, as prominently shown by Toch, no longer considers this argument compelling,[2] it has become so well rooted in the literature that it is still taught in schools and remains popular outside academic circles.

The theory of restrictions has several "fathers," such as the prominent historian Cecil Roth. Roth argued that the prohibition on owning land imposed by either the religious or secular authorities made European Jews forsake farming and become an urban population specialized in crafts and trade. Subsequently, the exclusive membership imposed by the craft and merchant guilds pushed European Jews into the only occupation outside the control of the guilds—moneylending.[3] Other scholars have proposed similar arguments.[4]

We leave these arguments aside for a moment to consider the way economics views the choice of an occupation. Economists model occupational choice as an individual decision based on two key variables: education/ skills and income. Occupations such as crafts, commerce, money changing, moneylending, banking, finance, and medicine require more literacy, education, and skills than rural occupations, such as farming, but they typically provide higher incomes. Someone with the education and skills to become, say, a banker or a diamond trader, would therefore generally prefer to do so than to become a farmer. Likewise, individuals without the education or skills to become bankers or diamond traders would become farmers or unskilled urban workers, even if no ban prevents them from engaging in high-skill occupations.

Suppose that the restrictions on Jewish landownership that Cecil Roth and other scholars maintained existed in medieval and early modern Europe had never existed or had been lifted at some point. Based on the economist's way of thinking about occupational choice, would Jews with the literacy, education, and skills to become artisans, traders, moneylenders, or physicians have chosen to become farmers? Clearly they would not have. Hence, to understand whether constraints and bans played key

[2]Baron (1928; 1937, vol. 2, p. 31; 1952, vol. 4, p. 194) was the first to argue against what he called the "lachrymose" view of Jewish history put forward by scholars influenced by the Zionist movement. More recently, Toch (2005, 2008, 2012) disputes the argument based on restrictions.

[3]Roth (1938, pp. 228–30; 1964, pp. 2–3).

[4]See, for example, Abrahams (1896); Mann (1917–1921); Parkes (1934, 1938); S. Katz (1937); Baer (1961); Bein (1990, chap. 3). Stow (1992, chap. 10; 2007) argues against the view that Jews entered trade and moneylending because they were prohibited from owning land but maintains that Jews were disadvantaged from profitably engaging in agriculture because they could not hire Christian agricultural laborers. See Engel (2006) for a survey of the historiography of Jewish history.

roles in the transition into and specialization of the Jews in urban skilled occupations, we investigate the following questions:

- Did restrictions on Jewish economic activities exist in the Roman, Byzantine, and Persian empires?
- Did these bans exist in the Muslim caliphates?
- Were restrictions imposed on Jews when they migrated to and within Europe during the early medieval period?
- Did these constraints exist later, for example, in the twentieth-century United States?

In pointed contrast to both conventional wisdom and generations of scholarly study, we show that no significant restrictions on Jewish economic activities existed in any of these locations or periods.

The Roman, Byzantine, and Persian Empires

Almost all of the Jews living in the Roman and Persian empires were farmers, and most of the Jews in the eastern continuation of the Roman Empire, the Byzantine Empire, were farmers (see table 1.3). The transition out of agriculture began in the fifth and sixth centuries in the large Jewish communities of Mesopotamia and Persia, reaching its full-fledged stage during the eighth and ninth centuries. The transition was not precipitated by legal codes, which placed almost no restrictions on the economic activities of the Jewish population under either the Parthian or the Sassanid rulers. Jews could own land, employ slaves, and engage in farming or any other occupation except the civil service (table 2.1).

Under Roman rule, no legal restrictions prevented Jews from farming land as sharecroppers, fixed-rent tenants, or agricultural laborers, or from engaging in any occupation. Before the two Jewish-Roman wars (66–73 CE and 132–35), Jews in the Roman Empire were also allowed to own land. After the two wars, the Romans confiscated some landholdings in Judea. Some of these confiscations were temporary; in other cases, the confiscated land was given to Roman citizens or military veterans but the earlier Jewish owners kept working as farmers. Many landholdings, though, were never confiscated.[5]

Similarly, no legal bans prevented the large Jewish community in the Byzantine Empire from farming or engaging in any occupation (table 2.2). Jews could own, purchase, and sell land as long as it did not belong to the Church. They could possess and employ slaves on their farms as long as the slaves were not Christians. They could be artisans, shopkeepers, traders,

[5] S. Safrai (1976b, pp. 314–56); Avi-Yonah (1984).

TABLE 2.1. Economic Activities Open and Closed to Jews in the Roman and Persian Empires, 1 CE–650

Activity	Roman Empire	Persian Empire
Own land[a]	✓	✓
Engage in farming[a]	✓	✓
Own slaves	✓[d]	✓
Engage in crafts, shopkeeping, trade, medicine, teaching	✓	✓
Engage in moneylending[b]	✓	✓
Work in civil service[c]	X	X

Sources: For the Roman Empire, Juster (1914), Baron (1937, vol. 1; 1952, vols. 1 and 2; 1971a), Tcherikover (1945, 1961), A. Jones (1964), M. Stern (1974, 1976), Applebaum (1976a, 1976b), S. Safrai (1976b), Avi-Yonah (1984), Kasher (1985), Hamel (1990), L. Jacobs (1990), Z. Safrai (1994), and Goodman (1998). For the Persian Empire, Newman (1932), Baron (1937, vol. 1; 1952, vols. 1 and 2; 1971a), Neusner (1965–70, vol. 1, pp. 94–99; vol. 2, p. 14; vol. 3, pp. 24–25; vol. 5, p. 134; 1990c; 1990e), Beer (1974), M. Stern (1974), Applebaum (1976b), and L. Jacobs (1990).

Notes: The Roman Empire included Italy, the Iberian Peninsula, France, Belgium, the Netherlands, Britain, the Balkans, and parts of Germany, Asia Minor, the Land of Israel, Syria, Lebanon, Egypt, and some areas in North Africa. The Persian Empire (under the Parthian and, later, the Sassanid dynasty) encompassed all of modern-day Syria, Iraq, Iran, Afghanistan, the Caucasus, southwestern Central Asia, part of Turkey, certain coastal parts of the Arabian Peninsula, the Persian Gulf area, and parts of southwestern Pakistan.

[a] "Own land" is distinguished from "engage in farming," because one can own land but have someone else cultivate his landed properties. Conversely, someone who does not own land can work as tenant, sharecropper, or agricultural laborer for a landlord. Therefore, "engage in farming" identifies the occupation of a farmer more precisely than "own land."

[b] Moneylending also includes banking, minting, tax collection, and working for the royal treasury.

[c] The civil service includes professionals directly involved with the state and public administration, such as judges, state and local bureaucrats, and military officials.

[d] Emperor Constantius (c. 337–61) issued the decree that prohibited Jews from owning and trading in slaves.

physicians, or moneylenders.[6] The only sector from which Jews were legally excluded in all three empires was the state bureaucracy, in which citizenship or adherence to the official religion was typically a prerequisite.

The Muslim Caliphates (622–1258)

The full-fledged transition of the Jews from farming to crafts and trade took place in Mesopotamia and Persia (where the majority of world

[6] S. Safrai (1976b, pp. 343–63); Avi-Yonah (1984); Bonfil, Irshai, Stroumsa, and Talgam (2011); Jacoby (2008, 2011).

TABLE 2.2. Economic Activities Open and Closed to Jews in the Byzantine Empire, 350–1250

Activity	350–650	650–1250
Own land	✓	✓
Engage in farming	✓	✓
Own slaves	✓	✓
Engage in crafts, shopkeeping, trade, medicine, teaching	✓	✓
Engage in moneylending	✓	✓
Work in civil service	X	X

Sources: Baron (1937, vol. 1; 1952, vols. 1 and 2; 1971a), Sharf (1966, 1971), Holo (2009), and Jacoby (2008, 2011).

Note: Until 650, the Byzantine Empire included the Land of Israel, Syria, Lebanon, Egypt, Asia Minor, and the Balkans, and during Justinian I's reign (527–65), Italy, a small area in southern Spain, and some regions in North Africa. After 650, the Byzantine Empire included mainly Asia Minor, Greece, and, until the early ninth century, southern and parts of central Italy. See notes to table 2.1 for descriptions of activities.

Jewry lived) from circa 750 to circa 900 and then spread to the vast territory under Muslim rule (see chapter 1). Did the Umayyad, Abbasid, and Fatimid caliphs enact laws that drove the Jews out of farming? The answer is an unequivocal no: there were no legal restrictions on any Jewish economic activity in the vast territory under Muslim rule (table 2.3). Jews were legally permitted to own land, to be farmers, to own and employ slaves in farming, and to engage in any occupation they wished.[7]

The only sector from which Jews and other non-Muslims were banned was the civil service, which was typically reserved to Muslims.[8] Ironically, as in the Roman, Persian, and Byzantine empires, the only legal constraint imposed on the Jews in the Muslim caliphates concerned neither land ownership nor farming but one of the very urban skilled occupations in which the Jews later excelled.

One could object that legal codes do not portray how people actually behaved, that unwritten social norms may have made it difficult for Jewish households to own land and farm in the Muslim Middle East. Fortunately,

[7]Baron (1952, vol. 4); Goitein (1967–88, vol. 1); Ashtor (1973–84); H. Ben-Sasson (1976, pp. 393–402); Gil (1992; 2004, pp. 273–90); M. R. Cohen (1994); Ashtor et al. (2007); Ashtor and Sagiv (2007); Ashtor, Yaari, and Cohen (2007).

[8]Despite the legal prohibition on entering the civil service, Jews entered and held prominent positions in the state bureaucracy of the Muslim caliphates (see Goitein 1967–88, vol. 1; Gil 1992; 2004; M. R. Cohen 1994). One of the most famous examples is Rabbi Samuel ha-Nagid, the merchant, scholar, and poet who became the chief minister in Granada.

TABLE 2.3. Economic Activities Open and Closed to Jews in the Muslim Caliphates, by Area, 650–1250

Activity	Land of Israel	Mesopotamia, Persia, Arabian Peninsula	North Africa	Syria, Lebanon	Iberian Peninsula, Sicily
Own land	✓	✓	✓	✓	✓
Engage in farming	✓	✓	✓	✓	✓
Own slaves	✓	✓	✓	✓	✓
Engage in crafts, shopkeeping, trade, medicine, teaching	✓	✓	✓	✓	✓
Engage in moneylending	✓	✓	✓	✓	✓
Work in civil service	X	X	X	X	X

Sources: Mann (1920–1922), Baron (1952, vol. 3; 1971a), Goitein (1967–88, vol. 1), Ashtor (1973–1984, 1976, 2007), H. Ben-Sasson (1976), Morony (1981), Udovitch (1981), Lewis (1984), Gil (1992, 2004), M. R. Cohen (1994), and M. Ben-Sasson (1992, 1996).

Note: See notes to table 2.1 for descriptions of activities.

evidence documenting the actual behavior and daily lives of the Jews is available. Many documents in the Cairo Geniza (including thousands of contracts, letters, business partnerships, account books, deeds, and wills) and the rabbinic responsa (comprising debates and court cases) refer to the sale and purchase of land and other transactions involving landholdings.[9] This wealth of evidence shows that landownership was not just a legal option but also a reality for the Jews living in the vast territory under Muslim rule. The right of Jews to own land and the actual ownership of land by Jews did not halt the occupational transition that in less than two centuries transformed the Jews of the Middle East from a population of farmers, like the rest of the population, to an urban population of craftsmen, traders, brokers, moneylenders, court bankers, and physicians.

Medieval Christian Europe (850–1492)

No restrictions were imposed on the Jewish artisans, shopkeepers, traders, moneylenders, scholars, and physicians who migrated to and within Christian Europe during the early Middle Ages. Many charters issued in the early medieval period (the mid-ninth through the thirteenth century) indicate that rulers invited Jews to settle in their lands in order to spur the development of crafts and trade (see chapter 7).

[9] See Goitein (1967–88); Gil (1992; 2004).

As well documented by Toch, the early medieval charters, as well as court records and rabbinic responsa, confirm that the Jews in Europe were permitted to own land and that a great number of them—especially in Italy, southern Spain, southern and east-central France, and Germany—possessed fields, gardens, and vineyards and owned, transferred, and mortgaged landholdings. Had they wanted to, they could have been farmers, like the majority of the population of medieval Europe.[10]

Restrictions on Jewish landownership began appearing in some charters issued in the late medieval and early modern period—centuries *after* the Jews had become specialized in crafts, trade, moneylending, and medicine. The timing of these restrictions indicates that they cannot explain why European Jews entered and then became prominent in these occupations. At the same time, it raises the question of why Jews were prevented from owning land in certain locations in late medieval and early modern Europe. We address this issue in chapter 8, where we also investigate the argument that craft and merchant guilds in medieval Europe excluded the Jews from many crafts and trade, allegedly leading to their further specialization in moneylending.

TAXATION DISCRIMINATION

Rulers may have affected the choice of occupation through the use of discriminatory taxation that made some occupations unprofitable for Jews. Baron, Ben-Sasson, and Gil argue that the Muslim caliphs ruined agriculture in Mesopotamia and Persia by taxing according to area instead of yield. The land tax levied on non-Muslim farmers weighed heavily on Jewish farmers. The outcome was that the Jews abandoned rural areas, moved to towns and cities, and entered the skilled occupations available there.[11]

There are some problems with this explanation. First, the vast urbanization in the Middle East that occurred with the founding of the Muslim caliphates could not have been sustained unless a productive countryside supplied the cities and towns with plenty of agricultural foodstuffs (see chapter 6). If agriculture in Mesopotamia and Persia declined, how did towns and cities blossom? Second, if land taxes on non-Muslims were as heavy as has been claimed, they should have led other religious minorities, not only the Jews, to quit farming and enter urban occupations.

---

[10] Toch (2005, 2008, 2010, 2011, 2012).

[11] See Baron (1952, vol. 4, pp. 151–53); H. Ben-Sasson (1976, pp. 393, 405); Gil (2004, pp. 287–90, 599–600). They also point out that the increasing urbanization in the Umayyad and Abbasid caliphates made this movement of the Jews to the cities reach a full-fledged stage.

Might another form of tax discrimination have made the Jews switch occupations? The Jews and other religious minorities (*dhimmis*) had to pay head taxes levied on all household heads. But the head tax was not an innovation of the Umayyad and Abbasid caliphs: their predecessors, the Sassanid rulers, had imposed such taxes on the non-Persian, non-Magian part of the population, which included the Jews.[12] Moreover, the head tax was much more modest than other taxes. During the eleventh century, for example, it amounted to 3.4 dirhams a month—about 5 percent of a teacher's monthly salary at the time. Most important, the head tax was levied regardless of the occupation of the household head: whether a Jewish household head was a farmer, a smith, or a silk trader, he still paid this tax.[13] Thus the head tax could not possibly have led the Jews to abandon farming and to become artisans, shopkeepers, traders, and moneylenders.

PHYSICAL VERSUS PORTABLE HUMAN CAPITAL

The view that persecuted minorities prefer to invest in human rather than physical capital is as popular as the explanation based on restrictions. Scholars such as Werner Sombart, Reuven Brenner, Nicholas Kiefer, and Yuri Slezkine have maintained that the Jews, like members of other persecuted religious or ethnic minorities, preferred to invest in education rather than land because human capital is portable and cannot therefore be expropriated.[14] The corollary of this argument is that by not investing in land, the Jews ceased being farmers; investing in literacy and education enabled them to specialize in crafts, trade, banking, finance, law, and medicine.

The theory has no problems from the point of view of internal consistency. The argument is problematic when one considers the salient facts of Jewish history, however, as the transition from farming to urban skilled occupations occurred in eighth- and ninth-century Mesopotamia and Persia, where the Jewish minority enjoyed significant security of life. When, beginning in the mid-ninth century, groups of Jewish migrants arrived from Mesopotamia and Persia to Yemen, Egypt, Libya, and the Maghreb, they were already literate artisans and traders, able moneylenders, and

---

[12] Morony (1974, p. 119).

[13] Goitein (1967–88, vol. 2, pp. 300–304).

[14] Sombart ([1911] 1913); Brenner and Kiefer (1981); Slezkine (2004, p. 4). Related to this argument, Kessel (1958, pp. 46–48) argues that centuries of discriminations (e.g., by the medieval craft guilds) and persecutions made the Jews develop attitudes and skills that were suitable for commercially oriented or high-skill occupations, such as the medical profession. See Ayal and Chiswick (1983) for a discussion of the portable human capital argument.

highly educated scholars and physicians. The Jews who migrated from North Africa to the Iberian Peninsula and later to Sicily, and those who migrated within the Byzantine Empire including southern Italy, and their descendants who moved north and set the foundations of a large portion of European Jewry, were literate craftsmen, merchants, and scholars. Also the Jews from France, who settled in England and Germany beginning in the eleventh and twelfth centuries, were literate and educated traders and merchants.

Systematic persecutions and mass expulsions came later, in late medieval and early modern Europe, when world Jewry already comprised a small population of highly literate and mobile craftsmen, traders, moneylenders, and physicians (see chapters 7 and 8). Moreover, had the Jews wanted to maintain the right to own and farm land, they could have converted. Conversions to other religions for economic motives were not unheard of: Christians and some Samaritans in the Land of Israel converted to Islam to escape persecutions. Some prominent Jews did so as well, to gain access to the high echelons of the state bureaucracy of the Muslim caliphates.[15]

Finally, many minorities have been persecuted throughout history but did not abandon farming. In the first century, the Samaritans shared the same religious norms and rules as the Jews and worked as farmers, exactly like the Jews. During the fifth and sixth centuries, the Byzantine rulers persecuted, forcibly converted, and massacred many Samaritans. They also confiscated their lands. Centuries later, the Samaritans suffered a similar fate under the Abbasid rulers,[16] but they remained farmers, never invested in portable human capital, never became an urban population engaged in crafts and trade, never migrated from the Land of Israel, and never generated a worldwide diaspora like the Jews did.

The early Christians also remained farmers, despite persecutions and massacres in both the Roman and the Persian empires. Their circumstances did not cause them to invest in literacy and education and to become mobile or urban. In recent times, the Roma (Gypsies) have been persecuted in, and expelled from, many countries, but they never became a literate population, much less a people of traders, bankers, financiers, lawyers, or physicians.

As we show in detail in chapters 3, 5, 6, and 7, the decision of the Jews to invest in literacy and education (first to sixth century) came centuries *before* their worldwide migrations (ninth century onward). The direction of causality thus runs from investment in literacy and human capital to voluntarily giving up investing in land and being farmers to entering

[15]Goitein (1967–88, vol. 2).
[16]Gil (1992, pp. 822–23).

urban occupations to becoming mobile and migrating—not the other way around.

SELF-SEGREGATED RELIGIOUS MINORITY

Max Weber recognized the paramount legacy of Judaism in world history. At the same time, he posed the question of how world Jewry developed into a "pariah people" with highly specific peculiarities.[17] His view was that the prophets and sages during the Second Temple period (515 BCE–70 CE) moved the emphasis away from theological discussions, endowing Judaism with a rational morality that promised future reward to Jews who strictly observed ritual correctness and the norms of behavior codified in the Written and Oral Torah.[18] Voluntary self-segregation for religious purposes had profound economic implications for the Jewish people in the long run. In Weber's words:[19]

> A truly correct observance of the ritual was made extremely difficult for peasants.... Observance of the true Levitical purity commandments, which the exemplary pious propagated increasingly, were well nigh impossible for the peasants in contrast to the city people.... Moreover, Jews living among foreign peoples could hardly maintain a ritually correct way of life in rural areas. The center of gravity of Jewry had to shift increasingly in the direction of a transformation into an urban pariah people—as, indeed, came to pass.

The Jews voluntarily chose to become an urban population, according to Weber, and to segregate in certain occupations in order to maintain their ritualistic correctness, dietary prescriptions, and Sabbath rules, which would have been impossible to observe in rural areas.

One can raise several objections to Weber's argument. First, for centuries after the period of the prophets in the sixth century BCE, the Jews maintained their way of life while working as farmers in the Land of Israel, where they formed the majority of the local population. When, in the early

---

[17] See Shmueli (1968). In 1904–5, Weber published his famous essay "The Protestant Ethic and the Spirit of Capitalism." In a nutshell, Weber's thesis maintains that a particular form of rationality developed in Western countries as a direct product of Protestant beliefs. The Protestant form of rationality and work ethic contributed to the rise of capitalism. In this work, Weber called the Jews simply a minority. He used the term "pariah people" to designate the Jews in his *Essays in Sociology* ([1915] 1980), where he stated his difference of opinion with Sombart, who had argued in *The Jews and Modern Capitalism* ([1911] 1913) that Judaism was the true father of the spirit of capitalism. In *Ancient Judaism* ([1917] 1952), Weber began a lengthy analysis of Judaism that was interrupted by his death in 1920.

[18] Weber ([1917] 1952, p. 336).

[19] Weber ([1917] 1952, pp. 363–64).

fourth century, they became a religious minority under Roman rule, they still remained mainly a population of farmers, all the while observing the ritualistic rules required by their religion. Jews had always been religious minorities in Mesopotamia and Egypt, the other two important Jewish communities in antiquity, where they earned their living from farming while preserving the Jewish rites and customs.

More than a thousand years separate the period of the Second Temple from the transition of the Jews from farming to crafts, trade, and banking. The occupational transition occurred first in Mesopotamia and Persia under Muslim rule during the eighth and ninth centuries, before spreading to all other locations where the Jews lived. During this long period, generations of Jews observed the strict rules of their religion while earning their living as farmers.

Second, other religious minorities had similarly demanding ritualistic rules, but they did not turn into a small group of highly specialized craftsmen, traders, and moneylenders. The Samaritans are the best example, because they observed Jewish customs regarding eating kosher food, observing the weekly Sabbath and the Sabbath year, and obeying the Torah. They remained farmers for centuries while conforming to most of the religious rules and norms of the Jews. The fact that a religious minority with strict rules can survive as farmers is also illustrated in modern times by the Amish in the United States.

The Economics of Small Minorities

Some scholars argue that the Jews are just one of the many examples of trade and commercial diasporas—ethnic or religious groups without a territorial base, whose social, economic, and political networks cross the borders of nation-states and whose members live in urban areas and specialize in trade and commercial activities.[20] From this perspective, the Jews are no different from the Parsi (Zoroastrian) diaspora from Persia, the Huguenots in early modern and modern western Europe, the Chinese in Southeast Asia from the fifteenth to the twentieth century, the Armenians and Greeks of the Ottoman Empire, the Germans in eastern Europe in modern times, the Lebanese Christians in eighteenth-century Egypt and contemporary West Africa, the Indian middlemen minorities of East Africa, or the Pakistanis in Great Britain.[21]

Baron partly shares this view in contending that the Jews, as a religious minority, moved to cities in order to protect themselves from potential

---

[20] For the most recent and forceful arguments, see Slezkine (2004) and Muller (2010).
[21] See Armstrong (1976) and the references therein.

outbreaks of violence from hostile rulers or unfriendly local populations and to maintain their cultural identity. Life in isolated rural villages exposed them to both the hazard of being physically threatened and the risk of losing their religious cohesiveness.[22]

The economist Simon Kuznets offers extensive data in support of this theory.[23] Unlike other scholars, who focus on the study of European Jewry in the late medieval and early modern periods, Kuznets analyzes the occupational structure of world Jewry in the 1920s, 1930s, and 1940s and shows the unique occupational distribution of the Jewish labor force. In the countries with the largest Jewish communities (the nations of eastern Europe, the Soviet Union, the United States, Argentina, and Canada), an astounding 91–99 percent of the Jewish labor force was engaged in occupations other than agriculture (table 2.4).

Kuznets could not rely on the explanation based on restrictions on land use, because in these countries in the early twentieth century, the Jews were legally permitted to own and farm land, as well as to engage in any occupation they wished. Therefore, he had to look for another explanation—what he called "the economics of small minorities." The basic observation was that Jews were a minority everywhere, as shown in the last column of table 2.4.

Like Weber, Kuznets contended that the occupational and residential structure of the Jewish people was the result of voluntary choice. Stripped to its essence, Kuznets's argument maintains that for noneconomic reasons, a minority group, such as the Jews, has distinctive cultural characteristics within a larger population. The goal of maintaining cohesion and group identity leads minority members to prefer to be concentrated in certain industries and occupations. As a consequence, members of the group end up living in cities, where these occupations are available. Kuznets claims that his explanation applies to any ethnic or religious minority, not just the Jews.[24]

The notion that the Jews are just one of many examples of ethnic or religious minorities specializing as urban and trade diasporas does not pass the test of historical facts. During the first millennium, the Jews in the Land of Israel were a population of farmers both when they formed the majority of the population (until the fourth century) and when they became a religious minority. Becoming a religious minority did not transform them into an urban commercial diaspora.

Mesopotamian, Persian, and Egyptian Jews were also mainly farmers, despite being religious minorities in the Persian and Roman empires. The

[22] Baron (1937, vol. 1).
[23] Kuznets (1960, 1972).
[24] Kuznets (1960, p. 1604).

TABLE 2.4. Percentage Shares of Nonagricultural Workers in Labor Force, c. 1930

Country	Year	Jews	Non-Jews	Jews as % of total population
Argentina	1935	94	—	2.0
Bulgaria	1926	99	31	0.9
Canada	1931	99	71	1.5[a]
Czechoslovakia	1930	91	73	2.4
Germany	1933	99	83	0.8
Hungary	1930	97	52	5.1
Latvia	1930	99	47	4.8[a]
Lithuania	1937	96	—	7.6[a]
Poland	1931	96	47	9.8
Romania	1930	96	37	4.2
Soviet Union	1926	96	27	2.1
United States	1940	98	82	3.7

Source: Kuznets (1960, p. 1608, tables 1 and 2).

Notes: The Jewish population in these countries (almost 13 million people) amounted to 87 percent of world Jewry (see Baron 1971b, table 3). Nonagricultural workers include individuals engaged in industry and crafts, trade and finance, transportation and communication, public service, professions, and domestic and personal services.

— Not available.

[a] For Canada, Latvia, and Lithuania, the percentages refer to 1941, 1935, and 1923, respectively.

Jews were a religious minority in the vast territory under Muslim rule during the eighth and ninth centuries, when they became an urban population of craftsmen, traders, physicians, and moneylenders (see tables 1.3 and 1.5). Hence their status as a religious minority that aimed to preserve its cultural identity could not have prompted their occupational transition.

Moreover, other ethnic and religious minorities kept their distinctive characteristics yet dwelled in villages and earned their living as farmers during the first millennium. The most striking examples are the Druse and the Samaritans in the Land of Israel, who kept their distinct religious identities as farmers and never became an urban or trade diaspora. The Coptic minority in Egypt also remained a population of farmers while preserving their religious identity under Muslim rule.

In more recent times, the Jews share some characteristics with other ethnic or religious trade diasporas that specialize in urban skilled occupations. The key distinction is that all the Jews, not just a small group, chose these occupations. In contrast, other ethnic or religious trade diasporas, such as the ethnic Chinese in Southeast Asia or the Indian middlemen in East Africa, represent a small percentage of the populations to which they belong.

SUMMARY

Why are there few Jews in farming? Why did the Jews create a world-wide urban diaspora? The theories set forth to address these questions can be grouped into two main categories: theories that highlight exogenous factors (restrictions, discrimination, persecution, massacres) and theories that emphasize endogenous choices (voluntary self-segregation because of religious rules, voluntary migration to the cities to preserve group identity). None of these theories is consistent with the historical evidence. None can explain why the Jews left farming or became a diaspora population.

CHAPTER 3

The People of the Book, 200 BCE–200 CE

> Make the study of the Torah your chief occupation.
> —*Shammai, c. 10 BCE*

> The Jews consider the birth of a child to be no occasion for
> festivity or an excuse for drinking to excess. The law ... orders
> that they shall be taught to read, and shall learn both the laws
> and the deeds of their forefathers, in order that they may imi-
> tate the latter, and, being grounded in the former, may neither
> transgress nor have any excuse for being ignorant of them.
> —*Flavius Josephus, c. 96 CE*

THE JEWS LOOKED, DRESSED, SPOKE, AND EARNED THEIR LIVING MAINLY
from agriculture like the rest of the population in the Hellenistic, Roman,
and Persian empires.[1] The key difference between Jews and non-Jews was
their religion. Solving the puzzles of Jewish economic and demographic
history therefore requires an investigation of the pivotal events, religious
leaders, and main characteristics of the Jewish religion from the founding of
the Second Temple in 515 BCE to the compilation of the Mishna circa 200.

THE TWO PILLARS OF JUDAISM FROM EZRA TO HILLEL (500–50 BCE): THE TEMPLE AND THE TORAH

During the first millennium BCE, the two pillars of Judaism were the
Temple in Jerusalem and the Torah. The first pillar made the Jewish religion similar to the pagan cults spread in the Mediterranean and the Middle East. In the times of both the First Temple (c. tenth to ninth century
BCE through 586 BCE) and the Second Temple (515 BCE–70 CE), ritual
sacrifices by a small elite of high priests were the predominant mode of
divine service.[2] Pilgrimage to Jerusalem and the offering of sacrifices in

---

[1] Breuer (2006, pp. 457–59); J. Schwartz (2006, pp. 433–53).

[2] For more than seventy-five years, archaeologists maintained that the First Temple had
been built during King Solomon's reign, during the tenth century BCE. Recent scholarship

the temple were considered paramount religious duties that all Jewish men had to perform.[3]

The second pillar of Judaism, the Torah, set the foundation for the entire body of Jewish law (halakha). The belief in the existence of one God and the gift of the Torah given by God to the Hebrews through the Mosaic covenant made Judaism profoundly different from the pagan cults. The Written Torah (the Five Books of Moses) acquired a central role in shaping all aspects of Jewish life during and after the Babylonian exile (586–538 BCE).[4] Alongside the Written Torah, the Oral Torah developed as the outcome of myriad discussions, judgments, and rulings of generations of prophets, scholars, and sages, who emerged as the new religious leaders during the Second Temple period.[5]

The Gospels provide a vivid portrait of the two pillars of Judaism during the Second Temple period. In several episodes, Jesus enters the Temple and teaches parables to clarify the Torah.

The Temple and particularly the Torah were the driving forces behind the development of Jewish educational institutions. The Torah highlights the importance of study throughout life and establishes a father's duty to teach his children the laws of Judaism.[6] However, it does not contain an explicit ruling or law requiring Jewish fathers to send their children to school to learn to read and to study the Torah.

---

has questioned the extent and power of David's and Solomon's united kingdoms of Israel and Judah and argued that the events described in the Bible as having occurred during their reigns, including the erection of the First Temple, actually happened a century later. See Finkelstein and Silberman (2001, 2006) and the references therein.

[3] Tadmor (1976); Cahill (1998).

[4] After the Torah was canonized, the eight books of Prophets (*Nevi'im*) were canonized (between 500 and 400 BCE). The eleven books of Scriptures (*Ketuvim*) were canonized between 100 and 200. The Tanakh (the Hebrew name of the Bible) consists of these three subdivisions. There is a debate among scholars about the dating of the Torah. Some scholars maintain that the Bible was written during the Persian period (fourth century BCE) or the Hellenistic period (third and second centuries BCE) and that people and facts mentioned in the Bible are pure fiction. Other scholars contend that the Torah was canonized sometimes during the sixth century BCE and is a fully reliable historical account of ancient Jewish history. See Friedman (1997) for an overview of this debate. Recently, Finkelstein and Silberman (2001, 2006) stated that the core historical books of the Old Testament were written earlier than previously thought, in the late seventh century BCE (in the time of King Josiah) as political propaganda to support his reforms.

[5] M. Stern (1976); Cahill (1998).

[6] Exodus (6:7), for example, states the commandment regarding the laws of God and commands Jews to "teach them diligently to your children." Deuteronomy (6:6–7) orders "And be it that these laws which I command unto you today, you shall teach them diligently to your children, and you shall speak of them, as you sit in your home and as you walk on your way outside, when you lie down and when you awaken."

An important step in making reading a central feature of Judaism took place when the priestly scribe Ezra (c. fifth century BCE) inaugurated public reading of the Torah as a new element in Jewish life. Henceforth, the Torah was read and explained on regular occasions in public. Before Ezra, most parts of the Torah were under the exclusive control of the high priests.[7]

The process of setting up Jewish institutions for learning was slow and long. The first phase started during the Soferim (scribes) period (c. 515– c. 200 BCE) with the establishment of academies for higher learning in Jerusalem that trained the high priests for the Temple. For this reason, access was restricted to a very small elite.[8] During the first century BCE, schools for higher education were founded in Jerusalem and later in other towns under the leadership of two of the main sages of the time, Hillel and Shammai.[9] Tuition, living and transportation costs, and tough entry requirements all turned out to be serious obstacles that prevented all but a small number of Jews from attending these schools.[10]

Under the influence of the president of the Sanhedrin, Simeon ben Shetah (about 65 BCE), free secondary schools for sixteen- and seventeen-year-olds were established throughout the Land of Israel. A two-level school system thus came into existence. In Jerusalem, a college for advanced students prepared students for the higher academies; across the Land of Israel, preparatory schools supplied free and compulsory education to all sixteen- and seventeen-year-old men. The secondary schooling system suffered a fundamental problem: orphans and children whose fathers did not have the time or knowledge to provide them with some basic literacy did not receive the primary education required to meet the

---

[7] Marcus, Hirschberg, and Ben-Yaacob (2007).

[8] Swift (1919, pp. 86–98); Ginzberg (1943, pp. 8–11); Demsky et al. (2007).

[9] S. Safrai (2007). Born in Babylon in about 90 BCE, Hillel descended from the tribe of Benjamin on his father's side and from the family of David on his mother's side. As an adult, he moved to Jerusalem to study, became the spiritual leader of the Jewish community, and founded one of the two leading academies in Jerusalem, known as the House of Hillel (Bet Hillel). He is considered one of the most important figures in Jewish history and the founder of a dynasty of sages that includes some of the most eminent leaders and scholars, such as Rabbi Gamliel I and Rabbi Judah haNasi. Hillel issued many important rulings on religious, social, and economic matters. Born in the Land of Israel in about 50 BCE, Shammai was the most eminent contemporary and the halakhic opponent of Hillel. Shammai's academy became known as the House of Shammai (Bet Shammai). After Hillel died, Shammai took his place as president of the Sanhedrin in Jerusalem. Although Hillel's grandson, Rabbi Gamliel I, became president after the death of Shammai in 30 CE, the Sanhedrin remained dominated by the House of Shammai until about 70 CE. After the destruction of the Second Temple, the dynasty and disciples of Hillel dominated rabbinic Judaism, overshadowing the legacy of Shammai.

[10] Perlow (1931); Drazin (1940); Ebner (1956); Morris (1977).

standards of admission to the secondary schools. Therefore, despite being free, these secondary schools attracted only a small minority of students.[11]

THE LEVER OF JUDAISM: EDUCATION AS A RELIGIOUS NORM

For almost any good or service, there is a market in which demand and supply interact to determine the quantities exchanged and the prices paid. Does it make sense to speak of a market for religion at the time of Hillel, Shammai, Josephus, and Jesus, a market in which different groups and sects competed with one another to attract followers and individuals shopped around to find the religious group that best suited their preferences and needs?

Like most religions today—including Judaism—Judaism during the Second Temple period was a constellation of many religious groups. The Sadducees and Pharisees, the two major Jewish groups, competed for leadership. Essenes, Sicarii, Zealots, Samaritans, and the many Jewish-Christian sects added to the constellation of Jewish groups that lived in the Land of Israel during the first century. Members of these groups lived side by side with the pagan population, which worshipped Greco-Roman, Semitic, Egyptian, and Syrian gods and deities in temples.[12]

Members of the various Jewish sects were almost indistinguishable from one another in terms of speaking, eating, dressing, working, marrying, and other daily matters. They grew increasingly distinct in the religious norms set by each group as the main requirements for membership. This variance in religious norms plays a pivotal role in our theory, as we show later.

The works of Josephus and the Gospels provide a vivid picture of the Jewish sects in the Land of Israel during the first century and show how belonging to one religious group entailed following distinctive norms and rulings, like being members of a club. This is how Josephus describes the three main groups within Judaism:[13]

---

[11]Greenberg (1960); Demsky et al. (2007).

[12]M. Stern (1976); Neusner (1990d); E. Sanders (1992); D. Schwartz (1992); Baumgarten (1997); S. Cohen (1987, 1999). Appearing as new groups at the beginning of the first century CE, the Sicarii and Zealots actively engaged in anti-Roman uprisings, which reached their climax with the first Jewish-Roman war (66–73 CE).

[13]The first part of the quote comes from *The Antiquities of the Jews* (bk. 13, chap. 5, sec. 9); the second part of the quote comes from *The Life of Flavius Josephus* (para. 2). Josephus also described the three sects in *The Wars of the Jews* (bk. 2, chap. 8). All his works have been edited and translated in Flavius Josephus (1998).

At that time there were three sects among the Jews, who had different opinions concerning human actions; the one was called the sect of the Pharisees, another the sect of the Sadducees, and the other the sect of the Essenes. . . .

. . . and when I was about sixteen years old, I had a mind to make trial of the several sects that were among us . . . for I thought that by this means I might choose the best, if I were once acquainted with them all. . . . I returned back to the city, being now nineteen years old, and began to conduct myself according to the rules of the sect of the Pharisees.

The Essenes became known as an ascetic and communalistic sect at the end of the Hasmonaean revolt (mid-second century BCE). The main group—who worked as farmers on the northwestern shore of the Dead Sea—saw themselves as the last generation before the coming of the Messiah. The discovery of the Qumran scrolls revealed that there were probably many small sects, including the Essenes, that expected the coming of the Messiah and had connections with the very first stages of the emergence of Christianity.[14] The main religious and political competition for leadership within the Jewish community was between the Sadducees and the Pharisees. Emerging as a group around the third century BCE, the Sadducees most likely derived their name from Zadok, the high priest in the days of King David and King Solomon. They consisted largely of the wealthy elite (priests, merchants, and aristocrats) and were associated with the first pillar of Judaism: the Temple. They dominated temple worship, rites, and sacrifices, and their power was tightly interwoven with the temple cult. One of their key tenets was that only the Written Torah was valid. Culturally, they were influenced by the spread of Hellenism in the Mediterranean.[15]

The Pharisees were closely associated with the second pillar of Judaism: the Torah. The meaning of the term "Pharisee" is uncertain. A widespread belief is that the name derives from the Hebrew stem *parash* ("to be separated"). The Pharisees emerged as a distinct religious and political group shortly after the successful revolt led by Judah Maccabee against the Hellenistic Seleucid rulers (165–160 BCE) and the consequent establishment of the Hasmonaean dynasty (140 BCE) that ruled Judea for 80 years. Considering themselves the descendants of the tradition tracing back to the priestly scribe Ezra and, therefore, to King David, they were the most rigid defenders of the Jewish religion and traditions. Unlike the Sadducees, they strongly opposed the influence of the Greek language and civilization in the Land of Israel.[16]

---

[14] Neusner (1990d); Baumgarten (1997).

[15] M. Stern (1976); Neusner (1990d); Baumgarten (1997); S. Cohen (1999); Mansoor (2007b).

[16] M. Stern (1976); Baumgarten (1997); Mansoor (2007a).

The Pharisees believed that both the Written Law and the Oral Law were authoritative. One of their main tenets was that as God was everywhere, he could be worshiped both in and outside the Temple and was not to be invoked by sacrifice alone. The Pharisees considered study, teaching, and preaching the law of God their paramount mission. They therefore established and fostered the synagogue as a place of worship, study, and prayer. In doing so, they aimed to undermine the monopoly of the Temple and to challenge the political and religious leadership of the Sadducees.[17]

One has to be careful in drawing sharp distinctions among the various Jewish religious groups (there were certainly high priests in the ranks of the Pharisees, for example). Nevertheless, it is accurate to observe that the Second Temple period witnessed the growth of increasingly different clubs (sects) within Judaism, each promoting its own religious rulings and social norms.

It is in this milieu of religious and cultural competition within the Jewish leadership that the revolutionary step toward the establishment of a unique Jewish educational system took place. About 63–65 CE, the Pharisaic high priest Joshua ben Gamla issued a religious ordinance requiring every Jewish father to send his six- or seven-year-old sons to primary school.[18] Some 200 to 300 years later, the Babylonian Talmud described this event as follows:[19]

> However, that man is to be remembered for good, and his name is Joshua ben Gamla; for were it not for him, Torah would have been forgotten in Israel. For at first he who had a father was taught Torah by him, and he who had no father did not study Torah. It was then decreed that teachers of children should be appointed in Jerusalem. However, he who had a father, the father would bring him to Jerusalem and have him taught, while he who had no father, would not come to Jerusalem to study. It was then decreed that teachers of the young should be appointed in every district throughout the land. But the boys would be entered in the school at the age of sixteen and seventeen and if the teacher would rebuke one of them, he would resent it and leave. Thus it was until Joshua ben

[17] M. Stern (1976); E. Sanders (1977); Neusner (1990d); Baumgarten (1997); S. Cohen (1999).

[18] Drazin (1940); Ebner (1956); Greenberg (1960); Morris (1977); Crenshaw (1998); Demsky et al. (2007). For Ebner (1956), the Jewish primary school was established about 70 BCE, a century earlier than the ruling of Joshua ben Gamla. Other scholars attribute the establishment of the Jewish primary school to the high priest Simeon ben Shetah, who lived in the second century BCE. For our main argument and theory, which will be outlined in chapter 4, it does not make any difference whether the religious norm regarding educating the children was enacted during the second or first century BCE, or during the first century CE.

[19] Babylonian Talmud, Baba Batra 21a, cited in Greenberg (1960, p. 1261). A similar quotation is in the Talmud of the Land of Israel (Ketubot 8, 12–32c).

Gamla decreed that teachers of children should be appointed in every district and every city and that boys of the age of six and seven should be entered.

Why did Judaism develop this emphasis on religious instruction? Was the religious ordinance of Joshua ben Gamla swiftly implemented? The historian Moshe Aberbach maintains that the strong economic conditions in the third to the first century BCE made it possible to expand the learning of the Torah and the educational system.[20] Baron attributes the increased emphasis on religious instruction to the competition between the Sadducees and the Pharisees for the leadership of the Jewish community.[21] To achieve their goal of expanding the study of both the Written and the Oral Torah among all Jews, the Pharisees laid the foundations for the primary and secondary school system in the Land of Israel. A third, speculative explanation is that the Pharisaic rabbis may have favored the educational reform and the expansion of schools because they increased both their revenues as teachers and their status among the Jewish people.[22]

Although Josephus solemnly claimed at the end of the first century CE that "children's education is the principal care among the Jews,"[23] there is no direct evidence that primary education became universal within either the large Jewish community in the Land of Israel or the Jewish communities of Mesopotamia and Egypt. In fact, the vast majority of the Jewish population in the Land of Israel during the first two centuries was probably illiterate.[24]

The slow implementation of Joshua ben Gamla's ruling regarding children's instruction is understandable if one remembers the historical context in which the new religious norm came into existence. The Pharisaic high priest issued this ruling at a time when the Jewish leadership was split between Sadducees and Pharisees. Joshua himself was forced out of the post of high priest after one year. There is no evidence that the Sadducees' high priests, who were then in power, accepted and supported this ruling. In his detailed historical accounts, Josephus, who called Joshua ben Gamla his friend, did not report any information regarding the establishment of primary schools in his time. Moreover, the first Jewish-Roman

---

[20] Aberbach (1982, p. 19). This view is consistent with the fact that many pagans converted to Judaism at that time because they saw that the Jews were doing well from an economic point of view.

[21] Baron (1952, vol. 2, pp. 274–79). See also Feldman (1996b); Baumgarten (1997).

[22] See Carlton and Weiss (2001) for an interesting economic analysis of the religious rulings regarding Jewish education and competition in Torah instruction.

[23] The quote comes from Josephus's *Against Apion* (bk. 1, sec. 12) edited and translated in Flavius Josephus (1998).

[24] Bar-Ilan (1992); Hezser (2001, pp. 39–59, 495–97); Demsky et al. (2007).

war, which broke out within a few years of Joshua ben Gamla's ruling, would have made it difficult to immediately implement the educational reform envisaged by the Pharisaic high priest.

Whether or not the ruling of Joshua ben Gamla was swiftly implemented into world Jewry in his time is irrelevant for the theory we present in the next chapter. What is important is that this ruling was issued in the form of a *takkanah*, a legislative religious enactment that every Jewish father had to obey. Religious instruction (i.e., learning to read and studying the Torah) for both children and adults became a religious norm that grew to be the "lever of Judaism" in subsequent centuries.

THE DESTRUCTION OF THE SECOND TEMPLE: FROM RITUAL SACRIFICES TO TORAH READING AND STUDY

The burning and demolition of the Second Temple was the most traumatic event in Jewish history up to the Holocaust. Josephus's detailed and accurate historical account of the first Jewish-Roman war indicates that for the internal dynamics of Judaism, both the war and the destruction of the Temple were pivotal events that profoundly altered the competition and equilibrium among the constellation of religious groups.[25] The Zealots and the Sicarii, the major instigators and supporters of the rebellion, were exterminated during the sieges of Jerusalem in 70 CE and of the fortress of Masada three years later. The aftermath of the war did not bring any major change for the Essenes, who never played an active role in the economic or political sphere. The Sadducees, whose leadership depended on the Temple cult based on ritual sacrifices, lost their source of wealth and power and disappeared as a separate group shortly after the revolt.[26]

The Pharisees (including the Tannaim, the scholars in the academies in Jerusalem), who did not participate in the revolt, survived the massacres and gained the religious and political leadership over the Jewish population in the Land of Israel. A key member of the Pharisaic group was Rabbi Johanan ben Zakkai, one of the most eminent scholars and strongest opponents of the Sadducees. During the siege of Jerusalem, he argued (in vain) in favor of peace. Perhaps in recognition of his efforts, the Romans granted him permission to leave the city and, later, to reconstitute the academy (yeshiva) of Jerusalem in the coastal town of Jabneh,

---

[25] Josephus, *The Wars of the Jews*, edited and translated in Flavius Josephus (1998).

[26] Some scholars maintain that the Sadducees had already lost their power before 70 CE. See Neusner (1990d) and Baumgarten (1997) for discussions of this issue.

which became the most important center of Jewish learning between 70 CE and 135.[27]

The establishment of the academy in Jabneh was, de facto, the reestablishment of the Sanhedrin in Jerusalem. One of the primary issues over which Johanan ben Zakkai and his fellow Tannaim debated and issued their rulings was how Judaism should deal with the loss of the sacrificial altars of the Temple. He apparently helped persuade the other scholars and rabbis in the academy to replace animal sacrifice with prayer. The newly established Jewish leadership consisting of Pharisaic scholars and rabbis thus replaced the pilgrimage to Jerusalem and rituals, sacrifices, and ceremonies that could be performed only by the priests in the Temple with the study of the Torah and learning.[28] The events in the following century gave a major push to this process.

Instruction meant religious instruction to prepare boys for the time when, as adults, they would read in the synagogue, which became the center of reading and learning the Torah.[29] Synagogues existed in the Land of Israel well before the destruction of the Temple.[30] After 70 CE, however, many more synagogues were built in towns and even villages in the Land of Israel, especially in the Galilee, where most Jews moved after the two Jewish-Roman wars.[31]

The Legacy of Rabbinic Judaism: The Mishna and Universal Primary Education, 10 CE–200

After the destruction of the Second Temple, the Pharisaic sect was reestablished as rabbinic Judaism, which ultimately produced normative Judaism, the basis for all contemporary forms of Judaism.[32] The relationship between the Pharisees and rabbinic Judaism (exemplified by the Talmud) is so close that many do not distinguish between the two.

Rabbinic Judaism had a profound and long-lasting impact on the Jewish people and religion. At the doctrinal level, the scholars and rabbis in

[27] According to the Talmud, during the siege Johanan ben Zakkai escaped from the city hidden in a coffin to negotiate with Vespasian, who he predicted would become emperor. In exchange, he was granted three wishes, one of which was to reconstitute the Sanhedrin in the town of Jabneh at the end of the war (S. Safrai 1976b, pp. 319–20).

[28] Drazin (1940, p. 25); Maller (1960); S. Safrai (1976b).

[29] S. Safrai (1968, 1976a).

[30] According to the Gospels, Jesus taught in synagogues in Judea and Galilee, confirming the archaeological finding that synagogues existed before the destruction of the Second Temple.

[31] Flesher (1998); Levine (2005).

[32] S. Cohen (1987); Neusner (1990d).

the academies in the Galilee left as a perpetual gift to the Jews the Mishna, the pillar of Jewish law and the basis for all subsequent commentaries and halakhic literature. At the institutional level, the legacy of the Pharisees was to transform into reality the religious norm of Joshua ben Gamla by making primary education almost universal in world Jewry.[33] The authority of the rabbis of the Land of Israel deeply influenced, and was accepted by, the Jewish communities in Mesopotamia and the rest of the Diaspora.

Judah haNasi and the World of the Mishna

The development of the Oral Torah did not cease when, in the aftermath of the events of 70 CE, Rabbi Johanan ben Zakkai relocated the academy in Jerusalem to Jabneh. The yeshiva functioned as an academy, a high court, and a legislative body, in which generations of Tannaim discussed religious, social, and economic matters submitted to them by ordinary people; interpreted the Bible and the sacred law; and issued rulings. Prominent among the Tannaim were Rabbi Akiva and his disciple Rabbi Meir, who started to systematically organize the vast body of Jewish Oral Law accumulated through the centuries.

When in the aftermath of the Bar Kokhba revolt in 135, the academy of Jabneh was closed, the work of the Tannaim did not come to an end but simply moved to the new center of gravity of Judaism, the Galilee, whose academies soon became the hub of Jewish learning. This is the intellectual milieu in which Rabbi Judah haNasi compiled the Mishna in about 200.

Born circa 135, Judah was the son of Rabbi Simeon ben Gamliel II, a descendant of Hillel and, therefore, of King David.[34] Judah's grandfather, the prominent Rabbi Gamliel II (the great-grandson of Hillel), was the political leader (*nasi*) of the Jewish community in the Land of Israel, as well as the head of the yeshiva in Jabneh. Gamliel II was succeeded by his son, Rabbi Simeon, who moved the rabbinic academy to the town of Usha, and later to Shefar'am, in the Galilee, after the disastrous end of the Bar Kokhba revolt.

Judah succeeded his father, Simeon, in the powerful political role of *nasi* of the Jewish community in the Land of Israel and in the prominent religious role of head of the rabbinic academy. Under his leadership, the academy moved first to Beth She'arim and later to Sepphoris, both in the Galilee. Because of his impressive qualities—scholarship, political prestige, and wealth—he was called *ha nasi* ("the prince"), *rabbi* ("teacher"), *rabbenu* ("our teacher"), and *rabbenu ha qadosh* ("our saintly teacher").

---

[33] Ebner (1956).

[34] See Wald (2007a) for a description of Judah haNasi's life and contributions to Judaism.

Judah's legacy to Judaism and the Jewish people rests in the Mishna, completed in about 200. The six volumes of the Mishna form the religious and legal canon on which all subsequent Jewish law and halakhic literature have been built. Since the days of Judah haNasi, the heads of the academies gained paramount influence on a wide spectrum of matters pertaining to the daily lives of the entire Jewish community.

To systematize and combine the tradition of Jewish Oral Law accumulated through the centuries and to make sure that it could be transmitted to future generations, Judah spent many years sifting through the immense body of debates, judgments, and rulings of earlier generations of prophets and sages. He then compiled them into six orders of laws related to agriculture (*Zeraim*), festivals (*Moed*), marriage (*Nashim*), civil and criminal law (*Nezikin*), sacrifices and temple service (*Kodashim*), and ritual purity (*Tohorot*).[35] The organization of the Mishna by subject matter followed the method of Rabbi Akiva and his student Rabbi Meir.

Judah's purpose was not only to preserve a storehouse of tradition and learning but also to determine which statement of *halakhot* (laws) was normative. He identified the rabbinic opinions he considered authoritative, carefully preserving minority opinions in case laws should be changed in the future and a precedent for the changes be required. He omitted laws that were obsolete or otherwise lacking in authority. The compilation of the Mishna did not put an end to the development of Jewish law; rather, it provided it with a solid foundation over which subsequent generations of scholars would debate, clarify, and issue further rulings.[36]

Judah haNasi, as well as the earlier and later generations of scholars in the academies, also played an influential role as an educational reformer, adopting a harsh attitude toward the unlearned, in both statements and rulings. For example, he exempted sages from city taxes, increasing the hostility between the sages and the illiterate.[37] In his time, the term *am ha-aretz* ("people of the land"), which in earlier times referred to a Jew who disregarded tithing and the norms of ritual purity and sacrifices (*am*

---

[35] Neusner (1998) and G. Cohen (2002).

[36] Wald (2007b). The Tannaim who were contemporaries and disciples of Rabbi Judah haNasi produced the other major collection of halakhic tradition, the Tosefta. The word *tosefta* (literally an "additional" or "supplementary" halakhic tradition—that is, one not included in the Mishna), eventually came to denote a particular literary work organized according to the order of the Mishna and serving as a companion volume to it. Though there may once have been other such collections, the Tosefta is the only such collection to have survived. The Hebrew language, content, terminology, and Tannaim mentioned in the Tosefta are the same as those in the Mishna. Hence the Tosefta was likely redacted in the same circles in which the Mishna was redacted—the school of Rabbi Judah haNasi—some forty or fifty years later, by his own disciples.

[37] Talmud, Baba Batra, 8a.

ha-aretz le-mitzvot), acquired the new meaning of "one who does not know and does not teach his sons the Torah" (*am ha-aretz le-Torah*). For Judah haNasi and his fellow scholars, an *am ha-aretz* was an outcast in the Jewish community. Being an outcast involved a long list of social penalties: *ammei ha-aretz* could not be elected judges, and fathers were discouraged from marrying their daughters to sons of *ammei ha-aretz*.[38]

Judah haNasi is one of the towering intellectual and religious authorities in rabbinic Judaism. He and generations of scholars before him and during his time—the Tannaim in the academies—contributed to the development of Judaism into a "club" that imposed a unique obligation on its members: the requirement to read and study the Torah and to send one's children to the synagogue or school to do the same.

Jewish Primary Education in Tannaic Times

During the Tannaic period (c. 10–c. 200), primary schools for boys began being established in the Land of Israel, although the disruption brought by the Jewish-Roman wars likely put an halt to this process. It is only starting from the early third century that the leadership and influence of Rabbi Judah haNasi and of subsequent generations of scholars and rabbis contributed to implement a system of organized primary education in the Land of Israel and the Diaspora.[39]

The content of Jewish primary education during the Tannaic period was dedicated mainly to reading, understanding, and studying the Torah and learning the *mitzvot* (that is, the right deeds and conduct). At the beginning of primary school (*bet hasefer* in Hebrew, "house of the book"), children were taught the Hebrew alphabet. They were then taught to read the Torah in both Hebrew and Aramaic (whose alphabet were very similar). Greek, geography, arithmetic, and natural sciences were not part of the curriculum at this time. Knowledge for its own sake was accepted only for the study of the Torah.

As for writing, scholars debate the extent to which Jewish children learned to write in primary school during the Tannaic period. Some scholars argue that writing may have been taught in some schools and in some periods but not in others. Other scholars maintain that the rudiments of writing (using Hebrew letters) were taught in many schools but that writing as an art, as it was taught in Greek schools, had no place in Jewish primary schools.

[38] Oppenheimer (1977); Haas (1989).

[39] Information in this section comes from Drazin (1940); Ebner (1956); Greenberg (1960); Maller (1960); S. Safrai (1976a); Morris (1977); Aberbach (1982); Crenshaw (1998); Millard (2000); Hezser (2001); Demsky et al. (2007).

JUDAISM AND EDUCATION: THE UNIQUE LINK IN THE WORLD OF THE MISHNA

After 70 CE, Judaism no longer centered on temple service and ritual sacrifices. Instead, it demanded that all of its members read and study the Torah, educate their male children, and invest in literacy and instruction.

No other religion required fathers to educate their sons. Pagan religions continued to worship their gods via sacrifices and votive offerings in the temples (Greek and Roman pagan cults, Zoroastrianism), initiation into mysteries and magic (Eleusinian mysteries, Dionysian and Orphic cults, Mithraism), or prayers and fasting (Manichaeism).[40]

Not even the monotheistic religions closest to Judaism, such as Christianity and Samaritanism, made children's instruction a religious norm that all fathers were supposed to obey. After the destruction of the Second Temple and the transformation of the Jewish religion into rabbinic Judaism, the key differences between Jews on the one hand and Samaritans and Christians on the other was that the Jews considered the reading and studying of the Torah and the education of their children to be *the* fundamental religious duties for any Jewish adult, and they relied on the Mishna as their guiding religious and legal canon. "Torah, work, and charity" were the three paramount duties of Jewish fathers, according to the Mishna. In contrast, a Samaritan or Christian was not required to read or study the Torah, was not obligated to send his sons to primary school, and did not recognize the Mishna as his religious and legal canon. The Samaritans retained the high priesthood and animal sacrifices in the temple on Mount Gerizim (whereas the Jews no longer had a temple) and did not establish any primary educational institution.[41]

Judah haNasi made illiterate Jews outcasts in the Jewish community. Paul (c. 5–67 CE), a Pharisaic Jew, pushed Christianity in the opposite direction. After his famous conversion to Christianity, Paul decided that non-Jewish Christians should not adhere to Jewish law. Under his influence, Christianity abolished many requirements imposed by Judaism, including circumcision for men and the reading and studying of the Torah. "Faith, hope, and charity" became the three main requirements for being a devoted Christian.[42]

This "mutation" in the Jewish religious norms is one of the two pillars of our theory. In order to understand our argument in the next chapter,

[40] See E. Ferguson (2003) and L. Jones (2004) for a description of these religions, which spread in the Middle East and the Mediterranean during the first half of the first millennium.
[41] Flusser (1988); Neusner (1990a, 1990b, 1991). Samaritan scriptures also include the Samaritan version of the Torah, the Memar Markah; the Samaritan liturgy; and Samaritan legal codes and biblical commentaries.
[42] Nock (1969); E. Sanders (1977); Flusser (1988); Stark (1996); E. Ferguson (2003).

we highlight a few important points here. The transformation of Judaism reflected a change in religious preferences that was not motivated by economic incentives. Before the destruction of the Second Temple, the Sadducees and the Pharisees argued over religious matters. The main point of contention was whether the core of the Jewish religion should be the sacrifices in the Temple performed by the high priests or the reading and studying of the Torah by any Jewish man. The competition between the two groups ended with the siege of Jerusalem and the burning and demolition of the Second Temple by the Roman army in 70 CE, after which the Pharisees became the religious leaders.

The goal of the Pharisees was to equip all Jewish males with the ability to read the Torah in Hebrew, so that they would learn and obey all the laws of their religion. The emphasis on Hebrew, rather than the spoken languages of the Jewish communities in the Land of Israel and the Diaspora (Aramaic, Greek, and Latin), is consistent with the notion that the goal of Jewish education was religious rather than worldly. Even if economic profit had motivated the decision to educate children, learning to read would probably not have been particularly useful, as neither the Land of Israel nor Mesopotamia were urban or commercial economies in the first half of the millennium. Most of the Jewish population consisted of illiterate farmers, for whom investment in children's religious literacy was a sacrifice that generated no economic returns.

Whether the distinction between Pharisees and Sadducees was really this sharp or whether Jews really identified themselves with one sect or another is irrelevant. What is relevant for the argument presented in the next chapter is that during the Second Temple period, different groups within Judaism chose different religious norms and social codes of behavior to create their own religious clubs. The tragic end of the siege of Jerusalem and the burning of the Second Temple by the Roman army allowed one group—the one that considered reading and studying the Torah the paramount duty of every Jewish man and boy—to establish itself as the religious leader within Judaism. Generations of scholars and rabbis in the academies during the first two centuries, epitomized by the intellectual eminence of Rabbi Judah haNasi, set the foundations for the implementation of this new religious club, whose paramount norm was literacy and education.

CHAPTER 4

The Economics of Hebrew Literacy in a World of Farmers

> Rabbi Yose said: Give yourself to studying the Torah, for it
> does not come to you by inheritance.
>
> —*Mishna, Pirkei Avot 2:1*

ONE CAN THINK OF RELIGION AS A CONSUMPTION GOOD: PEOPLE DERIVE
satisfaction—what economists call "utility"—by following the norms and
rituals established by their religion.[1] Obeying these norms may entail costs
(spending time in a temple instead of doing other activities, contributing
to the maintenance of a church or mosque or synagogue, restricting one's
diet). If these costs are lower than the utility derived from observing the
religious norms, individuals obey the norms. If the costs exceed the utility,
individuals may opt for another religious affiliation or decide not to belong
to any religion at all.[2] Different religions may impose different norms on
their followers in order to create unique and distinct clubs.[3]

In the aftermath of the destruction of the Second Temple and especially after the Bar Kokhba revolt in 135, Jews could choose to maintain
their affiliation to rabbinic Judaism (henceforth, Judaism)[4] or convert to
Samaritanism and Christianity, including a collection of Jewish-Christian
sects. A more radical choice was to become a pagan, like many people
in the Greco-Roman world in the Mediterranean. A key feature that set
Judaism completely apart from any other religious group at this time was

---

[1] See McCleary and Barro (2006) and McCleary (2011) for recent overviews on the growing field of economics of religion.

[2] If legal bans prevent people from changing their religious affiliation or they are forced
to convert, individuals have to obey the norms of the imposed religion even if these norms
generate enormous disutility. In the 1,500 years surveyed here, with the exception of a few
instances of forced conversions, Jews enjoyed religious freedom (see chapters 5, 6, and 7).

[3] Iannaccone (1992) started the economic literature that models religious affiliation as a
club.

[4] Throughout this chapter, when we refer to Judaism, we mean rabbinic Judaism—the
set of rules and norms sanctioned by the Pharisaic sect during the Second Temple period
and culminating with the redaction of the Mishna. As described in chapter 3, after 70 CE,
the sect of the Pharisees gained the religious leadership within the Jewish community in the
Land of Israel, and Judaism became identified with the rabbis and scholars in the academies.

the religious norm requiring Jewish fathers to send their sons from the age of six or seven to the synagogue or the school to learn to read and study the Torah (see chapter 3).

How would an economist interpret the different norms of the main religions in the Land of Israel from the time of Rabbi Judah haNasi to the time of Muhammad? In particular, what would be the demographic and economic implications of the religious norm requiring Jewish fathers to educate their sons? Would all Jews obey this norm? What would be the consequences of not investing in children's literacy and education? Is it more likely that Jews would convert to other religions or that Christians, Samaritans, and pagans would convert to Judaism? What would happen to Judaism and the Jewish people in the long run?

To address these questions, this chapter describes our economic theory narratively; the annex presents the formal model. To explain the rationale behind our theory, we put ourselves in the shoes of Jewish farmers living in the Galilee (the center of Jewish economic and intellectual life in the Land of Israel) from 200 to 650 in order to understand their economic and religious choices under the new norm imposed by Judaism.

Two caveats are in order. First, we focus on the choices of farmers because the overwhelming majority of the population in the period considered earned its living from agriculture and related occupations. Second, our goal is not to explain why Jewish scholars and rabbis in the academies pushed Judaism toward becoming a literate religion and enforced the religious norm requiring fathers to educate their children.[5] As shown in chapter 3, the transformation of Judaism into a literate religion was the outcome of an exogenous event (the destruction of the Second Temple), which destroyed one pillar of Judaism (the Temple) and made the other (the Written and Oral Torah) the surviving core of religious practice. The new Jewish religious leadership vested in the Pharisaic scholars and rabbis made the reading and study of the Torah the key requirement for belonging to their club. Whether they chose to do so for purely religious reasons or were motivated by economic incentives (as teachers of children they could earn income) is irrelevant for our argument. What is relevant is that Judaism transformed itself into a literate religion. The question we seek to answer is how this transformation affected the lives of the millions of Jewish farmers living in the Land of Israel and elsewhere.

---

[5] In economic jargon, our model is not a political economy model for studying the choices of the Jewish religious leadership on which religious and social norms to set as requirements of their religion. We take the religious norm regarding educating the children as given and investigate how the implementation of this norm affected the choices of Jewish farmers living at that time.

HETEROGENEITY AND THE CHOICES FACING
JEWISH FARMERS CIRCA 200

People have different tastes, aspirations, expectations, beliefs, and values. They also have different abilities, temperaments, earnings, and wealth levels. Throughout their lives, they experience different shocks (wars, droughts, floods, famines, diseases). In the language of economics, differences in tastes, religiosity, abilities, initial endowments of land and capital, fertility and mortality rates, productivity, earnings, taxes, and luck are captured by the word "heterogeneity." Heterogeneity in the characteristics of the population means that in the same environment, different individuals will make different choices.

To see how heterogeneity helps explain the history of the Jews during the first half of the first millennium, consider a hypothetical village in the Galilee circa 200. One resident, Simeon, is a wealthy farmer and devoted Jew.[6] He spends time in the local synagogue, where he listens to the rabbi, who reads and discusses the weekly portion of the Torah. As he hopes that his three sons, who are smart and diligent, will learn and study the Torah and obey all the laws of Judaism, he sends them to the primary school in the synagogue instead of employing them on his farm. Simeon never entertains the idea of choosing another religion, because as a pagan, Samaritan, or Christian, his sons would not learn and study the Torah, which would make him unhappy.

Another local farmer, Reuven, works on Simeon's farm as a wage laborer, earning 26 denarii a month.[7] Providing his family with food and shelter costs him about 24 denarii a month. His son would earn 8 denarii a month if he starts working. With his meager income, Reuven cannot afford to educate his son: a book costs 200 denarii, and tuition is expensive. Reuven would also have to forgo the money his son could bring in. The learned people call Reuven *am ha-aretz le-Torah* and tell him that following the ruling of the great Rabbi Judah haNasi, they would never let their daughters marry the illiterate son of an illiterate person. Despite this, Reuven would never leave Judaism, because his relatives and friends would stop talking to him or helping him if he lost his job.

---

[6] In the rabbinic debates in the Talmud, scholars resorted to hypothetical reasoning to discuss a specific issue by using Simeon or Reuven as fictitious names of Jews living in the Land of Israel or Mesopotamia.

[7] The information on prices and wages comes from data collected from primary sources by Sperber (1965, 1966, 1968, 1970). In the Roman currency system, the denarius was a small silver coin, first minted in the early third century BCE. It was the most common coin in circulation in the empire. It was slowly debased during and after Emperor Nero's reign (54–68 CE) and no longer minted after the mid-third century.

Near the farm of Simeon is the landed estate of another wealthy land-owner, Elisha, who employs many agricultural laborers. Elisha finds the scholars' discussions in the synagogue boring and prefers to spend his time in the beautiful bathhouse built by the Romans in the neighboring town of Beth Shean. He hopes that his two sons will work on his farm instead of wasting time in the synagogue. He does not understand why the rabbi insists that all children in the village learn to read and study the Torah in Hebrew, a useless language in daily life, as most people speak Greek or Aramaic. Even if all his fellow village dwellers could read books in Hebrew or any other language, they would not become better farmers and earn more. Elisha is thinking about whether to leave Judaism or to remain Jew but ignore most of its rules.

On the outskirts of the village live the brothers Eliezer and Thryphon, who own a small plot of land. Each of them has a son who is eager to learn and to go to school. Despite being illiterate, Eliezer strives to go to the synagogue whenever he can, because he enjoys listening to the rabbi explain the Torah. Half of Eliezer's meager earnings is typically spent on food, and about a third goes to the annual land tax.[8] Despite the cost, he hopes to send his six-year-old son to school. The expense is worth paying in order to see his son read and study the Torah in the synagogue in front of the entire community on the Sabbath. Eliezer is proud of being a devout Jew and would never leave his religion.

Eliezer's brother, Thryphon, is not fond of public Torah reading and does not want to send his son to school. He resents being called *am ha-aretz* by the rabbi and the other literate people in his village and is thinking about joining the sect of the Ebionim, who are kind toward poor and illiterate people and do not require fathers to educate their children.[9]

Why does the wealthy Jewish farmer Simeon decide to invest in his sons' literacy whereas the wealthy Elisha does not? Why does Eliezer, who is a poor farmer, do everything possible to send his son to school, whereas Reuven and Thryphon, who are equally poor, choose not to invest in their sons' literacy? Why do Elisha and Thryphon consider converting to another religion, whereas Simeon, Reuven, and Eliezer do not? The concept of heterogeneity helps explain the different choices Jewish farmers in the first half of the first millennium made.

[8] Z. Safrai (1994) estimates that in the Land of Israel during Roman times, 50 percent of the annual household income went to food and clothing and 30 percent to taxes.

[9] The Ebionim were one of the Jewish-Christian sects that emerged in the Land of Israel during the first and second centuries (see chapter 5).

The Economic Theory: Basic Setup

The way economists reason when they write a model to explain how individuals make choices is similar to the way of thinking and the "what if" type of reasoning that characterize the rabbinic discussions and debates in the Mishna and the Talmud. For any possible contingency in a given situation in daily life, the rabbis and scholars in the academies in the Land of Israel and Mesopotamia debated the pros and cons of the various options and analyzed what has happened or what could happen if a particular event occurred. Similarly, when economists write models to explain the decisions of individuals, they make hypotheses about individuals' preferences, skills, and incomes and on the economic environment in which they live and ask "what" is likely to happen "if" those hypotheses hold.

Economists assume that when making choices, individuals compare the benefits and the costs of the alternatives with the goal of selecting the option that yields the greatest utility.[10] A Jewish farmer (that is, a farmer who identifies himself with Judaism) living in a village in the Galilee circa 200 had to make two key choices. First, he had to decide whether to send his sons to work or to school (synagogue) to learn to read and study the Torah. Second, he had to choose whether to continue belonging to Judaism or to convert and become a Samaritan, a Christian, or a pagan. We begin by describing the benefits and the costs associated with the first choice.

Both Jewish and non-Jewish individuals derive utility from consumption. Jews differ from non-Jews in one key dimension: they also derive utility from being able to read and study the Torah and from having literate sons who can read and study the Torah.[11] As described earlier, people display heterogeneity in many dimensions, including their religiosity (that is, their attachment to the norms sanctioned by their religion). Depending on whether a Jewish farmer has (or has not) a strong attachment to Judaism, he may derive more or less utility from being able to read and study the Torah and from his sons being literate and able to read and study the Torah for a variety of reasons.[12] By getting religious instruction, children

---

[10] Reasoning that compares the benefits and the costs of various options when making a choice can also be found in the rabbinic debates. For example, the Mishna (Pirkei Avot 2:2) reports Rabbi Judah haNasi saying, "What is the proper path a person should choose for himself? . . . Consider the loss incurred for performing a mitzvah (commandment) compared to its reward, and the reward received for sinning compared to the loss."

[11] We assume that all the other norms Judaism imposes (e.g., eating kosher food, observing the Sabbath) yield the same utility (or disutility) as similar norms imposed by other religions.

[12] Positing that the utility of the father depends on both his own education and his sons' education translates into the language of economics the key feature of Judaism after

learn the laws of Judaism and are more likely to obey them, which in turn make their parents happy. When grown up, the sons may stand in front of the community in the synagogue and read the weekly portion of the Torah, making their parents proud.

Religious affiliation may be transmitted from parents to children, and parents typically impose their own religious affiliation on their children. Similarly, religiosity within a religious denomination may be transmitted from parents to children. This means that a child born to a Jewish father inherits some positive attachment to the religious norm regarding receiving religious instruction and learning to read and study the Torah; given heterogeneity, the level of this attachment/religiosity in each individual varies. A child born to a Samaritan, Christian, or pagan father does not inherit any attachment to the Jewish religious norm regarding education, as these religions do not impose this norm on their members. By obeying the religious norm and educating his children, the Jewish farmer gets an additional benefit: he avoids the social penalty inflicted on illiterate people (*ammei ha-aretz*) within the Jewish community.[13]

In order to learn to read and study the Torah in Hebrew, boys need to be sent to the primary school (typically inside or next to the synagogue), which is costly. Given the way farming and pastoral activities were organized during the first millennium, the Jewish farmer derives no economic benefit from sending his sons to school and having them learn to read and study the Torah in Hebrew. A farmer needs children with physical strength to work hard on his farm.[14] Literate sons do not make a farmer more productive or richer.

The Jewish farmer earns an annual income from his agricultural activity. If he owns and manages the farm, his income consists of the profits (revenues minus costs). If he does not own the farm, he may work on the farm of a landlord as wage laborer, sharecropper, or fixed-rent tenant,

---

it became identified with rabbinic Judaism: a good Jew was one who read and studied the Torah *and* sent his sons to the synagogue to learn to do so.

[13]The social penalty, or community sanction, on *ammei ha-aretz* could take several forms, as described in many rabbinic debates in the Mishna and Talmud (see chapter 3).

[14]Unlike in modern economies, in which various branches of agriculture and cattle rearing have become a field of study and farmers can read books devoted to the best practices to cultivate the land or raise cattle, no such books or scientific approach to agriculture existed in antiquity. Cato the Elder, Columella, Varro, and Pliny the Elder wrote manuals on farming (Pliny the Elder even wrote an encyclopedia consisting of hundreds of volumes) during the late Republic and early empire (White 1970; Mokyr 1990, chap. 1). The target audience of these books (written in Latin, not in Hebrew) was typically the circle of the authors' friends and the elite, however, not the average farmer. Moreover, given the prohibitively high cost of books before the invention of the printing press (see Buringh and van Zanden 2009), the average farmer could hardly afford to buy a book.

earning an income that depends on the type of contractual arrangement he has.[15]

With his income, the Jewish farmer buys food and clothing for his family and pays taxes. If he decides to send his sons to school, he has to incur the associated costs. He has to pay for books and contribute to both the teacher's salary and the maintenance of the synagogue where the school activities are typically held. In small communities, these expenses may represent a heavy burden on the household head. Given heterogeneity in individuals' abilities and temperaments, the cost of educating a child may decrease with his ability and diligence. The costs of educating one's son also include the forgone earnings the child could have earned by working on the farm rather than attending school—what economists refer to as "opportunity cost." Even if education is free (because, for example, the state provides books and pays all tuition), the opportunity cost of going to school makes educating children a burden for farmers, especially poor and middle-income ones. (Even today, many farmers in developing countries that provide free universal primary education keep their children out of school so that they can work on the farm.[16])

Next let us consider the benefits and the costs associated with the second choice the Jewish farmer has to make: whether to remain a Jew or to opt for another religion. The Jewish farmer can avoid following the rules set by Judaism, including the one requiring him to educate his sons, by converting to another religion. Doing so would free him of the costs of educating his children or suffering the social penalty inflicted on the illiterate. A Jew who converts, however, may suffer psychological or monetary costs, including losing the support of his Jewish friends and relatives. We call the costs associated with converting to another religion the "costs of conversion."

Religious affiliation typically requires some costly signal of belonging to a club or network; different religions may require their members to follow different rituals and adhere to different norms as a way to signal their membership in the club.[17] Investing in literacy and education, as Judaism requires, is a very costly signal for individuals and households living in farming economies in which there are no economic returns to literacy. As we show, the decisions to invest in a son's literacy and to remain or become a member of a religious group are related.

---

[15]As a wage laborer, he earns an annual wage that does not depend on how much is produced. As a sharecropper, he and the landlord divide the agricultural output (50–50 being common). As a fixed-rent tenant, the farmer pays a fixed rent to the landlord and keeps the entire agricultural output.

[16]The World Bank has programs (e.g., Mexico Opportunidadas) targeted to address this issue; the programs provide subsidies to rural households that send their children to school.

[17]Iannaccone (1992); Berman (2000).

The Economic Theory: Predictions

We first consider the decision of whether or not educate one's children. Given heterogeneity in people's tastes, religiosity, incomes, and the costs of educating children, our theory predicts that some Jewish farmers do not send their children to study in the synagogue because, for them, the marginal cost of doing so outweighs the marginal benefit. In particular, farmers with low attachment to Judaism will have less incentive to invest in their sons' religious literacy. Farmers with low incomes or with higher costs of educating children (e.g., farmers whose sons are not fast learners or do not like studying; farmers who live in small communities and therefore bear a higher share of the teacher's salary) will invest less in their children's literacy, up to the point at which they will not educate their children at all. In this way, they will save the cost of providing the basic (minimum) level of literacy. Regardless of heterogeneity, in bad economic conditions (e.g., when a drought or war causes a negative shock to the entire economy), fewer farmers will educate their sons.

Next we consider the decision to convert. A Jewish farmer converts to another religion if the utility he derives from remaining Jewish is less than the utility he derives from becoming a Samaritan, a Christian, or a pagan. Jewish farmers who educate their children have fewer incentives to convert, because other religions assign zero value to their religious literacy. Jewish farmers who do not educate their sons may or may not leave Judaism. Those farmers whose costs of conversion are higher than the social penalty imposed by the Jewish community on illiterate people are more likely to maintain their religious affiliation (these are the *ammei ha-aretz*). Conversely, farmers whose costs of conversion are lower than the social penalty are more likely to leave Judaism for another religion with less demanding requirements.

The main prediction of our theory regarding conversions is that in a farming society in which literacy has little or no economic returns, given heterogeneity, in each cohort some proportion of Jews convert. If the economy remains mainly rural—meaning that investment in literacy and education yields no direct economic returns—the size of the Jewish population will keep shrinking.

What are the dynamics of the conversion process predicted by our theory? First, as initially the proportion of Jews that is illiterate or has low devotion to the new religious norm is high, the absolute and relative rate of conversion is also high. As time passes, the proportion of literate Jews increases. The proportion of conversions therefore declines, but with sufficient heterogeneity in individuals' characteristics, conversions continue.

Second, each time there is an aggregate (macro) shock that negatively affects everyone's incomes, the rate of conversions increases, because the marginal cost of educating the children grows relative to the marginal benefit. More Jewish farmers will not educate their sons and convert to religions that do not impose this costly requirement. This process has an impact on the next generation, as more Jews become illiterate and convert to other religions. Hence in the long run, Judaism does not survive in farming economies that are subject to negative aggregate shocks and in which there are no economic returns to investment in religious and general literacy.

What about non-Jewish farmers? Our theory predicts that Christian, Samaritan, and pagan farmers will not educate their sons, because investing in literacy and education is costly and generates neither economic benefits nor a sense of satisfaction or pride for people affiliated with these religions. Furthermore, farmers from other religions will not convert to Judaism because, as illiterate people who do not educate their children, they would suffer the social penalty imposed by the Jewish communities on illiterate people and gain nothing from being part of the Jewish "club."

Life in a Village in the Galilee circa 200 through the Lens of the Theory

We now return to the hypothetical village in the Galilee circa 200, when Rabbi Judah haNasi was compiling the Mishna, to see how the economic theory helps explain the choices made by Simeon, Reuven, Elisha, Eliezer, and Thryphon. Simeon has such high religiosity—that is, he derives so much utility from reading and studying the Torah and having sons who can read and study the Torah—that he decides to educate them. He does not want to convert to another religion, because he derives great utility from following the rules of Judaism, including the rule requiring him to educate the children.

Reuven does not educate his son, because the additional (marginal) cost of educating his son is higher than the additional (marginal) benefit he would get from doing so, given his meager earnings. Because he does not opt to educate his son, he suffers the social penalty inflicted by the Jewish community on illiterate people (ammei ha-aretz). He still chooses not to convert, because the cost to him of doing so is higher than the social penalty imposed for not educating the son.

Elisha, who is wealthy, could certainly afford to educate his sons. However, he has very little religiosity and hence derives little utility from reading and studying the Torah or having children who can read and study the Torah. Hence he decides not to educate his sons. Given that the social penalty and the cost of conversion are more or less the same for him, he is thinking about whether or not to convert.

Although providing for his son's education imposes a heavy burden on Eliezer, who is poor, he is so devout that he is willing to afford the cost. Hence he chooses to educate his son. Because he decides to educate his son, he does not suffer the social penalty imposed on *ammei ha-aretz* and so remains Jewish and does not convert.

His brother Thryphon, who is equally poor but has low religiosity, decides not to educate his son. Given this decision, he suffers the social penalty imposed on illiterate people who do not educate their children. Because for him this penalty is larger than the cost of converting, he considers the possibility of leaving Judaism and joining the Ebionim (a Jewish-Christian sect), among whom he will no longer suffer the scorn of being illiterate and not educating his son.

Through the lens of economic theory, one can rationalize the behavior of these Jewish farmers encountered in this hypothetical journey back in time. But what about the historical evidence? Does it support the main predictions of our theory regarding educating children and converting? Did only a proportion of Jews invest in their children's literacy and education? Did the proportion of such Jews grow over time? Did Jewish farmers convert to other religions? Did the Jewish population shrink? If this were the case, would not Rabbi Judah haNasi and his fellow scholars have been able to predict this outcome and worried that Judaism would disappear through conversions if the many norms of Judaism, including the costly one requiring fathers to educate their children, were strictly enforced? Did non-Jews become Jews in subsequent centuries? Did the Jews remain mostly farmers, even though they were literate? What would happen if, suddenly, the economy became urban and there was a huge growth in the demand for literate and skilled occupations? This is what we are going to discuss in detail in the next two chapters.

ANNEX 4.A: FORMAL MODEL OF EDUCATION AND CONVERSION OF FARMERS

We assume that up to the year 200—that is, before the educational reform within Judaism—both Jews and non-Jews derived utility only from consumption, as no religion required literacy. For the purpose of argument, we assume that Jews and non-Jews had the same level of education and income.

We model the transformation of Judaism by assuming that Jewish farmers derived utility from their sons' and their own Hebrew literacy (education). Therefore, after the year 200, Jews received an exogenous taste parameter (an attachment index) $x > 0$, which weights the value of belonging to the "literate" Jewish religion in the utility function, interacted with the family literacy level. The taste parameter is set equal to 0 for an individual whose father is not Jewish (either because he was born non-Jewish or because he converted).

The basic setup is a two-period overlapping-generations model with no population growth.[18] An individual is assumed to live for two periods. In the first period, he lives with (and perhaps works for) his family and receives religion-related literacy and education e_s. In the second period, he becomes an adult with literacy and education level e who decides whether to keep or change his religion r (j = Jewish, n = non-Jewish), and whether and how much to educate his own sons.

Like Iannaccone (1992), we assume that utility comes from consumption and religious participation.[19] The utility of an adult has the following simple structure:

$$u^j(c, e_s; e, x) = \log c + x(e + 1)e_s - \varepsilon h \tag{4.1}$$

$$u^{jn}(c, e_s; e, x) = \log c - \pi x \tag{4.2}$$

$$u^n(c, e_s; e, x) = \log c \tag{4.3}$$

where c is family consumption, u^j is the utility of a Jewish individual, u^{jn} is the utility of a Jew who converts, and u^n is the utility of a non-Jew. In equation 4.1 the utility from being a Jew is increasing with an individual's literacy and education and those of his son.[20] This interaction of the preference parameter x with the level of literacy and education in the family is our way of modeling the transformation of Judaism from a religion based on sacrifices to a religion whose core became literacy and education. The term εh models the subsequent development within Judaism (beginning in the third century) that, under the leadership of rabbis and scholars,

[18] The hypothesis of no population growth is consistent with the fact that world population did not grow significantly during the first millennium. It would be straightforward to include fertility as an endogenous variable: the increased cost of raising children imposed by the religious requirement regarding education would make Jewish farmers less inclined to have children. This prediction would complement the one explored here regarding the decrease in the Jewish population as a result of conversions. The main reason why we do not make fertility an endogenous variable is that there is no historical evidence showing that Jews had lower fertility rates after the religious transformation.

[19] The model can be modified to resemble Iannaccone's model of religion as a club whose size is endogenously determined. Once the utility is specified as a general concave function, in equilibrium the utility and the cost of education can depend on the size of the Jewish population.

[20] Our specification implies that if $e_s = 0$, the individual derives no utility from being a Jew. This is an extreme version of the model, but it captures the paramount importance of educating children in Judaism after the educational reform.

imposed a social penalty on illiterate Jews. We set $h = 1$ if a Jewish father chooses not to invest in his son's literacy and education (i.e., if he is an *am ha-aretz*) and $h = 0$ otherwise. The community penalty for an illiterate Jew is expressed as $\varepsilon > 0$.[21]

Literacy and education do not enter the utility function of Jews who convert (equation 4.2) or of non-Jews (equation 4.3). This assumption models the fact that in the first millennium, no religion except Judaism assigned a positive value to the literacy and education of its followers. The term πx represents the disutility from conversion ($\pi \geq 0$).[22] The conversion of a non-Jew to Judaism is assumed to have zero cost.[23]

A Jew who follows the religious norm regarding children's literacy and education must provide at least a minimum level of literacy and education ($e^{min} > 0$) to his son, where the minimum level represents the ability to read and study the Torah. If $0 < e < e^{min}$, it is as if the literacy and education level is equal to 0. Without loss of generality, we normalize $e^{min} = 1$.

The cost of investing in one's son's (religious) literacy and education is given by $\gamma(e_s)^\theta$, where $\gamma > 0$ and $\theta > 1$. The cost of providing the minimum level of literacy and education is then equal to γ, which can be interpreted as the teacher's salary, the cost of books, and related expenses. It is possible that γ decreases with the size of the Jewish community, as each family will pay a smaller share of the teacher's salary in larger Jewish communities. From the viewpoint of the child, γ can be interpreted as the child's cognitive ability or diligence (with γ lower for high-ability and/or diligent children), the income forgone as a result of sending a child to school instead of work, and/or the cost of hiring a private teacher.[24]

A farmer's budget constraint is

---

[21] Making ε an increasing function of the proportion of literate Jews in the community would enhance the conversion result; it would also make the model closer to Iannaccone's (1992) model if one solves for the size of the Jewish community in the static model. An alternative way to endogenize the social penalty for being illiterate is to have the Jewish religious leaders set the level of ε that maximizes the size of the Jewish literate community in the static model. These extensions affect the proportion of educated individuals in the Jewish rural population in the static framework but not the dynamic implications on the reduction of the Jewish population in the long run, which is the main focus of our model.

[22] The inclusion of the disutility from conversion is not essential for our main result, but it helps us interpret the data in view of the model.

[23] We could model a positive cost for non-Jews converting to Judaism, but the results would not change. Even without this cost, there are no conversions to Judaism.

[24] By making γ a decreasing function and ε an increasing function of the number of Jewish children in school in the static framework, one can analyze the implications on the incentives to live in large and/or wealthy Jewish communities and also solve for the optimal community penalty that maximizes the proportion of educated Jews, the goal of the religious leaders in Talmudic times.

$$c + \gamma(e_s)^\theta + \tau^{rF} \le w^F \tag{4.4}$$

where τ^{rF} is the tax a farmer belonging to religion r pays and w^F is the farmer's income. Given the way agriculture was practiced in the first millennium (and even for most of the second millennium), literacy did not increase a farmer's productivity and earnings. For this reason, education does not affect a farmer's income; the model captures this feature of agriculture in the first millennium by making w^F exogenous.

Education

From equations 4.3 and 4.4, the optimal choice for a non-Jewish farmer is not to educate his sons ($e_s^* = 0$), because their literacy and education provide no benefit (either in utility or in production). To solve for the optimal level of literacy and education for Jewish farmers' sons, we let the budget constraint in equation 4.4 hold with equality. Then the optimal level of e_s is given by $e_s^* = 0$ if

$$x(e+1) < \frac{\gamma\theta}{w^F - \gamma - \tau^{jF}} \quad \text{and} \quad x(e+1) < \log\left[\frac{w^F - \tau^{jF}}{w^F - \gamma - \tau^{jF}}\right] - \varepsilon \tag{4.5}$$

If equation 4.5 does not hold, the optimal level of e_s is given by $e_s^* \ge 1$ and is the solution to

$$x(e+1) = \frac{\gamma\theta(e_s)^{\theta-1}}{w_F - \gamma(e_s)^\theta - \tau^{jF}} \tag{4.6}$$

The first inequality in equation 4.5 is a result of the corner solution at $e_s = 1$. The second inequality follows from the condition that the utility of a Jew with $e_s = 0$ must be larger than that of a Jew with $e_s = 1$.[25]

The two conditions yield testable implications on children's education. Jewish fathers will not invest in their sons' education if the marginal cost of providing basic Jewish education ($\gamma\theta$) is large and/or the level of family consumption ($w^F - \gamma - \tau^{rF}$) when the minimum level of education ($e_s = 1$) is provided is low. When do these conditions occur?

At the community level, γ is large in small Jewish communities. It is also large when the aggregate economic conditions in a given community

---

[25]The model could be simplified by assuming that education for farmers is a discrete choice of either 0 or 1. Then the optimal level of e_s is given by $e_s^* = 0$ if the second inequality in equation 4.5 holds and all the previously discussed implications hold. We prefer modeling education as a continuous variable, mainly for the sake of equivalence with the model for Jewish merchants presented later.

are bad. Negative aggregate shocks drive agricultural incomes (w^F) down, which can in turn reduce family consumption to a sufficiently low level that it would be almost impossible to invest in children's literacy and education.

At the individual level, families with low-ability sons or with sons who do not like studying (large γ), or families whose opportunity costs of sending their sons to school instead of having them work on a farm are high (again, large γ), will be less likely to invest in children's literacy and education. Fathers with low levels of attachment to Judaism (low x) and low levels of literacy and education (low e) will also be less likely to educate their sons.

Conversion

Conversion to another religion can be prompted by several factors, which we model as follows. A Jewish farmer converts if his utility as a Jew is lower than his utility as a converted individual—that is, if

$$u^j(c, e_s^*; e, x) < u^{jn}(c, e_s^*; e, x) \tag{4.7}$$

or

$$\log(w^F - \gamma(e_s^*)^\theta - \tau^{jF}) + x(e+1)e_s^* - \varepsilon h < \log(w^F - \tau^{nF}) - \pi x, \tag{4.8}$$

where a Jewish farmer's utility is evaluated at the optimal level of his child's education e_s^* as discussed earlier. Suppose that $\tau^{jF} = \tau^{nF}$. Then there are three cases:

- Jewish farmers whose parameters (w^F, γ, θ, x) are such that they educate their sons ($e_s^* \geq 1$) do not convert even if $\pi = 0$, because $u^j(c, e_s^* \geq 1; e, x) > u^{jn}(c, e_s^* = 0; e, x)$.
- Jewish farmers whose parameters (w^F, γ, θ, x) are such that they do not educate their sons ($e_s^* = 0$) convert if $0 \leq \pi x \leq \varepsilon$.
- Jewish farmers whose parameters (w^F, γ, θ, x) are such that they do not educate their sons ($e_s^* = 0$) do not convert if $\pi x > \varepsilon$.

Heterogeneity across individuals (different x, e, and γ) in each cohort as well as changes in aggregate economic conditions over time (a change in w^F, τ^{rF}, or γ) provide testable implications on conversions. First, because of heterogeneity across individuals, at a given point in time, a proportion of Jewish farmers educate their children and do not convert, a proportion of Jewish farmers do not educate their children and do not convert, and a proportion of Jewish farmers do not educate their children and convert. This reduces the Jewish rural population in any period. Conversions are more numerous when aggregate economic conditions are bad (low w^F, high τ^{rF}) and communities are small (high γ).[26]

Second, in the long run, Judaism cannot survive in a subsistence farming society, because the Jewish rural population shrinks each generation as a result of conversions. This process can be halted if Jewish farmers can migrate to locations with better economic conditions or larger Jewish communities, where the cost of educating the children is lower, or increased urbanization and the expansion of trade make available to the literate Jewish farmers skilled occupations with positive returns to education.

---

[26] If cognitive skills are inherited from fathers to sons, then our work shares some of the features of the natural selection model of Galor and Moav (2002).

CHAPTER 5

Jews in the Talmud Era, 200–650

THE CHOSEN FEW

> Theodotos son of Vettenos, priest and head of the synagogue,
> rebuilt the synagogue for the reading of the Law and for the
> study of the precept. . . .
>
> —*Theodotos Inscription, Jerusalem, c. 50*

> It was said in the name of Rabbi Hosea that in every synagogue
> there was an elementary school and a Talmud school.
>
> — *Talmud of the Land of Israel, Megilla 3:1, 73–74*

WAS THE RELIGIOUS NORM REGARDING THE READING AND THE STUDY of the Torah in the synagogue implemented in the centuries following the compilation of the Mishna? Did world Jewry implement universal primary education centuries before any other population? Do the historical facts support the prediction of our theory that because investment in religious literacy is a major sacrifice in farming economies in which there are little or no economic returns to literacy and education, a proportion of Jews convert, causing the Jewish population to decrease over time?

We examine whether our theory is consistent with the historical evidence by looking at the history of the Jews during the Talmudic and early Gaonic times, which scholars identify with the four centuries spanning from the early third to the mid-seventh century. During this period, the Land of Israel remained important as a center for the academies, but Mesopotamia grew in importance and soon overshadowed it as the hub of Jewish religious and economic life.[1]

It is in the religious and social milieu of Talmudic and early Gaonic times that world Jewry became a small population of literate individuals (the "chosen few"). The unintended consequences of the religious ruling that required Jewish fathers to invest in their sons' literacy and education fully displayed themselves in the centuries from the compilation of the Mishna to the rise of Islam.

[1] S. Safrai (1976b).

TABLE 5.1. Estimated Cost of Living in the Land of Israel, Egypt, and Mesopotamia during the First to Third Century (denarii)

Item in household budget	Land of Israel	Egypt	Mesopotamia
Monthly wage of an agricultural worker	24–48	4–32	72–96
Monthly wage of an urban skilled worker	48–72	6–40	—
Monthly wage of a boy on farm work	—	2–10	—
Monthly bread expenses (family of 4 people)	10–20	5–10	—
Cattle (ox or cow)	100–200	15–100	—
Suit/cloak	30	—	—
Monthly rent of a house	4	—	—
Book	200	—	80–120

Sources: Sperber (1965, 1966).

Note: The range of values encompasses the different figures mentioned in primary sources as well as the increase in wages and prices from the first to the third century.

— Not available.

An Increasingly Literate Farming Society

At the time of the destruction of the Second Temple, illiteracy was virtually universal among farmers, who formed the majority of the population. Pagan farmers in western Europe under Roman rule, Christian farmers in Judea, Zoroastrian farmers in Mesopotamia, and Jewish farmers in the Galilee, Mesopotamia, and Egypt shared one common trait: they were all illiterate.[2] For most of these farmers, investing in their sons' literacy was a sacrifice: both the direct costs (the purchase of books and the teacher's salary) and the opportunity costs (the forgone income from sending the children to primary school instead of employing them on farm work) were very high relative to average incomes (table 5.1).

Literacy did not make a farmer more productive or enable him to earn more. Moreover, in the rural economies of the first half of the first millennium, there were very few opportunities for literate people to enter crafts and trade. "Investment" in children's literacy and education thus represented a burden with no economic returns for almost all households whose incomes came from agriculture. Not surprisingly, the overwhelming majority of farmers—Jews and non-Jews—were illiterate, as they are today in most developing countries whose economies are mainly rural and agrarian.

[2]Bowen (1972–81, vol. 1); Harris (1991); Bar-Ilan (1992); Demsky (1997); Hezser (2001).

Commitment to Education

The Tannaim in the academies in the Land of Israel during the first two centuries CE encouraged the establishment of primary schools. Yet, the disruptions brought by the Jewish-Roman wars did not create the ideal environment for this process to blossom, and illiteracy was still widespread until the late second century. In the early third century, Rabbi Judah haNasi and his fellow scholars and subsequent generations of rabbis in the academies in the Land of Israel and Mesopotamia brought renewed emphasis on the implementation of a system of organized and universal primary education (see chapter 3).

We focus on the evidence from the third to the early seventh century. Three independent sources—the Talmud, the early Gaonic responsa, and the archaeological record—show unambiguously that a large proportion of Jewish farmers invested in their sons' literacy and education.[3] In this way, religious instruction and literacy spread among the Jewish communities of the Land of Israel and the Diaspora during the Talmud era.

EVIDENCE FROM THE TALMUD

The Talmud consists of the Mishna and the Gemara (the latter contains commentaries mostly on the Mishna, written by generations of scholars and rabbis in the academies in the Land of Israel and Mesopotamia).[4] The Talmud of the Land of Israel (Talmud Yerushalmi) was codified around 350–400; the Babylonian Talmud (Talmud Bavli) was codified around 450–550.[5] The Babylonian Talmud, which is broader than the Talmud of the Land of Israel, would eventually become the pillar of rabbinic Judaism for world Jewry.

Today each Talmud consists of many volumes of text in Hebrew and Aramaic. A Talmudic debate starts with a paragraph of the Mishna (in Hebrew), followed by the corresponding Gemara (typically in Aramaic). In the outer and inner margins appear the commentaries of the most eminent Jewish scholars of medieval Europe, such as Rashi and the Tosafists,

---

[3] Although information on the spread of literacy among women during the Talmud era is limited, it seems that girls received a more limited education than boys (S. Safrai 1968, 1976a).

[4] Segal (1991). The Gemara frequently refers to other rabbinical statements in addition to the ones from the Mishna in order to compare them with those in the Mishna. All such non-Mishnaic tannaitic sources are termed *baraitot* ("outside material"). The *baraitot* cited in the Gemara are often quotations from the Tosefta (a tannaitic compendium of halakha parallel to the Mishna) and the halakhic Midrashim (specifically Mekhilta, Sifra, and Sifre). Some *baraitot* are known only through traditions cited in the Gemara and are not part of any other collection.

[5] Scholars still debate the exact dating of the two versions of the Talmud.

as well as, in some tractates, the commentary of the North African commentator of the Islamic period, R. Hananel.[6]

The compilation of the Mishna did not stop the religious, academic, or legal activities of the academies. As the Mishna became the authoritative code of the Oral Law, the activity of the Amoraim (the scholars who succeeded the Tannaim) became devoted principally to interpreting this code. They did so in the academies (yeshivot) of Caesarea, Sepphoris, and Tiberias in the Land of Israel and Nehardea, Sura, Pumbedita, and other seats of learning in Mesopotamia.[7]

At this time, the yeshiva functioned not only as an academy of higher learning for advanced students. It was also a legislative body and religious court to which ordinary people brought matters and problems pertaining to any aspect of daily life and asked the scholars and religious authorities for advice or rulings. The matters brought before the academy ranged from questions on farming to issues related to division of property or damages, from problems arising from family matters (marriage, children, divorce, widowhood, bequests) to questions about eating, cleanliness, charity, or religious rituals. Questions regarding children's education and its practical implementation figured prominently among the matters brought to the attention of the scholars and discussed in the academies.[8]

The two functions of the yeshiva were strictly intertwined. The main object of the lectures and discussions of the scholars was to find the appropriate ruling in the Mishna to address the matter brought to the attention of the scholars by ordinary people, to interpret the often brief and concise sentences and rulings of the Mishna, to investigate its reasons and sources, to reconcile seeming contradictions, to compare its canons

---

[6] Segal (1991). The page format of the Babylonian Talmud has remained almost unchanged since the early printings in Italy. Some twenty-five individual tractates were printed by Joshua and Gershom Soncino between 1484 and 1519, culminating in the complete edition of the Talmud produced by Daniel Bomberg (a Christian) in 1520–30. These editions established the familiar format of placing the original text in square formal letters in the center of the page, surrounded by the commentaries of Rashi and the Tosafists, which are printed in a semi-cursive typeface. The page divisions used in the Bomberg edition have been used by all subsequent editions of the Talmud until the present day. Over the years several additions were introduced, including identifications of biblical quotes, cross-references to the Talmud and rabbinic literature, and to the principal codes of Jewish law. Almost all versions of the Talmud in current use are copies of the famous Vilna (Wilno, Vilnyus) Talmud, published in several versions from 1880 by the "Widow and Brothers Romm" in the renowned Lithuanian center of Jewish scholarship. While retaining the same format and pagination as the previous editions, the Vilna Talmud added several new commentaries along the margins and in supplementary pages at the ends of the respective volumes.

[7] Goodblatt (1974, 2006a); S. Safrai (1976b); Neusner (1987).

[8] Gafni (1990).

with those of sages not included in the Mishna, and to apply its decisions and established principles to new cases not yet provided for.

Much of the Gemara consists of legal analysis. The starting point for the analysis is usually a legal statement found in the Mishna. The statement is then analyzed and compared with other statements, often in the form of a debate between two (frequently anonymous and sometimes metaphorical) disputants, termed the *makshan* (questioner) and the *tartzan* (answerer). The Gemara also identifies the biblical basis for laws presented in the Mishna and the logical process connecting one with the other.

As an example, the Mishna (Baba Batra 20b–21a), reveals the following regarding children's instruction:[9]

> If a man desires to open a shop in a courtyard, his neighbor may prevent him on the ground that he will not be able to sleep through the noise of people coming and going. A man, however, may make articles in the courtyard to take out and sell in the market, and his neighbor cannot prevent him on the ground that he cannot sleep from the noise of the hammer or of the millstones or of the children.

On this ruling, the Gemara (Babylonian Talmud, Baba Batra 20b–21a) comments:[10]

> Why is the rule in the second case not the same as in the first? Abaye [Babylonian Amora, third and fourth centuries] replied: The second clause must refer to a man in another courtyard. Said Raba [Babylonian Amora, third and fourth centuries] to him: If that is so, the Mishnah should say, "In another courtyard is it permissible?"—No, said Raba: the concluding words refer to school children, from the time of the regulation of Joshua ben Gamla. . . . At length Joshua ben Gamla came and ordained that teachers of young children should be appointed in each district and town, and that children should enter school at the age of six or seven.
>
> Rab [Babylonian Amora, second and third centuries] said to Rabbi Samuel ben Shilath [Babylonian Amora, first half of the third century]: Before the age of six do not accept pupils; from that age you can accept them, and stuff them with Torah like an ox. . . .
>
> Raba further said: The number of pupils to be assigned to each teacher is twenty-five. If there are fifty, we appoint two teachers. If there are forty, we appoint an assistant, at the expense of the town. . . . Raba further said: A teacher of young children, a vine-dresser, a ritual slaughterer, a blood-letter, and a town scribe are all liable to be dismissed immediately if inefficient. The

[9] Gafni (1990, pp. 107–9).
[10] Feldman and Reinhold (1996, pp. 204–5).

general principle is that anyone whose mistakes cannot be rectified is liable to be dismissed immediately if he makes ones.

The Talmud does not contain discussions regarding highly speculative matters or abstract theological debates. It focuses on practical problems pertaining to daily life, making it an excellent source of information on the world in which the Jews in the Land of Israel and Mesopotamia lived during the first half of the first millennium.[11] It provides clear evidence of the growth of the number of students in the academies, the large number of detailed rulings dealing with the provision of education, and the scheduling of a central event in Jewish religious life, the *kallah* (discussed below). The growth of the academies in Mesopotamia documented in many passages of the Talmud indirectly suggests that more Jewish children must have received some primary education—a prerequisite for entering the secondary schools and then the academies.

Both the Talmud of the Land of Israel and the Babylonian Talmud are filled with discussions and rulings regarding schools, synagogues, pupils, books, duties and wages of teachers, duties of parents to provide for their children's Torah study, and duties of pupils toward their teachers. Such issues were unheard of in other rural civilizations of the time.[12]

The picture that emerges from this enormous body of discussions and rulings is one of a farming society that was setting up the economic, legal, and social tools to implement the religious ruling of Joshua ben Gamla and to make primary education universal among Jewish boys. For example, the Talmud of the Land of Israel reports that Hillel, the son of Gamliel III and grandson of Rabbi Judah haNasi, worked to establish an educational system despite the financial difficulties of his times. To accomplish this goal, he asked three distinguished scholars to travel to many locations and to appoint teachers of children in many towns and villages.[13] Some debates and rulings in the Talmud regulated the practical

---

[11] That the Mishna and the Talmud were devoted to daily practical matters and not to highly speculative subjects was recognized by Emperor Justinian when he passed the following law in 553 permitting the Jews to read the Holy Scriptures but prohibiting them from reading the Talmud: "We decree, therefore, that the Hebrews who wish so shall be permitted to read the Holy Scriptures in their synagogues—and generally where ever Jews are found—in Greek before those who agree so, or in the language of their fathers, or simply in any other language, according to the different places, and we decree that there shall be no freedom of speech to their commentators, who use only Hebrew in order to abuse it as they wish [in] what they call "Mishna," which however, we totally forbid, since it is not a part of the Holy Scriptures and was not received by the prophets, but was invented by people who chattered on earthly matters without anything divine" (Leibner [2006]).

[12] S. Safrai (1976a); Aberbach (1982).

[13] Aberbach (1982, pp. 30–31).

organization of primary instruction. One ruling, for example, established a communal tax to provide for the wages of teachers of the Torah and Mishna. Another ruling required that unmarried people with no children who resided in a town had to pay for the wages of teachers. A third ruling allowed the community as a whole to fire a teacher if he did not follow the parents' instructions.[14]

Both versions of the Talmud show the commitment of the Jewish communities to the implementation of the educational reform. The sages of the Land of Israel had different views from those in Mesopotamia, however. The Talmud of the Land of Israel describes the communal organization of primary education (including a communal tax for the wages of the teachers), whereas the Babylonian Talmud puts more emphasis on parents' responsibility for paying for their children's education, as clearly shown in the ruling requiring a father to pay for his son's education and to teach him, or have someone teach him, a craft.[15]

Similarly, the Talmud of the Land of Israel states that "a person's sustenance is decreed for the coming year, except for what the person pays out for food in celebration of the Sabbath, festivals . . . and for what the *tinokot* [children under seven or eight] bring to the house of their master as his tuition." On the same matter, the Babylonian Talmud has a different formulation: "A person's entire allotment for that year is determined [by God] between New Year's Day and the Day of Atonement, except for the expenses of celebrating Sabbaths and the expenses of celebrating festivals and the expense of educating his sons in Torah."[16]

The difference between the provision of education in the Land of Israel and Mesopotamia is consistent with the divergent economic conditions in the two locations. In the Land of Israel, the provision of education was publicly organized by the community, educational taxes were levied on everyone, and the education of poor and orphan children was subsidized. In contrast, children's education in Mesopotamia was provided mainly by private teachers for individuals or groups of households, so that almost every family had to bear the entire cost of teaching itself.[17]

The institution of the *kallah* also indicates that literacy was spreading among the Jewish population. The *kallah*, which appears to have begun in Babylon in the third century, was one of the central activities in the yeshiva.[18] During the months of March and August (Elul and Adar), large gatherings assembled at which men studied the Torah in the Mesopotamian

---

[14]Goodblatt (1980); Z. Safrai (1987, pp. 77–78); Gafni (1990, pp. 107–9).

[15]Goitein (1962, p. 121); Gafni (1990, pp. 107–9).

[16]Z. Safrai (1987, pp. 77–78 and n. 5).

[17]Aberbach (1982, pp. 30–35); Z. Safrai (1987, pp. 77–78); Gafni (1990, pp. 107–9).

[18]There are many conjectures about the etymology of the word *kallah* (Gilat 2007).

academies and listened to the scholars and sages, who read and discussed a specific section of the Talmud.[19] During the spring *kallah*, in addition to a portion of the Talmud, the scholars discussed and issued rulings on questions sent from Jewish communities everywhere. The questions concerned everything from economic and social matters to religious and ritualistic issues. The written answers (*teshuvot* in Hebrew, *responsa* in Latin) to these questions were then sent back to the Jewish communities through Jewish merchants. The rabbinic responsa are a unique feature of Judaism that played an important role in shaping the economic and social history of the Jews over time.

EVIDENCE FROM THE EARLY GAONIC RESPONSA

The rabbinic responsa existed in Talmudic times, but they did not constitute a separate body of literature from the Talmud. It is after the Babylonian Talmud was redacted and the Amoraim were succeeded by the Geonim as the new heads of the academies that the rabbinic responsa became a separate body of literature. For more than 500 years (from the mid-sixth to the eleventh century), the Gaonic responsa were one of the main sources of information on the social, religious, and economic life of the Jewish people.[20]

These documents illustrate the spread of literacy and primary education during the sixth and seventh centuries within the Jewish communities in Mesopotamia, where most of world Jewry was located in the century before the rise of Islam, as well as in the numerous locations of the Diaspora. Some responsa mention that teachers taught children in both towns and villages.[21] Other responsa point out that together with rabbis, judges, and heads of synagogues, teachers were among the community officials listed at the end of letters of excommunication the Geonim sent to the many Jewish communities in the world.[22] Teachers were also listed as synagogue officials, together with scholars, elders, administrators (*parnasim*), cantors (*hazzanim*), and caretakers (*shammashim*).[23]

The early Gaonic responsa document a key fact: an increasing number of Jewish farmers educated their children in the period before the rise of Islam and the vast urbanization that occurred in the newly established Muslim caliphates. The investment by a proportion of Jewish farmers in their children's literacy and education during these times should be viewed

---

[19] Neusner (1965–70, vol. 4, pp. 384–85); Goodblatt (1974, 2006a).

[20] Elon (1994, vol. 2).

[21] Assaf (2002–6, vol. 2, pp. 11–27).

[22] See Greenberg and Cohn (2007) for a description of the rules regarding excommunication within a Jewish community since biblical times.

[23] Levine (2005, pp. 412–52).

as a financial sacrifice made in order to obey the religious norm sanctioned by the Pharisaic leadership. It could not have been prompted by economic returns during the third to seventh century, as the ability to read and the study of the Torah in Hebrew yielded no monetary benefits (except, of course, to the rabbis, teachers, and other community leaders, the main promoters of the implementation of universal primary education).

SYNAGOGUES

The third type of evidence of the implementation of the religious norm regarding children's education comes from the literary sources and the wealth of archaeological discoveries that document the timing of the construction of synagogues.[24] As we show later, many discussions and rulings in the Mishna, Tosefta, and Talmud indicate that synagogues were primarily places where children and adults read and studied the Torah.[25]

The origins and the early history of the synagogue (*bet knesset*, or "house of gathering," in Hebrew) are still the object of academic debate. There is a consensus that the development of the synagogue followed the destruction of the First Temple, in 586 BCE, either during the Babylonian exile or soon after, when Jews returned to Judea during the Restoration period. For some 500 years, synagogues appear to have developed parallel to the Temple in Jerusalem, providing complementary religious and social services. During the Second Temple period, however, the synagogue never replaced the Temple as the cultic focus of Judaism.

A Greek inscription found in Jerusalem (called the Theodotos inscription, from the name of the person mentioned on it) provides the earliest

[24] See Ovadiah (1978); Kasher, Oppenheimer, and Rappaport (1987); Hachlili (1988, 1989); Feldman (1996a); Fine (1996); Rutgers (1996); Flesher (1998); Gafni (1998); Grabbe (1998); Oppenheimer (1998); Urman and Flesher (1998); Levine (1999, 2005); Olson and Zetterholm (2003). Sources documenting the existence and functions of synagogues for the pre–70 period include Josephus, Philo, the New Testament, and the Tosefta's description of a first-century synagogue in Alexandria. The archaeological material pre–70 includes a handful of synagogue buildings excavated in Judea and Delos and some inscriptions in Jerusalem, Asia Minor, Rome, Delos, Egypt, and Berenice in North Africa. For the period after 70, the remains of more than 100 synagogues have been identified in the Land of Israel, and about 200 inscriptions have been retrieved. Literary sources mentioning synagogues are scattered among the writings of Byzantine authors, Church Fathers, the Theodosian Code, Justinian's Novellae, and rabbinic sources. There is also abundant archaeological evidence from the Diaspora, where the remains of many buildings have been identified as synagogues and hundreds of inscriptions have been found, most of them dedicatory in nature and deriving from the synagogue buildings themselves, others stemming from a funerary context and mentioning someone associated with the synagogue.

[25] See S. Safrai (1976a); Aberbach (1982, p. 41); Z. Safrai (1987, 1998); E. Stern (1993); Gafni (1998); Oppenheimer (1998); Urman (1998); and Levine (2005) for detailed discussions of the functioning of synagogues as places of worship, the instruction of children and adults, and a variety of other social and community services.

(likely mid-first century) archaeological evidence of the existence of a synagogue in the Land of Israel.[26] The earliest literary sources referring to synagogues date from the first century. They describe synagogues both in the Land of Israel and throughout the Diaspora in the Roman Empire.

Scholars agree that the emergence of the synagogue was a revolutionary development in the history of Judaism for several reasons.[27] Unlike the Temple, which could exist only in Jerusalem, a synagogue could be built anywhere, in cities, towns, and villages in the Land of Israel as well as the Diaspora. The development of the synagogue enabled the Jews to organize their communal life, worship, and study of the Torah anywhere.

The priesthood in the Temple in Jerusalem was restricted to a small elite of men descended from the priestly class (Cohenim). In contrast, in principle, anyone could serve as the head of a synagogue. The congregation of devoted Jews was no longer relegated to the outer courtyards of the Temple, where they could have only a glimpse of the rituals performed inside; they were directly involved in all aspects of synagogue ritual, foremost Torah reading and study.

The synagogue provided a variety of religious services and public goods to the entire Jewish community living in a village, town, or city, including Sabbath and holiday services, prayer, sacred and communal meals, charitable activities, court services, and religious instruction for children and adults. It functioned as a general assembly hall as well as a repository for communal funds, a library, and a hostel. Some synagogues provided all these services; others performed only some of them.[28]

Public Torah reading became a prominent part of synagogue ritual in the first century. The midcentury Theodotos inscription mentions the study of the Torah and the fulfillment of the commandments as the principal activities of the synagogue. Josephus and the New Testament document that Torah reading in the synagogue was a common practice in the Land of Israel in the first century. Philo, the Jewish philosopher born in Alexandria circa 20 BCE, makes the same observation about Egypt.[29] There is scholarly consensus that although some of these activi-

[26] Griffiths (1998). The evidence of early synagogues in the Diaspora dates even earlier: for Egypt there are remains of synagogues dating back to the third and second centuries BCE, and for Delos to the first century BCE.

[27] Levine (1982, introd.).

[28] Levine (1987; 2005, pp. 135–72, 381–410); Oppenheimer (1998); Z. Safrai (1998); Urman (1998).

[29] Schiffman (1999, pp. 40–47). As Josephus writes in The Antiquities of the Jews (bk. 16, chap. 2, sec. 4), edited and translated in Flavius Josephus (1998), "We give every seventh day over to the study of our customs and law, for we think it necessary to occupy ourselves, as with any other study, so with these through which we can avoid committing sins." Philo places Torah reading in the synagogue when, in On the Embassy to Gaius (155–56), edited in Philo (1962), he writes "Augustus knew therefore that the Jews have houses of prayer and

ties revolved around the synagogue even before 70 CE, it became the place where both children and adults read and studied the Torah after the destruction of the Temple.

During the Talmudic period, the educational mission and focus of the synagogue grew even stronger under the leadership of rabbinic Judaism. The synagogue became the center for reading and studying the Torah. Instruction meant religious instruction to prepare boys to read, once adults, in the synagogue. An entire tractate of the Mishna (Megilla) and many passages in the Tosefta are devoted to the rules for public Torah reading in the synagogue.

Torah study in the synagogue took a variety of forms. For adults, on Mondays, Thursdays, and the Sabbath, a Torah scroll was taken out and a section of the weekly passage read in public. On the Sabbath, the reading and expounding of the selected section of the Torah was longer than it was during the week. Individuals wishing to study could also come to the synagogue to study by themselves, with others, or with a sage.[30]

In the *bet ha-sefer* (primary school) and the *bet ha-midrash* (high school as well as a study room for adults), children and young adults were taught to read and studied the Torah (and the Talmud, for those who decided to acquire more knowledge of the religious texts). Large communities could afford separate schools, but in most communities the classroom for children was inside the synagogue.[31] In the Land of Israel, where a communal organization of primary education existed, village and town leaders considered the organization, coordination, and funding of the educational system within or near the synagogue as one of their primary duties.[32]

Of the more than 100 synagogues that have been excavated in the Land of Israel, the largest number were built after the destruction of the Second

meet together in them, particularly on the sacred Sabbaths when they received as a body a training in their ancestral philosophy." A passage in Luke (4:16–21) refers to reading in the synagogue in Nazareth: "Jesus went to the synagogue, as his custom was, on the Sabbath day. And he stood up to read; and there was given to him the book of the prophet Isaiah. He opened the book and found the place . . . and he closed the book . . . and he sat down . . . and he began to say to them. . . ."

[30] Scholars disagree over whether the *bet ha-midrash* ("house of study" in Hebrew) existed inside the synagogue or in a separate building. Some scholars (e.g., Oppenheimer 1981) argue that it was inside the complex of the synagogue; others (e.g., Ilan 1998; Z. Safrai 1998; Urman 1998) argue that it was in a separate building and existed even during the Second Temple period. Oppenheimer and Z. Safrai agree that the *bet ha-midrash* existed only in large settlements and places where important scholars resided.

[31] In the Land of Israel, synagogues performed a variety of functions. In contrast, synagogues in Egypt served strictly as houses of prayer and Torah study (Kasher 1998). In Mesopotamia synagogues were used mainly for prayer; Torah study and other activities took place outside the synagogue (Gafni 1998).

[32] S. Safrai (1968, 1976a); Z. Safrai (1987, 1998); Urman (1998).

TABLE 5.2. Sample of Synagogues Built in the Land of Israel, 200–550

Region/century	Site
Galilee/Golan	
Third	Gush Halav, Kefar Bar'am, Kefar Hananyah, Kefar Kana, Nabratein (Nevoraya)
Third–fourth	Chorazin, Dabura, Hammat Gader, Hammath Tiberias, Khirbet Shema, Kokhav Ha-Yarden, Meiron, Rehov
Fourth	Arbel, Beth Alpha, Beth Shean, Beth She'arim, Caesarea, Capernaum, Horvat Ammudim, Merot, Ma'oz Hayyim
Fourth–fifth	Aphik, Assalieh, Ein Neshut, Horvat Kanef, Qatzrin, Zumimra
Fifth	Huseifa, Sepphoris, Yafia
Sixth	Dalton, Horvat Dikke, Umm el-Kanatir
Judea	
Third	Beth Guvrin, Ein-Gedi, Eshtemoa
Fourth	Anim, Ashkelon, Gaza, Horvat Rimmon, Ma'on (Nirim), Susiya, Na'aran

Sources: Levine (1982, 2005), Hachlili (1989), E. Stern (1993), Urman and Flesher (1998), and Fine (1999).

Note: Archaeologists are still debating the exact dating of the construction of some synagogues. Hence, the taxonomy of synagogues by century can be subject to slight variations. There is, however, consensus that synagogues were built in the first half of the first millennium in the locations listed in the table (as well as in many other locations in the Land of Israel not reported in the table).

Temple, especially in the third to fifth century (table 5.2, map 5.1). They were erected in towns but also in many villages and small rural communities in Judea, the Galilee, and the Golan. Their construction was funded mainly by farmers, who represented the overwhelming majority of the Jewish population in rural areas.[33] These farmers then relied on the many services and public goods provided by the local synagogues, including the provision of primary education for their children and religious instruction for themselves.

Archaeological remains of more than 200 synagogues have been found in the Diaspora (map 5.2).[34] Archaeological evidence has been discovered

[33] Levine (1982, 2005); Flesher (1998). The Tosefta provides evidence of a special communal tax for the building and maintenance of the synagogue: "The townsmen coerce themselves to build a synagogue and to buy Torah and the Book of Prophets" (see Z. Safrai 1987, pp. 78–79).

[34] Ovadiah (1978); Kasher, Oppenheimer, and Rappaport (1987); Gafni (1998); Oppenheimer (1998); Levine (1999, 2005).

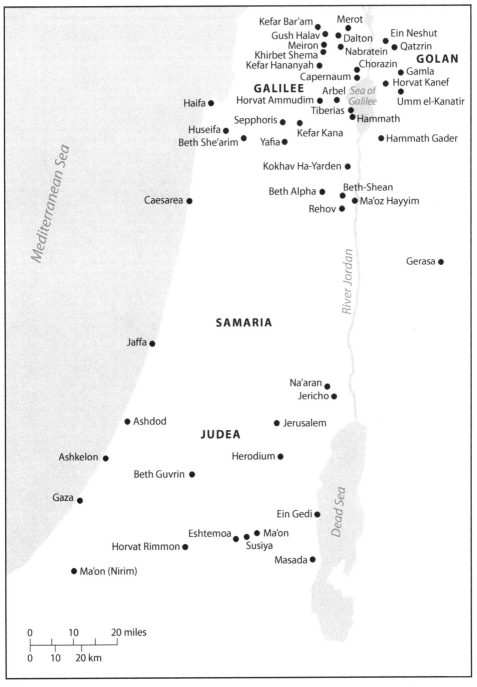

Kefar Bar'am ●   Merot ●
Gush Halav ●   ● Dalton   Ein Neshut ●
Meiron ●   ● Nabratein   ● Qatzrin
Khirbet Shema ●
Kefar Hananyah ●   Chorazin   GOLAN
        Capernaum ●   ● Gamla
                ● Horvat Kanef
GALILEE   Arbel   *Sea of*
Haifa ●   Horvat Ammudim ● ●   *Galilee*   Umm el-Kanatir ●
        Tiberias ●
Sepphoris ●   ● Hammath
Huseifa ●   Kefar Kana ●
Beth She'arim ●   Yafia ●   ● Hammath Gader

        Kokhav Ha-Yarden ●

        Beth Alpha ●   Beth-Shean ●
Caesarea ●   ● Ma'oz Hayyim
            Rehov ●

                    Gerasa ●

    SAMARIA

Jaffa ●

        Na'aran ●
        Jericho ●

● Ashdod   ● Jerusalem

    JUDEA

Ashkelon ●   Herodium ●

    Beth Guvrin ●

Gaza ●

            Ein Gedi ●
    Eshtemoa ● ● Ma'on
Horvat Rimmon ●   Susiya
            Masada ●

● Ma'on (Nirim)

Mediterranean Sea

River Jordan

Dead Sea

0   10   20 miles
0   10   20 km

Map 5.1. Ancient synagogues in the Land of Israel, selected sites. *Source*: Redrawn and adapted from Fine (1999).

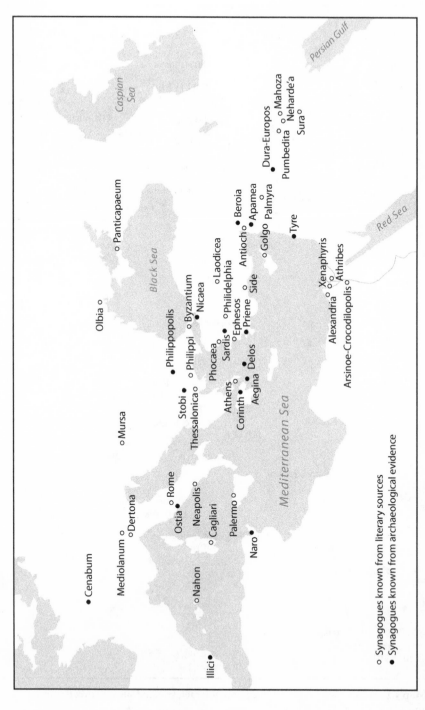

Map 5.2. Ancient synagogues in the Diaspora, selected sites. *Source:* Redrawn and adapted from Fine (1999).

○ Synagogues known from literary sources
● Synagogues known from archaeological evidence

Caspian Sea

Persian Gulf

Dura-Europos ●
Mahoza ○
Pumbedita ○ ○ Neharde'a
Sura ○

● Panticapaeum

Black Sea

Beroia ●
Antioch ●
Apamea ○
Golgo ● Palmyra
● Tyre

Olbia ○

Laodicea ○
Byzantium ○
Nicaea ○
Philippopolis ○
Philippi ○
Philidelphia ○
Phocaea
Ephesos ○
Sardis ●
Priene ○
Side ○
Delos ●

Xenaphyris ○
Athribes
Alexandria ○
Arsinoe-Crocodilopolis ○

Red Sea

Stobi ●
Thessalonica ○
Athens ●
Corinth ●
Aegina ●

Mediterranean Sea

● Cenabum

Mediolanum ○
Dertona ○
Mursa ○

Rome ○
Ostia ●
Neapolis ○
Cagliari ○
Palermo ○
Nahon ○
Naro ●

Illici ●

also in Mesopotamia (e.g., Dura-Europos), but one can infer the existence of many more synagogues there from the many references to them in the Babylonian Talmud.

That the provision and organization of universal primary education for children was a central goal of the Babylonian religious leaders is shown by the extensive power and functions assigned to the rabbis. During the Talmudic period, leadership of the Jewish communities in Mesopotamia was given over entirely to the religious leaders and the scholars in the academies. The exilarch, a Jew who held the political and administrative power over the Jewish community there, used the rabbis as judges in local courts, market inspectors, and poll tax collectors, handing over to them responsibility for managing communal institutions such as synagogues and schools.[35]

Literate Jews in a World of Illiteracy

The spread of literacy among the rural Jewish population is particularly impressive when contrasted with the lack of literacy among non-Jewish farmers at the time. In the Persian Empire under Sassanid rule, primary education was mainly a private enterprise, carried on in the home and in court schools for children of the upper classes.[36] In the Roman Empire, "illiteracy was widespread throughout the Mediterranean world . . . and the Imperial City itself had only begun to establish public schools for the wealthy and the middle class."[37] Primary schools existed in cities, but primary education was neither compulsory nor universal. Lower socioeconomic groups in cities and almost everyone in rural areas were illiterate.[38]

Literacy did not rise when the Roman Empire collapsed in the early fifth century and western Europe turned into an agrarian economy. Monks and clerics apart, virtually the entire population of western Europe was illiterate. The Church perceived the almost universal illiteracy of the population to be a major problem. In various councils and synods from the seventh to the ninth century, it encouraged the bishops to establish primary schools in towns and districts.[39] Even as late as 1500, though, the share of the literate population in most of western Europe did not exceed 10 percent.[40] When contrasted with these figures, the spread of literacy within world Jewry during Talmudic times—when the overwhelming majority of the

---

[35] Neusner (1965–70, vol. 4, p. 61; 1976, p. 135); Morony (1981, p. 317).

[36] Bowen (1972–81, vol. 1).

[37] Baron (1952, vol. 2, p. 279).

[38] Marrou (1982, chaps. 4 and 7); Harris (1991).

[39] Bowen (1972–81, vol. 1, chap. 13; vol. 2, pp. 29–31).

[40] Cipolla (1969); Bowen (1972–81, vol. 2); Reis (2004); Buringh and van Zanden (2009).

Jewish population were farmers, for whom literacy provided no additional productivity and income—is extraordinary.

Ammei ha-Aretz

According to our theory presented in chapter 4, Jewish farmers for whom the costs of investing in their children's literacy and education exceed the benefits of doing so do not send their sons to primary school. Is there historical evidence that supports this prediction?

The Talmud is filled with diatribes against the *ammei ha-aretz*, who, in the days of the Tannaim (first and second centuries), were identified as those Jews who were unable to read, did not study the Torah, and did not teach their sons the Torah.[41] For Rabbi Judah haNasi and his fellow scholars in the academies, *ammei ha-aretz* were to be considered outcasts in the Jewish community. Later, the Amoraim maintained the same harsh attitude toward illiterate Jewish fathers who did not send their sons to the synagogue to learn to read and study the Torah.

This negative attitude is clearly expressed in Talmudic excerpts, such as those that enjoin fathers not to allow their daughters to marry the sons of *ammei ha-aretz*, that prevent *ammei ha-aretz* from serving as judges, and that advise (literate) Jews to avoid eating or interacting with *ammei ha-aretz*.[42] These references indicate that universal literacy and religious instruction among male Jews remained one of the key concerns and goals of the Jewish leadership in the Talmud era. They also suggest that a certain proportion of Jews did not obey the religious norm regarding sending the children to primary school, which is consistent with the implication of our theory that some Jews found it too costly to obey this religious norm and did not invest in their children's literacy and education.

Implementation of the Jewish Educational Reform: A Summary

At the onset of Islam, in the early seventh century, the key difference between Jews and non-Jews was that a large fraction of world Jewry consisting mainly of farmers was able to read (some could also write), whereas the non-Jewish rural population was illiterate. The higher literacy of the

---

[41] Oppenheimer (1977); Haas (1989, p. 149).

[42] Oppenheimer (1977); Kalmin (1999). Babylonian Talmud (Pesachim 47, 72): "Who is *am ha-aretz*? He who cannot read the prayers . . . others say that even if he can read and was not a scholar (*talmid hacham*), then he is illiterate. R. Huna said: he who marries his daughter to an illiterate it is like he sent her to the lions. . . . A man should sell all his possessions and marry a scholar's daughter . . . but not to an illiterate's daughter, for they are detested and about their daughters he says: 'Damned he is who makes bestial intercourse.'"

Jewish people was the outcome of a religious and educational reform that the Pharisaic sect had started in the second and first centuries BCE. Literacy and education became primary goals of the Jewish religious leaders after the destruction of the Second Temple, when the redaction of the Mishna set the foundations of rabbinic Judaism. Although there is no evidence that the ruling of Joshua ben Gamla (c. 65 CE) requiring Jewish fathers to send their sons from the age of six or seven to the synagogue to learn to read and study the Torah was immediately implemented—most scholars maintain that the vast majority of the Jewish population in the Land of Israel in the first two centuries remained illiterate—his ruling became a religious law that all Jewish fathers were required to obey.[43]

The four centuries spanning from the redaction of the Mishna circa 200 to the rise of Islam in the mid-seventh century witnessed the implementation of Joshua ben Gamla's ruling and the establishment of a system of universal primary education centered on the synagogue. This sweeping change completely transformed Judaism into a religion centered on reading, studying, and implementing the rules of the Torah and the Talmud. A Jewish farmer going on pilgrimage to and performing ritual sacrifices in the Temple in Jerusalem was the icon of Judaism until 70 CE. In the early seventh century, the emblem of world Jewry was a Jewish farmer reading and studying the Torah in a synagogue and sending his sons to school or the synagogue to learn to do so.

CONVERSIONS OF JEWISH FARMERS

The other key implication of our theory is that a proportion of illiterate Jewish farmers will convert to other religions to avoid incurring the costs of obeying the laws and norms of Judaism, including the norm requiring fathers to send their sons to the primary school. Does the historical evidence support this implication? Is there evidence of conversions of Jews during Talmudic times?

Jewish Population Dynamics

In chapter 1 we pointed out that population estimates for ancient times are, at best, crude approximations. Whether one is inclined to accept Baron's estimate of 8 million Jews circa 65 CE; the much lower estimate of 2–2.5 million Jews proposed by Broshi, Hamel, and Schwartz; or the intermediate estimates of 4.5–5.5 million Jews proposed by DellaPergola

[43] Bar-Ilan (1992); Hezser (2001, pp. 39–59, 495–97); Demsky et al. (2007).

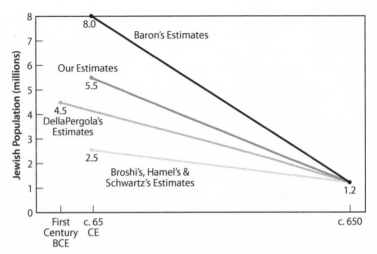

Figure 5.1. Estimates of Jewish population, c. 65 and 650 (millions). *Sources and notes*: See table 1.1.

and by us, there is consensus among scholars regarding the key trend: the steep decline in the Jewish population in the six centuries after the destruction of the Second Temple (figure 5.1).[44]

Baron proposes a higher estimate for the Jewish population in the first century CE and accepts the high estimates of war-related deaths proposed by the ancient historians Josephus, Tacitus, and Cassius Dio. Scholars such as Broshi, Hamel, and Schwartz, who maintain that the Jewish population in the first century CE was much smaller than Baron proposes, also contend that the massacres during the three Jewish-Roman wars did not take the huge toll claimed by the ancient historians. Yet *all* scholars reach the same conclusion: the Jewish population underwent a steep decline in the six centuries after 70 CE that war-related deaths and general population decline cannot completely explain. With this caveat in mind, we go back to the population figures we proposed in chapter 1 (tables 1.1 and 1.2) and try to explain this demographic puzzle.

In the five centuries from the end of the last Jewish-Roman war (the Bar Kokhba revolt) in 135 to the rise of Islam circa 650, the number of Jews in the world decreased by two-thirds, from about 3.1–3.3 million to 1–1.2 million (table 1.1). The Jewish population declined in relative terms as well,

---

[44]Baron (1971b); Broshi (1979, 1982, 2001); Avi-Yonah (1984); Hamel (1990); Herr and Oppenheimer (1990); DellaPergola (1992, 2001); Stemberger (2000); S. Schwartz (2001, 2006); Schiffman (2003); Goodblatt (2006c).

from about 5.3 percent to about 1.9–2.3 percent of the total population.[45] The number of Jews declined everywhere Jews lived.

What can account for this dramatic fall in the Jewish population? Three possible factors include deaths related to massacres and wars, the general decline in the population (e.g., as a result of famines or diseases), and a decline in fertility. Wars and related massacres help explain the decrease in the Jewish population mainly *before* 150 (see chapter 1). After 150, however, no comparable massacres occurred in the lands under Roman or Parthian rule.

General population decline—as a result of natural disasters, famines, and diseases, especially infectious diseases—could explain the absolute decline in the Jewish population during the Talmud era. In fact, the five centuries between 150 and 650 were marked by several traumatic events for the whole population, such as the plague of Justinian in 541. The Jews experienced the same famines and diseases as the rest of the population during these centuries. But the general population decreased by about 12 percent, whereas the Jewish population collapsed by roughly two-thirds during the same time span (table 1.1). There is no reason to think that the Jews suffered more from famines or infectious diseases than did the rest of the population.

A third candidate for the large absolute and relative decline in the Jewish population during the Talmud period is a fall in the fertility rate among Jewish women. Why would Jewish families have had fewer children than non-Jewish families? One could argue that if children became more expensive after the implementation of the religious norm requiring fathers to send their sons to primary school—in addition to feeding and clothing their children, fathers were also required to send them to school or the synagogue to learn to read and to study the Torah—some families, especially the ones with low incomes, might have decided to have fewer children in order to be able to obey the religious norm. That is, in economic jargon, rabbinic Judaism would have created a quality-quantity trade-off for parents.[46]

[45]Table 1.1 shows that circa 150, there were about 1.2 million Jews in the Land of Israel, 1–1.2 million Jews in Mesopotamia and Persia, and nearly 0.5 million in North Africa (mainly Egypt). Considering that circa 65 CE, there were 0.5–0.8 million Jews in the territory comprising Syria, Lebanon, Asia Minor, the Balkans, and western Europe and assuming that circa 150, this number was likely smaller because of war-related deaths, one can argue that circa 150, world Jewry amounted to roughly 3.1–3.3 million people. Given that circa 150, the total population amounted to about 58 million people, the percentage of the Jewish population over the total population was roughly 5.3 percent.

[46]Starting from the seminal article of Becker and Lewis (1973), a number of papers in economics assume that parents may decide on both the quantity and the quality of their children. As a consequence, they may reduce the number of children in order to invest in children's education.

To the best of our knowledge, there is no historical evidence showing that Jewish households reduced their fertility following the transformation of Judaism. The Talmud—which contains many detailed discussions and rulings regarding the age of marriage, sexual behavior between spouses, pregnancy, abortion, infertility, divorce, and the biblical requirement to "be fruitful and multiply" (*peru urevu*)—includes no discussion regarding reducing the number of children in order to fulfill the religious duty of educating one's sons. If this had been a major problem in the Jewish communities, one would expect it to have been brought to the attention of the scholars in the academies, been discussed, and found its way into the Talmud.

Some other factor or factors must account for the larger decrease in the Jewish population. Excluding a decrease in the fertility rate, conversion remains the only other factor that can explain the particularly large reduction of the Jewish population during the Talmud era.[47]

In the Land of Israel, the non-Jewish population grew from 500,000–600,000 Greeks, pagans, and some Christians circa 150 to 0.9–1.4 million people (mainly Christians) circa 650. Over the same period, the number of Jews (including 300,000 Samaritans) declined from 1.2 million to 100,000 (tables 1.1 and 1.2). The opposite trends in the Christian population, which more than doubled, and the Jewish population, which shrank by nearly 92 percent in these five centuries, seem to support the argument that a significant proportion of Jews converted to Christianity.[48]

Jews in North Africa (mainly Egypt), which consisted almost entirely of Hellenistic Jews who spoke Greek, almost disappeared—from about 500,000 circa 150 to no more than 4,000 before the Arab-Muslim expansion (table 1.1). This is the time in which Christianity spread in Egypt, laying the foundation of the Egyptian Coptic Church. Many of the early Hellenistic Christians were Jews by birth.[49]

Mesopotamian Jewry increased during the third and fourth centuries because better economic conditions prompted migrations of Jews from the Land of Israel and Egypt to Mesopotamia.[50] In the following three centuries, however, the number of Mesopotamian Jews decreased, despite

---

[47] DellaPergola (1992).

[48] Rabbinic sources in the Talmud indicate that a portion of Jews migrated from the Land of Israel to Mesopotamia during the third and fourth centuries because of better economic conditions in Mesopotamia. The scholars in the Land of Israel tried to stop these migrations, with no success.

[49] Harnack (1908); Latourette (1975); E. Sanders (1980); J. Sanders (2000); E. Ferguson (2003).

[50] See Leibner (2006, 2009) for a description of the economic conditions, settlements, and migrations of the Jews from the Land of Israel and Egypt to Mesopotamia.

the absence of massacres (tables 1.1. and 1.2).[51] At the same time, the Christian population became as numerous as the Jewish one, suggesting that a certain proportion of Jews under Sassanid rule converted to Christianity.[52]

The Jewish population in western Europe, Syria, Lebanon, Asia Minor, and the Balkans also shrank during this period. Circa 650, the Jews in western Europe numbered a few thousand (tables 1.1 and 1.2).[53] Some persecutions and forced conversions of Jews occurred in Syria, Lebanon, Asia Minor, and the Balkans in the early Byzantine period and in the Iberian Peninsula under Visigothic rule. However, the decline of the Jewish population in these areas started much earlier, in the second to fifth century. Simultaneously, Christianity was greatly spreading in these areas.

Christianity maintained the second pillar of Judaism—the laws sanctioned in the Written Torah with the related belief in one God. However, it changed some religious laws and norms imposed by Judaism. For example, Christians were not required to circumcise their sons or to eat kosher food. Moreover, under the leadership of Paul in the mid-first century, Christianity did not impose on its followers the Jewish norm requiring fathers to send their sons from the age of six or seven to the school or the synagogue to learn to read and study the Torah.

For many Jews during Talmudic times, conversion to Christianity probably did not appear as a major change: Christianity looked like a slightly different version of the Jewish religion, with the same core belief in one God and the Torah but with fewer demanding requirements. For many Jewish households that earned their living from farming—and especially the poorer ones that struggled to support their families and, as illiterate, were made to feel like outcasts (*ammei ha-aretz*) by the local rabbis and literate Jews—Christianity probably seemed a welcome change: it enabled them to believe in the same God without having to obey several costly norms, including the one that required fathers to educate their sons.

Literary and Epigraphic Sources

The demographic decline of Jewish communities in all locations provides indirect evidence of conversions of a large proportion of Jews to other religions, mainly Christianity. In addition, a wealth of literary and epigraphic evidence indicates that a relatively large percentage of Jews abandoned Judaism and embraced other religions during the first half of the

---

[51] There is virtually no record of large massacres against Jews in Mesopotamia (Gafni 1990, pp. 149–52).

[52] Gil (2004, pp. 57, 491).

[53] Toch (2005, 2012).

first millennium, both before and after the Edict of Milan and the Council of Nicaea.[54]

THE PERIOD 1–325

The two main competitors of Judaism were Hellenistic paganism and Christianity. In the three centuries before the Edict of Milan, in 313, Christians in the Roman Empire were persecuted. Conversions to Christianity must therefore have been voluntary. With the edict, Emperor Constantine I and Emperor Licinius, who ruled the western and the eastern part of the empire, respectively, granted religious tolerance. When, later, Constantine became the sole emperor, Christianity rose to become the dominant religion in the Roman Empire.

As highlighted in chapter 3, Judaism in the first century was a constellation of many religious groups that shared some basic features but were becoming increasingly differentiated in their religious norms, such as the one requiring fathers to send their children from the age of six or seven to school or the synagogue to learn to read and study the Torah. Christianity emerged as one of the many groups within Judaism in the first century; before becoming a predominantly Gentile religion, its main base consisted of Jewish Christians.[55] The early Christian community in Jerusalem consisted entirely of Jews and proselytes to Judaism.

The Jews and the early Jewish-Christian sects differed in at least one key aspect: Rabbi Judah haNasi made illiterate Jews outcasts in the Jewish community, whereas Paul worked hard to make the lower socioeconomic groups feel welcome in the Christian community.[56] Among the Jewish Christians, there were several subgroups—some closer to Judaism, others closer to Christianity.[57] The Ebionites (*Ebionim*, "poor people"), for example, accepted the Pharisaic form of Judaism (the Written and Oral Torah), practiced circumcision, and kept the Sabbath. They rejected Paul's doctrine but recognized Jesus as a prophet and the Messiah. They spoke

---

[54]The wealth of information on Jewish converts to Christianity in non-Jewish literary sources contrasts strikingly with the very few references to Jewish apostates or converts in both the Talmud of the Land of Israel and the Babylonian Talmud. One may wonder why the scholars in the academies who debated and issued rulings on an endless number of matters related to daily life did not seem concerned about conversions of Jews to Christianity or other religions. This attitude is actually consistent with the main goals of the Jewish leadership, from Rabbi Judah haNasi on, mentioned earlier: requiring every male Jew to read and to study the Torah so that he could learn and obey the laws and norms of the religion, and excluding the illiterate people (*ammei ha-aretz*) from the Jewish community. Hence, for scholars and rabbis, the conversion of illiterate Jews to other religions was not a major concern.

[55]Schiffman (1985, 2003).

[56]Danièlou and Marrou (1964); Nock (1969); Stark (1986, 1996); Lüdemann (1989).

[57]Danièlou (1964); Schoeps (1969); Neusner (1990a, 1991).

Jewish Aramaic and used both a Hebrew Bible and a Hebrew version of the Gospels. The Nazarenes were observant Jews who accepted Paul's doctrine and shared his hostility toward the Jewish scholars and the Pharisees. Other groups, collectively designated as Jewish Christian Gnostics, adhered to the laws of the Torah but rejected some part of the Bible (e.g., the part dealing with sacrifices), believed in Jesus as the Messiah, and shared gnostic elements with other non-Jewish sects. To these groups of Jewish Christians was addressed the substantial body of Jewish Christian literature (such as the Pseudo-Clementine literature), indicating the existence of Jews who were departing from Judaism and moving toward Christianity.[58]

Until the destruction of the Second Temple, Jewish religious leaders held ambivalent feelings, mostly of tolerance, toward the Jewish Christian sects. After the Bar Kokhba revolt, Jewish scholars declared the various sects of Jewish Christians outside the Jewish fold. To renounce Judaism for Christianity was condemnable, and apostates were regularly cursed in synagogues.[59]

Based on an enormous body of literary sources (including the Acts of the Apostles, Paul's letters, the works of early Christian writers and Church Fathers, the Coptic Bible, the canons of the synods, the Testament of the Forty Martyrs in Armenia, the Meletian Acts, and imperial decrees), a wealth of epigraphic evidence from hundreds of inscriptions, and archaeological findings on church buildings, scholars have documented three main patterns regarding the spread of Christianity from the Middle East to the West before 325, the year of the Council of Nicaea, the first of the great ecumenical councils.[60]

First, the Christian religion deeply penetrated towns, villages, and rural districts in locations where large Jewish communities existed, such as the Land of Israel, Syria, Armenia, Asia Minor, Egypt, parts of North

[58] Georgi (1995); F. Jones (1995). The Pseudo-Clementine literature is a main source of knowledge of several forms of early Jewish Christianity. The author of the source cited in Jones (1995) is identified as a Jewish Christian of about 200, possibly a Jewish-Christian presbyter or bishop in Jerusalem, who viewed Jewish Christianity as the only true form of Judaism.

[59] This harsh attitude toward apostates is captured by the cost of conversion π in the model presented in the annex to chapter 4.

[60] Harnack (1908, vol. 2, pp. 86–337); Wolfson (1947, chap. 1); Baron (1952, vol. 2); Neusner (1965–70, vol. 1, pp. 166–69); Latourette (1975, chaps. 1 and 5); E. Sanders (1980); Stark (1986, 1996); Stevenson (1987); Feldman (1993); Barclay (1996, 1998); Brown (1996); Frend (1996); Isaac (1998); J. Sanders (1999, 2000); Bar (2003a); E. Ferguson (2003); Zetterholm (2003, chap. 3, and pp. 216–35); Mullen (2004). There were no major church buildings before 150. The growth of the number of churches started toward the end of the second century and picked up especially during the reign of Emperor Gallienus (213–68) and continued in the next centuries.

TABLE 5.3. Extent of Christianity in Middle East, North Africa, and Europe, 1 CE–325

Group	Location	Extent
I	All provinces in Asia Minor (Armenia, Bithynia, Cappadocia, Caria, Diospontus, Galatia, Isauria, Lycaonia, Lycia, Lydia, Mysia, Pamphylia, Paphlagonia, Pisidia, Phrygia, Pontus); Cyprus; Thracia; towns and villages in the Land of Israel; Arbela and Edessa in western Mesopotamia	Nearly half the population was Christian, and Christianity was the most widespread religion
II	Villages in the Land of Israel, Syria, Egypt, Cyrenaica, Africa Proconsularis and Numidia, Achaia, Thessaly, Macedonia, central and southern Italy, Iberian Peninsula, southern Gaul	A large segment of the population was Christian
III	Galilee, Phoenicia, Mesopotamia, western Persia, Mauretania and Tripolitania, Epirus, Dardania, Dalmatia, Moesia, Pannonia, northern Italy	Christianity was thinly scattered
IV	Eastern Persia, Philistia, Dacia and northern coast of the Black Sea, eastern Europe, Germany, Raetia, central and northern Gaul, Belgium	A small segment of the population was Christian

Sources: Authors' compilation based on Harnack (1908, vol. 2, pp. 89–337), Wolfson (1947, chap. 1), Baron (1952, vol. 2), Neusner (1965–70, vol. 1, pp. 166–69), Latourette (1975, chaps. 1 and 5), E. Sanders (1980), Stevenson (1987), Stark (1986, 1996), Feldman (1993, chap. 2), Barclay (1996, 1998), Isaac (1998), J. Sanders (1999, 2000), E. Ferguson (2003), Zetterholm (2003, chap. 3 and pp. 216–35), and Mullen (2004).

Africa (Africa Proconsularis and Numidia), and Arbela and Edessa in western Mesopotamia (table 5.3 and map 5.3). In contrast, in areas where there were few or no Jewish settlements (e.g., eastern Persia, Mauretania and Tripolitania in North Africa, central and northern Gaul, Belgium, England, Germany, Raetia, and eastern Europe), Christianity spread very slowly or not at all before 325. This fact suggests that the growth of Christianity was fueled partly by Jews, who abandoned Judaism to embrace the new religion.

Second, Christianity grew primarily in areas where the Jewish settlements consisted of Hellenistic Jews, as well as pagans or descendants of former pagans who had converted to Judaism in earlier times (e.g., Syria, Lebanon, Asia Minor, Greece, North Africa, the Iberian Peninsula, central and southern Italy, and southern Gaul). The lower degree of observance of Jewish laws among the large Hellenistic Jewish communities in North Africa, Syria, and Asia Minor, as well as their close proximity to a society dominated by the Hellenistic religion and culture, favored conversions to Hellenistic paganism (especially in the first and second centuries)

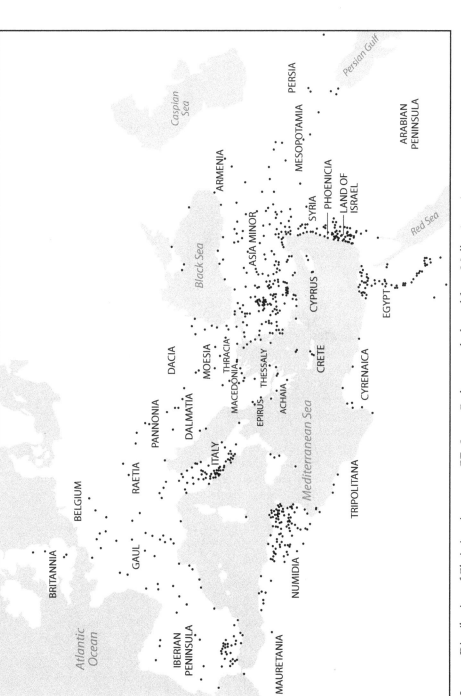

Map 5.3. Distribution of Christian sites to 325 CE. *Source:* Redrawn and adapted from Mullen (2004).

and to Christianity. Neither Asia Minor nor Egypt, which hosted large Jewish communities, ever had a Torah academy like those in the Land of Israel and Mesopotamia, and no students from Asia Minor are mentioned among those studying at these academies. These facts are consistent with the prediction of our model (see annex to chapter 4) that Jews who feel little attachment to their religion (i.e., with a low attachment parameter to Judaism) are more likely to convert.

Third, Christianity drew converts from a cross-section of the population, including middle-income and wealthy individuals.[61] However, passages by early Christian writers and Church Fathers indicate that most Jewish converts to Christianity were illiterate and poor.[62] This is not surprising, given that the majority of the Jewish population consisted of illiterate farmers until the fourth century. Therefore, most Jews who converted to Christianity must have been illiterate farmers.

The timing of the construction of synagogues in rural locations in the Land of Israel also supports the view that conversions of Jews to Christianity occurred predominantly among the low-income rural population. Most synagogues were built during the worst economic times for the Land of Israel—between the third and the fifth centuries—when some Jews migrated to Mesopotamia.[63] This timing implies that the Jews who funded the construction of synagogues in many villages across the Land of Israel were better off than those who left Judaism and embraced Christianity. All these facts are consistent with the prediction of our theory (see chapter 4) that Jewish farmers with low earnings and Jewish fathers who were less able to bear the opportunity costs of educating their sons were more likely to convert.

The second group that separated from the Jewish religion in the Land of Israel at this time was the Samaritans. Some Jewish rabbis and scholars in the second century still considered the Samaritans as belonging to the Jewish fold. But Rabbi Judah haNasi and later scholars considered them Gentiles. In the Talmudic period, Jewish scholars debated whether the Samaritans were *haverim* ("members of the community") or *ammei haaretz*. The number of Samaritans declined for two main reasons: massacres and conversions to Christianity.[64]

---

[61] Meeks (1983, pp. 54–72); Fox (1987, pp. 272–77).

[62] Harnack (1908, vol. 1, p. 47; vol. 2, pp. 33–34); Baron (1952, vol. 2, pp. 163–66); Latourette (1975, pp. 80–81); MacMullen (1984, p. 38); Fox (1987, p. 301); Theissen (1992, pp. 39–53); Stark (1996, pp. 19, 39, 46); Mullen (2004, p. 9) list the passages in these literary sources.

[63] S. Safrai (1976b, pp. 343–44); Leibner (2006, 2009).

[64] Montgomery (1968, chaps. 4–9); Sharf (1971); Alon (1980–84, vol. 2); Crown (1989); Herr and Oppenheimer (1990, p. 204); Crown, Pummer, and Tal (1993).

As for the conversion of non-Jews to Judaism, there is a debate among scholars about whether Jewish religious leaders encouraged proselytism during the Talmudic period.[65] Pagans converted to Judaism during the first century BCE and the first century CE.[66] In contrast, it seems that after the third century (i.e., after the compilation of the Mishna and the consolidation of the leadership of the scholars and rabbis in the academies), conversion to Judaism occurred only by coercion, as in the case of slaves owned by Jews.[67] The fact that pagans converted to Judaism before the destruction of the Second Temple but not afterward—when the rabbinic leadership imposed more demanding religious norms—is consistent with the prediction of our theory outlined in chapter 4.

THE PERIOD 325–700

With the Edict of Milan (313) and the Council of Nicaea (325), Emperor Constantine opened the way for Christianity to spread throughout the Roman Empire.[68] Before 325, the Christian religion was forbidden in the vast area under Roman rule, and Christians were persecuted. After 325, it was permitted in the Roman Empire and was gradually supported by subsequent Roman and early Byzantine emperors to the extent that the Byzantine Empire—identified with the eastern part of the Roman Empire—became the bastion of the new religion. Jews who converted to Christianity during this time were not forced to do so: neither Constantine nor subsequent emperors forced Jews to convert. All emperors imposed some restrictions on the Jews in the Roman and early Byzantine empires (such as the prohibition to buy Christian slaves or build synagogues), but they never imposed the Christian faith on the Jewish people.

Some Jews voluntarily left Judaism from the fourth to the seventh century. Roman and early Byzantine emperors issued decrees to protect Jewish converts to Christianity (table 5.4). There would have been no need to issue these laws unless the possibility that Jews might harm Jewish converts to Christianity was perceived as a major problem.

Samaritans were forcibly converted and massacred when the early Byzantine emperors crushed the Samaritan revolts in the fifth and sixth centuries. One of the cruelest repressions occurred under Emperor Justinian I

[65] Feldman (1993, chap. 9); Goodman (1994); S. Cohen (1999).

[66] Baron (1952, vol. 1, pp. 173–76).

[67] Schiffman (1985); S. Cohen (1999).

[68] The Council of Nicaea was the first of a series of ecumenical councils of bishops. Hundreds of bishops from all of Christendom gathered in this town located in the Roman province of Bithynia in Asia Minor (modern-day Turkey) and established the main theological tenets of the new religion.

TABLE 5.4. Legislation regarding Jewish Converts to Christianity, 300–600

Years	Emperor	Decree
311–37	Constantine	Death penalty imposed on Jews who harm Jewish converts to Christianity
364–75	Valentinian	Jewish parents banned from disinheriting children who converted to Christianity
379–95	Theodosius	Death penalty by fire imposed on Jews who harm Jewish converts to Christianity
395–423	Honorius	Jewish converts to Christianity permitted to revert to Judaism
395–408	Arcadius	Jews banned from becoming Christians for economic motives
527–65	Justinian	Jewish parents banned from disinheriting children who converted to Christianity

Sources: Parkes (1934), Alon (1980–84), and Linder (1987; 1997).

Note: The years refer to the length of an emperor's tenure. Emperors could ratify or annul the decrees of earlier emperors and institute new ones.

in 529, when tens of thousands of Samaritans were killed or enslaved. The Samaritan faith was virtually outlawed thereafter in the Christian Byzantine Empire, causing their numbers to dwindle to near extinction.[69]

As mentioned earlier, conversions of Jews to Christianity occurred in Mesopotamia in the first two centuries, but they were limited to some locations, such as Arbela and Edessa in western Mesopotamia (table 5.3). Christianity penetrated more widely and deeply into Mesopotamian Jewry during the fourth and fifth centuries.[70] Despite the migrations of Jews from the Land of Israel and Egypt to Mesopotamia as the outcome of worsened economic conditions, the number of Jews fell. Christians in Mesopotamia, including converted Jews, became as numerous as Jews.[71]

SUMMARY

Evidence from the Talmud, the early Gaonic responsa, and literary sources mentioning synagogues as well as archaeological remains of the synagogues themselves suggests that, during the Talmud era (third to sixth

[69] Montgomery (1968, chaps. 4–9); Sharf (1971); Alon (1980–84, vol. 2); Crown (1989), Herr and Oppenheimer (1990, p. 204); Crown, Pummer, and Tal (1993).

[70] Neusner (1965–70, vol. 2; vol. 4, p. 435).

[71] Gil (2004, pp. 57, 491).

century), Jewish communities in villages, towns, and cities in the Land of Israel, Syria, Lebanon, Mesopotamia, North Africa, Asia Minor, the Balkans, and western Europe implemented the first-century religious norm requiring fathers to educate their sons. During these centuries, a growing proportion of Jewish farmers invested in their children's religious literacy by sending their sons from the age of six or seven to the primary schools built inside of or next to the synagogues. This increase in religious and general literacy among the predominantly rural Jewish population occurred at a time when world Jewry was declining.

The growth of literacy among Jews and the decline in the number of Jews during the Talmud period are consistent with the predictions of our theory: (a) that a proportion of Jewish farmers obey the religious norm and send their children to school and (b) that a proportion of Jewish farmers do not educate their children and convert to another religion. Historically, this is what happened in the four centuries from roughly 200 to 600. A proportion of Jews educated their children and did not leave Judaism, whereas a significant proportion of Jews is estimated to have voluntarily converted to Christianity during this period—a phenomenon that, coupled with war-related deaths and general population decline, led to the near disappearance of the Jewish populations in the Land of Israel, Syria, Lebanon, Egypt, Asia Minor, the Balkans, and western Europe by 650. The Jewish community in Mesopotamia was also affected by a wave of conversions to Christianity, but it alone survived, becoming the new religious and economic center of world Jewry at the birth of Islam.

The demographic collapse of world Jewry partly as the outcome of voluntary conversions to Christianity in the agrarian economies of the Talmud period supports the main prediction of our theory presented in chapter 4 regarding the dynamics of the Jewish religion: in the long run, rabbinic Judaism, with its core emphasis on reading and studying the Torah in the synagogue, cannot survive in subsistence farming societies. The heavy costs imposed on Jewish families to obey the many norms set by their religion including the costly one requiring fathers to educate their sons and the lack of economic returns to this investment in literacy will prompt a proportion of Jews to leave Judaism and embrace other religions with less-demanding religious norms.

CHAPTER 6

From Farmers to Merchants, 750–1150

> The current situation in which most Jewish people do not own land explains why the Geonim of the two academies of Sura and Pumbedita in 787 abrogated a Talmudic law and decreed that debts from orphans and women's dowries could also be exacted from movable property, whereas before that time creditors could claim only landed property.
> —*R. Moses b. Jacob, Gaon of Sura, c. 832*

> Parents everywhere were bound by religious injunctions and pressure of society to send their children to school, at least for a number of years. The community made strenuous efforts to provide education for orphans and the children of the poor.
> — *Shelomo Dov Goitein, 1971*

By 650, the Land of Israel, Syria, Lebanon, Asia Minor, and North Africa (mainly Egypt) no longer hosted large Jewish communities, as they had done six centuries earlier. Nearly 75 percent of the roughly 1–1.2 million Jews in the world were living in Mesopotamia and Persia when Muhammad (c. 570–632) set the foundations of one of the largest empires in history.

What were the main features of world Jewry at the inception of Islam? Most Jews were still farmers, just like the rest of the population. In Mesopotamia and Persia, they were a religious minority in a largely pagan Zoroastrian society, living side by side with other religious minorities, such as the Christians, who were as numerous as the Jews.[1]

The transition away from agriculture into crafts and trade started in the late Talmud era (the fifth and sixth centuries)—mainly in Mesopotamia, where some Jews abandoned agriculture, moved to the towns, and became small shopkeepers and artisans in the tanning, linen, silk, glassmaking, and dyeing industries.[2] The Amoraim, the scholars in the academies, were the first to enter trade and commercial activities that required literacy.

[1] Gil (2004, pp. 57, 491).
[2] Baron (1937, vol. 2); Beer (1974); L. Jacobs (1990).

The specialization into urban skilled occupations reached its full-fledged stage after the establishment of the Abbasid caliphate, when the Jews in Mesopotamia and Persia migrated to the newly established cities and urban centers. This movement was so strong that by the late ninth century, the Jewish population in these locations was almost entirely urban.[3] The rural-urban migration coincided with the movement of the Jews out of agriculture, the main source of their income for centuries. This occupational transition took about 150 years: by 900 the overwhelming majority of the Jews in Mesopotamia and Persia were engaged in a wide variety of crafts, trade, moneylending, and medicine.[4] Once set in motion, this transition never reverted. The words "urban," "highly educated," "merchant," "trader," "broker," "banker," "physician," and "scholar" became permanently associated with the Jews up to today.

How does the theory outlined in chapter 4 apply to a context in which most Jews became craftsmen and traders? If literate Jewish farmers prefer to be merchants—as a simple economic argument will show—why were most literate Jews still engaged in farming in 650? Why, instead, did most Jews in Mesopotamia and Persia move from farming to crafts and trade between roughly 750 and 900? What are the implications of our theory regarding the investment of the Jews in children's literacy and conversions in an urban environment? Do the historical facts support the implications of our theory regarding the investment in literacy and education, and conversions for Jewish merchants?

The Economics of Hebrew Literacy in a World of Merchants

To address the questions set forth above, we imagine traveling back in time and putting ourselves in the minds of the Jews who lived in Mesopotamia and Persia between 650 and 900. Together the two areas were home to nearly 75 percent of world Jewry during this period.

In chapter 4, we posited that Jewish farmers living in a village in the Galilee circa 200 faced two key decisions: how much literacy and education to provide for their sons and whether to continue to adhere to rabbinic Judaism or convert. We enrich the economic analysis presented there by adding a third decision: whether to remain a farmer or to engage in occupations such as crafts, trade, and moneylending. To make the analysis as simple as possible without ignoring important aspects of the historical facts we aim to explain, we make some assumptions. These simplifications

---

[3] Gil (2004, pp. 491–92, 597–600).

[4] Baron (1952, vol. 4, chap. 22); Ashtor (1959b, pp. 147–54); H. Ben-Sasson (1976, pp. 388–400); Gil (2004, pp. 597–662).

turn out to be consistent with the descriptions of the economy of the Mediterranean area and the Middle East between the eighth and the twelfth
centuries presented by Goitein and Gil.[5]

The Economic Theory: Basic Setup

As during the first half of the first millennium, described in chapter 4, heterogeneity is a paramount feature of the world population during the second half of the first millennium. People differ in tastes, beliefs, religiosity,
abilities, attitudes to work, health, as well as earnings and incomes.

Like individuals in the first half of the first millennium, Jews and
non-Jews in the second half of the first millennium derive utility from
consumption. As before, Jewish farmers and merchants differ from non-
Jews in one key feature: they also derive utility from being able to read
and study the Torah and from having literate sons who can read and study
the Torah.[6] They continue to impose a social penalty on Jews who do not
obey the religious norm regarding sending their sons to school to learn
to read and study the Torah. The *ammei ha-aretz* continue to be outcasts.
Translated into economic jargon, the social penalty brings disutility to a
Jew who chooses not to invest in his children's literacy and education.

A Jewish farmer in Mesopotamia in the year 650 or 850 is not much
different from a Jewish farmer in the Galilee in the year 200.[7] Physical
strength, knowledge of the soil, the use of farming techniques passed on
from father to son, and hard work are required to be a productive farmer.
In the subsistence economies of the first millennium, most farmers work
their fields and raise cattle mainly for consumption, selling what is left
after providing for their families. They produce few cash-earning goods.
They rarely form business partnerships, write contracts, or engage in
transactions requiring sophisticated calculations. In the language of economics, literacy and education are not significant inputs into the production functions of farmers and, hence, do not make farmers—Jewish or
non-Jewish—more productive and wealthier.

How does literacy affect urban dwellers engaged in skilled occupations? Even illiterate craftsmen and merchants can earn good incomes:
a shoemaker can make shoes without being able to read or to write. For
the sake of simplicity, we assume that illiterate craftsmen and merchants

[5]Goitein (1967–88, vol. 1); Gil (1992, 2004).

[6]We assume that all the other norms Judaism imposes (e.g., eating kosher food, observing the Sabbath) yield the same utility (or disutility) as similar norms imposed by other
religions.

[7]Technical progress in agriculture took place during the first millennium (see Mokyr
1990, chap. 1) but not to the extent that agriculture became mechanized or the object of scientific study, as it did during and after the Industrial Revolution.

earn only as much as farmers.[8] This assumption seems a reasonable one, as were it not true, farmers would leave farming to become (illiterate) craftsmen and merchants.[9]

The nature of their work makes literacy extremely valuable to craftsmen, merchants, and moneylenders, who produce goods or provide services for sale on the market. Selling their goods or services, purchasing raw materials, using contracts, and being aware of market conditions are all central to their earnings. Many artisans, traders, and moneylenders benefit from establishing business partnerships and finding financiers. Writing and reading contracts, letters, deeds, business accounts, inventories, and lists of prices and exchange rates can greatly enhance the way individuals who work in these occupations do their business. In the language of economics, the literacy and education of an adult and his sons enter the production functions of craftsmen, merchants, and moneylenders, raising their productivity and earnings.

Just as today, an adult's literacy and education in the first millennium is determined by the investment made by his parents when he was a child. He may choose to become even more literate and educated, but without the initial investment made by his parents, he will be unable to enhance his own education as an adult.

Given this, Hebrew religious literacy has spillover effects on general literacy, as convincingly argued by economist Carmel Chiswick.[10] A Jewish man who obeys the religious norm set by Judaism and sends his sons from the age of six or seven to the synagogue or the primary school to learn to read and study the Torah in Hebrew greatly enhances the boys' ability to learn to read and study any other text written in Hebrew (and then in other languages as well). Moreover, learning to read helps people learn to write. It also helps develop numeracy and the ability to compute prices, costs, interest rates, and exchange rates and thus to keep account books. These skills are useless for farmers in the agrarian economies of the first millennium for the reasons mentioned earlier. They are key assets for craftsmen, traders, and moneylenders.

Thanks to the intellectual prominence of the scholars in the academies of the Land of Israel and Mesopotamia between the first and the sixth

---

[8] In the discussion here, we follow the assumptions of the model presented in the annex. We assume that there are only two occupations, farmers and merchants, and that there is no return to literacy for farmers for the sake of simplicity. Whether or not the return is actually zero is unimportant—the key point is that the return to literacy for farmers is less than that for urban skilled occupations.

[9] In occupational choice models, this is equivalent to the assumption of one-dimensional skill. Given that we consider only two occupations, this simplification is not restrictive.

[10] See C. Chiswick (1999, 2006) for an insightful discussion of the spillover effects between religious and general literacy in Judaism.

centuries, the Jews are also endowed with the Talmud, the responsa, and the rabbinic courts (see chapter 5). The canon of law universally accepted by all Jewish communities in the world (the Talmud); the supplementation of those rulings through the responsa written by the heads of the academies, who adapted Jewish halakha to new and unforeseen contingencies; and the rabbinic courts, which ensured that contracts were enforced—all of these institutions represent invaluable assets for Jews engaged in occupations that benefit from contract enforcement, such as crafts, trade, and moneylending.[11] Literacy is clearly a prerequisite for these institutions.

With the incomes they earn in their occupations, Jewish households living in Mesopotamia and Persia from the mid-seventh to the late ninth century purchase consumption goods for their families (food, shelter, clothing); they pay taxes; and, if they send their sons to primary school, they incur the direct expenses of their education (books, tuition) as well as the opportunity cost of the wages the children would otherwise have earned by going to work. Translated into economic jargon, each household has a budget constraint, which it allocates in various ways.

Given the opportunities and constraints they face, and given their preferences, aspirations, and religious devotion, what choices would Jews living in Mesopotamia and Persia under Muslim rule make regarding their occupation, religion, and investment in children's literacy and education?

The Economic Theory: Predictions

We first analyze the choice of occupation by applying the logic of Roy's model of occupational choice.[12] What occupation would a literate Jew choose? Given that earnings in crafts, trade, and moneylending increase with literacy and education and that Jews have contract-enforcement institutions that greatly benefit commercial and business transactions, all literate Jews would prefer to engage in crafts, trade, and moneylending, because they can earn more from these pursuits than from farming.[13] The first implication of our theory is thus that literate Jews will always be looking for the opportunity to find urban skilled occupations that yield high returns to their investment in literacy and education.

Who will enter these professions first? When the economy shifts from rural and agrarian to urban and commercial, literate Jewish farmers will

---

[11] Greif (1989, 1993, 2006) shows how these assets were key in fostering contract enforcement among the Maghrebi (Jewish) traders in the Mediterranean during the tenth and eleventh centuries. See below for an overview of Greif's argument.

[12] Roy (1951).

[13] For this result to hold, taxes paid by farmers and by merchants should be roughly the same or taxes paid by merchants should not exceed the difference in earnings between farmers and merchants.

be the first to become craftsmen, merchants, and traders. For non-Jewish farmers whose parents did not invest in their literacy, it is almost impossible to learn an occupation requiring literacy.

How many Jews will become urban dwellers engaged in skilled occupations? The demand for these occupations determines how many literate Jews can enter such fields. When few urban skilled occupations are available because the economy is still mainly agrarian, many literate Jews will be forced to remain farmers. When urbanization kicks off, new industries develop, trade and commercial activities expand and demand for a wide array of urban skilled occupations grows, many literate Jews will be able to enter these occupations. The second implication of our theory is therefore that urbanization and commercial expansion will enable a large share of the Jewish population to leave farming and specialize in crafts, trade, moneylending, and other skilled professions *before* any other ethnic or religious group.

Next we consider the decision of whether and how much to invest in children's literacy and education. The third implication of our theory is that the fact that literacy is useful to craftsmen, merchants, and moneylenders but not to farmers (regardless of religious affiliation) means that the former group has a greater incentive to invest in their children's literacy and education than farmers. The fourth implication of our theory is that as craftsmen, traders, and moneylenders, Jews will be more likely to invest in their children's literacy and education—and will invest more— than non-Jews because in addition to the earnings advantage literacy provides, Jews who obey the religious norm set by Judaism derive utility from being able to read and study the Torah in the synagogue and having their sons able to do the same.

Finally, we consider the choice of which religion to belong. Will Jewish craftsmen, merchants, and moneylenders voluntarily convert, as our theory predicts a proportion of Jewish farmers will? The answer is no. To understand why, we return to the rationale for conversions among Jewish farmers (see chapter 4). Literate individuals always prefer to be in urban skilled occupations than farming and will always invest in their sons' literacy and education. Assuming that the costs of acquiring literacy and education for Jews and non-Jews are the same and that the economic returns from literacy and education are the same for Jews and non-Jews, Jews will invest more in their children's literacy and education, because as members of a religion that highly values literacy, they reap additional benefits from obeying the religious norm and becoming literate.[14]

---

[14] Jewish craftsmen, traders, and moneylenders can in principle earn more than non-Jews in the same occupations because they are endowed with contract-enforcement institutions (the Talmud, the responsa, rabbinic courts). If non-Jews can also rely on similar

Moreover, as literate Jews, they are not subject to the social penalty inflicted by the Jewish community on illiterate Jews. Hence even with zero attachment to Judaism, Jews engaged in crafts, trade, and money-lending have no incentive to convert as long as they are not discriminated against. Unless Jews in skilled occupations have to pay higher taxes than non-Jews (or are subject to other forms of discrimination), they will derive no benefit from converting to another religion.[15] The last prediction of our theory, then, is that over time, the Jewish population as a population of urban, highly literate and educated individuals engaged in crafts, trade, and moneylending will remain stable, or grow, because few voluntary conversions will occur.

THE GOLDEN AGE OF LITERATE JEWS IN THE MUSLIM CALIPHATES

Do the assumptions of our theory match the main features of the society and economy in which the Jews in Mesopotamia and Persia lived from the mid-seventh to the late ninth century? Does the economic and demographic history of the Jews in that period support the five implications of our theory?

Hebrew Literacy

The first assumption of our theory is that Hebrew religious literacy (the ability to read and study the Torah in Hebrew) has spillover effects on general literacy (the ability to read, and then to write, any document written in Hebrew or any other language). The Hebrew, Aramaic, Greek, and Latin alphabets display strong similarities.[16] Hence, learning in childhood

---

contract-enforcement institutions—and they did—it makes sense to assume that Jews and non-Jews engaged in crafts, trade, and moneylending earn the same incomes from their businesses.

[15] This implication relies on the assumption spelled out in the model in the annex that the education of a father and of his son are complementary in the production function of merchants. The argument goes as follows: consider an educated Jewish individual who has no attachment to his religion and faces high costs of sending his sons to school (because, for example, his children lack motivation for or dedication to studying the Torah in the synagogue). Suppose that he would prefer to be a merchant than a farmer. In this case, he will invest in his sons' education exactly as a non-Jewish merchant does. As long as the tax differential between Jews and non-Jews is not larger than the social cost of leaving Judaism and losing the help and support of fellow Jews, a Jewish merchant has no incentive to convert.

[16] Daniels (1996); O' Connor (1996). Originated in what is modern-day Syria and derived from the North Semitic script, Aramaic became extremely widespread between 1000 and 600 BCE (especially after the Assyrian conquest of the Middle East), spoken from the Mediterranean coast to the borders of India. Its script, derived from Phoenician (from which

to read Hebrew in the synagogue enhanced the ability of Jewish boys and men to learn other alphabets and to read other languages used in the various locations where Jews lived.

Learning to read Hebrew also helped develop one's ability to write Hebrew (and other languages). The Jews' ability to write before most other people could do so is clearly shown in the description of the economic transactions by Jewish artisans, shopkeepers, long-distance traders, and moneylenders in the Middle East and North Africa under Muslim rule portrayed in the myriad documents of the Cairo Geniza.[17] Most of the business deeds and personal letters were written in a casual Arabic, heavily influenced by the spoken dialect, and transcribed into Hebrew letters (called Judeo-Arabic). This ability enabled Jewish craftsmen, traders, and moneylenders to conduct business transactions with non-Jews, because they knew the local spoken language (Arabic in the lands of the Muslim caliphates), even if they used Hebrew characters to write their documents.[18]

The second assumption of our theory is that literacy (the ability to read and to write) enhances the productivity and the earnings of artisans, merchants, traders, and moneylenders, for a variety of reasons. Almost all goods were custom made in the first millennium. Artisans and craftsmen such as goldsmiths, jewelers, blacksmiths, weapons producers, shoemakers, dyers, weavers, and tailors enjoyed an advantage from being able to read and write contracts, which specified the characteristics of the raw materials and the finished products. Such contracts were used in case of disputes between customers and sellers.

This positive economic return to literacy for craftsmen and traders is illustrated by three of the many letters found in the Cairo Geniza. The first letter was written circa 1030 by the Spanish-Jewish merchant Jacob b. Samuel, who lived in Palermo, to his Spanish-Jewish brother-in-law Joshua b. Nathan, who was living in Fustat (Old Cairo), Egypt:[19]

Greek is also considered to have derived) and first attested during the ninth century BCE, also became extremely popular and was adopted by many people, both with or without any previous writing system. The Aramaic alphabet consists of twenty-two letters, all indicating consonants, and it is written from right to left. It was also ancestral to the Nabataean and modern Arabic scripts, the Palmyrene alphabet, and the Syriac, as well as hundreds of other writing systems used at some time in Asia east of Syria. One of the most influential impacts of the Aramaic script was on the square Hebrew script. Writing, derived from Phoenician, began to appear in the Land of Israel around the tenth century BCE, and the Old Hebrew script was one of them. However, by the sixth century BCE, an Aramaic-derived script, appropriately called the Jewish script, began to replace the Old Hebrew script. It is the Jewish script that eventually evolved into the modern square Hebrew script.

[17] Goitein (1967–88); Gil (1992, 2004); M. R. Cohen (1994, 2006).

[18] Goitein (1967–88, vol. 2, pp. 191, 228).

[19] Goitein (1973, p. 116). The wimple mentioned in the letter was a female turban.

Kindly buy me a holiday robe with its wimple, made of fine linen, green with gold threads, worth between 8 and 10 dinars, made of dense fabric, so that it should be durable. Also (buy) two white wimples, six cubits long, for 2¼ to 2½ dinars, and a pair of . . . shoes.

The second letter was written by a Jewish merchant living in Tyre, Lebanon, during the eleventh century:[20]

In my previous letter, I have informed you about the arrival of the yarn. . . . immediately after its arrival, I delivered it to a trustworthy Jewish craftsman. Earlier, I showed it to various craftsmen, who told me that it would make a thousand robes of the bazaar type and slightly more of the homemade kind. Among the rolls of the yarn, there were four spoiled ones which were coarse and deformed. I also gave him (to the weaver) two robes of the bazaar type, in accordance with your instructions.

After each roll is finished, the craftsman is to receive 3 quarter dinars. The embroidering will require 1/6 dinar and 1/2 qīrāt, and the bleaching and pounding, 5 qīrāts, the total (for a roll) being 1 1/8 Nizāriyya dinars. . . .

The bleaching will not be completed until after Passover. For it is now winter, and God does not make bleaching possible in winter time, when it would not be as brilliant as during the summer. . . .

The third letter was written circa 1010 by Moses, son of Barhūn, the eldest of the Tāhertī family, one of the wealthiest and most influential households in Qayrawan, Tunisia. It is addressed to Sahl, the eldest of the Tustarī family, one of the wealthiest and most prominent families in Egypt:[21]

I would like the robe to be deep red, as red as possible, and the white and yellow also to be of excellent color. I did not like the color of the yellow which arrived. Also, the white robe which is to serve as mantle should be of the same quality. The best robes manufactured are the old ones. It should be cut in two pieces. Its price should be 2[5 dinars], or as you deem proper; 1 dinar more on a robe having your approval is preferable to one not so good.

The Sig[laton] robe is of extreme beauty, but it is not the color which they ordered. For this is white and blue, but instead I w[ished to have] one of the blue onion color, an open color, according to your taste. I wish to have the very best, as chosen by you.

I wish also to have two lead-gray robes with borders "filling your eyes," each worth about 25 dinars, or a little more, provided they are first class. . . .

[20] Goitein (1973, p. 108).
[21] Goitein (1973, p. 77). Qayrawan is located in the northern part of Tunisia and it was an important trading center at the turn of the millennium.

Literacy—and hence, the ability to read and write contracts, deeds, and letters—also greatly enhanced the establishment of business partnerships among traders, as shown by a typical letter from the Cairo Geniza. Written circa 1020 by the Jewish trader Abraham to the Jewish merchant Joseph Ibn Awkal in Fustat, the letter mentions twelve traders (eleven Jews and one Muslim) with whom Abraham was involved in business partnerships:[22]

> I inform you, my elder, that I arrived safely [in Alexandria]. . . . I loaded nine pieces of antimony (kohl), five in baskets and four in complete pieces, on the boat of Ibn Jubār... These are for you personally, sent by Mūsā Ibn al-Majjānī. On this boat, I have in partnership with you. . . . a load of cast copper, a basket with (copper) fragments, and two pieces of antimony. . . .
>
> I have also sent with [the sailor] Banāna a camel load for you from Ibn al-Majjānī, and a camel load for me in partnership with you. . . . He also carries another partnership of mine with Ammār Ibn Yijū, four small jugs (of oil).
>
> With Abū Zayd I have a shipload of tin in partnership with Salāma al-Mahdawī. Your share in this partnership with him is fifty pounds. I also have seventeen small jugs of s[oap]. . . . They belong to a man [called . . .]r b. Salmūn, who entrusted them to me at his own risk. Also a bundle of hammered copper, belonging to [a Muslim] man from the Maghreb, called Abū Bakr Ibn Rizq Allah. Two other bundles, on one is written Abraham, on the other M. . . . I agreed with the shipowner that he would transport the goods to their destination. . . .
>
> Please sell the tin for me at whatever price God may grant and leave its "purse" [the money received for it] until my arrival. I am ready to travel, but must stay until I can unload the tar and oil from the ships.

Literacy facilitated the acquisition of other skills, such as the ability to perform calculations, compute exchange rates, and produce written accounts of business transactions. The Geniza documents are full of descriptions of complicated calculations related to marriage contracts, contributions to the poor, accounts on payment by the community, wills, settlements, and myriad business activities.[23] Surprisingly, although Arabic numerals and algebra were known to readers of scientific books since the ninth century,[24] there is no evidence that Jewish traders, craftsmen, physicians, moneylenders, teachers, or scholars used Arabic numerals.[25]

---

[22] Goitein (1973, pp. 85–88).

[23] Goitein (1967–88, vol. 1, app. D).

[24] Levy (1996).

[25] Goitein (1967–88, vol. 2, pp. 177–78) maintains that craftsmen and traders in the Arab world adopted Arabic numerals from Europeans only in modern times. The origins of modern numeracy and algebra trace back to Muhammad ibn Musa Al-Khwarizmi's book (c. 825) *On the Calculation with Hindu Numerals*. *Al-jabar*, from which the word "algebra" comes, is the

The letters and account books preserved in the Cairo Geniza display addition and subtraction that relied only on Hebrew and Greek characters. Jewish as well as non-Jewish individuals who engaged in these occupations probably performed mental computations and, when necessary, used an abacus.

By enabling them to read and to write contracts and letters, literacy also helped Jews communicate at a distance. News about travel conditions, including safety from pirates and other dangers; demand for products in a particular location; changes in prices; arbitrage opportunities; and a wealth of additional information could be transmitted in writing from one location to another. Consider, for example, a letter written in Jerusalem during the mid-eleventh century:[26]

> You inquired about silk. Here, black and sky blue are mostly in demand, and, indeed, all colors. Crimson, however, does not sell in Jerusalem, but it might sell in Ramle or in Ascalon. Corals are weak in Jerusalem, for it is a poor town. In any case, bring them or a part of them, for success is in the hand of God. If Persians happen to arrive, they may buy them. . . .

Another letter was sent circa 1040 by the Tunisian-Jewish trader Yahyā, son of Mūsā, to his former apprentice and current partner, living in Egypt:[27]

> You wrote about the loss of part of the copper—may God compensate me and you, then—about the blessed profit made from the antimony and, finally, about the lac and the odorous wood which you bought and loaded on Mi'dād and 'Abūr. (You mentioned) that the bale on Mi'dād was unloaded afterward; I have no doubt that the other will also be unloaded. I hope, however, that there will be traffic on the Barqa route. Therefore, repack the bales into camel-loads— half their original size—and send them via Barqa. Perhaps I shall get a good price for them and acquire antimony with it this winter. For, dear brother, if the merchandise remains in Alexandria year after year, we shall make no profit.

Arabic term introduced by Al-Khwarizmi to refer to the transformation used to solve a quadratic equation. During the early thirteenth century, the Italian mathematician Leonardo Fibonacci, arguably the most talented mathematician of the early Middle Ages, introduced algebra in Europe after meeting Muslim scholars during his travels in North Africa.

[26] Goitein (1973, p. 107). Ramle and Ascalon were towns located in the central and southern parts of the Land of Israel, respectively.

[27] Goitein (1973, p. 103). The letter was written between 1038 and 1042, when the great Byzantine attack on Muslim Sicily led to the fall of Syracuse, Messina, and other towns connected with the countries along the southeastern shores of the Mediterranean. The Byzantine navy's presence on the direct route of trade between Egypt and Tunisia made traders reluctant to travel along that route.

> Only small quantities of odorous wood are to be had here, and it is much in demand. Again, do not be remiss, but make an effort and send the goods on the Barqa route—may God inspire you and me and all Israel to do the right thing.

In addition to basic literacy, Jews who learned the Talmud acquired skills in rational thinking and problem analysis. These analytical skills could be helpful when handling commercial and business transactions.[28] In fact, many traders were also learned people; some were even scholars, versed in Jewish law and lore, as shown from the legal opinions they wrote on the reverse sides of business letters they received that are preserved in the Cairo Geniza.[29]

To sum up, religious literacy—the ability to read and study the Torah in Hebrew—had several positive spillover effects on general literacy that increased the ability of Jews to profitably engage in crafts, trade, and moneylending. The close link between religiosity and trade skills of Jewish traders is epitomized in a letter written circa 1120 by a Jewish merchant of Persian origin, Isaac ben Simhā al-Nīsābūrī, living in Alexandria, to a Jew of Syrian (Damascus) origin, Abu el-Alā Sāid ha-Levi, son of Joseph, almoner and trustee of the court in Fustat:[30]

> Abu 'l-Hasan Caleb b. Nathan arrived some time ago and told me that he had carried with him a note with the measurements for the pair of mats which your honor had ordered to make; he had lost it and also did not remember the measurements. . . .
>
> I ask you also to meet with R. Abraham the Rūmī, the scribe, who wrote the Torah scroll in Tinnīs, and this year, too, I have heard that he wrote two others in Fustat. Formerly we did not have here in Alexandria a Torah scroll on parchment. But now, with the support of the Creator, we have obtained parchment and are resolved. . . . to carry this matter through. Therefore I ask your honor to meet with the aforementioned R. Abraham and make an agreement with him regarding his remuneration and all his expenses. He should come here as early as possible. Here are many scribes, but our endeavor in this matter is that the scroll of the congregation should have the very best script . . .
>
> I have learned what you have done to extricate that load of brazilwood. May I never be deprived of your kindness.

Contract-Enforcement Institutions

The third assumption of our theory is that Jews were equipped with contract-enforcement institutions that were useless to farmers but clearly

---

[28] Agus (1965, p. 7); Goitein (1967–88, vol. 1).
[29] Goitein (1967–88, vol. 2, p. 9).
[30] Goitein (1973, pp. 251–52).

benefited the business transactions of people engaged in crafts, trade, and moneylending. During the first half of the first millennium, the scholars in the academies in the Land of Israel and Mesopotamia endowed the Jewish people with three levers for contract enforcement: the Talmud, the rabbinic academies and courts, and the responsa (see chapter 5). Through the Talmud, the Jewish leadership created a body of norms, religious rulings, and legal precedents that enabled the Jewish communities scattered across the Mediterranean world and the Middle East to share a common written language (Hebrew) and a common legal framework irrespective of the political, economic, and religious environments in which they lived.

The academies also acted as rabbinic courts that offered Jews advice on specific matters and helped resolve legal controversies or litigation pertaining to daily economic, social, or religious matters. Wherever Jews lived—in sixth-century Babylon, eighth-century Fustat, or eleventh-century Córdoba—the rabbinic courts provided a judicial and arbitration body that relied on the Talmud as the binding legal code but adapted its rulings to the contingent economic and social environments in which the Jews were living.

This process of applying the legal canon set forth in the Talmud to new problems and specific contingencies was facilitated by the rabbinic responsa.[31] In the leading academies of Sura and Pumbedita in Mesopotamia, the scholars discussed each problem, using the Talmud as the guiding legal paradigm, before issuing written rulings, which were then dispatched to all Jewish communities in the Diaspora through the network of Jewish traders.[32] The typical structure of a responsum consisted of a ruling, a concise reason for it, supporting citations from the Talmud, and often a refutation of any possible objection. The services were not free: individuals who sent in questions paid for the responsum. The payments helped support the academies and the scholars. The responsa indicate that some contracts between Jews and non-Jews included a clause explicitly mentioning

---

[31] Goitein (1967–88, vol. 1, app. C) reports eleventh and twelfth-century responsa dealing with business partnerships between Jewish craftsmen and traders in which scholars including Moses Maimonides provided legal advice and judges in the rabbinic courts settled matters according to Talmudic law.

[32] Elon (1994); Brody (1998); Gil (2004, pp. 117–206). Each responsum was given by the Gaon, as R. Natan the Babylonian describes (Elon 1994): "[S]uch was the habit in responsa questions. Each Adar [March, one of the kallah months], the head of the yeshiva would bring out all the questions which he received and let the students answer them. And they would refuse until the head of the yeshiva would attack them, and then each one of them would state his opinion. The head of the yeshiva would listen to them until he gets to his conclusion and orders the scribe to write down the answer. Such was their habit each day until they would answer all the questions they received and by the end of the month they would read all the responsa in front all of them and the head of the yeshiva would sign them and send them away."

the use of a rabbi as an arbitrator in case of disagreement. The value of these arrangements and agreements was high, because the rabbis had a record of previous decisions, were familiar with traders' activities, and could safely transfer their written replies through the traveling merchants.

Having a communal written alphabet (Hebrew) that could be used to write any language, literacy, a common legal canon (the Talmud) and judicial institutions (the rabbinic courts), and a process for adapting the Talmud to the economic, social, and political environments in which they lived (the responsa) created a powerful networking mechanism that helped the Jews excel in a variety of crafts, trade, moneylending, and other skilled occupations.

Avner Greif has shown how this network externality enabled the Maghrebi traders (Jewish traders based in North Africa) during the eleventh and twelfth centuries to overcome the absence of a state as a contract-enforcement mechanism, to impose collective punishment within a community of Jewish merchants, and to enforce the laws of the Talmud within Jewish communities scattered across the Mediterranean.[33] These Jewish traders succeeded, according to Greif, because, as a small but distinctive minority, they could reduce opportunistic behavior by fellow members by excluding or ostracizing those who deviated from mutually agreed norms of economic behavior or abused the trust of other members of the Diaspora. Once trust existed among members of a small group and cooperative norms were established, members of the Jewish Diaspora were well equipped to take over long-distance trade, because they could find kinsfolk abroad whom they knew would not behave opportunistically.

Only a Jewish merchant who could read was able to enforce sanctions on Jewish traders who cheated and acted opportunistically toward other Jewish merchants. Thus literacy was a precondition for the application of community sanctions, Jewish court rulings, and the rulings of the scholars in the academies in Mesopotamia.

Earnings across Occupations

The fourth assumption of our theory is that literacy enters the production functions and raises the earnings of individuals engaged in crafts, trade, and moneylending, whereas it brings no returns to farmers. Hence, wages and earnings in farming are, on average, lower than in occupations that benefit from literacy.

Table 6.1 shows some data supporting this hypothesis. In the Land of Israel during the first centuries of the first millennium, an urban skilled

---

[33]Greif (1989, 1993, 1994, 2006).

TABLE 6.1. Rural and Urban Wage Differentials in Selected Locations and Years

Location/period	Agricultural worker	Urban skilled worker
Middle East		
Land of Israel, 1 CE–300	24–48	48–72
Mesopotamia, 1 CE–300	72–96	—
Egypt, 1 CE–300	4–32	6–40
Tuscany		
c. 1290	35	60
c. 1350	30	90
c. 1430	120	240
England		
1750–59	5.57[a]	11.14–16.70[b]
Japan		
1880–84	4.94	7.44

Sources: For the Land of Israel, Mesopotamia, and Egypt, Sperber (1965, 1966). For medieval Tuscany, Malanima (2005, 2007). For England and Japan, Allen (2001, tables 1 and 2; 2005, app., tables 5.3 and 5.4).

Notes: Figures for the Land of Israel, Mesopotamia, and Egypt are average monthly nominal wages in denarii. Figures for Tuscany are average annual nominal wages in lire. Figures for England and Japan are average daily wages expressed in grams of silver per day.

— Not available.

[a] The figure refers to Oxford.

[b] The two figures refer to Oxford and London, respectively.

worker earned twice as much as an agricultural worker. The same is true for other locations and periods.[34]

The Slow Transition to Urban Occupations

Under the four assumptions made above, our theory predicts that literate Jewish farmers would prefer to leave farming and to engage in crafts, trade, and moneylending because they can earn more. Why did it take so long for literate Jewish farmers to become urban dwellers engaged in these profitable occupations? Why did the full-fledged occupational transition from farming to crafts, trade, and moneylending occur in the Muslim Middle East during the eighth and the ninth centuries and not the fifth and the sixth centuries, when most Jews were already literate in a world of almost universal illiteracy?

[34] Allen (2001, 2005) and van Zanden (2009) analyze a lot of historical data on the wages of agricultural workers and urban unskilled and skilled workers in Europe and Asia and discuss the skill premium in early modern and modern times.

The historical evidence helps solve the puzzle. With the exception of Constantinople, which grew spectacularly and became the center of a vibrant commercial economy under Byzantine rule, no major urbanization occurred in Mesopotamia, Persia, the Land of Israel, Syria, North Africa, or western Europe between the third and the early seventh centuries. The economy of Mesopotamia and Persia under Sassanid rule was mainly rural and agrarian, and no new cities were built. The Amoraim, the scholars in the academies in Mesopotamia, with their high literacy and human capital, were the first to abandon agriculture and become craftsmen and merchants, during the fifth and sixth centuries. This occupational transition affected only a small segment of Mesopotamian Jewry, however.[35]

Under late Roman and then Byzantine rule, the Land of Israel entered a period of decline: towns and villages were disappearing rather than growing (see chapter 1). The economies of Egypt and the western Roman Empire were also deteriorating.[36] The fall of Rome, in 476, marked the end of the western half of the Roman Empire; the subsequent invasions of Germanic populations from central and northern Europe brought on the so-called Dark Ages in western Europe, characterized by predominantly agrarian economies and few urban commercial centers.

With no major urbanization occurring between 200 and 650, the demand for urban skilled occupations in 650 was roughly what it had been in 200 or 400. Meanwhile, the supply of literate Jews who were able to become craftsmen, merchants, and traders rose rapidly between the third to the late sixth century, as a result of the implementation of the Jewish religious norm imposing fathers to educate their sons. With no new cities built and the economy being mainly agrarian between the time of Rabbi Judah haNasi and the time of Muhammad, there was excess supply of literate Jewish farmers who wanted to engage in crafts, trade, and moneylending but could not find jobs in these occupations. This situation changed dramatically in the seventh century, when Muhammad set the foundations for one of the largest, most urban, and most commercial empires in premodern history.

Urbanization, Commercial Expansion, and Jewish Occupational Transition

From the point of view of the Jewish people, the founding of the Muslim caliphates was a "historical accident"—an exogenous event set in motion by the Arabs under Muhammad's leadership. This historical accident interacted with the internal dynamics of Judaism to lead to an unprecedented

[35] Neusner (1965–70); Beer (1974); Gafni (1990); L. Jacobs (1990).
[36] Avi-Yonah (1976); Herr and Oppenheimer (1990); Leibner (2006, 2009); Gil (2008).

and long-lasting change in the occupational and residential structure of world Jewry.

After Muhammad's death in 632, Muslim religious leaders aspired to make Islam a universal religion as well as a world empire. At the height of its territorial expansion under the Umayyad and subsequently the Abbasid dynasty, the empire embraced a vast territory stretching from the Iberian Peninsula to India, within which it was relatively easy to move or migrate. Muslim rule, which imposed a common language (Arabic) and a uniform set of institutions and laws over an immense area, greatly favored trade and commerce.[37]

The Abbasid period was marked by spectacular developments in science, technology, and the liberal arts. The reigns of Harun al-Rashid (786–809) and Mamun (813–33) were periods of extraordinary economic, technological, scientific, philosophical, and literary splendor. The Muslim world adopted papermaking from China, improving Chinese technology with the invention of paper mills many centuries before paper was known in the West.[38] Muslim engineers made innovative industrial uses of hydropower, tidal power, wind power, steam power, and fossil fuels. The industrial use of water mills dates back to the seventh century; horizontal-wheeled and vertical-wheeled water mills have been in widespread use since at least the ninth century. By the eleventh century, industrial mills were operating in every province in the Islamic world. Muslim engineers invented crankshafts and water turbines, employed gears in mills and water-raising machines, and pioneered the use of dams as a source of waterpower. Such advances made it possible to mechanize many industrial tasks that had previously been performed by manual labor.[39]

Important advances were made in irrigation and farming, using new technologies such as the windmill. The Arabs brought crops such as almonds and citrus fruit to Europe through the Iberian Peninsula and introduced sugar cultivation in Europe.[40] Rising agricultural productivity fostered the growth of cities and industries throughout the Middle East.[41]

---

[37] Lewis (2002). Persians continued to use their native language, as did Persian Jews, writing it in Hebrew characters (Judeo-Persian).

[38] Goitein (1967–88, vol. 1); Mokyr (1990, chap. 6). The knowledge of gunpowder was also transmitted later on from China via Islamic countries.

[39] Mokyr (1990, chap. 6).

[40] Watson (1974); Mokyr (1990, chap. 6); Decker (2009).

[41] Mokyr (1990, chap. 6). Products of these early industries included astronomical instruments, ceramics, chemicals, distillation technologies, clocks, glass, mechanical hydropowered and wind-powered machinery, matting, mosaics, pulp and paper, pharmaceuticals, rope-making, shipbuilding, silk, sugar, textiles, weapons, and the mining of minerals such as sulfur, ammonia, lead, and iron.

Large factory complexes were built for many of these industries, and knowledge of these industries were later transmitted to medieval Europe.

With technological progress, trade expansion, and economic growth came vast urbanization.[42] New towns and cities were founded in both Mesopotamia and Persia, with Baghdad—the new capital of the empire— becoming one of the largest cities in the world (about 1 million people) during the ninth century (see table 1.4). From an economic point of view, the major consequence of the urbanization of the Middle East was that it vastly increased the demand for skilled occupations in the newly established cities, to which Jews in Mesopotamia and Persia flocked. This movement was so overwhelming that by the late ninth century, the Jewish population in the Middle East was almost entirely urban.[43]

Jews who moved to cities and towns became engaged in hundreds of urban occupations, including crafts, shopkeeping, trade, moneylending, tax collection, teaching, and medicine. The documents of the Cairo Geniza cover about 450 occupations (including about 265 manual occupations, such as crafts; 90 occupations related to commerce and banking; and about 90 bureaucratic or teaching professions, including scribes, state and local bureaucrats and officials, religious functionaries, teachers, rabbis, and educators). Never before had so many occupations existed in a single place.[44]

This residential and occupational transition took about 150 years: by 900, few of the Jews in Mesopotamia and Persia were farmers, as their ancestors had been for centuries. They were wine sellers, corn and cattle dealers, builders, clothiers, booksellers, agents and brokers, makers of water clocks, dealers in houses, innkeepers, tanners, manufacturers of silk and purple cloth, glass manufacturers, skilled artisans and craftsmen, shipowners, pearl dealers, shopkeepers, goldsmiths, physicians, local merchants, long-distance traders, and court bankers.[45]

The timing (eighth and ninth centuries) and location (the Muslim Middle East) of the occupational transition of the Jews is consistent with the first two implications of our theory regarding the choice of occupation: when urbanization kicked off, trade and commercial activities greatly expanded, and a wide array of urban skilled occupations became available, many literate Jews were able to enter these occupations *before* any other ethnic or religious group.

---

[42] Baron (1952, vol. 4, pp. 150–227); Stillman (1995); Gil (2004, pp. 491–92).

[43] Baron (1952, vol. 4, pp. 150–227); Ashtor (1959b, pp. 147–54); H. Ben-Sasson (1976, pp. 388–94); Gil (2004, pp. 491–92, 597–600).

[44] Goitein (1967–88, vol. 1).

[45] Baron (1952, vol. 4, chap. 22); Ashtor (1959b, pp. 147–54); H. Ben-Sasson (1976, pp. 388–400); Gil (2004, pp. 603–62).

The length of the Jewish occupational transition—about 150 years—is consistent with the length of the transition from rural to urban occupations observed during the Industrial Revolution in western Europe during the eighteenth and nineteenth centuries, as the economist Robert Lucas shows.[46] Lucas built his argument on a theory of human capital accumulation as the main mechanism for the transition from rural to urban societies. The intuition in his model is that it takes some time for literate people to learn the skills that enable them to move from rural to urban occupations. As a result, a lag exists between the point at which individuals become literate and the point at which they change location (rural to urban) and occupation (unskilled to skilled).

Universal Primary Education among Jews

The third implication of our theory is that once most Jews are urban dwellers engaged in crafts, trade, moneylending, and medicine, they increase their investment in their children's literacy and education. The historical evidence fully supports this implication. Primary education became almost universal in the Jewish communities of the Muslim Middle East. As Goitein notes, "Knowledge of Hebrew was . . . nearly universal among Jewish males, at least at the minimal level of the ability to read the Bible, which formed the core of the Jewish primary education."[47]

The two main primary sources documenting the spread of literacy and education among the Jews are the Gaonic responsa and the documents of the Cairo Geniza. The existence and extent of the responsa is by itself evidence of the spread of literacy in the Jewish communities throughout the Diaspora. Many responsa referred to schools, teachers and their salaries, pupils, and books. Some letters refer to teachers and tutors being appointed even in small towns and villages. Some responsa indicate that Jewish children in synagogues learned Hebrew and Arabic script, as well as arithmetic.[48] Other responsa mention that non-Jewish families were interested in sending their children to synagogues to learn nonreligious topics.[49]

---

[46] Lucas (2004).

[47] Goitein (1967–88, vol. 2, pp. 171–83).

[48] Goitein (1967–88, vol. 2, p. 177). Letters in the Cairo Geniza also confirm this. For example, in a letter written by the wealthy Jewish trader and scholar Halfōn b. Manasse ha-Levi (1100–39), a widow contracts the merchant to instruct her son in Arabic calligraphy and arithmetic. For successful teaching the instructor's remuneration would be two dinars.

[49] Assaf (2002–6, vol. 2, p. 27). Rabbi Hai, the head of the academy in Pumbedita in the late tenth to early eleventh century, notes that children may study "Arabic script and arithmetic as an addition to the study of the Torah. But without the teaching of Torah, one should not teach these" and that "one should avoid, as far as possible, teaching the children of gentiles in the synagogues; but if there is a fear it may cause outrage, then it should be permitted, so as to keep the peace."

The Cairo Geniza also includes a wealth of information confirming the universality of primary education among Jewish children. The budgets, letters, and contracts of both wealthy and modest households, even households from small towns and villages, contain numerous references to teachers and school fees.[50]

Many letters and court records attest to the centrality of education in Jewish household life. For example, a woman from a modest family tried to prove in a trial that her husband did not have the rights of a husband because he did not pay for the education of his children (she paid herself). In a settlement, a woman confirmed that she had paid the expenses associated with food, drink, clothing, living quarters, and education of their three children. A letter by a Jewish man, probably in response to his wife's complaint that the workload imposed by teachers on their children was too heavy, notes that "the knowledge we acquire as children is the only thing that makes others respect us. . . . [T]he teacher should be respected and the children should be sent to school (in the synagogue) every morning and every evening."[51]

In a business letter, a Jewish merchant advises his correspondent to make sure that his son does not interrupt his studies; if the need arises, his friend was asked to advance the school fees. Several letters by fathers traveling abroad give instructions to their wives or other relatives regarding the proper education of their children. One Jewish merchant complains bitterly about his wife, who let the children miss school and play in the streets. In the same letter he sends his brother fifteen dirhams for his children's teacher and a fine piece of clothing for his son, to encourage him to attend school.[52]

Jewish communities made strenuous efforts to provide education for orphans and the children of the poor. In addition to the school fees for one's own children, each household head was required to pay an education tax to finance the primary education of orphans and poor children. Records from Fustat, Jerusalem, Damascus, and Baghdad mention "teachers of the orphans" supported by this communal tax.[53] Every household head who had resided for twelve months or longer in a given location had to pay an education tax to finance the schooling of orphans and poor children. This document from the Cairo Geniza provides evidence of households' expenditures for their own children and that of orphans and poor children in a Jewish community:[54]

[50] Goitein (1962). In addition to living expenses and the head tax, education took up the major portion of the family budgets found in the Cairo Geniza.
[51] Goitein (1962, pp. 34–35; 1967–88, vol. 2, p. 174).
[52] Goitein (1962, pp. 34–35; 1967–88, vol. 2, p. 174).
[53] Goitein (1967–88, vol. 2, pp. 174–93).
[54] Goitein (1962, p. 40); M. R. Cohen (2003).

Account of the teaching of children in Torah School of R. Nisim son of Ibrahim the community leader from Shabat Bereshit until Shabat Va-Yoshea—16 weeks . . . 8 dirhams

Son of the carpenter, called Chayoun the Mugrabi for 4 months . . . 8 dirhams

Three sons of Calaf from the town of Almachla for 12 weeks . . . 15 dirhams

Chayoun the Mugrabi the orphan, from the month of Av until the end of Shabat Va-Yoshea—5 months . . . 10.5 dirhams

Sons of the shoemaker's wife and a little boy of R. Yehosua, for 10 weeks ending with Shabat Va-Yoshea . . . 15 dirhams

Son of Mechsan the shamash and the son of Baha the shomer [kashruth supervisor] for 12 weeks ending at the same time . . . 12 dirhams

Goitein explains this letter as follows. The teacher received his salary at the end of the teaching period. Teachers likely stipulated that children will learn for a certain period and were paid by its end. The weekly payment for a child was 0.5 dirham. If the teacher had forty pupils, he received twenty dirhams by the end of the week. The community paid for the son of the *shomer* and the son of the *shamash*, as well as for the son of one of the community leaders.

How was the instruction of children and adults organized in the world described in the Cairo Geniza? Recall that the primary goal of educating Jewish children was to prepare them to take an active part in the synagogue service. The Five Books of Moses (the Pentateuch) were read and studied in their entirety from a sacred scroll, written in the ancient fashion, without vowels or signs for cantillation. A Jew wishing to participate in the synagogue service also had to be fluent in the readings of the Prophets, as well as the Aramaic translation (Targūm) of the Prophets, and some other books of the Bible. A boy chanting the Targūm "on the Torah"—that is, reciting the ancient Aramaic translation of the Hebrew lection read by an adult verse by verse—was the pride of his parents, as shown in a long business letter sent from Cairo to a merchant on a trip to India, in which the writer notes, "Your boy Faraj now reads the Targūm accompanying the lections—as I guaranteed you he would."[55]

This close link between religion and literacy explains why Jewish education was organized in the way described in the records of the Cairo Geniza. A boy spent his childhood in a school attached to the synagogue or in a private house of study at the residence of the teacher; children of wealthy parents were provided with private instruction.[56] The primary school, which typically hosted children of mixed ages, was meant to prepare young children for participation in worship in the synagogue.

---

[55] Goitein (1967–88, vol. 2, p. 175).
[56] Goitein (1967–88, vol. 2, p. 177).

Learning to read and study the Torah in Hebrew was the main part of the program. The exercise books found among the documents of the Cairo Geniza show that reading was taught by teaching letters together with other symbols used in Hebrew and their various combinations. In order to make teaching more entertaining and to enhance the likelihood that children learned, teachers drew large calligraphic outlines of the letters, which children filled in red and brown colors.[57]

There is some evidence that young girls attended school with young boys, at least in Alexandria. In prominent households, especially when there were no sons, girls received a high level of Jewish literacy and education. The Geniza contains several accounts of women who were teachers.[58]

The size of the Jewish community affected the way primary education was organized. In smaller settlements, a single teacher was hired and paid by the community collectively. In larger communities, teachers were free to compete for students. Sometimes the Jewish communities paid a fixed salary to the teacher; sometimes they paid a salary based on the number of orphans and poor students in the classroom.

The documents in the Cairo Geniza also reveal the different social statuses accorded to *melamedei tinokot* (teachers of young children), *talmidim* (scholars), and *haverim* ("accredited" learned men). *Melamedei tinokot*, although respected, were at the bottom of the social ranking; *haverim* were at the top of the social standing within the Jewish communities described in the Cairo Geniza.[59] The Jewish community carefully controlled the teachers, provided for the education of the poor and the orphans, and regulated teachers' salaries.

After attending primary school, where he acquired basic literacy in Hebrew and Arabic, the ability to read and study the Torah in Hebrew, and some arithmetic skills, a Jewish boy was supposed to learn a craft or a trade, as indicated in the Talmudic passage (Kiddushin 19a) requiring a Jewish father to pay for his son's education and to teach his son a craft or trade. This ruling did not obligate the father to teach the son a craft himself. Crafts were typically taught by craftsmen, who received payment for their teaching. As this on-the-job training for craftsmen was usually done orally, there is little evidence of this practice in the documents of the Cairo Geniza. Because the nature of their work required merchants to write more, these documents provide more evidence of training for commerce.[60]

[57] Goitein (1967–88, vol. 2, p. 178).
[58] Goitein (1962, p. 64). It is not clear whether Jewish girls received instruction in the primary school before the Muslim period, because there are no surviving records such as the Cairo Geniza documents.
[59] Goitein (1967–88, vol. 2, pp. 185–90).
[60] Goitein (1962, pp. 116–25).

Skills such as the ability to perform sophisticated calculations involving prices, the future value of goods bought and sold at different times, interest rates, and exchange rates were not taught in primary schools (or even in the academies of higher learning). Older children and young adults learned these computational skills while learning business practices in their fathers' businesses or from other artisans, merchants, traders, and moneylenders to whom they were sent to learn a craft or a trade.[61]

The same documents shed little light on higher stages of education (religious or secular) to which some Jewish young adults devoted themselves after primary school. They provide no information on the academies as learning institutions for young adults. This is not surprising, given that the academies were originally intended as assemblies for scholars. The language of instruction in the academies was Aramaic mixed with Hebrew. Higher secular studies were typically conducted in Arabic (although the Geniza includes some documents on medicine and science written in Hebrew). These studies were interdenominational. Jews studied with Muslim and Christian teachers, and Jewish physicians instructed people of other faiths.[62]

Study was not deemed a duty only of children. Given that it was considered an act of worship of God, study continued throughout the entire lives of all Jewish men. The documents of the Cairo Geniza provide much evidence of the commitment of adult Jews to reading and studying the sacred texts. The spiritual leader in the Geniza period was called a *dayyan* (judge) rather than a rabbi. His main duty was to educate adult men. Teaching was done on the Sabbath and holidays; there were also regular classes on weekdays, especially at night. In one Geniza document, a Jew from the eleventh century writes, "Just as the body needs food, so the soul needs learning. Therefore, part of man's time should be dedicated to learning, meaning in the free time, Sabbath and the holidays."[63] In a letter from Tunisia, a Jew wrote, "You wrote that you had gone over the Bible a second time and knew it, and, furthermore, that you studied the Mishna and the Talmud. You made me extremely happy . . ."[64]

Members of almost all professions were involved in learning and educational activities. Goitein portrays in detail the educational process of scholars, judges, preachers, cantors, other religious functionaries, scribes, copiers, physicians, druggists, pharmacists, perfumers, preparers of potions, and so on.[65] Most literate people were from the middle and upper

---

[61] Goitein (1967–88, vols. 1 and 2).
[62] Goitein (1962, pp. 140–45).
[63] Goitein (1962, p. 129).
[64] Goitein (1967–88, vol. 2, pp. 192–95).
[65] Goitein (1967–88, vol. 2, pp. 171–262).

classes, but Geniza records also provide evidence of craftsmen who were accredited learned men. Jewish traders were typically the most highly literate and educated scholars within the Jewish communities.

The ninth to twelfth century also witnessed the growth of Hebrew poetry and literature that remains a landmark of Jewish higher education up to today.[66] The growth and spread of Hebrew knowledge was thus not limited to commercial or economic purposes.

Urbanization and the growth of local trade and long-distance commerce made literacy and education more valuable for both Jews and non-Jews in the vast Muslim caliphates. Both groups therefore increased their investment in education. To spread Islam, Muslim rulers promoted the establishment of primary schools (*maktab* or *kuttab*); by the end of the eighth century, the number of such schools had grown.[67] Unlike Judaism, however, Islam did not require Muslims to provide their sons with primary education, so that whereas all Jews invested in children's literacy and education, only some non-Jews did so. Moreover, most of the Muslim primary schools were devoted to memorizing the Koran; few of them taught children to read or write.

Intellectual Prominence: The Geonim

The central place of learning and scholarship within the Jewish communities during the Muslim period is best epitomized by the powerful role held by the Geonim, the heads of the academies of Sura and Pumbedita in Mesopotamia.[68] From the end of the sixth century until the middle of the eleventh century, they were recognized as the highest authority of instruction within world Jewry.

During the Talmud period (third to sixth century), the scholars of the academies appointed the heads of the academies. In contrast, the Geonim were appointed by the Babylonian exilarch, the political leader of the Jewish community in Mesopotamia, after consultation with the group of scholars. If the exilarch and the scholars could not agree on a candidate, the appointment might drag on until one of the candidates died. The Geonim played a powerful role at the side of the Babylonian exilarch. The recognition of their prominent political role is attested to by the fact that on the death of the exilarch, his income was given to the Gaon of Sura until the appointment of a new exilarch. Through the Jewish community in Baghdad, which had representatives at the court of the caliphs, the

---

[66] Baron (1952, vol. 3).

[67] Nakosteen (1964, pp. 44–47).

[68] See Elon (1994); Brody (1998); and Gil (2004, pp. 117–206) for thorough descriptions of the rise of the Geonim and the development of the responsa literature.

Geonim also attempted to influence the policy of Muslim caliphs toward the Jews in the vast empire.

The academies provided an array of fundamental services for world Jewry. First and foremost, they interpreted the Talmud, with the aim of making it the accepted code of law in all social and religious matters and of spreading its knowledge to all Jewish communities.

They also acted as a supreme court and a provider of legal services. They issued new rulings and norms to regulate contingencies not dealt with in the Talmud. Their ordinances (*takkanot*), dispatched to Jewish communities in the vast territory under Muslim rule through the responsa, had legal religious validity throughout the Jewish world. The Gaonate also had jurisdiction over the organization of local rabbinic courts throughout Mesopotamia. With the approval of the Geonim, the exilarch appointed the judges of these courts.[69]

The multiple tasks carried on by the Geonim required a large and learned bureaucracy. Their expenditures were covered by taxes levied by the Jewish authorities in the locations under their jurisdiction. In addition, the communities that addressed their questions to the Geonim paid for these services. In rare instances, the Geonim would turn to the communities in the Diaspora with a request for financial support, requests that were usually honored. Real estate (landholdings and houses) also served as a source of income for the academies.

Stable Jewish Population

The last implication of our theory is that Jewish urban dwellers who engage in crafts, trade, and moneylending have no incentive to voluntarily convert to another religion unless there is a significant difference between the taxes they pay and the taxes levied on non-Jews (or they face other forms of discrimination). Hence, once the Jews have completed their transition from farming into these occupations, few or no conversions will occur and the Jewish population should remain stable or grow.

From the mid-seventh to the mid-twelfth century, the total population in Mesopotamia, Persia, the Land of Israel, Syria, Lebanon, North Africa, Asia Minor, the Balkans, and Europe increased from about 51 million to roughly 70 million (figure 1.1 and table 1.6). Most of this population growth occurred in western Europe at the turn of the millennium, as urbanization expanded and commerce blossomed. The Jewish population in these areas also grew (from 1–1.2 million circa 650 to 1.2–1.5 million circa 1170). Natural growth due to the high standards of living of many

---

[69] Elon (1994, vol. 2).

Jews in the Muslim caliphates (the so-called golden age of Jewish history) was offset by the losses caused by deaths and forced conversions. Jewish settlements suffered severe blows in the waves of intolerance that swept through the seventh century Iberian Peninsula under Visigothic rule, Merovingian France, and Langobard Italy. Some Jewish communities in Germany were massacred in the late eleventh and early twelfth centuries, at the time of the Crusades.[70]

Forced conversions also took a toll on some Jewish communities. The most severe persecutions and forced conversions of Jews (and especially Christians) occurred in the early eleventh century in Egypt, under the Fatimid caliph al-Hakim. In the Iberian Peninsula and North Africa under Muslim rule, the Almohad rulers massacred Christians, Jews, and dissenting Muslims and forced Christians and Jews to convert to Islam.[71]

In contrast, no mass voluntary conversions of Jews to Islam occurred once the Jews became engaged in urban skilled occupations. This observation is supported by the thousands of letters and documents from the Cairo Geniza and the responsa literature, in which episodes of voluntary conversions of Jewish individuals to Islam are mentioned as exceptional cases that mainly involved prominent members of Jewish communities who converted in order to enter prestigious positions in the bureaucracy of the Muslim caliphate.[72] Such conversions were rare and quite different from those of Jewish farmers to Christianity in the agrarian economies during the Talmud era—conversions that were, we posit, also the outcome of the need to implement the costly religious norm requiring fathers to educate their sons.

The head tax (equal to about 5 percent of a teacher's salary, according to the documents of the Cairo Geniza) was a significant liability for poor households, as evidenced by documents describing cases in which the entire Jewish community helped poor families pay the tax.[73] The head tax was not a significant burden for Jewish craftsmen, traders, moneylenders, court bankers, tax collectors, and physicians, however; given the size of the tax, it is unlikely that it would have motivated large numbers of middle-class and wealthy Jews to convert. Consistent with the last implication of our theory, Jewish urban dwellers who engaged in high-skill occupations such as crafts, trade, and moneylending did not convert to other religions, especially given the positive network externality in trade, highlighted by Greif, of being a Jew.[74]

---

[70] Baron (1971b).

[71] Baron (1952, vol. 17, pp. 181–83); Goitein (1967–88, vol. 2, pp. 299–303).

[72] Goitein (1967–88, vol. 2, pp. 300–4).

[73] Goitein (1967–88, vol. 2, pp. 300–4).

[74] Greif (1989, 1993, 2006).

Summary

The higher literacy of the Jewish people, coupled with a set of contract-enforcement institutions (the Talmud, the rabbinic courts, the responsa), gave the Jews a comparative advantage over non-Jews in crafts, trade, commerce, and moneylending once the spectacular urbanization and the growth of commerce and trade in the newly established Muslim caliphates during the eighth and ninth centuries created a huge demand for these occupations.

The eighth through twelfth centuries marked the intellectual golden age of the Jewish communities in the Middle East, an age characterized by universal primary education among the Jews, growing investment in higher literacy and education by a large segment of the Jewish population, and the prominence of the academies of Sura and Pumbedita headed by the Geonim.

Urbanization and commercial expansion in the Muslim caliphates also helped the Jewish population stabilize. The Jewish population grew from the eighth to the twelfth century because once they became literate and urban dwellers working in myriad crafts and commercial activities that enjoyed contract-enforcement institutions as members of the same religious community, Jews had little incentive to voluntarily convert to other religions.

Once this occupational and residential transition was set in motion, it never reverted but rather became even stronger. From then on, the Jews became a small population of highly literate people, who continued to search for opportunities to reap returns from their investment in literacy and contract-enforcement institutions.

Annex 6.A: Formal Model of Education and Conversion of Merchants

By the eighth and ninth centuries, the occupational transition of the Jews was completed, and most Jews were engaged in crafts and trade. To take account of this transition, we modify the model presented in the annex to chapter 4 to study their choices in light of their changed circumstances. Given that the change in religious preferences after 200 occurred among all Jews, regardless of their occupation, our assumptions concerning the utility functions of Jewish and non-Jewish merchants are the same as those discussed in the annex to chapter 4 in the model for farmers.

Hebrew religious literacy and education have spillover effects on general literacy and education, which in turn increase the productivity of urban skilled workers. As before, we assume that w^F is the earnings (productivity) of an individual without literacy or in an occupation in which literacy and education do not enhance productivity. We model the assumptions on the impact of literacy and education by having earnings depend on the literacy and education of adults and their sons, independent of religious affiliation:

$$w^M(e, e_s) = w^F(1 + Ae_s^\alpha e^{1-\alpha}) \qquad (6.1)$$

where $Ae_s^\alpha e^{1-\alpha}$ is the additional earnings (productivity) of a literate and educated merchant, A is an exogenous productivity parameter, e and e_s are the literacy and education of an adult individual and of his son, and α measures the weight of the contribution of a son's literacy and education to his father's productivity. A merchant's budget constraint is given by

$$c + \gamma(e_s)^\theta + \tau^{rM} \le w^F(1 + Ae_s^\alpha e^{1-\alpha}) \qquad (6.2)$$

where τ^{rM} is the tax paid by a merchant of religion r.

Education

Our main prediction is that Jewish merchants invest more in their children's literacy and education than non-Jewish merchants do, because a Jewish merchant's taste parameter for Judaism (i.e., his attachment parameter to Judaism), x, is positive. The first-order condition that gives the optimal level of a child's literacy and education for any merchant (Jewish or non-Jewish) can be written as

$$x(e+1) + (-\theta\gamma(e_s)^{\theta-1} + w^F \alpha A e_s^{\alpha-1} e^{1-\alpha}) \frac{1}{w^M - \gamma(e_s)^\theta - \tau^{rM}} \le 0. \qquad (6.3)$$

Consider first the steady-state education level ($e = e_s = e^*$) of non-Jewish merchants, whose exogenous taste parameter for Judaism is (by definition) 0. Then, from equation 6.3, $e = e_s = e^* = (w^F A\alpha/\theta\gamma)^{1/\theta-1}$. In the steady state, non-Jewish merchants educate their sons (i.e., $e_s^* \ge e^{min} = 1$) if the parameters satisfy $w^F A\alpha > \theta\gamma$—that is, if the marginal product of education is greater than or equal to the marginal cost of education at $e_s = e = e^{min} = 1$. The better the aggregate economic conditions, the higher the earnings of merchants ($w^F A\alpha$) and hence the more likely it is that both non-Jewish and Jewish merchants invest in their sons' literacy and education.

Let us assume that before the implementation of the religious norm requiring Jewish fathers to educate their sons, the literacy and education levels of both Jewish and non-Jewish merchants were positive. Literacy and education have a positive effect on merchants' productivity and earnings regardless of which religion a merchant belongs to. However, after the religious transformation of Judaism, Jewish merchants will invest more in their children's literacy and education than non-Jewish merchants, because they also derive direct utility from children's literacy and education at the rate x (see the utility equation of a Jewish father in the annex to chapter 4).

Conversion

The main prediction regarding conversion is that if there is a small (or no) tax difference between Jewish and non-Jewish merchants, no Jewish merchant will convert. If taxes on Jewish merchants are significantly higher than those on non-Jews, Jewish merchants with low levels of attachment to Judaism (low x) will convert. Hence given that some Jewish farmers convert (see annex to chapter 4) and Jewish merchants do not (unless the tax differential is high), the model predicts that the proportion of merchants in the Jewish population will increase over time.

Formally, a literate ($e^j \geq 1$) Jewish merchant converts if the utility of remaining a Jew is lower than the utility of becoming a non-Jew—that is, if

$$u^j(c, e_s; e, x) < u^{jn}(c, e_s; e, x)$$

or

$$\log[w^F(1 + A(e_s^j)^\alpha (e^j)^{1-\alpha}) - \gamma(e_s^j)^\theta - \tau^{jM}] + x(1 + e^j)e_s^j < \\ \log[w^F(1 + A(e_s^n)^\alpha (e^n)^{1-\alpha}) - \gamma(e_s^n)^\theta - \tau^{nM}] - \pi x. \tag{6.4}$$

Assuming that the level of literacy and education of Jewish merchants before the implementation of the religious norm requiring fathers to educate their sons, e^*, is greater than or equal to 1, equation 6.4 implies that if taxes on Jewish and non-Jewish merchants are the same ($\tau^{nM} = \tau^{jM}$), then a literate Jewish merchant does not convert.

To show why this is true, we start with the extreme case of $x = 0$, in which a Jew places no value on the educational requirement established by Judaism. In this case, by equation 6.4, a Jewish merchant's investment in his son's literacy and education will be identical to that of a non-Jewish merchant, and the Jewish merchant will be indifferent regarding conversion because he derives the same utility irrespective of his religious affiliation. As the attachment to Judaism index, x, increases, the utility from being Jewish increases with the literacy and education level of the child e_s^j. Therefore, a Jewish merchant who educates his children will not convert. Moreover, the higher the attachment index, the greater the cost of conversion (πx). As a result, no Jewish merchant will convert if the tax differential between Jews and non-Jews is zero or small.

CHAPTER 7

Educated Wandering Jews, 800–1250

> This is to announce [to] you, my brother, that I have left India
> and arrived in Aden . . . safely with my belongings, life, and
> children. . . . I have to reproach you . . . because you got as far
> as Egypt and did not come to Aden. I sent you to Egypt with
> a shipment of my master, Sheikh Madmûn, about fifty ounces
> of civet perfume worth 40 dinars. . . . Afterward, I learned . . .
> that the civet arrived duly in Fustat; however, as they did not
> find you there, they forwarded it to you to Sicily with a trust-
> worthy Jew called Samuel, himself a Sicilian.
> —*Abraham Ben Yijū, 1149*

> The greatest misfortune that has befallen me during my entire
> life . . . was the demise of the saint . . . who drowned in the
> Indian sea, carrying much money belonging to me, to him,
> and to others. . . . How should I console myself? He grew up
> on my knees, he was my brother, he was my student; he traded
> on the markets, and earned, and I could safely sit at home. He
> was well versed in the Talmud and the Bible, and knew Hebrew
> grammar as well. . . . Whenever I see his handwriting or one of
> his letters, my grief awakens again. . . .
> —*Moses Maimonides, c. 1170*

BY THE LATE TWELFTH CENTURY, THE WORLD'S 1.2–1.5 MILLION JEWS
were scattered across three economic and intellectually independent centers: Mesopotamia, Persia, and the Arabian Peninsula under Muslim rule,
which was home to about 70 percent of world Jewry; the Iberian Peninsula (partly under Christian and partly under Muslim rule), which hosted
wealthy communities in hundreds of cities and towns; and Christian
France, England, Germany, and Italy where small Jewish communities,
whose size varied from a handful of families to a few hundred households,
lived in hundreds of locations (see table 1.6, map 1.3, and appendix, tables
A.1 and A.2). Small Jewish communities existed in myriad locations all
over Bohemia, Poland, Hungary, the Balkans, Asia Minor, the regions
located between the Black and Caspian Seas, Syria, Lebanon, the Land of
Israel, Egypt, the Maghreb, Central Asia, China, and India.

Was the scattering of the Jewish communities in the early Middle Ages the outcome of restrictions, persecutions, and expulsions, or did it instead reflect the free and voluntary choices made by a people endowed with some distinctive characteristics? Were there economic and cultural connections between the Jews living in Baghdad and the Jews living in Alexandria, between the Jews living in Tangiers, Palermo and Salonica and the Jews living in Granada, Troyes, and Mainz?

We address both questions by presenting a wealth of historical evidence. We follow the "educated wandering Jews" first in their migrations within the vast territory of the Muslim caliphates, then in their migrations within, from, and to the Byzantine Empire, and next in their migrations to and within Christian Europe. This journey—in the company of Jewish merchants, traders, coin minters, physicians, skilled craftsmen, moneylenders, and scholars—reveals some key developments in the history of the Jewish people that support our theory that first- and second-century rabbinic Judaism, with its emphasis on literacy and learning, permanently endowed the Jews with some distinctive skills that enhanced their mobility and facilitated their migration.

Wandering Jews before Marco Polo

Before describing the salient features of the migrations of the Jewish Diaspora in the early Middle Ages, we present portraits of one Jewish group and three Jewish individuals. These portraits are emblematic of the radical change that transformed the Jews from a population of illiterate farmers, fishermen, and shepherds, as described by Josephus in the first century, into a small population of literate and highly mobile urban dwellers engaged in high-skill occupations.

The Radhanite Traders of the Ninth Century

During the ninth century—more than four centuries before Marco Polo's journey to China—Jewish traders known as the Radhanites, very likely originating from Mesopotamia, traveled over a vast territory and connected the Middle East to Europe, North Africa, and Asia through their trading routes.[1] The activities of the Radhanites were documented by Abū

---

[1] Several etymologies have been suggested for the word "Radhanite." Most scholars, including Gil (1976; 2004, pp. 615–37), believe it refers to a district in Mesopotamia called "the land of Radhan" in Arabic and Hebrew texts of the period. Alternative views maintain that their center was the city of Ray (Rhages), in northern Persia, or the Rhône River valley in France (*Rhodanus* in Latin), as all their trade routes began there (see Bareket [2002] for an overview of the debate).

al-Qasim Ubaid Allah ibn Khordadbeh, the director of posts and police for the province of Jibal under the Abbasid caliph al-Mu'tamid, in his book *Kitab al-Masalik wal-Mamalik (The Book of Roads and Kingdoms)*, circa 850. Ibn Khordadbeh described four main routes used by the Radhanite traders in their journeys, connecting lands as far distant from one another as China and India in the east and France in the west. The Radhanites carried highly valued goods, including spices, perfumes, furs, jewelry, steel weapons, oils, incense, silk, and slaves.

According to ibn Khordadbeh,[2]

The Route of the Jewish Rādhānite merchants who speak Arabic and Persian and Rūmī (= Greek), and Ifranjī (probably Latin) and Andalusī (= Spanish) and Slavic. They travel from east to west and from the west to the east, by land and by sea. They market slaves from the west and maidservants and boys, and silk cloth, and rabbit hides and sable furs and swords. They sail from Firanja in the western sea[3] and leave from Faramā [= Pelusium in north-eastern Egypt] and transport their goods on the backs (of beasts of burden) to Qulzum [= village in northeastern Egypt near the Suez Canal], whereas there is (between these two places) a distance of 25 parasangs (about 150 kilometers); then they sail in the eastern sea, from Qulzum to al-Jār and to Judda [in the Arabian Peninsula], then pass on to Sind and to Hind [= the northern regions of India] and to China. They transport from China musk, aloe wood, camphor, cinnamon, and more (goods than they regularly) transport from those areas; they then return to Qulzum and then transport them to Faramā, then they set sail in the western sea; sometimes they turn to Constantinople with their merchandise and sell it to the Byzantines; sometimes they travel with it to the king of Firanja and sell it there. And if they wish, they transport their goods from Firanja, in the western sea, and they go for Antioch (in Asia Minor) and travel by land three *marhalas* (a marhala, a distance of one day, about 50 kilometers) to Jābiya [in Syria], and from there they sail the Euphrates to Baghdad, and from there they sail the Tigris to Ubulla [in Mesopotamia], and from Ubulla to Ummān and to Sind and to Hind and to China. All this is done consecutively, one after the other. Those of them who go from Andalus [= Iberian Peninsula] or Firanja cross (the sea) to Sūs al-Aqsā [in North Africa] and arrive at Tanja [= Tangiers] and from there to Ifrīqiya and from there to Egypt (or: Fustat) and from there to Ramla and from there to Damascus and from there to Kūfa and from there to Baghdad and from there to Basra and from there to al-Ahwāz [in Persia] and from there to Fāris and from there to Kirmān [in Persia] and from there to Sind and from there to Hind and from there to China. Some of them turn to beyond Byzantium to the land of the Slavs and from there to Khamlīj the city of

---

[2] Gil (2004, p. 618).

[3] The western sea is the Mediterranean. Firanja has been identified with either France or Italy under Frankish control (Gil 2004, p. 627).

the Khazars and from there in the sea of Jurjān (= Caspian) and from there to Balkh and to what is beyond the river (=Transoxania) and from there to Wurut Tughuz Ghuzz and from there to China.

The beginning of the description points to a key feature of these Jewish traders: their ability to speak several languages. Their itineraries indicate that as early as the mid-ninth century, they had established a trading network that bought and sold goods in the Abbasid caliphate; the Frankish kingdom; the Byzantine Empire; and the Slavic states, including the kingdom of the Khazars, all the way to the empires of the Far East.

Jewish Traders in the Indian Ocean: Abraham Ben Yijū

The importation of spices, pharmaceuticals, dyes, and other materials from India formed the backbone of the medieval economy, especially in the Islamic world. Letters written in Judeo-Arabic (Middle Arabic written in Hebrew characters) in the eleventh and twelfth centuries shed light on myriad details of Jewish traders in the Indian Ocean and their families in the territories from the Far East to southern Arabia and Egypt. They also provide valuable information on Jewish, Islamic, and Mediterranean cultures.[4]

One Jewish trader whose documents were preserved in the Cairo Geniza was Abraham ben Yijū.[5] Born circa 1100 in Mahadia, a large town and a major center of Jewish culture on the coast of Tunisia, Abraham probably derived his family name, ben Yijū, from a Berber tribe that was once the protector or the patron of his lineage. His father, Perahyah, was a rabbi and a respected scholar who earned his living in trade.

Abraham received an excellent education that could have made him a rabbinical scholar had he not been attracted by the lucrative business opportunities offered by the eastern trade. To pursue these opportunities, he first moved from Tunisia to Fustat in Egypt. Circa 1120, he moved to Aden, in Yemen, which was one of the busiest ports in the most important sea route from the Middle East to the Indian Ocean. In Aden, Abraham met his mentor and, later main partner in business, the wealthy and prominent Jewish trader Madmûn ibn al-Hasan ibn Bundâr. Following in his father's footsteps, Madmûn became the *nagid* in Aden, the head of the city's wealthy Jewish community. The earliest correspondence between Abraham and Madmûn dates from the period after Abraham's departure from Aden, when he was engaged in setting up business on the Malabar

---

[4]Goitein and Friedman (2007) edited and translated into English a huge number of these letters.

[5]Ghosh (1992) and Goitein and Friedman (2007) describe Abraham ben Yijū's life in detail.

coast in western India. The letters of this period are full of detailed commercial instructions, as well as affection.

Abraham also corresponded with two other wealthy Jews in Aden—Yousuf ibn Abraham, a judicial functionary and trader, and Khalaf ibn Ishaq, a trader and close friend of Abraham. The fortunes of these two Jews derived from the trade between India and the Middle East, in which they served as brokers and financiers rather than traders. From the letters requesting shipments, it is clear that both men, as well as Abraham, were extremely rich.

Two of Madmûn's friends were among the most well-traveled men in the Middle Ages. The first was a prominent figure in the Jewish community in Fustat, Abû Sa'îd Halfon ben Nethan'el ha-Levi al-Dimyâti, a wealthy merchant, scholar, and patron of literature.[6] His journeys to Egypt, India, East Africa, Syria, Morocco, and the Iberian Peninsula can be compared with the travels of both Marco Polo and Ibn Battûta.[7] The second of the great travelers of Madmûn's circle was Abu Zikri Judah ha-Kohen Sijilmasi. Born in the desert town of Sijilmasa, in Morocco, he migrated to Fustat and rose to power within the Jewish community, eventually becoming chief representative of the Jewish merchants. He, too, traveled between Egypt, Yemen, the Iberian Peninsula, France, Italy, Greece, and India.

Sometime before 1132, Abraham moved to and settled along the Malabar coast in western India. One of Madmûn's letters to Abraham reveals that Abraham's departure for, and long permanence in, India was not entirely voluntary (the most obvious explanation is that his departure had to do with a debt, a financial irregularity, or unpaid taxes). Only in 1149, almost two decades after he had left, did Abraham return to Aden, bringing back all his goods and two adolescent sons.

Rabbi Samuel ha-Nagid and the Golden Age of Iberian Jewry

Abraham ben Yijū, his friend Madmûn, and their circle of Jewish traders represent the combination of prominence in trade and patronage of Jewish scholarship that characterized the golden age of the Jewish Diaspora.

---

[6]He was a friend and patron to one of the greatest Jewish poets, Judah ha-Levi, who wrote a number of poems in his honor. Judah ha-Levi's poems are so important that they are part of the baccalaureate exams in contemporary Israeli high schools. Almost every town in Israel has a street named for the poet.

[7]Ibn Battûta (1304–c. 1368) is one of the most famous medieval travelers. Born in Tangiers, he went to Mecca to study law and complete his Muslim education. From there, he began his long journey that brought him to Yemen, Kenya, India, Ceylon, Malaysia, Java, Sumatra, China, and back to Africa, where he visited Timbuktu. He then returned to Morocco where he spent the last years of his life.

Rabbi Samuel ha-Nagid ("the prince") epitomizes the mix of scholarship and political prominence that was also a common feature of the Jews in the Muslim world. Samuel ha-Nagid was a Talmudic scholar, grammarian, philologist, poet, warrior, and statesman who lived in Córdoba and Granada.[8]

The Arab-Muslim occupation of the Iberian Peninsula, Al-Andalus in Arabic, which began in 711, set the stage for the establishment of an Islamic kingdom similar to the kingdoms that flourished in Damascus under the Umayyad dynasty in the seventh and eighth centuries. Within a century, the Umayyad and then Abbasid rulers developed a civilization based in the capital of Córdoba that had no rivals in Europe. From the end of the eighth to the early twelfth century, the Iberian Peninsula under Muslim rule was the most populous, cultured, and commercial economy in Europe. It was during this time of economic expansion that Jewish craftsmen and traders from Egypt and the Maghreb migrated to and settled there.[9]

Jewish prominence in trade grew together with Jewish scholarship. A translating program was established in Toledo, where Jews translated Arabic books into Romance languages; they also translated Greek and Hebrew texts, including many major works of Greek science and philosophy, into Arabic. Jews studied and contributed to mathematics, medicine, botany, geography, poetry, and philosophy. It was at this time that the study of medicine expanded to produce a large number of exceptional Jewish physicians.[10]

In the caliphate of Córdoba, the Jews became increasingly important, reaching the peak of their prominence during the tenth century. They lived among themselves in a walled area known as the *aljama* (Jewish quarter) and managed their communal affairs through the rabbinic court.

It is in this economic and cultural milieu that Shmuel Halevi ben Yosef ha-Nagid, better known as Rabbi Samuel ha-Nagid, was born, in 993. In 1013, when Berber rebels sacked Córdoba, Samuel was forced to leave the city, together with other Jews. With the decline of Córdoba, the city of Granada, the new capital of the Arab kingdom, gradually became the new leading center of Jewish life. Like other Jews, Samuel settled in Granada, where he continued his studies of the Talmud and the sciences.

He soon became known as a great poet and writer, not only in Hebrew but also in Arabic and Latin. His perfect mastery of the Arabic language and deep understanding of Arabic grammar and literature became known to the vizier Abu-al-Qasim-ibn-al-Arif. The vizier was so impressed by his scholarship and wisdom that he appointed him as his personal secretary

---

[8] H. Ben-Sasson (1976, pp. 454–58) describes Samuel ha-Nagid's life and accomplishments.
[9] Baron (1952, vol. 3, chap. 22); Beinart (2007a).
[10] H. Ben-Sasson (1976, pp. 400, 452–58).

and adviser. Years later, when the vizier died, the Berber ruler Habus appointed Samuel ha-Nagid in his place. The office of vizier was that of minister of state, the highest office next to the ruler himself. Samuel ha-Nagid accepted the position and retained his posts as the rabbi of the flourishing Jewish community and the director of the Talmudic academy of Granada. Under his leadership, Granada became one of the world's leading centers for the study of the Talmud.

When the Berber ruler died, his son and successor, Badis, entrusted his Jewish vizier with managing all the affairs of state. Samuel ha-Nagid's fame grew even further. He financially supported and helped many scholars and invited to Granada Jewish Talmudists, philosophers, poets, and scribes to copy important Hebrew books.[11]

Great Medieval Travelers: Benjamin of Tudela

That at least some Jews in the early Middle Ages were highly mobile is documented by one of the most famous travelers of all times, Benjamin of Tudela. Born in the town of Tudela in the Navarra region of Spain, Rabbi Benjamin undertook a long journey in the mid-1160s. From the city of Saragossa in Spain, he proceeded north to France. From Marseilles he sailed to Genoa, Pisa, Rome, southern Italy, Greece, and Constantinople before traveling across the Middle East, visiting Lebanon, the Land of Israel, Syria, and northern Mesopotamia before reaching Baghdad. Very likely, he did not visit but only heard of the Jewish communities in Persia, Yemen, Central Asia, Far Eastern Asia, and on his way back to Europe, Germany, and northern France; his descriptions for these areas are much shorter, much less detailed, and in some instances he even confused one region (Yemen) with another one (India). He probably cut back across the Arabian Peninsula to North Africa and Sicily, returning to the Iberian Peninsula a few years later, during the early 1170s.

The goal of his journey was likely to make a pilgrimage to the Holy Land, to learn about how Diaspora Jews lived, and to describe the many prosperous Jewish communities in the world. When he arrived in a town, he went to the local synagogue and asked the rabbi how many Jewish households were associated with the synagogue and what their occupations were. In his famous *Sefer ha-Masa'ot* (*Book of Travels*), written in Hebrew and later translated into Latin, he recorded detailed geographic, economic, and demographic information on the more than 300 towns and cities he visited, as well as on other regions he heard of during his travels, including China and Tibet (see map 1.3, as well as appendix table A.2). For

---

[11]Among the writers translated was the great Andalusian Hebrew poet and philosopher Rabbi Solomon ben Judah ibn Gabirol, who brought the knowledge of Platonic philosophy to early medieval Europe.

the locations Benjamin actually visited and described in detail (Europe, the Balkans, Asia Minor, Lebanon, the Land of Israel, Syria, Mesopotamia, and some locations in Egypt), his estimates should be interpreted as the number of Jewish *households* living there. Hence, in the excerpts of his travel itinerary reported below, one should multiply the numbers of Jews Benjamin recorded by roughly a factor of five (i.e., assuming that each household consisted, on average, of five people).[12]

His book offers vivid and sometimes colorful descriptions of Jewish and non-Jewish life. The portrayals of Jewish communities highlight the importance these communities assigned to learning, the high consideration in which rabbis and scholars of the Talmud were held, the scholarship and knowledge of the Talmud displayed by many Jewish traders, and the wealth of Jewish leaders and their connections to local rulers as well as Jewish merchants and scholars in other communities.

Benjamin of Tudela's account of Rome is remarkable for his description of the freedom and power the small community of Jews there enjoyed[13]

> Rome is the head of the kingdoms of Christendom, and contains about 200 Jews, who occupy an honorable position and pay no tribute, and amongst them are officials of the Pope Alexander, the spiritual head of all Christendom. Great scholars reside here, at the head of them being R. Daniel, the chief rabbi, and R. Jechiel, an official of the Pope. He . . . has the entry of the Pope's palace; for he is the steward of his house and of all that he has. . . .

He also writes of the benevolence of the Abbasid caliph in Baghdad toward the Jews; the wealth and intellectual prominence of the very large Jewish community in Baghdad; and the power of the exilarch, the political leader of the Jewish communities in the Abbasid caliphate:

> There the great king, Al Abbasi the Caliph (Hafiz) . . . is kind unto Israel, and many belonging to the people of Israel are his attendants; he knows all languages, and is well versed in the law of Israel. He reads and writes the holy language (Hebrew). . . .
>
> In Bagdad there are about 40,000 Jews, and they dwell in security, prosperity and honor under the great Caliph, and amongst them are great sages, the

---

[12] See the appendix for a discussion of how we and other scholars have interpreted Benjamin of Tudela's numbers. For example, Benjamin's figure of 40,000 Jewish households in Baghdad and its surrounding area is consistent with the figure of 36,000 Jewish taxpayers right before the Mongol invasion of Mesopotamia in the early 1250s (see Gil 2004). Other historical sources document that Baghdad was one of the largest cities in the Middle East before the Mongol Conquest. Benjamin's very detailed description of Baghdad shows that he actually visited the city, unlike his brief and imprecise descriptions of the Arabian Peninsula with exaggerated population figures.

[13] Benjamin's descriptions of the Jewish community in each location are much longer. Here we report only the relevant passages, which can be found in Benjamin of Tudela ([c. 1170] 1983).

heads of Academies engaged in the study of the law. In this city there are ten Academies. . . .

These are the ten Batlanim, and they do not engage in any other work than communal administration; and all the days of the week they judge the Jews their countrymen, except on the second day of the week, when they all appear before the chief rabbi Samuel, the head of the Yeshiva Gaon (Jacob). . . . And at the head of them all is [the exilarch] Daniel the son of Hisdai, who is styled "Our Lord the Head of the Captivity of all Israel." He possesses a book of pedigrees going back as far as David, King of Israel . . . and he has been invested with authority over all the congregations of Israel at the hands of the Emir al Muminin, the Lord of Islam. . . .

In respect of all these countries the Head of the Captivity gives the communities power to appoint rabbis and ministers. . . .

He owns hospices, gardens, and plantations in Babylon, and much land inherited from his fathers, and no one can take his possessions from him by force. He has a fixed weekly revenue arising from the hospices of the Jews, the markets and the merchants, apart from that which is brought to him from far-off lands. The man is very rich, and wise in the Scriptures as well as in the Talmud. . . .

The Exilarch appoints the Chiefs of the Academies by placing his hand upon their heads, thus installing them in their office. The Jews of the city are learned men and very rich.

In Bagdad there are twenty-eight Jewish synagogues, situated either in the city itself or in Al-Karkh on the other side of the Tigris. . . .

The vastness of the territory under Muslim rule over which the Jews were scattered is clear from this description:

The authority of the Head of the Captivity extends over all the communities of Shinar, Persia, Khurasan and Sheba which is El-Yemen, and Diyar Kalach (Bekr) and the land of Aram Naharaim (Mesopotamia), and over the dwellers in the mountains of Ararat and the land of the Alans, which is a land surrounded by mountains and has no outlet except by the iron gates which Alexander made, but which were afterward broken. Here are the people called Alani. His authority extends also over the land of Siberia, and the communities in the land of the Togarmim unto the mountains of Asveh and the land of Gurgan, the inhabitants of which are called Gurganim who dwell by the river Gihon, and these are the Girgashites who follow the Christian religion. Further it extends to the gates of Samarkand, the land of Tibet, and the land of India.

In many of the locations he visited, Benjamin of Tudela found great Jewish scholars, who in some instances owned land:

A three days' journey takes one to Narbonne [in France], which is a city preeminent for learning; thence the Torah (Law) goes forth to all countries. Sages and great and illustrious men abide here. At their head is R. Kalonymos, the son of the great and illustrious R. Todros of the seed of David. . . . He possesses hereditaments and lands given him by the ruler of the city, of which no man can forcibly dispossess him. . . . At the present day 300 Jews are there. . . .

. . . From Montpellier it is four parasangs to Lunel, in which there is a congregation of Israelites, who study the Law day and night. Here lived Rabbenu Meshullam the great rabbi, since deceased, and his five sons, who are wise, great, and wealthy. . . . He is a great scholar of the Talmud. . . . The students that come from distant lands to learn the Law are taught, boarded, lodged and clothed by the congregation, so long as they attend the house of study. . . . The congregation consists of about 300 Jews.

. . . The kingdom of France, which is Zarfath, extends from the town of Auxerre unto Paris, the great city—a journey of six days. The city belongs to King Louis. . . . Scholars are there, unequalled in the whole world, who study the Law day and night. . . .

At the same time, he noted that the knowledge of the Talmud was weak in locations far away from the great centers of Jewish learning, as this description of the Jewish community in India shows:

Thence it is seven days' journey to Khulam [Quilon] which is the beginning of the country of the Sun-worshippers. These are the sons of Cush, who read the stars, and are all black in color. They are honest in commerce. . . .

. . . Pepper is found there. . . . Calamus and ginger and many other kinds of spice are found in this land.

. . . And throughout the island, including all the towns there, live several thousand Israelites. The inhabitants are all black, and the Jews also. The latter are good and benevolent. They know the law of Moses and the prophets, and to a small extent the Talmud and *halakha*.

The variety of skilled occupations in which the Jews were engaged is shown by his description of Thebes, Salonica, and Constantinople:

. . . the great city of Thebes, where there are about 2,000 Jews. They are the most skilled artificers in silk and purple cloth throughout Greece. They have scholars learned in the Mishnah and the Talmud, and other prominent men, and at their head are the chief rabbi R. Kuti and his brother R. . . .

From there it is two days' voyage to the city of Salonica. . . . It is a very large city, with about 500 Jews, including the chief rabbi R. Samuel and his sons, who are scholars. . . . The Jews are oppressed, and live by silk-weaving. . . .

. . . Constantinople . . . is the capital of the whole land of Javan which is called Greece. Here is the residence of the King Emanuel the Emperor. . . .

. . . All sorts of merchants come here from the land of Babylon, from the land of Shinar, from Persia, Media, and all the sovereignty of the land of Egypt, from the land of Canaan, and the empire of Russia, from Hungaria, Patzinakia, Khazaria, and the land of Lombardy and Sepharad. It is a busy city, and merchants come to it from every country by sea or land, and there is none like it in the world except Bagdad, the great city of Islam. . . .

...Wealth like that of Constantinople is not to be found in the whole world. . . .

. . . No Jews live in the city, for they have been placed behind an inlet of the sea. . . . In the Jewish quarter are about 2,000 Rabbanite Jews and about 500 Karaïtes, and a fence divides them. Amongst the scholars are several wise men, at their head being the chief rabbi. . . . And amongst them there are artificers in silk and many rich merchants. No Jew there is allowed to ride on horseback.

The one exception is R. Solomon Hamitsri, who is the king's physician, and through whom the Jews enjoy considerable alleviation of their oppression. For their condition is very low, and there is much hatred against them. . . . Yet the Jews are rich and good, kindly and charitable. . . .

The description of the Jewish communities in Thebes, Salonica, and Constantinople highlights an important feature of the history of the Jewish people to which we return in chapters 8 and 10: the wealth and high standards of living they enjoyed coexisted with discrimination and oppression in some locations at given times. In Constantinople, for example, where the Jews were rich and prominent, they were prohibited from living inside the city or to ride on horseback.[14]

The long list of places Benjamin visited (see appendix, table A.2) indicates the vast extent and richness of the Jewish Diaspora during the late twelfth century. Jews were almost everywhere, most of them were devoted to learning and implementing the laws laid down in the Talmud, and some of them were wealthy and well connected to rulers.

What were the common patterns and distinctive features of the Jewish communities in the hundreds of locales in which Jews lived? Could the Jews freely migrate within the vast territory under Muslim rule? Could they easily settle, buy land, and engage in any occupation in the countries of Christian Europe? Did the Jews migrate from the Byzantine Empire to Italy (and from there to other places in Europe), from Mesopotamia and Persia to Egypt and the Maghreb, from North Africa to the Iberian Peninsula and Sicily, from France to England and Germany because they were persecuted? Or did some distinctive characteristic of the Jews act as the engine of their migration in the early Middle Ages?

JEWISH MIGRATION WITHIN THE MUSLIM CALIPHATES

The rise of Islam in the early seventh century shaped the Jews' residential, economic, and demographic destiny in a unique way. Muhammad founded a unified polity in the Arabian Peninsula, which expanded dramatically

---

[14]The prohibition against riding on horseback was also imposed on the large, wealthy, and prominent Jewish community in the Abbasid Empire (Goitein 1955).

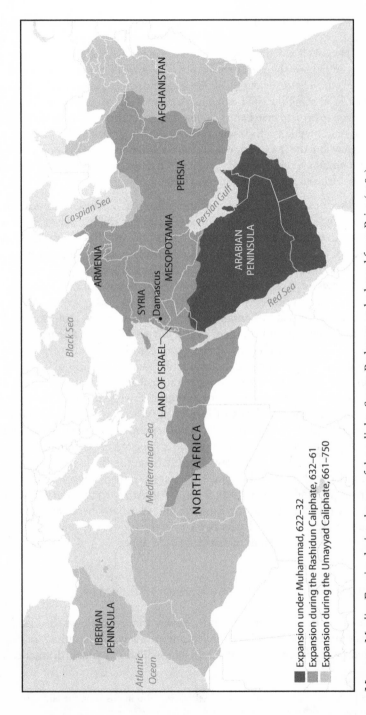

Map 7.1. Muslim Empire during the age of the caliphs. *Source:* Redrawn and adapted from Brice (1981).

Legend:
- Expansion under Muhammad, 622–32
- Expansion during the Rashidun Caliphate, 632–61
- Expansion during the Umayyad Caliphate, 661–750

Map labels: IBERIAN PENINSULA, Atlantic Ocean, Mediterranean Sea, Black Sea, Caspian Sea, NORTH AFRICA, LAND OF ISRAEL, SYRIA, Damascus, ARMENIA, MESOPOTAMIA, PERSIA, AFGHANISTAN, ARABIAN PENINSULA, Persian Gulf, Red Sea under the Rashidun and Umayyad caliphates. In 750, when the Umayyad caliphate fell and the Abbasid caliphs rose to power, the empire stretched from northwest India, across Central Asia, Persia, Mesopotamia, North Africa, Sicily, southern Italy, and the Iberian Peninsula to the Pyrenees (map 7.1). The vastness of the empire, coupled with the uniformity of laws, language, and freedom of mobility, greatly contributed to the rise and expansion of trade between the seventh and twelfth centuries.

Men, goods, money, books, and knowledge traveled far and freely throughout the Mediterranean area. In the words of Goitein, "In many respects, the area resembled a free-trade community."[15] Along the dense network of trade routes in the Mediterranean, regions under Muslim rule traded with one another and, later, with European powers such as Genoa, Venice, and Catalonia. The Silk Road crossing Central Asia passed through the Abbasid caliphate between China and Europe. Trade also flourished in the Indian Ocean, where Jewish and Muslim traders played leading roles for centuries.

Muslim Attitudes toward Religious Minorities

For more than 500 years, the Jews in the Muslim caliphates enjoyed demographic stability, economic prosperity, and religious autonomy. Beginning in the mid-seventh century, Muslim rulers regulated the political, economic, and social standing of religious minorities (foremost, Christians and Jews) through the *dhimma*, which granted them protection in exchange for the payment of special taxes. The religious groups that were permitted to live according to this status were termed *ahl al-dhimma* (the "protected people"); individuals belonging to these groups became known as *dhimmi*. As long as they paid the head tax (*jizia*) levied on all male non-Muslims age fifteen and older, *dhimmi* enjoyed protection as well as freedom of worship.[16]

Freedom extended to the economic sphere. *Dhimmi* could buy, own, and sell land. They could engage in farming and pastoral activities, as well as in any craft, trade, or other high-skill urban occupation they wished (table 2.3).[17] The only occupations closed to non-Muslims were civil service and bureaucratic positions (the same profession from which Jews were excluded under the Roman, Byzantine, and Persian empires). Despite this ban, some Jews (such as Rabbi Samuel ha-Nagid, described

---

[15] Goitein (1967–88, vol. I, p. 66).

[16] Goitein (1955); H. Ben-Sasson (1976, p. 405); M. R. Cohen (1994, chap. 4). The head tax on ethnic and religious minorities already existed under Sassanid rule before the Arab conquest of the Middle East. In 1046, the head tax levied in Egypt was 2.5 dinars, a substantial but still reasonable amount, according to Goitein (1967–88, vol. I, p. 63).

[17] M. R. Cohen (1994, chaps. 5 and 7); Gil (2004, pp. 273–86, 597–662).

earlier) held prominent positions in the bureaucracy of the Abbasid Empire. Few Jews converted to Islam in order to gain powerful positions within the Muslim bureaucracy.[18]

Free and Voluntary Jewish Diaspora

From the ninth century onward, larger and larger numbers of Jews began migrating from Mesopotamia and Persia to Yemen and other regions in the Arabian Peninsula, Syria, Lebanon, the Land of Israel, Egypt, and the Maghreb. From North Africa, Jews migrated to the Iberian Peninsula and, later, Sicily and southern Italy under Muslim rule.[19] This Jewish Diaspora was free and voluntary.

It was free because both the *dhimmis* and the Muslim population were legally permitted to move and to migrate. A Jewish artisan or scholar from Baghdad, or a Jewish trader or physician from Basra, could freely migrate to, and settle in, Damascus and Aleppo in Syria, as well as Alexandria in Egypt or Qayrawan in Tunisia. In their new location, they would find the same language, the same laws, and the same set of institutions, and they would enjoy the same status as a protected religious minority they enjoyed anywhere else within the empire.

The Jewish Diaspora within the Muslim caliphates was also voluntary, prompted by the search for new economic opportunities by people with skills. When, for example, the Fatimid Muslim caliphs moved the center of their power from Tunisia to Egypt in the eleventh century and the center of gravity of trade shifted toward Egypt, many Jewish artisans and traders moved there.[20]

Jewish Population Dynamics

How did the rise of Islam and the establishment of the Muslim caliphates affect the demography and geographical distribution of world Jewry? In the early seventh century, nearly 75 percent of the world's 1–1.2 million world Jews lived in Mesopotamia and Persia. Individual Jewish communities in the Land of Israel, Syria, Lebanon, Asia Minor, the Balkans, North Africa (mainly Egypt), once among the largest in the world, ranged from 4,000 to no more than 100,000 people (table 1.6).

Four centuries later, when Benjamin of Tudela undertook his long journey from the Iberian Peninsula to Mesopotamia, the geographical

[18]Baron (1952, vol. 3, chap. 17); Goitein (1955; 1967–88, vols. 1 and 2).
[19]H. Ben-Sasson (1976, pp. 393–94); M. Ben-Sasson (1991, 1992, 1996); Simonsohn (1997–2010, 2011); Abulafia (2000).
[20]Goitein (1967–88, vol.1, chap. 1); M. Ben-Sasson (1991, 1992, 1996).

distribution of world Jewry had changed only slightly: the largest Jewish community in 650 (consisting of 700,000–900,000 Jews in Mesopotamia and Persia) was still the largest community in 1170, having grown only slightly in 500 years (table 1.6 and appendix, table A.1). At this time, a sizable Jewish community (probably numbering 100,000 to 120,000 people) also dwelled in Yemen, with cities like Aden and Sana'a hosting Jewish merchants, who traded from the Mediterranean all the way to the Indian Ocean. (Very likely, Benjamin of Tudela did not visit the Arabian Peninsula. He provided exaggerated figures for the Jews in this area, whereas he failed to provide population estimates for cities, such as Aden, in which it is known from many other sources that large Jewish communities dwelled. The appendix provides a discussion of how we interpreted and revised his population figures for the Arabian Peninsula.) By 1170, the Jewish population in the Land of Israel had almost disappeared (numbering just 6,000 people), whereas the number of Jews had grown to about 70,000 in Egypt and roughly 55,000 in Syria, largely as a result of the migration of Jews from Mesopotamia and Persia to North Africa and the Levant.

EGYPT AND THE MAGHREB

Jews lived in North Africa before the Arab Conquest. Writers in antiquity mention Jews in North Africa as having connections with Italian Jewry during the Roman era.[21] During the Muslim period, primary sources began referring to Jewish immigrants. During the ninth century, some of these long-distance traders stopped in Tunisia, temporarily settling among the Jewish communities.[22]

What were the main occupations of the Jewish immigrants to North Africa? Did any restriction prevent them from entering any occupation? Beginning in the ninth century, most Jewish craftsmen and traders arriving in Egypt and the Maghreb came from Mesopotamia and Persia; only a few came from the Land of Israel, which hosted a very small Jewish community at that time. Initially, they acted as agents in their new location while their families remained back home. There is no evidence that these migrations were forced or prompted by persecutions of the Jews by local rulers.[23]

During the ninth century, Jewish immigrants became involved in crafts and local trade, sometimes in partnership with non-Jews. The first evidence of Jewish involvement in long-distance trade in Egypt and the Maghreb dates from the ninth century, along the trading route linking Baghdad,

[21] Tcherikover (1961); Kasher (1985).
[22] M. Ben-Sasson (1992, 1996); Schulman et al. (2007).
[23] M. Ben-Sasson (1996, pp. 38–44); DellaPergola (2001).

Morocco, and the Iberian Peninsula. These traders did not own the trading routes or the caravans; they joined the caravans of other traders.

Jewish immigrants soon began to play leading roles in long-distance trade, often buying and selling on credit and extending loans. Jewish traders and moneylenders kept meticulous documentation of their loans (lending money without a proper note was a crime).[24] The large number of loan contracts and the need to have written records of these transactions presented a problem for local people, most of whom were illiterate. The Jews' ability to read and write—the legacy of the religious norm requiring fathers to educate their sons beginning in childhood—gave them an important comparative advantage in shopkeeping, long-distance trade, moneylending, and other occupations in which literacy was valuable.

Jewish immigrants from Mesopotamia and Persia to North Africa founded synagogues and rabbinic courts, which adhered to the cultural, legal, and religious tradition of the Babylonian Talmud. Jewish immigrants from Syria (and the few from the Land of Israel) to Egypt and the Maghreb founded their own synagogues and rabbinic courts, which followed the tradition of the Talmud of the Land of Israel.[25] Most Jewish traders were also scholars, well versed in Jewish law. Documents from the Cairo Geniza indicate that academies of higher learning were also established in this period in North Africa. Sometime after 1057, a Jewish chief judge of al-Mahdiyya, a town in Tunisia, wrote:[26]

> I was much pleased to read in your letter about the dedication to the study of the Torah and the zeal for learning shown by the son of our master Nathan of blessed memory, the head of the yeshiva. May God keep his youthful zeal and support him. And may be protect the life of our lord, the Rāv, may his honored position be permanent and may be always receive God's favors. For through him God has revived learning in Egypt, illuminated the community and fortified the religion.

Muslim rulers imposed no restriction on the way Jews conducted business. Jews were, however, required by their religion to obey the laws and norms set out in the Talmud. Jewish traders sometimes tried to avoid some of these restrictions, either through new interpretations of Talmudic restrictions or by establishing business partnerships with Muslims.

The economic, social, and religious condition of the Jews in Egypt and the Maghreb improved even further with the conquest of the region by

---

[24] M. Ben-Sasson (1996, pp. 40–58).

[25] Because most Jewish migrants came from Mesopotamia and Persia, the halakhic literature developed in North Africa shows a stronger influence of the Mesopotamian academies than of the academies of the Land of Israel.

[26] Goitein (1973, p. 166–67). The Rāv mentioned in the letter was Rabbi Nissim b. Jacob, one of the greatest rabbinical authorities of all times.

the Shia Muslim dynasty of the Fatimids, a rival of the Abbasid caliphate, in 969. Egypt became the center of a vast and powerful kingdom, which, at the end of the tenth century, included almost all of North Africa, Syria, Lebanon, and the Land of Israel. A period of prosperity in industry and commerce, as well as of great religious tolerance, ensued, from which the Jews also benefited.[27]

The economic structure of the Jews in North Africa during the Fatimid period was highly diversified. According to the lists of Jewish taxpayers and charitable donors, the majority were engaged in local trade; a minority were long-distance merchants, trading as far away as the Indian Ocean.[28] The Fatimid rulers had succeeded in diverting trade between India and the Middle East from the Persian Gulf to the Red Sea, which became the main artery of international trade. Many Jewish merchants, of varying degrees of wealth, participated in the India trade, as illustrated by the story of Abraham ben Yijū presented earlier. The Jewish communities in North Africa and Syria were headed by a *nagid* chosen by the Fatimid caliph from prominent Jews, very often court physicians. The *nagid* was to some extent similar to the exilarch who headed the Jewish community in the vast Abbasid caliphate, although there were also some important differences.[29]

The Fatimid dynasty began to weaken at the end of the eleventh century, but the condition of the Jews did not worsen. During this period and in the following century, the Jews of Egypt and the Maghreb prospered in every sphere, as the description of the Jewish communities given by Benjamin of Tudela, circa 1170, clearly shows.[30]

With the end of the Fatimid dynasty in 1171, North Africa, Syria, and the Levant fell under the control of the Sunni Muslim dynasty of the Ayyubids, who ruled during the twelfth and the thirteenth centuries. The Sultan Saladin and his successors were less tolerant toward the religious minorities than were their Fatimid predecessors, although they did not persecute non-Muslims.

Jewish communal life, economic prosperity, and cultural activities continued under the Ayyubid sultanate. During this period a number of Jewish scholars from Christian countries, including Anatoli b. Joseph and Joseph b. Gershon from France, settled in Egypt, taking an active part in communal life. Among the most famous Jews who migrated from the Iberian Peninsula to Egypt at this time was Moses Maimonides, one of the most eminent Jewish scholars of all times.

[27] Mann (1920–22); Ashtor (1976, chap. 3).
[28] Ashtor (1942, p. 142); Brasalawsky (1942).
[29] M. R. Cohen (1980); Bashan and Bareket (2007).
[30] Ashtor (2007).

To sum up, from the ninth to the thirteenth century, Egypt and the Maghreb witnessed the arrival of many Jewish immigrants from Mesopotamia and Persia; later, Jews also emigrated from Syria, Sicily, the Iberian Peninsula, and the Land of Israel. These immigrants became prominent in a variety of urban and high-skill occupations. The primary sources from the ninth, tenth, and eleventh centuries show no evidence of involvement in agriculture by Jewish immigrants in North Africa. Despite their need for kosher products, they stayed away from farming, preferring to purchase their dairy products from the local population.[31] To the extent that Jewish immigrants were involved in agriculture at all, it was always in connection with trade in agricultural products.[32]

No legal ban prohibited Jewish settlers in North Africa from buying land or engaging in farming. Their comparative advantage in literacy was the lever of their prominence in crafts, trade, and moneylending. Literacy and education, coupled with the availability of contract-enforcement institutions (the Talmud, the responsa, and the rabbinic courts in each location) enhanced their geographical mobility, which in turn made it possible to establish new Jewish communities in many locations in Egypt and the Maghreb, as described by Greif.[33] The trading network based on business partnerships across these locations fostered Jewish participation in long-distance trade within the vast territory under Muslim rule. Jewish mobility within the empire also helped Jews living in different places get news from other Jewish communities and exchange responsa with other Jewish centers.

THE IBERIAN PENINSULA UNDER MUSLIM RULE

The historical record indicates the presence of Jews in the Iberian Peninsula since Roman times. Their numbers probably dwindled during the fifth and sixth centuries, as the small number of epigraphs and references to Jews in law codes and canons seem to suggest. In contrast, many references to Iberian Jewry survive for the period between the Visigoths' conversion to Catholicism, in 589, and the Arab Conquest of 711. Migrations to the Maghreb and Egypt occurred as early as the sixth and seventh centuries, when some Jews fled to North Africa to escape persecutions by the Visigoths.[34]

After the Umayyad dynasty conquered southern Spain, in 710–12, a large number of Jews from North Africa settled there, initially as holders of the Muslim military posts. With the establishment of the Umayyad

---

[31] In ninth-century Qayrawan, in Tunisia, Jews were permitted to use butter produced by non-Jews (M. Ben-Sasson 1996, p. 42).

[32] Ashtor (1976, chap. 2); M. Ben-Sasson (1992, 1996).

[33] Greif (1989, 1993, 1994, 2006).

[34] Baron (1952, vol. 4, chaps. 20 and 22); Ashtor (2007).

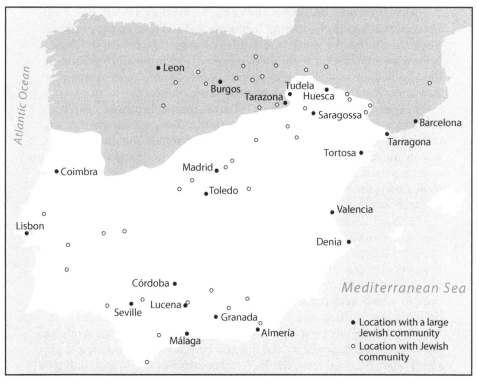

Map 7.2. Jewish communities in the Iberian Peninsula, c. 1030. *Source*: Redrawn and adapted from Ashtor et al. (2007). White = Regions under Muslim rule. Dark grey = Regions under Christian rule.

kingdom in 756, Córdoba became the largest and one of the most commercial cities in Europe, hosting about half a million people toward the end of the tenth century. A few decades after the Arab conquest of the Iberian Peninsula, sources in three languages (Latin, Arabic, and Hebrew) start including references to the Jews. In these documents, the Jews bear Arab names and speak and write in Arabic.[35]

This sizable immigration of Jews from Egypt and the Maghreb established the Sephardim—a new Iberian Jewry with a distinctive culture and the largest community after the one in the Middle East.[36] Soon, Jewish communities were established in many towns, including Badjana, Calsena, Calatayud, Córdoba, Elvira, Granada, Illiberi, Jaén, Lucena, Mérida, Pechina, Saragossa, Seville, and Toledo, as well as in villages (map 7.2).

[35] Baron (1952, vol. 4, chaps. 20 and 22); Goitein (1967–88, vols. 1 and 2); Toch (2005).
[36] Toch (2005, 2012).

Many references document the continuous contacts and migrations between the Jews in the Iberian Peninsula and the Jews in Egypt and the Maghreb during the ninth and tenth centuries. Qayrawan, in Tunisia, became an important stop for Iberian-Jewish traders traveling to and from the Middle East as well as an important point of connection between Iberian Jewry and the Jewish academies in Mesopotamia.[37]

The Jewish immigrants who settled in the Iberian Peninsula specialized in a large set of crafts and skilled occupations, held dominant roles in local trade, and gained a near monopoly in long-distance commerce.[38] These Jewish migrants were not farmers who moved there and then became craftsmen and traders. They were already urban dwellers engaging in skilled occupations, who freely and voluntarily moved to the Iberian Peninsula in search of business opportunities.

Jews also shared in the lively intellectual life that characterized the Iberian Peninsula in the five centuries after the Arab Conquest. As in southern Italy and Sicily, the Jewish culture that developed in the Iberian Peninsula initially drew from the centers of learning and law in Mesopotamia. However, later Iberian Jewry developed a distinctive profile of its own, in which Arab influences were a major component. These were the beginnings of the golden age of Sephardic Jews (as discussed later).[39]

Migration in this period was not unidirectional: during the tenth and eleventh centuries, Jewish craftsmen, teachers, scholars, traders, and physicians also migrated from the Iberian Peninsula to the Maghreb, Egypt, and Syria, creating a continuous and bidirectional flow of literate and highly skilled individuals within the vast territory under Muslim rule.[40]

MIGRATION OF BYZANTINE JEWRY

Between the early seventh and the late twelfth centuries, Byzantine Jewry remained fairly stable in both absolute and relative size. Circa 650, Jews in the Byzantine Empire amounted to roughly 0.4–0.5 percent of the population. Five centuries later, at the time of Benjamin of Tudela's journey, they were 0.3–0.4 percent of the population (table 1.6). The opposite directions of the Jewish Diaspora in the Mediterranean in these centuries contributed to the demographic stability of the Jews living under the rule of Constantinople.

[37] M. Ben-Sasson (1996, pp. 40–65).
[38] Ashtor (1973–84; 2007); H. Ben-Sasson (1976, pp. 393–402).
[39] H. Ben-Sasson (1976, pp. 439–61); Ashtor (2007).
[40] Ashtor (1973–84); H. Ben-Sasson (1976, pp. 393–402); M. Ben-Sasson (1996, pp. 60–93).

Persecutions and forced conversions by some of the Byzantine emperors from the early seventh to the late tenth century, as well as the parallel Arab expansion and the rise of the Muslim caliphates in Mesopotamia, North Africa, the Iberian Peninsula, Sicily and southern Italy, made a proportion of Byzantine Jews migrate all over the Mediterranean world. Beginning in the late tenth century and picking up during the eleventh century, the political decline of the Abbasid caliphate in North Africa (with related episodes of persecutions of Jews and Christians, for example, by Caliph al-Hakim in early eleventh-century Egypt), and the concomitant revival of the Byzantine economy, reversed the direction of Jewish migrations. Constantinople and other bustling cities under its dominion (e.g., Salonica or Seleucia) became attractive destinations for a number of Jews from Egypt and the Maghreb.[41]

Jewish migrations from, to, and within the Byzantine Empire share one feature: Jewish craftsmen, traders, physicians, and scholars generated this Jewish Diaspora. Primary sources, including letters from the Cairo Geniza, indicate that when they settled in the new locations, these Jewish immigrants were well-off and maintained economic and cultural relations with the Jews in their native homes.

Jewish Migration to and within Christian Europe

Jewish migration to Europe in the ninth to twelfth century shares some salient features of the Jewish Diaspora to, from, and within the Muslim caliphates and the Byzantine Empire. In all cases, the migrations involved the most literate and skilled individuals (artisans, teachers, scholars, merchants, traders, coin minters, moneylenders, and physicians), who moved to new locations in search of business opportunities. The migrations of the Jews to Europe also present some distinctive features that shaped the history of European Jewry in the subsequent centuries.

The Origin of Jews in Medieval Europe

Josephus, the Jewish military commander and historian, died in Rome circa 100, after having spent about thirty years under the patronage of the Roman emperors Titus and then Domitian. Josephus was not an isolated case. Many literary sources, as well as inscriptions and archaeological findings on synagogues, document that Rome, and central and southern Italy in general, hosted a large Jewish community. In Roman times, Jewish

[41] Holo (2009); Jacoby (2011).

communities also existed in the Iberian Peninsula, southern France, Germany, and the Balkans (see chapter 1).

A thousand years later, the Jewish traveler Benjamin of Tudela found Jewish communities in Barcelona, Narbonne, Marseilles, Rome, Naples, Salerno, Palermo, Lepanto, Thebes, and Corinth, to name just a few of the places he visited (see appendix, table A.2). Most of these Jews were craftsmen, traders, physicians, teachers, scholars, coin minters, money changers, moneylenders, tax collectors, diplomats, translators, or court bankers. Few were farmers or engaged in agricultural occupations.[42]

Were these Jews in twelfth-century Europe the descendants of the Jews who inhabited Italy, the Iberian Peninsula, France, Germany, and the Balkans under Roman rule during the first and second centuries? Most of them were probably not. As carefully documented by Toch, only in Italy from Rome southward and in a few places in southern France and eastern Spain did Jews seem to have lived continuously from late antiquity through circa 800.[43]

During the ninth and tenth centuries, the number of Jews in Europe grew significantly, as a consequence of both the establishment of the Córdoba caliphate in the Iberian Peninsula and the migration of Jews from Egypt and the Maghreb to the Iberian Peninsula and, later, to Sicily and southern Italy. From the Iberian Peninsula and southern Italy, some Jews likely migrated to central Italy and southern France. Beginning in the mid-ninth century, these movements extended the Jewish Diaspora beyond the vast territory under Muslim rule, with its common language, laws, and institutions, into the politically fragmented Europe that was the bastion of Christianity.[44] Moreover, migrations of Jews within and from the lands of the Byzantine Empire, which included southern Italy, may have also set the foundations, via Italy, for much of European Jewry.[45]

Also in central and northern France and western Germany, medieval Jews do not appear to have been descendants of Jews who lived there under the Roman Empire. There is almost no evidence of Jews living in these areas during the seventh and eighth centuries. Their presence in the Champagne and Rhineland area, and later in central Europe, was likely the outcome of the migration of Jews from southern Europe that began in the ninth and tenth centuries.[46]

The distinct patterns of Jewish settlement in southern Europe and in central and northwestern Europe left a permanent mark on their subsequent history. As shown by Toch, "during the early Middle Ages, the

[42] H. Ben-Sasson (1976, pp. 385–402).
[43] Toch (2005, pp. 547–48; 2012).
[44] Baron (1971b); DellaPergola (2001); Toch (2005, pp. 547–55; 2012).
[45] Toch (2005, pp. 549–55; 2012).
[46] Baron (1952, vol. 4, chaps. 20 and 22); Toch (2005, pp. 547–55; 2012).

Mediterranean-Hellenistic Jewry of antiquity separated and developed into Byzantine–southern Italian, Roman, Catalan–southern French, and Arabic-Sicilian branches. Subsequently, Ashkenazi (northwestern and northern European) and Sephardi (Iberian) Jewry became distinctive communities," as described later.[47]

Europe from Charlemagne to Frederick II (800–1250)

How did southern Europe look to the ninth-century Jewish craftsmen, traders, physicians, and scholars from Egypt and the Maghreb who sailed toward its shores with the intention of settling and starting up their business in Córdoba or Toledo or Palermo? How did Europe appear to the Jews from the Byzantine Empire who settled in Italy, and whose descendants likely migrated to the rest of Europe later on? How did Europe look to the Jews who migrated within the various regions of Europe in the following four centuries?

A PATCHWORK OF COMPETING KINGDOMS

With the collapse of the western part of the Roman Empire in the early fifth century, cities, trading networks, and urban infrastructure declined everywhere in Europe over the next 400–500 years. Unlike the Muslim caliphates, which were highly urban and commercial societies under a unified political leadership, Europe became an agrarian economy and a rural society after the fall of the Roman Empire. Land, the main source of wealth and political power, was dispersed among a variety of kingdoms, duchies, counties, independent city-states, and ecclesiastical municipalities.[48]

When Charlemagne was crowned emperor by Pope Leo III in 800, the major political players in Europe were the Umayyad Emirate of Córdoba, which imposed Muslim rule on most of the Iberian Peninsula; Anglo-Saxon England; the kingdoms of the Danes and Vikings in Scandinavia; and the Carolingian Empire, which covered a vast area including northern Spain, France, the Low Countries, northern Italy, Germany, and Austria. The Balkans and parts of southern Italy belonged to the Byzantine Empire. The Church held power in central Italy, the Bulgars in the Bulgarian Khanate, and the Magyars in Hungary. Germanic and Slavic tribes in Bohemia and eastern Europe completed the geopolitics of Europe when the first groups of Jewish immigrants—whether from the Byzantine Empire or from North Africa—arrived on the northern shores of the Mediterranean in the early and mid-ninth century. Political fragmentation was exacerbated by the fact that within each kingdom, an array of local rulers—princes, counts, dukes, noblemen, free assemblies of

[47]Toch (2005, p. 547).
[48]Le Goff (1988, chap. 2).

citizens, bishops, and abbots—held power and jurisdiction over a variety of economic, social, and religious matters.

Political division went hand in hand with linguistic, religious, legal, and economic fragmentation. A Jewish trader or craftsman could travel from Samarkand to Córdoba and still speak and hear the same language (Arabic) and be subject to a uniform set of laws and customs inspired by the Koran. In contrast, a Jew who settled in Aachen, York, Trier, or Pisa would hear different local languages, encounter different rulers, and be subject to different codes of laws.

In 1250, when the Holy Roman Emperor Frederick II died, the fragmentation of Europe was even greater than it had been four centuries earlier. The Holy Roman Empire extended from the North Sea to the Mediterranean and comprised the Low Countries, Germany, Austria, Bohemia, southeastern France, and northern and southern Italy, including Sicily and Sardinia. The rest of Italy was split into several kingdoms, including the Papal State in central Italy, the Venetian territories, and the County of Savoy in northwestern Italy. The kingdom of France, which covered only a portion of the regions that today belong to France, was ruled partly by the Capetian dynasty and partly by the Angevin monarchy of England. The Iberian Peninsula was fragmented into several Christian kingdoms, including Andalusia, Aragon, Castile, Leon, Navarre, and Portugal, whereas the Muslims retained only the kingdom of Granada in southeastern Spain. In Scandinavia, the Baltic states, eastern Europe, and the Balkans, various rulers reigned, people spoke different languages, and different laws were in place.[49]

THE POWER OF THE CHURCH

One of the important political players in Europe was the Catholic Church, which operated through the centralized administration based in Rome and its network of bishops, abbeys, and monasteries. Bishops often played a significant role in governance, whereas abbeys and monasteries acted as land trusts for powerful families, centers of propaganda and royal support in newly conquered regions, and bases for proselytizing. They were also the main outposts of education and literacy. In an early medieval Europe that was almost entirely illiterate, the Church carried out the important role of preserving Latin learning and maintaining the art of writing.[50]

In addition to dealing with political matters, the Church regulated many aspects of the daily lives of the millions of people living in early medieval Europe. From imposing monogamy to making Christians pay tithes, from issuing bans against lending at usurious interest rates to

[49] Baron (1952, vol. 9, chaps. 40, 41, 42, 43, 44); Le Goff (1988, chap. 3); Abulafia (1997).
[50] Pirenne (1954, pp. 270–82).

fighting heresy, the Church affected the daily lives of Europeans, dictating what was permitted and what was not.[51] The Jews migrating to and within Europe did not escape the Church's regulatory powers, which added to the secular regulations imposed by kings, princes, and local rulers and made the migrations of the Jews in Europe different from the migrations of their co-religionists within the Muslim caliphates.

URBANIZATION AND THE COMMERCIAL REVOLUTION

The breakdown of Roman society after the fall of the Roman Empire in the early fifth century had dire consequences for western Europe. The patchwork of rulers that came to power was incapable of supporting libraries and major educational institutions, to the extent that intellectual development suffered a major blow. Lack of safety led to a collapse in manufacture, local trade, and long-distance commerce. By the end of the eighth century, what had once been the western Roman Empire was politically decentralized and overwhelmingly rural.[52]

Because of the absence of major plagues or other major demographic shocks from the late eighth throughout the ninth century, the population of Europe was growing by the tenth century.[53] The rise in agricultural productivity—achieved by the reclamation of lands that had been left uncultivated, the drainage of marshes, the restoration of irrigation works, and the use of new agricultural tools and techniques—fueled and fostered the rise of towns, fair centers, trade posts, and cities.[54] Urbanization, the rebirth of crafts and industries, and the revival of local trade and long-distance commerce beginning in the tenth century made Europe an attractive place for people with the literacy, education, and skills required to succeed in crafts, trade, moneylending, medicine, and other high-skill professions.

[51] Stow (1981); Le Goff (1988, chap. 8); Lynch (1992); Ekelund et al. (1996).

[52] Lopez (1976); Le Goff (1988, chaps. 1 and 2).

[53] Between the mid-eighth century, when the last of the pestilences that swept through Asia and Europe took place, and the mid-fourteenth century, when the Black Death hit Eurasia and North Africa and started a cycle of recurrent pandemics that ended only in the late seventeenth century, Europe enjoyed almost six centuries with no major plagues or epidemic diseases. A variety of conquerors threatened Europe during these centuries. The Scandinavians raided western Europe, settled in Russia, and colonized Iceland and Greenland during the ninth and tenth centuries; the Slavs pushed westward; the Magyars settled in the Danubian region; the Muslims conquered the major islands of the Mediterranean. Their military expeditions and geographical expansions did not take a higher toll in terms of population decline than the earlier invasions by the Goths, Franks, Huns, or Arabs, however.

[54] Lopez (1976); Braudel (1982, pp. 231–49); Le Goff (1988, pp. 195–255); Mokyr (1990, chap. 3); Abulafia (2000); Hodges (2000).

Geography and Timing of the Jewish Diaspora

Who were the Jews from North Africa who settled in the Iberian Peninsula, Sicily, and southern Italy in the early Middle Ages? Who were the Jews from the Byzantine Empire who migrated to southern Italy and whose descendants later settled in other regions of Europe? Who were the Jews who migrated from France to England and Germany? Why did the Jews migrate to and within Europe? How did they typically arrive and settle? Could they freely settle in any European town or location? Could they acquire and own land, and engage in any occupation? How did rulers in medieval Europe view the Jews? How similar and different were the migrations of the Jews within the vast territory under Muslim rule and their migrations within the politically fragmented Christian Europe?

The timing and circumstances of the Jewish settlement in each country varied significantly. European Jews spoke various local languages, practiced different religious customs and rituals, worked in different occupations, and had different legal standing. Despite the differences, however, there were some common features that Iberian, Italian, French, German, and Anglo Jewry shared.

JEWS IN THE IBERIAN PENINSULA UNDER CHRISTIAN RULE

During the long period of the Reconquista (started in the late eighth century and completed in the mid-thirteenth century), Spanish monarchs of Christian faith regained control and established Christian rule over the regions of the Iberian Peninsula previously under Muslim authority.[55] Unlike the Visigoths, who had persecuted the Jews during the seventh century, the Christian rulers governing parts of the Iberian Peninsula during the ninth and tenth centuries tolerated the Jews and actually invited them to settle in their territories. Beginning in the ninth century, Jews started migrating to the areas of the Iberian Peninsula under Christian rule. Small numbers of Jews, some of them with Arabic names, appeared in northeast Spain, in Barcelona, Gerona, Tarragona, Tortosa as well as in the countryside; in the north, in Belorado, Castrojeriz near Burgos, León, Puento Castro, and Sahagún; and in the west, in Béja, Coimbra, Corunna, and Mérida (map 7.2).[56]

At the beginning of the eleventh century, concomitant with the decline of the caliphate of Córdoba, the Christian hold on the Iberian Peninsula increased through the initiative of King Alfonso V of León, who sought to attract settlers to his lands by granting them privileges and freedom. Among these new settlers were numerous Jews (probably including many

[55] Baer (1961).
[56] Toch (2005, p. 552; 2012).

leaving the portion of the peninsula under Muslim rule), who shared the same rights as the Christians.[57]

The attitude of the Christian monarchs toward the Jewish population was sometimes ambivalent and their actions inconsistent. In 1091, for example, King Alfonso VI was in desperate need of money to raise an army against the Almoravids (a Berber dynasty from North Africa). He therefore granted the population of the town of León a charter that provided them with various advantages over the Jewish population in exchange for financial support. A similar policy was adopted in 1114 for the town of Tudela. The outcome was that many Jews fled these towns. But, recognizing the important role the Jews played in the national economy and royal finances, Alfonso also provided the Jews with charters that enabled them to prosper economically.[58]

The Jews in the Iberian Peninsula played an important role as mediators in the transition from Muslim to Christian rule, and they helped the Christian rulers adopt the former state administration and bureaucracy of the Muslim rulers.[59] In many towns, they were granted charters that regulated the terms under which they were allowed to live and conduct business in a given location. These early medieval charters, such as the one granted to the Jews in Barcelona in 1053, in Tudela in 1116, and in many other cities between the mid-eleventh and mid-thirteenth centuries clearly show that the Jews could acquire and own land and be farmers, freely travel and trade, and lend money at interest.[60] In fact, tax records, court cases, and the responsa literature show that not only could Jews own land and engage in any occupation they wanted but also that they did so. In the eleventh and twelfth centuries, for example, the Jews owned about a third of the estates in Barcelona, which explains why the second Council of Gerona demanded that they continue to pay the tithes due to the Church on land they had purchased from Christians.[61]

ITALIAN JEWRY

Jews have lived in Italy continuously for twenty-one centuries, with the community dating back to the Roman Republic (the second and first centuries BCE). Probably preceded by individual Jews who visited Italy as traders, a Jewish embassy was dispatched to Rome in 161 BCE by Judah Maccabee to conclude a political treaty with the Roman Senate. From then on, other Jewish immigrants freely and voluntarily arrived in Italy,

[57] Ashtor et. al (2007).

[58] Baer (1961).

[59] Baer (1961); Ashtor (2007); Sapir Abulafia (2011).

[60] Parkes (1934, 1938); Marcus (1938); Pakter (1988); and Linder (1997) edited many of these charters.

[61] Baer (1961); H. Ben-Sasson (1976, pp. 462–76); Ashtor et al. (2007).

establishing sizable communities south of Rome, especially in urban locations in Apulia, Calabria, and Sicily.[62]

A certain number of Jews were deported as slaves to Italy after the siege of Jerusalem and the destruction of the Second Temple, but there were no mass deportations at this time. Moreover, the Jews who were brought forcibly to Italy regained their freedom after a few years. In the first century CE, the Jewish population in Italy amounted to nearly 50,000 people, half of whom were concentrated in or around Rome. Their occupational structure was quite diversified, including farmers, artisans, and traders.[63]

Central and southern Italy were the economic and religious centers of Jewish life in Italy in Roman times and remained so until the early seventh century.[64] Jews are mentioned in historical records in Lazio (Ostia, Terracina); Campania (Capua, Naples, Nola, Pompeii, Salerno, Venafro); Apulia and Basilicata (Bari, Oria, Otranto, Taranto, Venosa); Sicily (Agrigento, Catania, Palermo, Syracuse); Sardinia (Cagliari); and other locations in Campania and Sicily under papal rule.

The disintegration of the western Roman Empire in the early fifth century; the subsequent conquests of different regions of Italy by Huns, Ostrogoths, Vandals, Visigoths, and the Byzantine Empire; and the rising power of the Church led to continuous changes in the situation of the Jews in Italy during the fifth and sixth centuries. Peaceful conditions alternated with isolated episodes of forced conversions (by, for example, some Byzantine rulers in some towns in southern Italy).[65]

Epigraphic records and literary sources fall silent on the Jews during the seventh and eighth centuries, making it difficult to ascertain whether they left these locations or continued to live there but left no trace in the historical record. (An exception is Venosa, where there is almost unbroken archaeological and written evidence of Jewish settlement, including in villages around the town.[66])

Subsequent migrations of Jews from the eastern and southern shores of the Mediterranean contributed to the growth of Jewish communities south of Rome from the ninth century onward. Jews arrived to southern Italy from the Balkans and Asia Minor under Byzantine rule.[67] Parallel to this movement, when the Arabs began their conquest of parts of southern Italy and Sicily and Muslim rule brought political stability and economic

---

[62] Milano (1963); Toch (2005, p. 549; 2012); Milano et al. (2007).

[63] Baron (1952, vol. 2; 1971b, p. 874).

[64] Toch (2005; 2012). In northern Italy, there are fewer traces of Jewish presence during Roman times. Inscriptions and literary sources mention Jews in Aquileia, Brescia, Civitavecchia, Ferrara, Milan, and Pola.

[65] Milano (1963); Milano et al. (2007).

[66] Toch (2005, pp. 549–50).

[67] Toch (2005); Holo (2009); Jacoby (2011).

prosperity to these areas, an increasing number of Jewish immigrants from Egypt and the Maghreb settled in Sicily and parts of southern Italy, as amply documented by the documents of the Cairo Geniza. By the ninth and tenth centuries, more and more sources begin mentioning the presence of Jewish communities in places like Bari, Benevento, Capua, Gaeta, Lavello, Naples, Oria, Otranto, Salerno, Siponto, Trani, and Taranto, as well as Catania, Palermo, Ragusa, and Syracuse.[68]

As part of one large commonwealth, the Jews who migrated from North Africa to Sicily and parts of southern Italy did not require any permit or charter to settle and set up their businesses in the new locations. They could own and acquire land and engage in any occupation they wished, as clearly illustrated by their very diversified economic structure, similar to that of the Jewish communities in Mesopotamia, Persia, North Africa, and the Iberian Peninsula. They were skilled artisans, local merchants, long-distance traders, physicians, scholars, and moneylenders.[69]

The Jewish communities in Sicily and southern Italy reached the height of their prosperity in the first half of the thirteenth century under the Holy Roman Emperor of Norman descent Frederick II, who extended his personal protection to the Jews, granted them the monopolies in the silk weaving and dyeing industries and foreign commerce, and took a personal interest in promoting Jewish culture.[70] This culture had changed markedly since ancient times. In late antiquity, Jews in southern Italy spoke Greek, like the other Jewish communities in the Hellenistic-Byzantine Diaspora. In contrast, Jews in Muslim Sicily and southern Italy used Hebrew in their writings, relied on the rabbinical vocabulary and tradition of the Mesopotamian academies, and developed a rich religious poetry drawing from sources from the Land of Israel.[71]

North of Rome, Jewish communities are still mentioned in the early sixth century in Genoa and Milan but then disappear from the record. References to individual Jews appear in epigraphic evidence from eighth-century Asti and Pavia. Beginning in the tenth century, references to Jews in Ancona, Lucca, Pavia, Ravenna, Rimini, Treviso, and Verona appear.[72] Beginning in the twelfth century, Jews from southern Italy started moving northward. Unlike the Jews in southern Italy and Sicily under Muslim rule, the Jews could settle in the towns in central and northern Italy

[68] Roth (1946, 1966b); Goitein (1967–88, vol.1); M. Ben-Sasson (1991); Simonsohn (1997–2010, 2011); Gil (2004, pp. 535–93); Toch (2005, 2012); Abulafia (2008).

[69] Goitein (1967–88, vol. 1); M. Ben-Sasson (1991); Gil (2004, pp. 593–692); Toch (2005, 2012).

[70] Milano (1963); Abulafia (2000); Milano et al. (2007); Simonsohn (2011).

[71] M. Ben-Sasson (1991); Abulafia (2000, 2008); Gil (2004, pp. 535–93); Sapir Abulafia (2011).

[72] Toch (2005, pp. 551–52; 2012).

through charters and permits granted by local Christian rulers. These rulers were often keen on inviting Jewish merchants and traders (and later, moneylenders) to settle in their jurisdictions to help the local economies.[73]

Circa 1170, Benjamin of Tudela documented this uneven distribution of Italian Jews south and north of Rome (see appendix, table A.2). According to his account, 3,000 Jews lived in Salerno and 7,500 in Palermo; Pisa and Lucca hosted a mere 100 and 200 Jews, respectively. In the subsequent three centuries, Jewish communities varying in size from a handful of families to a few hundred households spread and grew all over Italy (map 7.3). The Jews in southern Italy and Sicily remained engaged in a wide variety of crafts and commercial activities, whereas the Jews in northern and central Italy became increasingly specialized in moneylending (see chapter 8).

FRENCH JEWRY

From the time of the Roman conquest by Julius Caesar in 58–51 BCE until its invasion by Burgunds, Franks, Huns, and Visigoths in the fourth and fifth centuries, Gaul shared its history with Rome. Inscriptions and archaeological findings indicate that the Jews, who probably settled in Gaul as itinerant merchants, did so as Roman citizens or protégés.[74] They benefited from certain rights and privileges deriving from their Roman citizenship, granted in 212 by Emperor Caracalla to all inhabitants of the empire. These rights included freedom of worship, as well as access to public office and to the army. Beginning in the fourth century, documents mention a Jewish presence, albeit small, in the region. Jewish settlements correspond to the routes taken by the Roman legions, which Jews followed as soldiers, tradesmen, and merchants.[75]

During the fifth century, the Franks, a loose confederation of tribes arriving from the lower Rhine, conquered the north of Gaul. Clovis I (481–511), the founder of the Merovingian dynasty, unified the confederation of the Frankish tribes into a single political unity. By converting to Christianity, he created an alliance with the Church and opened the way for the spread of Christianity in Gaul (henceforth France).

It is from roughly this time that written records documenting the presence of Jewish communities in various locations in France (Agde, Arles, Avignon, Clermont-Ferrand, Marseilles, Metz, Orleans, Poitier) become abundant. The Jews were engaged mainly in commerce, but there were

---

[73] Baron (1952, vol. 4, chaps. 20 and 22); Milano (1963); Simonsohn (1977, 1982–86, 1988–91); Stow (1995–97); Toch (2005, 2012); Milano et al. (2007); Sapir Abulafia (2011).

[74] Benbassa (1999, chap. 1); Blumenkranz et al. (2007). Little information is available on the numbers of Jews in Roman times.

[75] Blumenkranz et al. (2007).

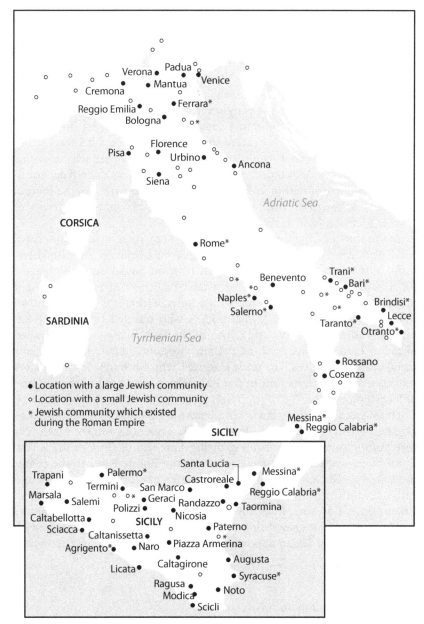

Map 7.3. Major Jewish communities in Italy, 1450–1550. *Source*: Redrawn and adapted from Milano (1963).

already Jewish physicians and even sailors. Despite Clovis's conversion, the legal status of the Jews in France did not change, and they continued to live in accordance with their customs.[76] During the sixth and early seventh centuries, French Jewry increased rapidly, especially through immigration, first from Italy and the Byzantine Empire and then from the Iberian Peninsula, especially after the persecutions of Iberian Jews by the Visigothic king Sisebut in the early seventh century.[77]

The condition of the Jews in France deteriorated during the seventh to eighth century. Some Jews were forced to convert to Christianity, but they were often allowed to return to Judaism (by subsequent rulers or even the same ruler). France seems to have experienced a sharp decline in the number of Jews within its borders except in areas close to the Iberian Peninsula. Between the mid-seventh and mid-eighth centuries, almost no sources mention Jews in Frankish lands.[78]

At the time of Charlemagne's reign (771–814), there is some anecdotal and legislative evidence of Jews in the emperor's entourage and elsewhere. From this time, their numbers began to grow under favorably peaceful circumstances.[79] Soon the Jews established themselves as prominent merchants. The Radhanite traders mentioned earlier are the best-known example of ninth-century Jewish traders who traveled from Mesopotamia to France in the West and China in the East. The goods they traded included luxury items, such as balsam, brocades, dates, furs, precious metals, silk, and spices. The trade in spices, which brought Jewish traders into contact with physicians in the East, also contributed to the training of Jewish physicians.[80]

During and after the reign of Charlemagne's son, Louis the Pious (814–40), the Jewish community in France grew. Evidence from the ninth century points to sizable, probably growing numbers of Jews in the south. From there, settlements spread out along the Rhone River to the center of France, to Châlons, Lyons, Mâcon, and Vienne. During the tenth and early eleventh centuries, communities were established in Bourgogne, Champagne, Lorraine, Maine-Anjou, and Normandy (map 7.4). Parallel to this demographic growth, legal and religious Jewish literature by Jewish scholars in France began appearing. By the eleventh century, the French

---

[76] Bachrach (1977); Benbassa (1999, chap. 1).
[77] Toch (2005, 2012); Blumenkranz et al. (2007).
[78] Toch (2005, pp. 547–50).
[79] Baron (1952, vol. 4, chap. 20).
[80] Baron (1952, vol. 4, chap. 20); Blumenkranz et al. (2007). At that time, medicine required the knowledge of herbs and spices, which were then employed as medicaments. The professions of physician and of seller of spices often went hand in hand.

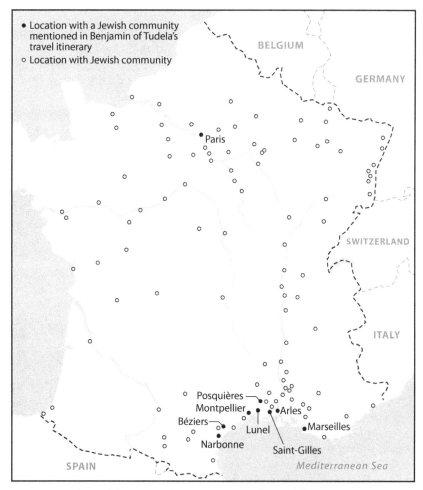

Map 7.4. Main Jewish communities in France in the Middle Ages. *Source*: Redrawn and adapted from Blumenkranz et al. (2007).

yeshivot were prominent enough to gain intellectual independence from the academies in Mesopotamia.[81]

As in other countries in Europe, Jews could not freely migrate to and settle in France unless they were invited by the local rulers. As elsewhere, their settlement was regulated by charters. The first surviving charter dates to circa 825, when Louis the Pious accorded individual Jews who

---

[81] Baron (1952, vol. 4, chap. 20); Benbassa (1999); Toch (2005, 2012); Blumenkranz, Steinberg, and Bensimon-Donath (2007); Blumenkranz et al. (2007).

came into the Carolingian Empire as merchants a number of privileges, including exemption from certain tolls and other duties on the transport of merchandise as well as royal protection of their lives and property. These privileges suggest that Jewish merchants played an important role in trade and commerce. That charter was followed by similar charters in Grenoble (894), Narbonne (899), Gironne (922), and France as a whole (1190). These early medieval charters document the wide spectrum of economic possibilities granted to the Jews who settled in France. Despite the opposition shown by the ecclesiastical authorities, they could own and farm land, travel freely, engage in trade and moneylending, own and import slaves from abroad (but not for selling them in other countries), and employ free Christians.[82]

French Jews practiced a variety of trades. During the ninth, tenth, and eleventh centuries, they possessed buildings, fields, orchards and vineyards, garden farms, and mills, which were typically worked by Christians.[83] Some Jews managed the assets of bishops and abbots, others were in the service of kings. They played an important role in trade, practiced medicine, and worked in fabric dyeing and the tanning and currying of leather. By the late tenth to early eleventh century, the occupational distribution of French Jewry had changed, with many Jews becoming moneylenders, as chapter 8 describes.[84]

GERMAN JEWRY

Sources indicate the presence of Jews in Cologne and Trier during Roman times. Nothing, however, indicates that these early Jewish communities were connected to the Jews living in Germany in the early Middle Ages: the record of German Jewry is scant during the fifth and sixth centuries and falls silent during most of the seventh and eighth centuries.[85]

The growth of German Jewry is closely connected to the development of French Jewry in northern France beginning in the ninth century. At first arriving from Italy and France and settling as individual or small groups of itinerant merchants during the reigns of Charlemagne (771–814) and Louis the Pious (814–40), the Jews emerged as organized communities in German locations more than a century later. The first Jews who came to Germany (e.g., the Kalonymos family from Lucca that settled in Mainz in the tenth century) were the extended families of long-distance traders, accompanied by servants and rabbis. These groups established small communities, which were protected by the Christian elite.[86]

[82] See Parkes (1934, 1938); Marcus (1938); Pakter (1988); Limor (1993); Limor and Raz-Krakotzkin (1993); and Linder (1997) for these and other charters.
[83] Toch (2005, p. 557; 2012).
[84] Baron (1952, vol. 4, chaps. 20 and 22); Taitz (1994); Benbassa (1999); Toch (2005, 2012).
[85] Baron (1952, vol. 4, chaps. 20 and 22); Toch (2000b, 2005, 2008, 2011, 2012).
[86] H. Ben-Sasson et al. (2007).

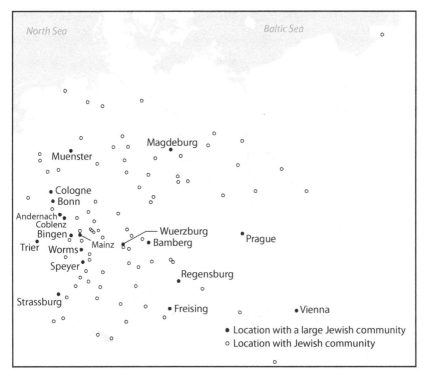

Map 7.5. Major Jewish communities in Germany in the thirteenth century. *Source*: Redrawn and adapted from H. Ben-Sasson et al. (2007).

By the late eleventh century, large and thriving communities had developed in the most important economic and political centers of Germany, such as Cologne, Magdeburg, Mainz, Regensburg, Speyer, Trier, and Worms. Circa 1100, there were about 1,000 Jews in Mainz and the same number in Worms. Many Jews migrated within Germany during the Middle Ages. In the twelfth and especially the thirteenth centuries, Jewish settlements in Germany grew rapidly (map 7.5). In 1238, Jews lived in about ninety towns and villages in Germany (table 7.1). By 1348, there were more than 1,000 Jewish communities in Germany.[87] The first half of the fourteenth century until the Black Death marks the high tide of Jewish settlement in medieval Germany, reaching a geographical extent unmatched until the nineteenth century.

During the tenth to twelfth century, Jews settled along the trade routes and by the Rhine and Danube Rivers. The prominence of these early Jewish communities in trade and commerce directed them to settle where

[87] Toch (2005, 2008, 2012); Sapir Abulafia (2011).

TABLE 7.1. Estimated Number of Locations in Germany in Which Jews Lived, 950–1300

Year	Number of new locales
950	5
1050	8
1100	5
1150	11
1200	62
1250	260
1300	509

Sources: Blumenkranz (1966), Baron (1971b), Toch (2005, 2008), H. Ben-Sasson et al. (2007).

the growth of new towns and urban centers created profitable business opportunities. In the Hebrew record from the second half of the tenth century onward, shopkeeping, local trade, long-distance commerce, toll-collection, minting, and money changing were the main occupations of German Jews. They also could and did own land, gardens, orchards, and vineyards, in which they employed Christian tenants and agricultural laborers. Soon thereafter, many German Jews became heavily engaged in lending money at interest (see chapter 8).[88]

The first reports of persecution of Jews in Germany date from the eleventh century (e.g., the expulsion of the Jews of Mainz in 1012), and the first written guarantees of rights, granted to them by emperors and bishops, also date from that century. In Germany, as in other locations in Europe, the Jews were often invited by local rulers, and their activities were regulated through charters, such as the one granted by Bishop Rudiger of Speyer in 1084, one of the earliest German charters:[89]

> In the name of the Holy and Indivisible Trinity, I, Rudiger, surnamed Huozmann, Bishop of Speyer, when I made the villa of Speyer into a town, thought I would increase the honor I was bestowing on the place if I brought in the Jews. Therefore I placed them outside the town and some way off from the houses of the rest of the citizens, and, lest they should be too easily disturbed by the insolence of the citizens, I surrounded them with a wall. Now the place of their habitation which I acquired justly (for in the first place I obtained the hill partly with money and partly by exchange, while I received the valley by way of gift from some heirs) that place, I say, I transferred to them on condition

[88] Baron (1952, vol. 4, chaps. 20 and 22); Toch (2000a, 2000b, 2003, 2005, 2008, 2010, 2012); H. Ben-Sasson et al. (2007).
[89] Cave and Coulson (1965, pp. 101–2).

that they pay annually three and a half pounds of the money of Speyer for the use of the brethren. I have granted also to them within the district where they dwell, and from that district outside the town as far as the harbor, and within the harbor itself, full power to change gold and silver, and to buy and sell what they please. And I have also given them license to do this throughout the state. Besides this I have given them land of the church for a cemetery with rights of inheritance. This also I have added that if any Jew should at any time stay with them he shall pay no thelony [tolls]. Then also just as the judge of the city hears cases between citizens, so the chief rabbi shall hear cases which arise between the Jews or against them. But if by chance he is unable to decide any of them they shall go to the bishop or his chamberlain. They shall maintain watches, guards, and fortifications about their district, the guards in common with our vassals. They may lawfully employ nurses and servants from among our people. Slaughtered meat which they may not eat according to their law they may lawfully sell to Christians, and Christians may lawfully buy it. Finally, to round out these concessions, I have granted that they may enjoy the same privileges as the Jews in any other city of Germany.

Lest any of my successors diminish this gift and concession, or constrain them to pay greater taxes, alleging that they have usurped these privileges, and have no episcopal warrant for them, I have left this charter as a suitable testimony of the said grant. And that this may never be forgotten, I have signed it, and confirmed it with my seal as may be seen below. Given on September 15th, 1084.

Other examples of these charters are the one of Trier (919), Magdeburg (965, 973, 979), Speyer (1090), Worms (1074, 1090, 1157), Ratisbon (1182, 1216, 1230), and Vienna (1238). These charters document that in the early Middle Ages, German Jews could own land, engage in trade (and later, in moneylending), and enjoy religious freedom and the ability of regulating matters pertaining to the community according to their laws. It also shows that Bishop Rudiger, as well as the other German secular and religious rulers, was eager to invite the Jews for the skills and potential income they would bring to their towns. In 1090, Emperor Henry IV issued charters of rights to the Jews of Speyer and Worms, and succeeding emperors followed his example.[90] One of the most prominent Jewish communities in the German area was the one in Vienna. Documentary evidence points to the first settlement of Jews there in the twelfth century. They owned houses and a synagogue and were mainly traders, money changers, and moneylenders. A prominent Jew was Solomon, mint master, and financial adviser to Duke Leopold V.[91] Between 1177 and 1230, more Jews settled in Vienna as experts in coinage and moneylending (see chapter 8). Under Leopold VI (1198–1230), a second synagogue was erected. In 1235, a Jew

[90] Parkes (1934, 1938); Marcus (1938); Pakter (1988); Linder (1997).
[91] Bato, Adunka, and Lehman (2007). Solomon and fifteen other Jews were murdered by participants in the Third Crusade.

named Teka (Tecanus), who lived in Vienna, acted as financier and state banker for Austria.

In 1238, Emperor Frederick II granted the Jews a charter of privileges that gave their community extensive autonomy. In the late thirteenth and fourteenth centuries, Vienna was home to about 1,000 Jews, making it the leading community of German Jewry. Economic prominence went hand in hand with intellectual leadership: the cultural and legal influence of the Jewish scholars of Vienna spread outside the city and was long lasting.

During the thirteenth century, the Jews migrated eastward, to Bohemia, Silesia, and Pomerania, then, by the fourteenth century, to other parts of Poland. Earlier migrations of Jews from the Byzantine Empire to eastern Europe, as well as the migrations of Jews from Germany eastward, established the basis for the rise of the large and prominent Ashkenazi Jewish communities in these areas in subsequent centuries.[92]

ANGLO JEWRY

Unlike the Jews in continental Europe, whose history covers a long period from the early Middle Ages to the early modern era, the history of the Jews in medieval England spans only a bit more than 200 years—from 1066 to 1290. After 1290, only sporadic records of Jews living in England survive; only in the seventeenth and eighteenth centuries are sizable Jewish communities established again in England.[93]

Jewish traders and moneylenders from Rouen in northern France—an important commercial center at that time—first arrived in England soon after the Norman Conquest in 1066. They freely migrated to England in search of profitable opportunities. The first mention of the "street of the Jews" in London is found about 1128. The Jews rapidly dispersed across the country, establishing relatively large (albeit small in absolute terms) communities in London and other major towns, such as Bristol, Gloucester, Lincoln, Northampton, Norwich, Oxford, York, and Winchester and in very small numbers (sometimes just a family or two) in some 200 rural villages at one time or another (map 7.6).[94]

Reliable information on Anglo Jewry starts with the reign of King Henry I (1100–35), who issued a charter to the Jews in 1120. The original text is lost, but the charter is mentioned and imitated in similar royal documents, including the charters granted by Henry II (1170), Richard I (1190), John (1201), and Edward I (1275).[95]

Henry I's charter in 1120 granted the Jews liberty of movement throughout the country, exemption from ordinary tolls, protection from

[92] Baron (1952, vol. 4, chap. 22); Toch (2005, 2012).
[93] Roth (1964); Toch (2005, p. 554).
[94] Roth (1964, pp. 31–32).
[95] J. Jacobs (1889, 1892, 1893, 1898).

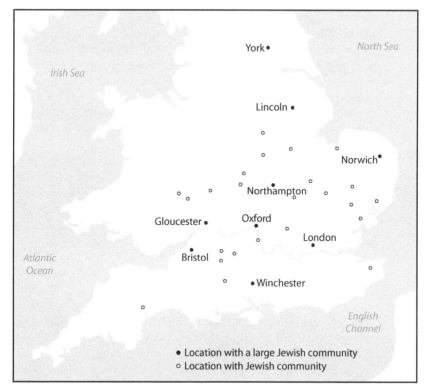

Map 7.6. Jewish communities in England before the expulsion of 1290. *Source*: Redrawn and adapted from Roth et al. (2007).

mistreatment, free recourse to royal justice in the case of disputes and responsibility to no other person but the king himself, permission to retain land taken in pledge as security, and special provisions to ensure fair trials. The terms of the charter confirmed the privileged status of the Jewish community.[96] Similar terms were granted to the Jews by King Richard I. This charter provides primary evidence that the Jews were permitted to own land and to engage in trade and moneylending under the protection of the king:[97]

> Richard, by the grace of God, King of England, duke of Normandy, &c., to his archbishops, bishops, &c., greeting:
>
> I. Know ye that we have granted and, by the present charter, confirmed, to Ysaac, son of Rabbi Joe, and his sons and their men, all their customs and

---

[96] Baron (1952, vol. 4, chaps. 20 and 22); Roth (1964).
[97] J. Jacobs (1893, pp. 134–36).

liberties just as the Lord King Henry, our father, granted and by his charter confirmed to the Jews of England and Normandy, namely: to reside in
our land freely and honorably, and to hold all those things from us which
the aforesaid Isaac and his sons held in the time of Henry the King, our father, in lands, and fiefs, and pledges, and gifts, and purchases, viz., which
Henry, our father, gave them for their service, and Thurroc, which the said
Isaac bought of the Count of Ferrars, and all the houses, and messages, and
pledges which the said Isaac and his sons had in our land in the time of King
Henry, our father.

II. And if any quarrel arise between a Christian and Ysaac, or any of his children or heirs, he that appeals the other to determine the quarrel shall have
witnesses, viz., a lawful Christian and a lawful Jew. And if the aforesaid
Ysaac, or his heirs, or his children, have a writ about the quarrel, the writ
shall serve them for testimony ; and if a Christian have a quarrel against the
aforesaid Jews let it be adjudicated by the peers of the Jews.

III. And if any of the aforesaid Jews shall die let not his body be kept above
ground, but let his heir have his money and his debts so that he be not disturbed if he has an heir who can answer for him and do right about his debts
and his forfeits, and let the aforesaid Jews receive and buy at any time whatever is brought them except things of the church and bloodstained garments.

IV. And if they are appealed by anyone without a witness let them be quits of that
appeal on their own oath upon their book [of the Law] and let them be quits
from an appeal of those things which pertain to our crown on their own oath
on their roll [of the Law]. And if there be any dissention between a Christian
and any of the aforesaid Jews or their children about the settlement of any
money, the Jew shall prove the capital and the Christian the interest.

V. And the aforesaid Jews may sell their pledges without trouble after it is cer-
tified that they have held them a year and a day. . . .

VI. Let them go whithersoever they will with all their chattels just like our own
goods and let no one keep them or prevent them. And if a Christian debtor
dies, who owes money to a Jew, and the debtor has an heir, during the minority of the heir let not the Jew be disturbed of his debt unless the land of
the heir is in our hands.

VII. And we order that, the Jews through all England and Normandy be free
of all customs and of tolls and modiation [tax] of wine just like our own
chattels. . . .

The prominence in trade and moneylending of the Jews in England
during the twelfth century, and the high standards of living they reached,
coexisted with isolated episodes of violence and persecutions (see chapter 8).
Nevertheless, the community grew in wealth and numbers, and its financial
importance became increasingly recognized and exploited by the Crown.[98]

---

[98] Roth (1964); Shatzmiller (1990); Mundill (2010); Sapir Abulafia (2011).

Rights and Regulation of Jews

To sum up, the freedom of mobility allowed to the Jews within the Muslim caliphates was in striking contrast with the situation of the Jews in politically fragmented Europe, where migration often started with a single Jewish individual or family asking the local ruler or bishop to reside in a given location or with a king or prince inviting one or more Jewish households to settle in his country or region. Like the migrations of other foreign craftsmen, traders, and moneylenders (Venetian and Genoese traders, Tuscan bankers, Flemish merchants), the migrations of the Jews to England, France, Germany, the Iberian Peninsula, and Italy, were regulated through special charters or privileges issued by kings, bishops, and local rulers.

These early medieval charters established no restrictions or prohibitions on the type of occupations in which Jews could engage. Almost all of them enabled Jews to settle in a town (or country), acquire real estate and land, freely move within the country's geographical boundaries, and trade in goods as they wished. As documented by Toch, the charters of the ninth to twelfth century, litigation cases from the responsa literature, and formularies[99] of Hebrew deeds all indicate that the Jews in southern and east-central France, Germany, Italy, and the Iberian Peninsula owned, transferred, and mortgaged landholdings. Land ownership did not imply that the Jews were farmers: their lands, more often vineyards than fields, were worked by non-Jewish tenants and agricultural laborers.[100]

Standards of Living

Just as they did in the Iberian Peninsula under Muslim rule, Jews achieved high standards of living in all of the other European countries in which they settled. Jewish communities paid taxes of 15,000 solidi in Saragossa, 10,000 in Catalayud, and 5,000 in Valencia, where the community was more recently established.[101] In England between 1239 and 1260, the Jews contributed roughly one-sixth to one-fifth of the crown revenues, despite representing just 0.01 percent of the population.[102] A partial list of imperial revenue in Germany, dating from 1241, documents that in twenty-five Jewish communities, the Jews paid 857 marks, amounting to 12 percent of the entire imperial tax revenue for the year and 20 percent of the total raised in the German cities.[103]

[99] A formulary is a medieval collection of models for the execution of documents (*acta*), public or private.
[100] Soloveitchik (2003); Toch (2005, 2008, 2010, 2011, 2012).
[101] Baron (1952, vol. 10, pp. 128–33).
[102] Elman (1937, p. 146).
[103] H. Ben-Sasson et al. (2007).

Narrative evidence of the high standards of living of the Jews in medieval Europe is given in the chronicle of the monk Rigord (*Gesta Philippi Augusti*), written in 1186, which describes the events leading to the expulsion of the Jews from France. In one passage, Rigord notes:[104]

> At this time [1180–81] a great multitude of Jews had been dwelling in France for a long time past, for they had flocked thither from divers parts of the world, because peace abode among the French, and liberality; for the Jews had heard how the kings of the French were prompt to act against their enemies, and were very merciful toward their subjects. And therefore their elders and men wise in the law of Moses, who were called by the Jews didascali [teachers], made resolve to come to Paris. When they had made a long sojourn there, they grew so rich that they claimed as their own almost half of the whole city, and had Christians in their houses as menservants and maidservants.

Migration to and within Europe: Push or Pull?

The Jews arrived in England, France, Germany, the Iberian Peninsula, and Italy from different places, at different times, and under different circumstances. Despite these differences, the Jewish communities they formed in early medieval Europe shared certain characteristics.

Like the migrations of the Jews within the Muslim caliphates during the ninth, tenth, and eleventh centuries, the Jewish Diaspora to and within Europe from 850 to 1250 was mainly a voluntary process set in motion by highly literate and skilled individuals in search of business opportunities. Jewish migrants were not farmers when they left their countries of origin, and they did not become farmers once settled in their new locations in Europe. They were skilled craftsmen, shopkeepers, local merchants, long-distance traders, coin minters, moneylenders, physicians, and scholars, who voluntarily moved to take advantage of the opportunities offered by expanding urbanization and the growth of a commercial economy. The Jews from Muslim Egypt and the Maghreb were by no means "pushed" toward the Iberian Peninsula and Sicily. Similarly, the Jews who arrived from the Byzantine Empire to southern Italy, and those who migrated within the countries of Europe, were in search of business opportunities. As a highly literate and skilled group of craftsmen, shopkeepers, merchants, traders, minters, money changers, physicians, and scholars, they were "pulled" toward the lucrative business opportunities offered by the rise of the urban and commercial economy in these regions.

Equally motivated by economic incentives were the European rulers who, beginning in the ninth century, invited the Jews to settle in their

[104] Marcus (1938, pp. 24–27).

lands. Bishops, kings, and local rulers were eager to attract the human capital and skills of the Jews in order to foster the economic growth and political power of their towns and countries and to earn the revenues from the taxes they imposed on them.

The outcome of this mutual economic attraction—the Jews toward the blossoming European urban economies, European rulers toward the highly literate and skilled Jews—was that in England, France, Germany, the Iberian Peninsula, and Italy, Jews held prominent positions in highly technical specialized branches, such as dyeing, silk weaving, and tanning. Many were craftsmen (smiths, bookbinders, sculptors, armorers, stone engravers, makers of scientific instruments, tailors, goldsmiths, glaziers, grinders); others were local and long-distance traders, moneylenders, tax collectors, court bankers, royal treasurers, vintners, coiners, spice importers, scholars, scribes, physicians, and booksellers.[105]

The fact that from the second half of the tenth century onward, commerce was the primary mainstay for French and German Jewry was summarized by Gershom ben Judah (Light of the Exile) of Mainz, the foremost Ashkenazi religious authority of his time (c. 960–1028) when he wrote, "[The Jews'] livelihood depends on their commerce/merchandise."[106] Within a politically fragmented Europe, the Jews created a trading and communication network that crossed the rival kingdoms.

MIGRATION OF THE JEWISH RELIGIOUS CENTER

Between 900 and 1200, the three main economic centers of Jewish life also became the three leading centers of Judaism. The migration of the center of Jewish life and Jewish wealth toward the Iberian Peninsula and then western Europe also moved the centers of Jewish learning. Although the academies in Mesopotamia led by the Geonim maintained their leadership for a long time, the academies in the Iberian Peninsula on the one hand and France and Germany on the other grew in prominence, gradually separating from the centers of learning in Mesopotamia. The rabbis and scholars in Europe were facing a completely different political, economic, and religious environment, which required different answers to the issues and questions regarding the daily lives of Jewish communities living in, say, Córdoba or Florence, London or Mainz, Narbonne or

---

[105]Baron (1952, vol. 4, chap. 22); Roth (1964; 1966a, p. 29; 1966b, pp. 102–12); Blumenkranz (1966, pp. 169–71); Kestenberg-Gladstein (1966, pp. 314–15); Scheiber (1966, p. 310); Schwarzfuchs (1966a, pp. 129–34; 1966b, pp. 151, 159); Toch (2005, 2011, 2012).
[106]Toch (2005, p. 558).

Prague. Once the center of Jewish wealth had moved to the West, so did the center of Jewish scholarship and learning.[107]

Jews shared in the lively intellectual life that characterized the Iberian Peninsula under Muslim rule. The founding of an academy in Córdoba in 929 created a gradual separation between the large Jewish community in Mesopotamia and Persia and the smaller but prominent Jewish population in the Iberian Peninsula.

This period of spectacular intellectual fervor culminated with the contribution of Rabbi Moses ben Maimon (called Maimonides or the Rambam), one of the greatest figures in Judaism.[108] Maimonides was born in 1138 in Córdoba, where his father was a *dayyan* (judge) and renowned scholar. As a result of the fall of Córdoba to the Almohads (a Berber dynasty), the family had to leave Córdoba. For eight or nine years, they wandered from place to place in the Iberian Peninsula (and possibly Provence) before settling, in 1160, in Fez in Morocco.

During this period, Maimonides acquired his vast and varied learning and began his literary work. In 1158 he started the draft of the *Sirāj*, his important commentary on the Mishna, as well as a short treatise on the Jewish calendar and another on logic. He completed the notes for a commentary on a number of tractates of the Babylonian Talmud and a work whose aim was to extract the halakha from the Talmud of the Land of Israel. While working on his commentary on the Mishna, the Rambam continued his general studies, particularly medicine. In his medical works, he frequently refers to the knowledge and experience he gained among the Muslims in North Africa.

In 1165, Maimonides's family left Fez and settled for a few months in Akko (Acre). From there they visited Jerusalem and a few other places before sailing for Egypt. After a short stay in Alexandria, they moved to Cairo, taking up residence in Fustat, the Old City of Cairo. With the financial support of his brother David, who dealt in precious stones, Maimonides was able for about eight years to devote himself entirely to preparing his writings for publication and to his work as both religious and lay leader of the community. His commentary to the Mishna was completed in 1168.

The following year, Maimonides suffered a crushing blow. His brother David drowned in the Indian Ocean while on a business trip, leaving a wife and two children. With him was lost not only the family fortune but also money belonging to others (see the epigraph at the beginning of this chapter). Opting for the medical profession, Maimonides became a court

---

[107] Baron (1952, vol. 4, chaps. 20 and 22); Kanarfogel (1992); Toch (2005, 2012); Ashtor et al. (2007); H. Ben-Sasson et al. (2007); Blumenkranz et al (2007).

[108] See Stroumsa (2009) for an overview of the life and contributions of Maimonides.

physician to the vizier of the sultan Saladin and, circa 1171, the head (*nagid*) of the Egyptian Jewish community.

It was during these years—when he was busy with his medical practice and the affairs of the Jewish community in Egypt, writing his extensive correspondence and responsa to every part of the Jewish world (apart from the Franco-German area)—that Maimonides wrote the two monumental works upon which his fame chiefly rests, the *Mishneh Torah* (compiled in 1180) and the *Guide* (compiled sometime between 1185 and 1190).[109] His literary work came almost to an end, but he continued to correspond with the scholars of Provence.

Maimonides died on December 13, 1204. Public mourning was ordained throughout the Jewish world. In Fustat, mourning was ordained for three days; in Jerusalem, a public fast was ordered. Maimonides's remains were taken to Tiberias, in the Galilee, where his grave is still an object of pilgrimage.

The influence of Maimonides on the future development of Judaism is enormous. He wrote works in Hebrew, Arabic, and Judeo-Arabic. In the fourteen-volume *Mishneh Torah*, he codified the immense body of Jewish law. The document was written for the believing Jew untroubled by the apparent contradictions between revealed law and contemporary philosophy. Its aim was to tell such a person how he should conduct himself in his desire to live according to the law. As its name conveys, the *Guide* was designed for people whose faith had been weakened by contemporary philosophical doctrines or other religions. Its aim was to explain why Jews should adhere to traditional Judaism. Both the *Mishneh Torah* and the *Guide* left a profound and long-lasting legacy within and also outside Judaism, although Maimonides's attempt to place Judaism on a rational Aristotelian basis was unsuccessful. The religious and intellectual tradition of Maimonides became the backbone of the cultural and religious milieu of the Sephardi Jewish communities.

In Christian Europe, numerous Jewish communities in England, France, Germany, and Italy blossomed intellectually.[110] Universal primary education—provided by private tutors or by schools funded and organized by the local community—was a distinctive feature of the Jews in comparison with the rest of the population, as this quote by a student of the French scholastic philosopher and theologian Peter Abelard (early twelfth century) nicely illustrates:[111]

---

[109] This sentence in one of Maimonides's letters, "Then I go forth to attend to my patients, and write prescriptions and directions for their various ailments," shows the importance of literacy also in the medical profession at this time.

[110] Agus (1965); Kanarfogel (1992); Limor (1993); Limor and Raz-Krakotzkin (1993).

[111] Kanarfogel (1992, p. 16).

If the Christians educate their sons, they do so not for God, but for gain, in order that the one brother, if he be a cleric, may help his father and mother and his other brothers. . . . But the Jews, out of zeal for God and love of the law, put as many sons as they have to letters, that each may understand God's law.

A Jew, however poor, if he had ten sons would put them all to letters, not for gain, as the Christians do, but for the understanding of God's law—and not only his sons, but his daughters.

After acquiring literacy and knowledge of the Torah, a number of Jews continued their education with the study of the Talmud and other religious commentaries in the houses of eminent scholars or in the academies. European Jewry's most important intellectual movement began to thrive when Rabbenu Gershom ben Judah (960–1028) founded an academy in Mainz that attracted Jews from all over Europe. Study of the Talmud flourished, and by the twelfth century the German academies in Mainz and Worms overshadowed those in Mesopotamia.

One of the most famous students attending the academies of Mainz and Worms was Solomon ben Isaac, universally known as Rashi.[112] Rashi was born in 1040 in Troyes, the capital of Champagne, the region that hosted the annual fairs and attracted merchants from many countries. In this economic milieu, Rashi, the son of a Jewish scholar, learned about different currency standards, banking, trade, engraving, the weaving of figures into material, the embroidering of silk with gold, agriculture, and husbandry.

After his initial education in Troyes, he went to study in the great German academies. He returned to Troyes circa 1065 but remained in touch with his teachers in Germany. About 1070, he founded a school in Troyes that attracted many students. Thanks to his intellectual eminence and influence, the academies in Troyes and then of northern France soon overshadowed those in Germany.

Rashi's three daughters married prominent scholars and gave birth to equally eminent scholars and rabbis. Jochebed married Rabbi Meir b. Samuel, who attended the Mainz academy. All four of their sons became famous scholars, members of the outstanding group of French scholars of the following generation who founded the school of the Tosafists. Another daughter, Miriam, married Judah b. Nathan, whose commentary is included in all editions of the Talmud. They had a learned son, Yom Tov, and a daughter, from whom Dulcea, the wife of Rabbi Eleazar of Worms, was descended.

The intellectual legacy of Rashi rests especially on his commentaries, which cover most, if not all, the books of the Bible. These commentaries,

---

[112] Information on the life and intellectual contribution of Rashi comes from Rothkoff et al. (2007).

particularly those on the Pentateuch, enjoyed an enormous circulation. More than 200 commentaries were written on his Pentateuch commentary, some by distinguished halakhists, such as Joseph Caro. The study of Rashi's commentary spread to such an extent that he was accorded the title of *Parshandata* ("the expounder of the law," "the commentator par excellence").

Christian scholars were also influenced by Rashi's commentary. Their interest in his work grew in the fifteenth century; from the seventeenth century onward his commentary began to be translated. Rashi's commentary on the Pentateuch is the first Hebrew work known to have been printed (in 1475). Since that time, hardly an edition of the Hebrew Bible for Jewish use has appeared without his commentary.

Rashi's most important contribution was his commentary on the Babylonian Talmud, which was published with the first printed edition of the Talmud. Except for modern editions of a few tractates, no edition of the Talmud has appeared without it. Although it was not Rashi's main aim in his commentary on the Talmud to determine the halakha, practical halakhic rulings are scattered here and there. His commentary on the Talmud became the basis for all later literary activity in this field in France and Germany. His students and their students did not hesitate to query his comments, disagree with them, and suggest alternatives.

Rashi's intellectual eminence was such that shortly after his death in 1105, his responsa, teachings, communications, and practices were assembled in different collections. This literature, the greater part of which has survived, has acquired the title of "the school of Rashi." The leadership of Rashi, of his grandsons (especially Rabbenu Tam), and contemporary and later generations of the scholars known as the Tosafists laid the foundations for the Ashkenazi Jewish communities, which separated themselves, both economically and intellectually, from the large Jewish community in Mesopotamia, Persia, and North Africa. By refusing the teachings of Maimonides, they also grew distinct from the wealthy and prominent Jewish community in the Iberian Peninsula.[113] During the twelfth and thirteenth centuries, the rabbis and scholars that followed Rashi's and Rabbenu Tam's tradition established a dense web of communications among the Jewish communities of Austria, England, France, Germany, and Italy.[114]

---

[113] Grossman (1992, 1999); Kanarfogel (1992); Limor (1993); Limor and Raz-Krakotzkin (1993). In the mid-thirteenth century, the scholars in the French and German academies that followed Rashi's intellectual legacy declared a boycott and punishment of those who read Maimonides's works. This ruling was reversed by Ashkenazi rabbis only in the nineteenth century.

[114] Goldin (1996).

SUMMARY

Jewish migrations from the Byzantine Empire to southern Italy in the early Middle Ages set the foundations for the rise of European Jewry. From Egypt and the Maghreb, Jews migrated to the Iberian Peninsula and, later, to Sicily and southern Italy. From southern Europe, some of them or their descendants likely found their way to France and, later, from France to Germany and England. These migrations to and within Europe established a permanent connection among the Jewish communities of the Diaspora.

Interestingly, studies by biologists and genetic experts show that contemporary Jewish populations show a closer genetic link to Jews from far away locations than to their neighboring non-Jewish populations.[115] The Ashkenazi Jews of eastern Europe, for example, are genetically closer to Jews from the Middle East, the Mediterranean basin, and North Africa, as well as to other non-Jewish Middle Eastern populations, than to non-Jewish populations in eastern Europe. This suggests that most European Jews migrated from the same original locations.

Why did the Jews in Europe not settle in a single city or a small number of cities within one country? Why were they scattered as small communities in myriad cities and towns? Was this pattern a result of restrictions or choice? We argue that the small size of the hundreds of Jewish communities in medieval Europe had to do with the Jews' voluntary specialization in the highest-skilled urban occupations, such as crafts, trade, money changing, moneylending, and medicine. In each location, the demand for these occupations, as well as the state of the local economy, limited the number of individuals who could enter and profitably earn from these highly skilled and lucrative occupations. Jews themselves could and did prevent fellow Jews from settling in the same location and competing with them. These two factors—the demand for skilled occupations and the state of the local economy—enhanced Jewish mobility and the need to migrate in search of locations that offered the possibility of profitably engaging in crafts and trade and, later, in the highest-skilled and most profitable occupation: moneylending.

[115]There is a large body of literature on this topic, including Bonné-Tamir et al. (1978); Karlin, Kennet, and Bonné-Tamir (1979); Bonné-Tamir, Zoossman-Diskin, and Ticher (1992); Bonné-Tamir and Adam (1992); Ritte et al. (1993a, 1993b); Hammer et al. (2000).

CHAPTER 8

Segregation or Choice?

FROM MERCHANTS TO MONEYLENDERS, 1000–1500

> Money lent on interest is profitable, because the pledge
> remains in the hand of the creditor, and the principal increases
> without effort or expense.
> —*Rabbi Joseph b. Samuel Tov Elem Bonfils, c. 1040*

> Today [Jewish] people usually lend money on interest to Gen-
> tiles . . . because we have to pay taxes to the king and princes
> and everything serves to sustain ourselves.
> —*Rabbenu Tam, c. 1160*

> His occupation is to lend against interest, and this is the main
> occupation of Jews that live in these [German] lands.
> —*Rabbi Joseph Colon, c. 1450*

CIRCA 1000, THE MAIN OCCUPATIONS OF THE LARGE JEWISH COMMU-
nity in the Iberian Peninsula and the comparatively smaller Jewish communities in France, Germany, and southern Italy were shopkeeping, local
trade, long-distance commerce, crafts, and medicine. As merchants, shopkeepers, traders, and skilled artisans, European Jews were often involved
in credit transactions, because in medieval times, sellers frequently sold
their goods or services by extending credit to buyers. Specialization in
moneylending was not yet a distinctive mark of European Jewry.[1]

Circa 1100, lending money at interest was *the* occupation par excel-
lence of the Jews in England, a very important occupation of French
Jews, and one of many professions of the Jews in Germany, the Iberian
Peninsula, and southern Italy. By 1300, almost all Jews in France, Ger-
many, and northern and central Italy were engaged in moneylending.[2] The
Rothschild banking dynasty, founded in the second half of the eighteenth

[1] Toch (2000b, 2005, 2012).
[2] Baron (1952, vol. 4, chaps. 20 and 22); J. Katz (1961, chap. 3); Toch (2005, 2008).

century by the German banker Mayer Amschel Rothschild, can be viewed as the heir of the Jewish moneylenders who extended credit in hundreds of villages and urban centers in medieval Europe.

Why did the words "Jew" and "moneylending" become almost synonymous in medieval Europe? Was the entry and further specialization into moneylending the outcome of economic restrictions, legal prohibitions, and discrimination? Or did the Jews voluntarily enter and specialize in moneylending and, later, banking and finance because they had skills and assets that gave them a comparative advantage in these professions? If the latter is the case, which skills and assets were needed to become a successful moneylender in medieval Europe? To answer these questions and explain some key features of the economic history of the Jewish people from 1000 to 1500, we first illustrate how money and credit markets functioned in medieval Europe, which increasingly became the new economic and intellectual center of world Jewry during this period, as described in chapter 7.

The Economics of Money and Credit in Medieval Europe

Although they lacked some of the sophisticated tools of the twenty-first century, money and credit markets in the Middle Ages shared many features with contemporary financial markets.[3] Consider a twelfth- or thirteenth-century European peasant who did not have enough money to feed his family or pay his taxes before he harvested his crops, or who wanted to buy an ox or seeds for the next year. If he worked as a tenant for a landlord or the local monastery, he could ask his employer to provide him with food or lend him money, which he would repay after the harvest. Shopkeepers and merchants could also sell their goods to him on credit. Better-off friends or fellow peasants could also help the peasant who was short of cash. Each of these transactions involved an implicit or explicit loan.

If none of these options was viable, the peasant could turn to a professional Christian or Jewish moneylender in the nearby town if there was one.[4] Similarly, urban workers, artisans, and merchants temporarily short of cash could borrow money from fellow workers, craftsmen, and merchants by pledging their equipment or houses as collateral. Alternatively, they could borrow funds from local moneylenders. These moneylenders

---

[3] See N. Ferguson (2008) for a history of financial markets from the second millennium BCE to today, in particular for the similarities and differences between financial markets in medieval Europe and today.

[4] Duby (1968); Cipolla (1976); Fossier (1988); Spufford (1988).

could settle in a given location through a permit (license) that regulated the annual interest rate ceiling the moneylender could charge (from 8 percent to 133 percent, depending on the location and period); the type of collateral he could accept as guarantee for the loan (land, pawn, guarantor, written guarantee); the rules regarding the repayment of the loan; and the consequences if the borrower failed to pay his debt, partly or in full (see below for details).[5]

Until the late fifteenth century, there were no other financial institutions to which a peasant or an urban dweller could turn for a loan. Banks accepting deposits from and granting loans to the local population did not exist until the early modern period. Banks such as the famous Florentine houses of the Bardi and Peruzzi in the fourteenth century or the Medici bank in the fifteenth century financed international trade and lent to European monarchs and popes.[6]

Christian loan banks (called *montes pietatis*, *monti di pietà*, or *mons de pietè*) were established in many Italian, and later, other European towns under pressure from the Franciscan monks beginning in the late fifteenth century; the monks' goal was to eradicate what they considered the nefarious practice of charging usurious (exorbitant) interest rates, which had dire consequences especially for the poor. The institutions accepted deposits from the local population and extended loans guaranteed with a pawn; they typically charged 5 percent a year in interest. Rural credit cooperatives appeared in Europe only in the nineteenth century.[7]

The need for money and credit did not arise only in the local community. The growth of money and credit markets in early medieval Europe was also fueled by the increasing demand for money and loans concomitant with the revival of trade and commerce during the so-called Commercial Revolution of the tenth through thirteenth centuries. Many credit transactions occurred among long-distance traders, who met at annual fairs in many locations in medieval Europe. On these occasions, traders settled their balances by carefully recording their purchases, sales, credits, and debts in their account books. They relied on loans from one year to the next and were required to perform complex calculations of interest rates and exchange rates among coins minted in different countries. The need to move large sums of money over space and time to settle the business transactions at the annual fairs, coupled with the desire to avoid carrying large quantities of coins, led to the development of sophisticated

[5] De Roover (1948); Lopez (1976); Braudel (1982).
[6] De Roover (1948, 1966); Spufford (1988); Goldthwaite (1995); Mueller (1997).
[7] See Pullan (1971) and Mueller (1972) for the historical developments of *monti di pietà*, and Guinnane (2001) for the rise of rural credit cooperatives in modern Europe.

financial tools, such as the bill of exchange, that contributed to the further development of financial markets in medieval and early modern Europe.[8]

At the heart of the functioning of money and credit markets was the interest rate. From this point of view, medieval artisans, shopkeepers, traders, and professional moneylenders performed very similar economic activities. Artisans, shopkeepers, and merchants selling on credit implicitly or explicitly charged an interest payment that took into account their time preferences, the value of the goods they sold over time (selling goods today and receiving immediate payment is worth more than selling goods today and receiving the payment in the future), and the risk that the buyer would be unable to repay the loan, partly or in full.[9] Shopkeepers and merchants extended loans even when no exchange of goods was involved, charging interest just as they did when they sold merchandise on credit. Similarly, professional moneylenders charged interest rates that incorporated their time preferences, the rate of return on alternative investments, the risk that the borrower would be unable to repay his loan partly or in full, and the resale value of the pawn posted as collateral for the loan that the moneylender would sell in the case of the borrower's default.

Interest rates were affected by the demand and supply of funds. As the famous scholar Rabbi Abraham b. Mordecai Farissol explained during a disputation attended by many prominent people at the court of Duke Ercole I d'Este in Ferrara, Italy, circa 1480, "One need not ponder over the interest rates charged, because they are agreed upon by the communities who require money from the Jews. They fluctuate according . . . to the availability or scarcity of silver and gold and the demand for it."[10]

To sum up, money and credit markets partly fueled the growth of economic activities in medieval Europe. The rise of towns and cities, the

[8] De Roover (1948, 1966); Cipolla (1976); Lopez (1976); Braudel (1982); Spufford (1988); Sargent and Velde (2002); Munro (2003). The bill of exchange or *lettre de change* was an informal letter by which one merchant ordered his agent-banker in some other city to make payment on his behalf to a merchant in that distant city. Basically unchanged from the fourteenth to the eighteenth century, the bill of exchange was a dual-functioning international banking instrument that involved a loan of funds in one city and the transfer or remittance of funds from that city to a city in some foreign country. The funds lent through this bill were to be repaid at some specified later date in the foreign city in the foreign currency of that city. A loan made in country A's domestic currency and repaid in country B's currency obviated the need to ship specie and bullion between countries. The bill of exchange, as a credit and transfer instrument, required four parties—two principals and two agents—in two cities, using two different currencies.

[9] The time preference expresses the fact that one dollar today is worth more than one dollar at a later point because the borrower has immediate access to the funds. The interest rate also incorporates the real rate of return on an investment, which economists call the marginal product of capital.

[10] Ruderman (1981); Stein (2007).

expansion of crafts, and the revival of trade that swept southern and western Europe from roughly 950 to 1350 were all made possible by the expansion of minting and coinage and the granting of loans to households and businesses. Credit markets also helped peasants and urban dwellers in times of economic hardship. The size and condition of the local economy, as well as fluctuations caused by annual fairs, religious festivals, pilgrimage, wars, epidemics, or famines, all affected the demand and supply of money and credit and, hence, the demand for the services of professional moneylenders. Like today, money and credit markets were fragile in medieval times, as the failures and bankruptcies of moneylenders and banking houses show.[11]

Reading, Writing, and Computing

Buying and selling goods on the spot does not require a written contract, because the economic transaction between the buyer and the seller ends at the moment the good is exchanged for cash. In contrast, selling on credit typically requires recording the transaction in a written document, which in the Middle Ages would have been the shopkeeper's account books. A written document was the best way of proving that the buyer had borrowed money on particular terms from the seller. In this respect, moneylenders were no different than craftsmen, shopkeepers, local merchants, and long-distance traders selling on credit. Moneylending was just a sophisticated version of trade and selling on credit.

A moneylender would carefully record his loans in account books by listing the name of the borrower, the amount of the loan, the type of collateral, the interest rate, and any other relevant information. If required by local customs or laws, he would provide the borrower with a written note as proof of the loan and the collateral involved.

To extend credit, a lender had to be able to read and to know the local laws, so that in the case of a dispute with the borrower, he would be able to apply to the local court to have the terms of the loan contract enforced. Loan contracts and account books were critical pieces of evidence. A medieval moneylender had to be able to estimate the value of collateral, so that in the case of default of the borrower, he could recover the full value of the money lent.

---

[11] Hunt (1994); Goldthwaite (1995); Mueller (1997); Tirole (2011). One of the most famous examples was the banking houses of the Florentine Bardi and Peruzzi families, the major financiers of the English Crown during the early and mid-fourteenth century. When King Edward III defaulted on his debts in 1340–43, the Bardi and Peruzzi banking houses almost went bankrupt.

Like merchants and traders, moneylenders were required to perform complicated calculations. Money markets in medieval Europe were extremely complicated. The circulation of coins of different types of metals (gold, silver, and copper) and different currencies and frequent episodes of government debasements that changed the metallic content (and thus the value) of the coins in circulation made the computation of interest rates and exchange rates challenging.[12] (The development of algebra in medieval Europe by the Pisan merchant and mathematician Leonardo Fibonacci in the late twelfth and early thirteenth centuries arose from the mathematical and computational problems encountered by medieval merchants and traders in their daily business transactions.) Just as today, highly skilled individuals were engaged in financial intermediation.[13]

Asymmetric Information, Networking, and Arbitrage

Asymmetric information—the situation in which one party in an economic transaction has more information than the other—was a salient feature of medieval money and credit markets, as it is today. Minters and money changers had more information regarding the metallic content and value of the coins they minted and exchanged than anybody else. Borrowers had better information than lenders regarding their ability of repaying their debts or the use they made of the funds they borrowed. At the same time, lenders might have more information than the rest of the population on money and credit markets both locally and elsewhere. In fact, information on market conditions in the local economy and in other locations was not easily available to anyone and was costly to acquire. In the language of economics, all these contingencies are described as situations of asymmetric information, in which the party that has more information can exploit this advantage.[14]

In the presence of asymmetric information, sophisticated traders and moneylenders with networks and information on market conditions

---

[12] See, among others, Cipolla (1982); Lane and Mueller (1985); Spufford (1988); Mueller (1997); Sargent and Velde (2002).

[13] See Philippon and Reshef (2009) for a recent study on the education and skill level of individuals working in the financial sector in the twentieth-century United States. They show that conditional on skills, the earnings in finance are higher and very cyclical.

[14] See Stiglitz (2002) for a survey of the literature on asymmetric information. Economists distinguish between adverse selection (a situation in which one party has more information than the other regarding the characteristics that are the object of the economic transaction) and moral hazard (a situation in which one party has more information than the other regarding the actions that are the object of the economic transaction). In some instances (e.g., the market for lemons), asymmetric information may lead markets to perform inefficiently or even cease to exist if the uninformed party is afraid of being cheated by the informed party and therefore refuses to take part in the economic transaction.

across locations, access to capital, and the ability to swiftly pool wealth if necessary and move it quickly from one place to another could reap huge profits. In the language of economics, networking abilities in the presence of asymmetric information facilitate arbitrage across locations in which market conditions may differ (higher demand for credit in one location, because of, say, famine or the annual fair, for example), and enabled traders and moneylenders to earn enormous profits.[15]

Because full-fledged banks accepting deposits and extending loans did not exist in early medieval times, moneylenders had to be able to raise capital or pool funds across different locations. A medieval moneylender typically needed to remain in a given location in order to be able to assess the customers' creditworthiness and recover his loans. If he did not have enough capital to meet local demand for credit, he would likely form business partnerships with either local merchants or moneylenders who had capital to invest or with moneylenders in other locations. Networking was also vital to acquire contacts and information about market conditions across different locations and forecast changes in economic and political scenarios.

To form business partnerships, moneylenders needed to draft written contracts detailing the terms of the business partnership (the amount of capital each partner would contribute, how losses and profits would be shared). To send and receive information in order to profit from arbitrage opportunities, moneylenders sent and received letters from business partners.

Government Finance

Medieval monarchs were sometimes short of cash, for both ordinary expenditures, such as the lavish expenses of their splendid royal courts, and extraordinary expenses, such as the provision of food to their subjects during famines or plagues. They also often waged wars, which they needed to finance.[16]

When tax revenues (or other sources of revenues, such as the income from royal estates) were not enough to fund these expenses, where would medieval kings, prices, dukes, or town governments turn to get financing? One option was to borrow money from wealthy citizens or professional

---

[15] Some of the letters found in the documents of the Cairo Geniza clearly show the importance of networking abilities and the arbitrage opportunities for the Jewish merchants involved in the Mediterranean, the Red Sea, and the Indian Ocean trade in the tenth, eleventh, and twelfth centuries (see chapter 6).

[16] See N. Ferguson (2008) and Reinhart and Rogoff (2009) for historical evidence on government defaults and financial crises in the past eight centuries.

moneylenders and, later, banking houses. English monarchs, for example, borrowed large sums of money from Jewish moneylenders during the twelfth and the thirteenth centuries and from Florentine bankers during the first half of the fourteenth century. The Medici bank financed European monarchs during the fifteenth century.[17]

Another option was to force citizens to lend money—that is, to impose "forced loans." Governments usually paid interest on and repaid such loans, distinguishing forced loans from taxation. By consolidating these forced loans into publicly funded debts, several Italian city states during the fourteenth and fifteenth centuries, and later other European states, issued government bonds that citizens could buy, sell, and bequeath. Annual interest rates of 5–10 percent were typically paid on these bonds.[18]

Secular authorities were not the only ones in search of financing. Religious powers—including the Papal State—also participated in medieval credit markets, as both lenders and borrowers. To build a church, a medieval bishop could turn to the local Jewish moneylender for a loan. Some European monasteries, abbeys, churches, and cathedrals were partly financed in this way. One of the most famous cases is the story of the wealthiest and most prominent Jewish moneylender of his time, Aaron of Lincoln (1123–86). His recorded transactions extended over a great part of England, and his clients included bishops, earls, and barons. Aaron advanced money to the English Crown on the security of future national revenues; he also lent to various ecclesiastical foundations, such as the Monastery of St. Alban, to finance their ambitious building programs. Nine Cistercian abbeys owed him 6,400 marks for the acquisition of properties to which he held mortgages.[19]

Contract-Enforcement Institutions

The promulgation of law codes, statutes, and edicts by monarchs, governments, and the Church provided the legal framework within which money and credit markets functioned in medieval Europe. The existence of courts, judges, notaries, and arbitrators, who helped enforce these laws, increased the probability of well-functioning credit markets and profitable moneylending.[20]

---

[17] De Roover (1948; 1966); Barzel (1992).

[18] Molho (1971, 1995); Kirshner (1977, 1993); Mueller (1997); Boone, Davids, and Janssens (2003); Pezzolo (2007).

[19] Roth (1964).

[20] De Roover (1948); Spufford (1988).

Regulations through legal codes and contract-enforcement covered a variety of details and contingencies pertaining to credit transactions. In particular, both secular and religious authorities heavily regulated interest rates. Lending per se was never prohibited. Beginning at the end of the twelfth century, the Church enforced usury bans prohibiting Christians and Jews from charging interest on consumption loans. The Church recognized, however, that trade and other business activities required credit in order to run smoothly. The Scholastic doctrine on usury, on which the Church's policy was based, permitted the charging of interest on loans to merchants advanced for investment purposes. In these cases the risk involved in the transaction justified the charging of the interest to compensate the lender for the risk that he might not recover his loan.[21]

Despite the ban on consumption loans, Christians in medieval Europe both lent and borrowed at interest for consumption purposes, both when usury bans were not strictly enforced (from the tenth to the twelfth century and during the fifteenth century) and when they were enforced (during the thirteenth and fourteenth centuries). The fact that Christians circumvented the Church's ban on lending is indicated by medieval wills in which the deceased donated money to the Church or to the poor as a way of gaining forgiveness for having committed the sin of lending at interest. To avoid the Church's sanctions, lenders sometimes disguised loans in ingenious ways. A peasant would, for example, perform a fictitious sale of his plot of land to another farmer or to a wealthy artisan, use the cash from the sale for consumption, and then buy back the same piece of land from the same person at a higher price—the price difference representing the interest rate on the disguised loan.

Jewish Prominence in Moneylending: Hypotheses

Scholars have put forth various hypotheses to explain the prominence of European Jews in moneylending. All but one of these arguments center on the idea that Jews in Europe became gradually more discriminated against and persecuted and, hence, segregated into moneylending. We first present these hypotheses and assess whether they pass the test of the historical evidence. We then present our argument, based on the economic theory outlined in chapter 6, to explain why Jews became specialized in moneylending in medieval Europe.

---

[21]Noonan (1957); Todeschini (1989, 2008); Glaeser and Scheinkman (1998); Reed and Bekar (2003).

Guilds and Usury Bans

The most popular view, first put forward by historian Cecil Roth, maintains that Jews in medieval Europe became segregated in moneylending because craft and merchant guilds in many European towns and cities during the Middle Ages, with their exclusive membership requirements, pushed the Jews out of many urban skilled occupations in which they had been previously engaged, leaving moneylending as the only available profession for them.[22] Complementing this argument, other scholars contend that restrictions on the economic activities of non-Jews excluded them from certain occupations, which Jews therefore performed. For example, the Islamic rule banning Muslims from lending money at interest paved the way for the Jews to become moneylenders in Muslim caliphates.[23] Similarly, usury bans on Christians sanctioned by the Church in medieval Europe left the profession open to Jews.[24]

Persecutions and Portable Human Capital

An alternative view outlined in detail in chapter 2 is that the Jews, like members of other persecuted religious or ethnic minorities, were often forced to leave and to migrate in search of a safer location where to settle and to earn their living. Hence, they preferred to invest in human rather than physical capital because human capital is portable and, therefore, cannot be expropriated. By investing in literacy and education, they ended up in occupations that require or benefit from literacy, such as moneylending and finance.[25]

From Wine Trade to Moneylending

The historian and halakha expert Haym Soloveitchik has recently argued that Jewish laws concerning wine are the missing link that can explain the movement of German Jewry into moneylending between the eleventh and the fourteenth centuries.[26] During the Middle Ages, wine was an important commodity in southern and central Europe, and even common people drank large quantities of it (in northern Europe, beer was the main beverage). Trade in wine represented a very profitable business

---

[22] Roth (1938, p. 228; 1960a, p. 229; 1964, pp. 2–3). See also H. Ben-Sasson (1976, p. 470).
[23] Baron (1952, vol. 4, p. 200).
[24] Schwarzfuchs (1966b, p. 151).
[25] Sombart ([1911] 1913); Brenner and Kiefer (1981); Slezkine (2004).
[26] Soloveitchik (1985, 2003). The main sources he studied are the Talmud and the works of the most prominent Jewish rabbis in medieval Europe.

opportunity. As wine production was subject to short-term fluctuations, it generated a large demand for credit from farmers who owned vineyards and produced wine.

Laws laid out in the Talmud forbade Jews from drinking or touching wine produced by Gentiles, even wine a Gentile had merely touched.[27] This prohibition caused three potential problems to Jews in medieval Europe. First, it made them buy and own vineyards so that they could produce their own wine. By the eleventh century, Jews in several countries in Europe employed Gentile agricultural laborers to work these vineyards.[28] Second, Jews who wanted to engage in the profitable trade of selling wine to Gentiles in Europe faced a dilemma: how could they engage in this lucrative business without violating the Talmudic laws? Third, how could the Jews accept payments from Gentiles in wine instead of cash? How could they accept vineyards as collateral without breaching the Talmudic laws regarding drinking or touching Gentile wine?

Prominent Jewish scholars and rabbis in France and Germany during the eleventh and twelfth centuries began addressing these issues. Law books written during the late eleventh century indicate that Jews began to trade in wine that had been touched by Gentiles. Initially, this trade was restricted to wine touched by a Gentile without the Jew's knowledge or consent, but later this restriction was softened.

The eminent scholar Rashi (1040–1105) argued that Gentiles could repay their debts to Jews with wine but forbade Jews from drinking or selling this wine. This ruling meant that debt payments in wine from Gentiles were worthless to Jewish lenders. To address this contradiction, Rashi stated in a subsequent ruling that Jews should sell the wine obtained as payment of loans made to Gentiles as soon as possible to prevent them from either losing or profiting from this trade. Nearly 100 years later, the rabbis in the main centers of Jewish life in Germany lifted almost all the restrictions regarding the use of Gentile wine as a mean of repaying loans, so that Jews could receive wine as collateral from Gentiles.

Soloveitchik contends that because of the Talmudic restrictions regarding drinking or touching Gentile wine, the Jews could engage in wine production and trade only through credit transactions with Gentiles. This "missing link," according to Soloveitchik, explains the voluntary occupational transition of Jews into moneylending in Germany from the eleventh to the fourteenth century.

---

[27] This prohibition dated back to antiquity, when Gentiles offered few drops of wine to their gods. In Hebrew these drops are called *neshech*, the name of these Talmudic laws.

[28] Toch (2005, 2008, 2010).

THE DYNAMICS OF JEWISH MONEYLENDING IN MEDIEVAL EUROPE

Which of the three explanations for the Jews' specialization in money-lending passes the test of the historical evidence? To answer this question, one needs to understand the circumstances under which Jews became prominent in credit markets in the different countries of Europe.

Jewish moneylending in medieval Europe emerged in different periods and circumstances. European countries experienced urban growth and the revival of trade at different times. Fluctuations in the economy varied from country to country. Moreover, the availability of local Christian traders or moneylenders who could supply funds and grant loans determined whether the services of Jewish moneylenders were needed. It is, then, not surprising that Genoa, one of the most vibrant commercial economies in medieval Europe, with its wealthy overseas traders and bankers, never invited Jewish moneylenders to settle in the city.[29]

Jews specialized in moneylending almost from the beginning of their settlement in England after 1066. The next center of Jewish moneylending was northern France and the Rhineland; in the rest of Germany and central Europe, the specialization of Jews into moneylending was much more gradual. In central and northern Italy, the specialization of Jews into moneylending occurred much later, during the late fourteenth and fifteenth centuries. In southern Italy, as in the Iberian Peninsula, the Jews never specialized in moneylending; until their expulsions in the late fifteenth century, they engaged in a wide spectrum of occupations, including crafts, shopkeeping, trade, and medicine, as well as moneylending.[30]

England

Soon after their arrival in 1066 as a group of traders and moneylenders, Anglo Jews became specialized in moneylending, although some also remained engaged in trade. The earliest documents referring to Jewish involvement in moneylending and finance date to 1131 in the earliest records of the Exchequer, the Pipe Roll of the twenty-first year of Henry I's reign. The charter issued in 1190 by King Richard I (the Lionheart) to the Jews of England recognized moneylending as their main occupation (see chapter 7). This charter and the one issued in 1201 by King John confirmed the privileges promulgated by earlier English monarchs

---

[29] S. A. Epstein (1996).
[30] Parkes (1938); Abulafia (2000); Toch (2005, 2011); Sapir Abulafia (2011).

and highlighted the important role of the Jews as a group specialized in moneylending.[31]

The importance of Jewish moneylending for the revenues of the English Crown is demonstrated by the extent to which the monarchy protected the Jewish lenders' account books and the records of their business from the risk of being destroyed during episodes of violence or riots. In 1194, the *Capitula de Judaeis* were issued as a result of the destruction of the Hebrew deeds during the riots of 1193. Later, special centers were appointed for registering deeds of loans. From this, the Exchequer of the Jews ultimately came into being.[32]

The charters, the responsa, and court records show that the Jews in England made mortgage loans to landowners and provided smaller loans on the security of pledges to poor and middle-income households. Monasteries, abbeys, churches, and clergy featured among the clientele of the Jewish lenders. Anglo Jews also helped finance several undertakings of the monarchy, including the Crusades, as well as the building of cathedrals and abbeys.[33]

That the business was very lucrative is shown by the fact that when the most prominent moneylender, Aaron of Lincoln, died in 1186, he was probably the wealthiest person in England in liquid assets. His outstanding credits amounted to £15,000, the equivalent of three-fourths of royal income in a normal year. Moneylending earned high returns but also bore high risks. The high standards of living reached by the Jews through lending money at interest did not protect them from sudden outbreaks of violence.[34] Their profession and the wealth they accumulated may have paved the way for episodes of violence, such as the first recorded blood libel in Norwich in 1144,[35] the attack in Gloucester in 1168, the massacre of almost all Jews in Norwich in 1190, or the notorious massacre of York in 1190, when during a riot sparked by citizens who owed money to the

---

[31] Parkes (1938, p. 168); Baron (1952, vol. 4); Roth (1964); Fuss (1975). The first charter to the Jews of England was issued by Henry I in 1120 and was confirmed by Henry II in 1170. None of these earlier permits survive; their existence is known because later charters refer to, and mostly confirm, them.

[32] J. Jacobs (1892, 1893, 1898); Roth (1964). At the beginning of the thirteenth century, in both France and Spain it was ordered that every town should appoint one notary to record all Jewish debts.

[33] Roth (1964); Shatzmiller (1990); Mundill (2010).

[34] Baron (1952, vol. 4, chaps. 20 and 22); Roth (1964).

[35] Limor and Raz-Krakotzkin (1993). A "blood libel" is a false accusation or claim that religious minorities, almost always Jews, murder children to use their blood for religious rituals or during specific holidays. The Jews of Norwich were accused of ritual murder after the body of a boy was found with stab wounds. The boy, William, became a martyr, and crowds of pilgrims visited and brought wealth to the local church. Similar blood accusations were raised against the Jews in other locations in medieval Europe.

agent of Aaron of Lincoln, almost all 150 Jews of York killed themselves rather than face the mob.[36]

The history of medieval Anglo Jewry ended in 1290. In 1275, King Edward I issued the *Statutum de Judaismo*, which forbade Anglo Jews from lending money at interest. The most astonishing feature of the statute is that the king granted permission to the Jews to engage in trade and crafts and even to rent farms for a period not exceeding ten to fifteen years. Apparently, the Jews refused (or failed) to engage in farming, crafts, or trade. Acknowledging the failure of his policy, on July 18, 1290, the king decreed that all Jews should leave England before All Saints' Day of that year. Some scholars argued that there was no need for the decree of expulsion and that the community of a few thousand Jews residing in England preferred to leave the country and migrate to France, Germany, the Iberian Peninsula, and other locations rather than give up moneylending and become farmers or artisans.[37]

The Jewish moneylenders were replaced first by the Lombards, then by the Tuscan banking houses. This transition occurred during the late thirteenth century and first half of the fourteenth century, exactly at the time when the Church was strictly enforcing the usury ban on Christians. When in the early 1340s King Edward III defaulted on the huge loans he owed to the Tuscan banking houses of the Bardi and Peruzzi, it was an English merchant, William de la Pole, who emerged as the Crown's principal source of loans. Medieval England attracted a variety of other Christian moneylenders, who lent to the rich and the poor despite the Church's ban.[38]

The Lombards, the Tuscan banking houses, and William de la Pole had the four assets for being successful players in credit markets: capital, networking, literacy, and contract-enforcement institutions secured from the English Crown. As such, they became the main competitors of the Jews in the lucrative business of moneylending in medieval England.

---

[36] This is the account of the episode by a contemporary Jew, Rabbi Ephraim of Bonn (cited in Roth 1964, chap. 2): "Afterwards, in the year 4551 (1190) the Wanderers came upon the people of the Lord in the city of Evoric (York) in England, on the Great Sabbath and the season of the miracle was changed to disaster and punishment. All fled to the house of prayer. Here Rabbi Yom-Tob stood and slaughtered sixty souls, and others also slaughtered. . . . The number of those slain and burned was one hundred and fifty souls, men and women, all holy bodies. Their houses moreover they destroyed, and they despoiled their gold and silver and the splendid books which they had written in great number, precious as gold and as much fine gold, there being none like them for their beauty and splendor. These they brought to Cologne and to other places, where they sold them to the Jews."

[37] Elman (1937); Roth (1964); Singer (1964).

[38] See Shatzmiller (1990) and Barzel (1992) for a description of credit markets and moneylenders in competition with the Jews in medieval England.

France

The early medieval charters granted by the French monarchs to the Jews settling in France enabled them to engage in a wide variety of occupations (see chapter 7). In their capacity as traders, they entered the business of moneylending early, by selling on credit and advancing loans to customers.

Starting in the late tenth and early eleventh centuries, French Jews became increasingly specialized in lending money at interest. This transition accelerated during the early twelfth and thirteenth centuries, concomitant with the rise of the annual fairs in Champagne. The huge demand for credit that the fairs brought created a vast opportunity for wealthy Jewish traders and merchants to provide the much-needed credit and specialize in moneylending.[39]

The regulation of Jewish moneylending in France began at the end of the twelfth century, with treaties of agreement between the king and his barons and the Jewish lenders. Moneylending quickly became the most important occupation of French Jews. A canon at the Council of Poitiers in 1280 complained that nearly all the Jews in the diocese of Poitiers were moneylenders.[40]

The identification of French Jewry with moneylending coincided with the beginning of repeated episodes of expulsions that characterized their history during the fourteenth century. The earliest surviving charter is the one granted by Louis X in 1315, after the banishment of Jews from France in 1306. They were allowed to return for a period of twelve years and were promised that they would receive a year's notice in future expulsions. They were permitted to settle in any town that previously had a Jewish community. The next expulsion occurred in 1322, when Philip V died. His successor, Charles IV, expelled the Jews and replaced them with the Lombards as licensed moneylenders until they were also expelled in 1330.[41]

In 1360, the Jews were invited to resettle in France. At the time, during the Hundred Years' War, King John II of France was held prisoner in England. As ransom, he had to pay three million gold crowns. To help put together this enormous sum of money, Charles the Dauphin decided to recall the Jews and grant them a new charter for twenty years. On admission, each head of family had to pay fourteen gold florins for himself and his wife and one florin for each child or dependent. The charter permitted them to charge interest at four pence per pound per week (about 86 percent annually) on their loans. They could also acquire houses and land,

---

[39]Taitz (1994); Benbassa (1999); L. Glick (1999, chap. 9); Toch (2005).

[40]Parkes (1938, pp. 170–77, 344).

[41]Blumenkranz et al. (2007).

settle anywhere in France, and govern their communities according to their laws and with great internal autonomy. These charters granted Jews every possible protection, in return for which the Jews agreed to pass on a substantial portion of the wealth generated by their lending activities to the royal treasury.[42]

Although the charter of 1360 remained valid until the final expulsion in 1394, the Jews suffered greatly in the last decades of the fourteenth century, when many borrowers started refusing to pay back the money they owed Jewish moneylenders. As a result, the revenues the Crown was eagerly expecting to collect plummeted. The king ordered his officers to enforce payment of debts, but this policy failed. In 1394, he ordered the expulsion of the Jews, replacing them with an influx of Lombards.[43]

Germany, Austria, and Central and Eastern Europe

During the twelfth and thirteenth centuries, especially the latter, money-lending became the main occupation of German Jews. Local authorities (e.g., town governments, bishops, princes) issued the first charters; later the German emperors became involved directly in dealing with the Jews. In 1090, Emperor Henry IV gave similar charters to the Jews of Worms and Speyer. In 1157, the Holy Roman Emperor Frederick I gave a charter, based on Henry IV's privileges, canceling the previous charters granted by local authorities. This marked the beginning of a more centralized way of regulating Jewish settlement and economic activities in German lands.[44]

When moneylending became the main occupation of German Jews, their history became punctuated by repeated episodes of temporary expulsions from one location followed by their return and subsequent expulsions and readmission. Unlike elsewhere in western Europe, there was never a total expulsion of Jews from Germany, probably because of its political fragmentation. Most Jews did not leave the country but rather kept moving within Germany.[45]

For example, by the fourteenth century, the Jewish community in Cologne was one of the largest and most prosperous in Germany. But in 1349, concomitant with the spread of the Black Death, a mob attacked the Jewish quarter, set fire to synagogues (with the Jews inside), and burned Jewish property and debt bills. In 1372, the Jews were invited to resettle in Cologne, where they stayed for fifty years, until their expulsion in 1424. During this period, the Jews received a new charter. For the right to live in

[42] Parkes (1938); Benbassa (1999); Blumenkranz et al. (2007).
[43] Benbassa (1999); Blumenkranz et al. (2007).
[44] Toch (2005, 2008, 2012).
[45] H. Ben-Sasson et al. (2007).

the city, every Jew paid seventy marks, as well as a yearly tax. The Jews were allowed to rebuild their synagogues, to be judged in Jewish courts, and to engage in moneylending. The new community was much smaller (about thirty-four families) than the old one. In 1424, the city leaders decided not to renew the privileges. This decision meant that the Jews were expelled from Cologne. They were permitted to return to the city only during the eighteenth century.[46]

Between 1300 and 1350, Germany ceased to be a destination for Jewish immigration, becoming instead a source of emigration. A few Jews migrated to the Land of Israel, mainly for religious purposes. A number of emigrants from Germany went to Poland. The most important destination of Jews who left Germany was Italy. German Jews first relocated to towns such as Bassano, Cividale, Treviso, and Trieste in northeastern Italy. From the mid-thirteenth century, they appear in greater numbers, with some migrating as far as the Venetian colonies, such as the island of Crete. From the mid-fifteenth century, some Jews even settled in the Ottoman Empire. These Jewish migrants were rich moneylenders and finance experts.[47]

Similar developments occurred in the Jewish community in Austria. In 1244, Duke Frederick II of Austria nullified the imperial privileges of 1238, granting his own charter to the Jews living in his duchy. (The charter, which formed the basis for privileges given to Jews all over eastern Europe in the subsequent centuries, appears in the annex to this chapter.) The charter recognized that the primary occupation of the Jews in Austria was no longer local trade or long-distance commerce but moneylending. The Jews were dependent on the duke and his chamberlain. They were free to travel throughout the duchy and were exempt from municipal and local tolls. They could lend on anything brought to them (except bloody or wet clothes), without any question regarding its origin. Violent theft, the retraction of a pledge, or an attack on a Jew in his home were to be punished like an assault on the treasury. Jews could charge an annual interest rate of 173.333 percent on their loans (eight pence per talent or pound per week). A series of clauses that established provisions for the settlement of disputes about loans were written in a way that favored Jewish moneylenders.[48]

From 1250 onward, the Jews in Vienna became heavily engaged in moneylending, extending loans to both lower- and upper-class borrowers. At the onset of the plague of 1348, the Jewish community in Vienna was the largest in the Holy Roman Empire.[49]

[46] Parkes (1938); Berenbaum and Carlebach (2007).
[47] Toch (2005, 2008); Milano et al. (2007).
[48] Baron (1952, vol. 4, chap. 22).
[49] Bato, Adunka, and Lehman (2007).

The German Jews migrating to central and eastern Europe during the thirteenth and fourteenth centuries were already specialized in moneylending. At the same time, the backwardness of central and eastern Europe brought them more opportunities to engage in a wider spectrum of urban high-skill occupations, including crafts and trade. Later, the rulers of Bohemia, Hungary, Lithuania, Pomerania, Romania, Russia, and Silesia that granted charters to the Jews also invited German artisans and traders. This competition made the Jews specialize in financial intermediation to the royal and noble estates.[50]

The Iberian Peninsula

In the Iberian Peninsula in the eighth through twelfth century, moneylending was one of the many occupations in which the prosperous Jewish community was engaged. Unlike in England, France, or Germany, where moneylending became the Jewish occupation par excellence during the Middle Ages, Iberian Jews engaged in skilled crafts, shopkeeping, long-distance commerce, medicine, and the state bureaucracy as well as moneylending.[51]

In the middle of the thirteenth century, when the Reconquista was completed (with the exception of Granada), regulations were imposed in both Castile and Aragon on the conditions of Jewish settlement. In all legal matters, Jews and Christians possessed equal rights. This climate would soon change. Like King Louis IX of France, the kingdom of Aragon initiated a large-scale campaign to convert the Jews by exposing the "Jewish error." In 1250 the first Spanish blood libel was made, in Saragossa. After the famous disputation that took place in Barcelona in July 1263, forced conversion of Jews to Christianity remained prohibited but Jews were compelled to attend Christian sermons.[52]

In 1267, Pope Clement IV granted the Inquisition the freedom to interfere in Jewish affairs by allowing inquisitors to pursue converted Jews who had reverted to their old religion, Christians who had converted to Judaism, and Jews accused of exercising undue influence over Christians and their converted brethren. Hostility toward the Jews from the religious authorities was growing. Yet the economic usefulness of the Jews was still considerable: in 1294, revenue from Jews accounted for 22 percent of total revenue in Castile. Despite mounting hostility on the

---

[50] Parkes (1938, pp. 178–81); Baron (1952, vol. 4, chap. 22).
[51] Baer (1961); Ashtor et al. (2007).
[52] Baer (1961); Ashtor (1973–84); Toch (2005, 2011, 2012); Ashtor et al. (2007).

part of the local population and the Church, the secular rulers were reluctant to give up such a valuable source of income.[53]

During the fourteenth century, attitudes toward the Jewish population began deteriorating. Both commercial and religious complaints by Christians grew until the end of the century, when violence broke out against Spanish Jews. In 1391, there were massacres in both Castile and Aragon, after which thousands of Jews nominally accepted Christianity. The Crown and landowners—the main beneficiaries of the revenues brought in by the Jews in both taxes and loans—suffered an economic loss. By the beginning of the fifteenth century, a number of privileges were issued to encourage the Jews to resettle. Despite these measures, their economic and social standing steadily deteriorated, culminating in the mass expulsion of 1492 described in chapter 1.[54]

Jewish Moneylending in Medieval Italy: A Detailed Analysis

Thanks to the wealth of archival data, it is possible to analyze the minutest details of Jewish moneylending in medieval and early Renaissance Italy. Hence, we devote a separate section to the dynamics of Jewish moneylending in Italy, and in particular, Tuscany, one of the most vibrant and commercial economies of the Middle Ages. What we find for medieval Italy can shed light on Jewish moneylending in other European countries, given that money and credit markets worked in a similar manner all over Europe, as described earlier in this chapter.

During the fourteenth and fifteenth centuries, many Jews came to Italy after their expulsion from France, Germany, and the Iberian Peninsula (see map 7.3). It is at this time that Jewish moneylending reached its apogee in central and northern Italy. Italian town governments regulated Jewish lending in their domains. Jews could settle and lend money at interest through a *condotta*, a bilateral contract between the town government and the Jewish lender. *Condotte* were long-term charters, binding both parties for a period of five to twenty years, that could be renewed upon expiration. In many locations, a Jewish lender wishing to establish his business in the same town as another Jewish lender had to receive permission from the incumbent.[55]

[53] Ashtor et al. (2007).

[54] Baer (1961); Gampel (1989, 1998); Limor (1993); Limor and Raz-Krakotzkin (1993); Beinart (1998); T. Glick (1998).

[55] Simonsohn (1977, 1982–86, 1988–91); Milano (1963); Milano et al. (2007). In some towns there was more than one Jewish lender. The monopoly right prohibited other Jews from freely settling and lending money in a town without the permission of the local Jewish community and without being regulated and taxed by the local town government.

Jewish moneylenders had to pay an annual tax and agree to lend (sometimes at favorable terms) to the town governments.[56] The tax was typically a lump sum paid at the beginning of each year or at specified interim dates. It ranged from 55 gold florins in San Gimignano in 1425 to 1,200 gold florins in Florence in 1448 to 4,000 gold ducats in Venice in 1382. (To give an idea of how profitable Jewish moneylending was, 1,200 gold florins in Florence in 1448 amounted to roughly forty times the average annual wage of an urban unskilled worker and twenty times the average annual wage of an urban skilled worker.[57])

The charters also regulated the annual interest rate ceiling, which was, for example, 10–12 percent in Venice in 1382, 60 percent in Città di Castello in Umbria in 1402, 42 percent in Spoleto around 1416, 30 percent in most Tuscan towns, and 15–20 percent in most towns on the Venetian mainland in the fifteenth century. These percentages applied to loans to local citizens; Jews were allowed to charge whatever interest rate they wished to people from other towns, whose creditworthiness was harder to assess.

In some towns, the interest rate ceiling also varied with the size of the loan. In 1421, for example, Jews in Gubbio could charge 50 percent on loans smaller than one florin, 45 percent on loans between one and seven florins, and 33 percent on loans larger than seven florins. In other towns, the interest rate ceiling varied according to the type of collateral. In 1382, for instance, Jewish lenders in Venice could charge 10 percent on loans against pawn and 12 percent on loans guaranteed with a written bond.

As for collateral, people could borrow from Jews by pledging movable objects—such as clothes, shoes, jewels, and working tools—as pawns. Alternatively, borrowers could provide a written promise of repayment to the Jewish lender. In some instances, the borrower himself wrote this deed; in other cases, a notary drafted the promise of repayment before two witnesses. A borrower could also name a guarantor, who ensured repayment of a debt if the borrower became insolvent. In some instances, Jews lent money on trust, without asking the borrower for any guarantee at all.

Many charters explicitly banned Jewish moneylenders from mortgage lending. Other charters simply did not mention land among the permitted types of collateral; by remaining silent on lending on mortgage while

---

[56] Botticini (2000) collected information on the annual taxes and the interest rate ceilings in the charters for Tuscany housed at the State Archives of Florence (henceforth ASF), *Statuti delle comunità autonome e soggette*, and for other Italian towns from secondary sources. See Toaff (1992–94) for information on Umbria, and Mueller (1972, 2008) for Venice.

[57] See Malanima (2007) for data on wages in early Renaissance Florence.

TABLE 8.1. Participation of Tuscan Households in Borrowing and Lending, 1427
(% of all households)

	Lenders	Nonlenders	Total
Borrowers	29.3	25.5	54.8
Nonborrowers	10.1	35.1	45.2
Total	39.4	60.6	100.0

Sources: State Archives of Florence, *Catasto* 207, 208, 213, 214, 215, 216, 219, 233, 234, 235, 236, 248, 249, 252, 253, 254, 257, 258, 266, 269; State Archives of Pisa, *Archivio Fiumi e Fossi, Serie Catasto* 532, 533, 535, 552, 557, 558.

Note: Sample size is 7,793, the total number of households residing in nine of the largest Tuscan towns (Arezzo, Castigion Fiorentino, Cortona, Montepulciano, Monte San Savino, Pescia, Pisa, Pistoia, and San Gimignano) as well as smaller towns and rural villages in the countryside surrounding these towns.

going into detail in spelling out other types of collateral, the charters implicitly excluded Jews from lending on mortgage.

Few account books of Jewish moneylenders in medieval Europe have survived. For medieval Tuscany, we uncovered detailed microdata in the State Archives of Florence. The primary source from which these data come from is the Florentine Catasto of 1427, a census and property survey of nearly 60,000 households (260,000 people) living throughout Tuscany, in which each head of household reported his landholdings, houses, credits, debts, shares of public debt owned, shops or other commercial partnerships, occupation, and family composition. Among the debts recorded are the loans obtained from local Jewish moneylenders. Together with other new and unpublished primary sources, these data provide a detailed picture of the functioning of credit markets and the role of Jewish moneylenders in late medieval and early Renaissance Italy.[58]

What are the key facts that emerge from these new primary sources and microdata? Table 8.1 indicates that two-thirds of the households living in nine Tuscan towns and hundreds of nearby villages were involved in credit transactions (as lenders, borrowers, or both)—an indication that credit was a vital part of the medieval economy.

Most households actively participated in credit market transactions. People borrowed for various purposes (to buy seeds and working tools, to provide their daughters with dowries at the time of the marriage, to buy food while awaiting the next harvest). One-third of the loans to peasant households were advanced by fellow peasant households subject to correlated shocks (table 8.2).

[58] Botticini (1997; 2000).

TABLE 8.2. Loans to Peasant Households, by Creditor Type, Tuscany, 1427 (%)

Type of creditor	Loans to peasants
Peasant	35
Merchant	30
Jew	22
Other[a]	13
Total	100

Source: See table 8.1.

Notes: Number of loans = 2,587. This table refers to peasant households borrowing from Jews in the Tuscan towns of Castiglion Fiorentino, Cortona, Montepulciano, Pescia, and San Gimignano.

[a] Includes artisans, notaries, clergy, nobles, charitable institutions, and monasteries.

Tuscan credit markets were local and isolated, especially for peasant households: in 99 percent of the 2,587 loans shown in table 8.2, the lender and the borrower lived in the same town. Households whose main source of income and wealth came from agriculture and that therefore were subject to correlated shocks, nevertheless lent and borrowed locally. Peasants lacked access to regional or larger credit markets, because neither rural banks nor credit cooperatives existed there. As a result, peasants in Pescia did not lend to people living in Montepulciano, peasants in Cortona seldom borrowed from people living in San Gimignano, and so on.

Institutional barriers and information costs were responsible for the local character of rural credit markets. During the fourteenth and fifteenth centuries, town governments did their best to keep their economies isolated, both to implement protectionist policies and to pursue their strong parochialism. Statutes prohibited foreign citizens from lending money against pawn to local citizens. Local citizens could not sell their lands to foreigners, effectively disallowing one potential source of credit. Above and beyond these rules, other transaction costs prevented the development of a regional capital market. Travel costs, for example, were an important concern in this period, when it took a long time for peasants to cover even short distances.

A more important reason for the lack of nonlocal credit markets was information. People were known quantities in their own towns; elsewhere their creditworthiness was largely conjectural. Unlike merchants, who had developed a good communication system through which they could relay information about other merchants' reputations, peasants had no such network. They had to wait four more centuries before the invention of credit cooperatives overcame problems of asymmetric information in rural credit markets.[59]

The isolated character of rural credit markets implied a welfare loss to these local economies, especially in the presence of aggregate shocks. In fifteenth-century Tuscany, these aggregate shocks stemmed from three sources. First, weather produced both aggregate and idiosyncratic shocks. Thunderstorms hit specific land plots, but a sudden frost could destroy all the vines in a village. Second, the Florentine town government's increasing needs for ready cash to finance its wars often resulted in new taxes for citizens living in all Florentine territories. Third, enemy troops besieging a town would often burn crops and kill cattle in the surrounding countryside; sometimes peasants themselves destroyed their crops and cattle to keep enemy armies from seizing them. All these ravages were common. In the presence of these aggregate shocks, access to an external source of credit was crucial, but it was hindered by the institutional barriers and information problems described above.

This is where the economic role of Jewish lenders came into play. Jews had two comparative advantages over other potential lenders. First, their wealth was liquid, consisting mostly of cash and easy-to-sell objects pledged as pawns. Because Jewish wealth was not invested primarily in land, it was not affected by aggregate shocks in the same manner as other people's: it was relatively immune to weather shocks, enemy plunder, and the land taxes frequently levied by Florence.

Second, Jewish lenders had an asset that other lenders lacked: strong economic and social ties among themselves. Substantial evidence documents the close family ties and economic connections linking Jews living in different towns and regions of Italy.[60] Through this thick network of social relationships and economic partnerships, Jewish lenders shared risk and afforded borrowers access to external sources of credit.

One might argue that merchants living in different towns could have provided a similar financial network and that in times of widespread economic distress, these merchants could have borrowed and lent among themselves and then to their unluckier fellow townsmen, either by advancing money or selling on credit. Merchants in Montepulciano, for example, bought goods on credit from merchants living in Florence and Siena. Distance seems to have mattered, however, and merchants typically chose to buy goods on credit and borrow from nearby places. At most, merchants in these peripheral towns exchanged goods and money with merchants in other Tuscan towns. Meanwhile, Jews living in Bologna, Mantua, Milan,

---

[59] Guinnane (2001).

[60] Luzzatto (1902); Molho (1971); Mueller (1975, 2008); Simonsohn (1977, 1982–86; 2011); Pini (1983); Muzzarelli (1984, 1994); Segre (1986–90); Cozzi (1987); Luzzati (1987, 1996); Toaff (1992–94); Bonfil (1994); Stow (1995–97); Botticini (1997); Pisa (1997).

Rome, Tuscan towns, and Venice had strong family and economic ties and often formed partnerships to run pawnshops. Consequently, they could quickly transfer substantial sums of money from one town to another. In the presence of aggregate shocks, Jews alone could connect a local town economy to external sources of credit.

Monti di pietà could have provided an alternative source of credit in these economies. Organized by town governments, these local credit institutions collected deposits from citizens willing to invest part of their wealth and made loans, typically at an annual interest rate of 5 percent. Created under the pressure of Franciscan preachers who wanted to ban Jewish moneylending from towns, *monti di pietà* had to provide loans on pawn mainly to poor people at advantageous terms. However, as many studies pointed out, *monti di pietà* never competed with Jewish lenders, who continued carrying on their business even after the establishment of these public banks. The services offered by Jewish lenders and *monti di pietà* were complements rather than substitutes.[61]

The advantages of inviting and hosting Jewish moneylenders were well recognized by citizens and rulers of towns belonging to the Florentine dominion. When requesting Florence's permission to admit a Jewish lender into their town, representatives always emphasized "the financial distress that the paupers experience because of the absence of a Jewish lender." The focus on the needs of paupers reflected the ban the Church had imposed against lending money at interest. To avoid the Church's punishment, town governments resorted to "the needs of the poor" in granting the charters to Jewish lenders. Once settled in these towns, Jewish lenders advanced credit to much larger segments of the population. However, they never reached even close to monopoly power in moneylending, as the data below clearly show.

Jewish lending in Tuscan credit markets was significant. A large proportion of households—one-third in Castiglion Fiorentino, one-fourth in Montepulciano, almost one-fifth in Monte San Savino, one-fifth in Pescia, and one-sixth in San Gimignano—borrowed from Jewish lenders (table 8.3). Loans from Jewish moneylenders amounted to roughly 10 percent of the total debt of all households. The average value of the loans was roughly equivalent to the average annual salary of an urban worker in Florence in 1427.

---

[61] Milano (1956, p. 216); Pullan (1971, 1987); Fornasari (1993); Menning (1993). The size of loan extended by *monti di pietà* was limited; for larger loans, people had to turn to Jews. Moreover, especially in the very early phases of their development, the *monti di pietà* suffered the constant problem of raising sufficient funds to satisfy the demand for loans, because their depositors were subject to correlated shocks. In times of widespread hardship, the depositors could hardly provide funds to the *monti di pietà*. In contrast, Jewish lenders could easily provide access to an external source of credit, thanks to the widespread economic and social networks that existed among Jews.

TABLE 8.3. Scale of Jewish Lending in Tuscan Towns, 1427

Town	Households borrowing from Jews		Debts to Jews	
	Number	% of total	Amount (gold florins)	% of total debt
Arezzo[a]	217	18.2	5,261	11.6
Castiglion Fiorentino	165	30.2	1,652	14.9
Cortona	118	6.1	1,892	5.1
Montepulciano	180	26.4	2,501	14.8
Monte San Savino	62	22.4	516	25.3
Pescia	197	20.3	1,896	8.8
Pisa[a]	80	4.7	1,704	0.6
San Gimignano	99	17.2	2,456	8.4
San Miniato	44	13.6	670	4.4
Total	1,160	14.8	18,548	8.2
Total excluding Cortona and Pisa	962	23.3	14,955	10.3

Source: See table 8.1.

[a] The figures for Pisa and Arezzo include citizens living in town, not those living in the countryside. For all other towns, figures refer to citizens living in towns and in the villages in the corresponding countrysides.

Who borrowed from Jews in late medieval Tuscany? According to the Florentine Catasto of 1427, the median and mean wealth of those who borrowed from Jewish lenders was greater than the median and mean wealth of those who did not (table 8.4). About 13.5 percent of households borrowing from Jewish lenders had wealth valued at more than 500 florins; among households not borrowing from Jews, the corresponding figure was 4.7 percent.

These findings contradict the common opinion that Jews specialized in small consumption loans to poor people. While the "needs of the paupers" may have been a valid concern of town governments when inviting Jewish lenders to settle in their towns, middle-class and wealthy citizens also benefited from their presence. These findings are even more important if one considers the use borrowers made of these loans. Data from the Catasto of 1427 indicate that artisans, and to a larger extent merchants, borrowed to finance productive investments. Among their creditors were Jews.

Analysis of two other economic indicators—occupation and land ownership—casts more doubts on the contention that poor urban workers and humble peasants were the primary clientele of Jewish lenders. Loans

TABLE 8.4. Wealth of Households Borrowing and Not Borrowing from Jews, Tuscany, 1427 (gold florins)

Town	Wealth of households borrowing from Jews (N = 1,160)		Wealth of households not borrowing from Jews (N = 6,633)	
	Mean	Median	Mean	Median
Arezzo	431.9	178	201.7	76
Castiglion Fiorentino	231.2	152.2	112	75
Cortona	181.8	114.8	115	40
Montepulciano	195.7	152.7	112	68
Monte San Savino	163.9	81.5	61.5	45
Pescia	246.4	189	164	121
Pisa	412.7	179.5	356	75.5
San Gimignano	489.3	256.4	232	58
San Miniato	280.6	113	178.3	39
All towns	293.9	132.5	200.2	55

Source: See table 8.1.

Note: A difference-of-means test on all towns yields a *t*-statistic of 4.33 (the 1 percent critical value is 2.32).

to households that earned their living from agriculture (e.g., agricultural workers, farmers, sharecroppers, and tenants) were by far the most numerous (see figure 8.1). Given that the majority of Tuscan households derived their income and wealth from agriculture, this finding is hardly surprising. What is striking is that artisans, merchants, notaries, and physicians—people with the greatest wealth and highest social standing—received loans that were fewer in number but significant in size.

Examining the household structure of the Jews' clientele reveals that loans were sought especially by households with daughters: Jewish loans amounted to 17 percent of debts of households with daughters, compared with 12 percent of debts of households with only male children and 8 percent of debts of households without children. Dowries provided by parents to their daughters at the time of the marriage played an important role in increasing the likelihood of marriage.

To evaluate the economic role of Jews in these medieval and Renaissance economies, it is essential to study their lending policies. Did Jewish lenders vary their interest rates according to the wealth of the borrower? Did they require different types of collateral from different borrowers?

In principle, nothing prohibited Jews from charging different interest rates to different borrowers. The charters established maximum annual interest rates but left Jews free to charge lower rates. In the Florentine

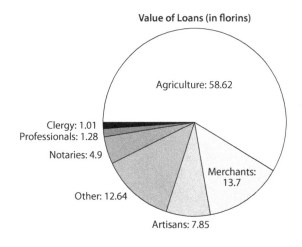

Value of Loans (in florins)

Agriculture: 58.62

Clergy: 1.01
Professionals: 1.28

Notaries: 4.9

Other: 12.64

Merchants: 13.7

Artisans: 7.85

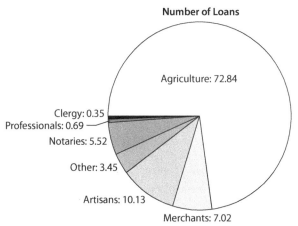

Number of Loans

Agriculture: 72.84

Clergy: 0.35
Professionals: 0.69

Notaries: 5.52

Other: 3.45

Artisans: 10.13

Merchants: 7.02

Figure 8.1. Clientele of Jewish lenders in 1427 Tuscany, by occupation. *Sources*: Adapted from figure 1 in Botticini (2000). Data from State Archives of Florence, *Catasto* 207, 208, 213, 214, 215, 216, 219, 233, 234, 235, 236, 248, 249, 252, 253, 254, 257, 258, 266, 269. *Note*: The data refer to the towns of Castiglion Fiorentino, Cortona, Montepulciano, Pescia, and San Gimignano. Each number in the upper diagram indicates the percentage value of the loans extended by Jewish moneylenders to borrowers by type of occupation. For example, 58.62 percent of the total value of the loans extended by the Jewish moneylenders went to households that earned their living from agriculture. Similarly, each number in the bottom diagram indicates the percentage of loans extended by Jewish moneylenders to borrowers by type of occupation. For example, 72.84 percent of the loans extended by Jewish moneylenders went to households that earned their living from agriculture.

TABLE 8.5. Number of Household Debts Owed by Tuscan Households, by Interest Rate and Creditor Type, 1427

Annual interest rate (%)	Debts to citizens (N = 18)	Debts to Jews (N = 69)
6	1	—
7	1	—
7.5	1	—
8	3	—
9	2	—
10	4	—
12	2	—
13	1	—
14	2	—
15	1	1
20	—	7[a]
25	—	2
30	—	59

Source: See table 8.1.

[a] Five loans were extended in Montepulciano, where the interest rate ceiling on Jewish loans was set at 20 percent.

Catasto of 1427, some borrowers specified the interest rate they paid on their debts. Table 8.5 indicates that interest rates on loans from Tuscans to Tuscans ranged from 6 to 15 percent, whereas Jews always charged the maximum interest rate allowed. Both bad and good risks paid the same interest rate: the fifty-nine borrowers who paid the maximum interest rate on loans from Jews (30 percent in all Tuscan towns except in Montepulciano) included both wealthy and poor citizens.

In contrast, Jewish lenders appear to have accepted different types of collateral based on the affluence of the borrower. Poor people mostly borrowed against pawn, while rich households could borrow on a written promise of repayment, a guarantor, or even on trust, not providing any formal guarantee at all (table 8.6).

Why, from a borrower's perspective, was a loan against pawn less desirable than a loan guaranteed with a private deed or by a guarantor? Pawns limited the size of loans, because the amount lent could not typically exceed two-thirds of the value of the pawn. Although movable items like clothing, swords, shoes, or hammers were easily pledged, their value hardly allowed borrowers to obtain large loans. Moreover, the borrower had to relinquish the pawn until the complete repayment of the loan. Table 8.6 confirms that the median and mean size of loans against pawn was smaller than that of loans guaranteed with private deeds or by guarantors.

TABLE 8.6. Type of Collateral Required by Jewish Lenders in Tuscany, by Borrower's Wealth and Value of the Loan, 1427

Type of collateral	Number of loans	Borrower's wealth (gold florins)		Value of loans (gold florins)	
		Mean	Median	Mean	Median
Pawn	133	365	72	46	20
Other types of guarantees	73	535	113	122.3	50

Source: See table 8.1.

Notes: A difference-of-means test for borrower's wealth yields a *t*-statistic of 2.03 (the 5 percent critical value is 1.66). A difference-of-means test for the value of loans yields a *t*-statistic of 3.01 (the 5 percent critical value is 1.66).

Table 8.6 also indicates that Jewish lenders discriminated among their customers by asking different borrowers for different forms of collateral. By asking a borrower to pledge a pawn, Jewish lenders indirectly limited the size of the loan. Prohibited from charging bad risks higher interest rates than the ceiling set in the charters, Jewish lenders rationed credit to these borrowers by asking them to guarantee their debts with pawns. Meanwhile, good risks could obtain larger loans, because Jewish lenders provided loans guaranteed with less restrictive collateral.

The important economic role of Jews was not limited to the private sector. The public finances of Italian towns also benefited from Jewish lending. In the fourteenth and fifteenth centuries, taxes and forced loans from citizens were insufficient to finance ordinary expenses such as officials' salaries. Money was also required to finance warfare against neighboring towns and to subsidize food in times of widespread dearth. Table 8.7, based on data from Perugia, indicates the various ways in which Jewish loans helped the public finances of Italian town governments. Similar data are available for other Italian towns.

In addition to providing large loans, Jewish lenders also contributed to the finances of the towns in which they resided through the annual tax they paid for the privilege of settling in a town and lending money. This tax seems to have depended on both the size of the town (and thus the prospective clientele) and the interest rate ceiling Jewish lenders were allowed to charge (see table 8.8).

The historical evidence indicates that in several instances, town governments raised the ceiling in order to appropriate part of the rent earned by Jewish lenders on their loans. This argument rests on three findings. First, town governments allowed Jews to charge interest rates above the rate set

TABLE 8.7. Jewish Loans to Perugia, 1284–1434

Year	Size of loan (gold florins)	Characteristics of the loan
1284	600	Guaranteed by five citizens
1284	400	Guaranteed by five citizens
1284	510	Guaranteed by five citizens
1287	1,000	—
1293	150	—
1312	600	Guaranteed by five citizens
1312	200	To pay a mercenary soldier army in the war against Spoleto
1315	1,000	To finance the war against Gubbio
1377	1,000	For the contract service of the rights and products of the lake
1381	500	On the occasion of a five-year charter granting the Jews permission to reside and lend money
1384	1,000	To pay soldiers to defend the town
1385	500	To finance military expenses to subdue the villages of Montone and Fratta
1385	545	To celebrate a victory
1386	500	To pay soldiers to help Siena
1389	700	To buy food for citizens
1392	500	To finance military expenses and to send an envoy to Pope Boniface IX
1392	500	To meet financial difficulties
1392	500	To pay honors bestowed to the pope visiting the town and to subdue a castle
1416	100	To defend the town from Braccio Fortebracci
1423	231	Jewish share of a 12,000-florin exaction by Braccio Fortebracci, Lord of Perugia, to arm troops
1428	500	To finance military expenses to defend the town of Città di Castello
1434	600	—

Source: Toaff (1975).
— Not indicated.

by usury laws. At the time of the Catasto of 1427, for example, shares of the Florentine public debt paid 5, 8, and 10 percent interest. The average interest rate on citizen-to-citizen debt was roughly 10 percent (table 8.5). Meanwhile, Jewish lenders were allowed to charge 30 percent in most Tuscan towns.

Second, thanks to this privilege and to their lending policies, Jewish lenders likely earned rent on most of their loans. They lent to good risks at the same rate they charged bad risks, but they minimized the potential losses on high-risk loans by demanding pawn. In several instances, town governments raised the interest rate ceiling for Jewish lenders with the

TABLE 8.8. Interest Rate Ceilings and Annual Taxes Paid by Jewish Moneylenders in Early Renaissance Italy

Region	Town	Year of charter	Interest rate ceiling (%)	Annual tax[a]
Tuscany	Castiglion Fiorentino	1414, 1419	30	80
	Cortona	1422	30	150
		1466	30	150
	Montepulciano	1429	20	60
	Prato	1437	30	800
	San Gimignano	1425	30	55
	Florence	1437	20	800
		1448–59	20	1,200
		1471	15	0
		1471–91	20	1,200
	Volterra	1408–47	30	100
Veneto	Venice	1382	11[b]	4,000
		1387	9[b]	0
		1513	17.5[b]	6,500
Romagna	Bologna	1399	30	607
		1406	30	552.5
		1418	25[b]	339

Sources: For Castiglion Fiorentino, Cortona, Montepulciano, and San Gimignano, data from State Archives of Florence (*Statuti* 201, fol. 482; 280, fol. 251; 501, fol. 158; 759, fol. 201), from Archivio Storico del Comune of Cortona (Manuscript F), and Biblioteca dell'Accademia Etrusca of Cortona (*Codice Cortonese*, Manuscript 520, *Capitoli del Monte Pio*). For Florence and Prato, data from Cassuto (1918, pp. 85, 120). For Volterra, data from Luzzati and Veronese (1993, pp. 57–87). For Venice, data from Mueller (1972, pp. 63–64) and Pullan (1971, pp. 674–75). For Bologna, data from Muzzarelli (1994, pp. 15–40).

[a] Figures are in gold florins for Tuscan towns and Bologna and in gold ducats for Venice.

[b] These interest rates are averages of two different rates applied to loans of different size or guaranteed with different types of collateral. For example, Jews could charge 30 percent on loans against pawns and 20 percent on loans with written guarantees or with a guarantor. In other towns, different rates were applied to loans of different sizes: 30 percent on loans below a certain amount, and 20 percent on loans above a certain amount.

explicit purpose of enabling them to earn a higher rent. For example, in Spoleto in 1416, Jewish lenders were allowed to charge a higher interest rate (42 percent versus 30 percent) for six months in order to provide the town government with a 50 gold florin loan. Third, by taxing and borrowing from Jewish lenders, town governments appropriated part of this rent.

Table 8.8 shows another interesting fact: the interest rate ceiling Jews were allowed to charge was lower in larger towns such as Florence or Venice, where Jews likely faced more competition from Christian banks. Florence and Venice were successful in negotiating a lower interest rate ceiling for their own citizens, but they let Jewish moneylenders charge higher interest rates in the smaller towns of their domains.

The charters and the detailed microdata on Jewish moneylending in medieval and early Renaissance Italian towns highlight some striking facts. First, moneylending was the primary occupation of the Jews. Second, the legal restrictions spelled out in the charters regulated the terms at which the Jews could engage in moneylending. The primary goal of these restrictions was not to prohibit Jews from owning land per se or from farming but rather to prevent the Jews from acquiring a lot of land and real estate through their moneylending business. Third, the Jews were not monopolists in this business: credit was also provided by local shopkeepers, traders, notaries, charitable institutions, and even monasteries. Fourth, Jewish moneylenders helped finance local governments through direct loans in case of need, as well as through the taxes they paid. Fifth, thanks to their family and business connections, Jewish moneylenders dwelling in different locations gained significantly from networking and arbitrage opportunities, which made their business very profitable.

ATTITUDES TOWARD MONEYLENDING

The attitudes of the Church authorities and of Jewish scholars toward lending money at interest were both similar and different during the Middle Ages. Did the differences in these attitudes contribute to the entry and specialization of the Jews into moneylending in medieval Europe?

Jewish Attitudes toward Moneylending

Did the Jews ever consider lending money at interest a sin? Was there any religious law or social norm in Judaism against lending money to Jews and Gentiles? Did the attitude and the rulings of subsequent generations of leading rabbis and scholars toward lending money at interest have any impact on the entry and specialization of European Jewry into moneylending in medieval times?

The ban on usury among Jews (as well as among Christians and Muslims) comes from Deuteronomy 23:20–21, which states, "Thou shalt not lend upon interest to thy brother: interest of money, interest of victuals, interest of anything that is lent upon interest. Unto a foreigner [Gentile] thou mayest lend upon interest; but unto thy brother thou shalt not lend upon interest." Other references to moneylending rarely occur in the Bible.

During the Talmudic period, the scholars in the academies in the Land of Israel and Mesopotamia offered different opinions regarding lending money at interest. Some rabbis were against the taking of interest from any borrower, whereas others allowed taking interest from Gentiles. In an often-quoted passage of the tractate Baba Metzia, lending at interest to Gentiles was left an open issue. Interestingly, in a Talmud filled with rulings regulating every aspect of the daily economic, social, and religious life of the Jewish communities, there was no final and accepted ruling forbidding lending at interest.[62]

During the Gaonic period (seventh to eleventh century), some sources mention that Jews in Mesopotamia were engaged in moneylending. The Koran (4:160) is the first source accusing the Jews of usury. There are also references in the rabbinic responsa. For example, a responsum by Amram ben Sheshna Gaon, the prominent head of the Jewish academy in Sura in Mesopotamia in the mid-ninth century, prohibited Jews from accepting interest from a Gentile even if it was economically necessary. During the tenth century, a Jew asked whether a Jew who takes interest from a Gentile should be excommunicated. The answer—written at a time when Jews were court bankers in the Abbasid caliphate—was that "this is a small matter, because God has never forbidden charging interest to a non-Jew. However, if one is strict he should refrain from doing so."

In general, the Geonim held an ambivalent attitude toward lending money at interest. On the one hand, they seemed to favor the idea that "even if a Jew has an opportunity to lend money to a Gentile at interest, a Jew in need of money, who need not pay the lender interest, must be given preference."[63] On the other hand, they permitted Jewish scholars to accept interest from Gentiles, because they thought that a scholar would not be influenced by Gentile practices when coming into contact with them.

During the eleventh and twelfth centuries, as the Jews in England, France, and later Germany established themselves as leading moneylenders, eminent Jewish rabbis and scholars in Europe shaped and adapted the Jewish law regarding the charging of interest on loans to Gentiles in order to fit the actual practice of the moneylending business. The first leading figure who took a stand on this matter was Rabbenu Gershom ben Judah (960–1040) of Mainz, who addressed the issue of loans extended to Gentiles through a Jewish intermediary. Because a Jew was prohibited by his religion from acting as a Gentile's middleman, this situation created a potential problem: by biblical rule, a loan at interest from a Jew to a Jew was prohibited. Rabbenu Gershom solved this problem by changing the role of the Jewish partner to that of "mediator." This was the first step toward permitting loans at interest between Jews.

---

[62] On the Jewish attitude toward moneylending, see Stein (1955, 2007); Soloveitchik (1985, 2005); J. Katz (1995).

[63] Stein (2007).

A few decades later, Rashi (1040–1105), the most influential scholar among Ashkenazi Jews, faced the reality that "we [Jews] cannot maintain ourselves unless we do business with them, because we live amongst Gentiles." During his time, European Jews had become heavily involved in moneylending, debt transactions, mortgages, and other forms of intertemporal trade and payments.

Among the hundreds of responsa Rashi wrote, many deal with issues related to credit transactions and lending money at interest.[64] The main problem was that Jews were permitted to charge interest to Gentiles but not to other Jews. To address this issue, Rashi ruled that a Gentile could serve as a "straw man" in a lending transaction between two Jews. Many contemporary rabbis felt uneasy with this ruling, but the necessity of making a living in medieval Europe made them accept and implement it.

One unresolved issue was that Rashi's ruling demanded that the lender not know that the Gentile was a mediator, something that was impossible in small communities. In addition, when two Jews had the opportunity to make a deal, they had to wait until they could find a Gentile mediator. This costly delay made Jewish moneylenders violate Rashi's ruling.

The watershed ruling that opened the way for the full involvement of Jews in credit markets came from Rabbi Jacob ben Meir (1100–71), known as Rabbenu Tam, who was Rashi's grandson. Rabbenu Tam was one of the first leading Baalei Tosafot—the Ashkenazi rabbis who issued rulings from the twelfth to the fourteenth century. He became so influential that to this day, his commentaries appear next to those of Rashi on each page of the Talmud. Rabbenu Tam sanctioned that Jewish lenders did not need to know that the Gentile was a mediator in a credit transaction. This ruling put a formal end to the delay in making a moneylending deal between Jews and enabled them to lend money to one another without violating Jewish law. The ruling merely legitimized practices that were already used: at the time Rabbenu Tam issued this ruling, leading Jewish moneylenders had networks of Jewish middlemen across cities. The most famous were Aaron of Lincoln (England), Karslin of Provin (France), Wiwilin of Strasbourg (Germany), and the family of Al-Constantini (Spain).

The ruling of Rabbenu Tam on transfers of pawns and debts between Jews cleared the way to all moneylending transactions between Jews and Gentiles. One factor that enabled acceptance of this ruling was the writing by another rabbi (R. Yitzhak) that he and Rabbenu Tam exchanged pawns and debts and loaned to each other with interest.

Circa 1100, lending money at interest was already the primary occupation of the Jews in England. The rulings by Rashi and Rabbenu Tam helped spread this business among Jews in France and Germany. Although

[64] H. Ben-Sasson (1976, pp. 398–400).

the rulings were criticized by several rabbis, they were accepted by Jewish traders and moneylenders, as well as by other important rabbis all over Europe, including the Iberian Peninsula. That Jews ignored any religious restriction on financial transactions is clear from this quotation about Provence by a prominent thirteenth-century scholar, Menachem ben Solomon Meiri:[65]

> In our days nobody cares about refraining from business dealings with and loans to Gentiles, even on their festivals—not a Gaon, not a rabbi, not a scholar, not a pupil, not a Hasid, and not one who pretends to be a Hasid. All these laws refer only to idolaters and their images, but all transactions with Christians are perfectly legal.

Laws and rulings typically follow established practice. Given that most eminent Jewish scholars and rabbis during the eleventh and twelfth centuries were discussing and issuing rulings regarding lending at interest to Gentiles, it is reasonable to argue that loans between Jews and from Jews to Gentiles were already a widespread practice *before* the Church started enforcing usury bans on Christians.

Christian Attitudes toward Moneylending

For Christians, the prohibition against lending at interest comes from the passage in the Deuteronomy mentioned earlier, as well as from the Gospel of Luke (Luke 6:35 "Lend, hoping for nothing in return"). In medieval Europe, the Church regulated many aspects of the daily lives of millions of people. The main tool of the Church's control over financial transactions was the issuance of bans against lending at usurious interest rates.

Until 1050, there were no formal prohibitions on lending at interest, usury was poorly defined, and the Church itself was heavily involved in both borrowing and lending money through mortgages (see table 8.9).[66] Between 1050 and 1175, usury was declared a sin and the Church introduced—although it did not immediately enforce—the first formal prohibitions against lending at interest on consumption loans. From roughly 1200, the bans started being enforced, with usurers condemned by the religious courts of committing a sin. The enforcement of the usury bans on consumption loans came in full swing between 1200 and 1400, coinciding with times of economic hardship such as the ones before and after the Black Death of 1348. During the fifteenth century, the

---

[65] J. Katz (1961, chap. 10).

[66] The literature on the Church's attitude toward lending money at interest and usury bans on Christians is vast. See, among others, Noonan (1957); Nelson (1969); Todeschini (1989); Glaeser and Scheinkman (1998); Munro (2003); Reed and Bekar (2003).

TABLE 8.9. Usury Bans on Christians, 300–1500

Period	Papal bull or bishops' council	Type of restriction
300–1050 Prohibitions applied primarily to clerics; usury itself poorly defined	Council of Nicaea (325)	Clergy banned from charging interest
	Nec hoc quoque by Pope Leo the Great (c. 450)	Christian laymen banned from charging interest
1050–1175 Usury declared a sin		Usury by all Christians formally prohibited, but ban not enforced
1175–1350 Usury an important concern of the Church; prohibitions on consumption loans, not investment loans	Third Lateran Council (1179)	Usury declared a sin prohibited in both Old and New Testaments; interest rates higher than zero considered usurious; usury punished by refusal of confession, absolution, and Christian burial; invalidation of wills; excommunication of rulers or communities that permitted usury
	Second Council of Lyon (1274)	Usurers banned from renting houses, expelled within three months, and never readmitted
	Council of Vienne (1311–1312)	Moneylenders compelled by ecclesiastical censure to open their account books when there was question of usury; persons claiming that usury was not sinful were punished as heretics
1400–1500 Enforcement of prohibitions relaxed in a variety of ways	Late 15th century	Professional usurers allowed to participate in church services and be buried in church graveyards; numerous types of loan contracts explicitly declared nonusurious; sin of usury increasingly applied only to excessive interest charges; Church helped create the *monti di pietà* and declared that such credit organizations did not provide any incentive to sin if they receive, in addition to the capital, a moderate sum for their expenses and by way of compensation

Sources: Noonan (1957), Todeschini (1989), Glaeser and Scheinkman (1998), Munro (2003), and Reed and Bekar (2003).

enforcement of prohibitions against lending at interest became relaxed in a variety of ways.

FACTS AND COMPETING HYPOTHESES

Did Jews in medieval Europe become segregated into moneylending because they were excluded from other occupations? Did they specialize in moneylending because of usury bans on Muslims and Christians? Did the fear of attack during the Crusades or episodes of banishment make them prefer to invest in portable human capital instead of physical capital (e.g., land), and did this, in turn, foster their entry and then specialization in moneylending? Did the Jews become skilled moneylenders in medieval Europe because of their earlier involvement with wine making and wine trading? As this section shows, the historical evidence supports none of these hypotheses.

Exclusion from Guilds

The timing of the rise and expansion of the craft and merchant guilds cannot explain the specialization of the Jews into moneylending, because the guilds came to dominate manufacturing, trade, and commerce at least two centuries after the Jews had entered and become prominent in moneylending (see table 8.10). Jews in England, France, and Germany were already involved in moneylending during the eleventh, twelfth, and thirteenth centuries. Craft and merchant guilds were neither widespread nor powerful in European towns and urban centers until the thirteenth century, by which time the Jews were already specialized in moneylending.[67]

Merchant guilds appeared first in many Italian cities in the twelfth century. Craft guilds became ubiquitous during the succeeding century. The number of guilds in Europe continued to grow after the Black Death of 1348. For nearly two centuries, they dominated life in medieval towns. They controlled and regulated entry into manufacturing and commerce, the quality and standards of production, and prices. They also dominated local politics and influenced national and international affairs.

[67]Lopez (1976); Gustafsson (1987); Mokyr (1990); S. A. Epstein (1991); S. R. Epstein (1998); Richardson (2004). Few written records survive from the twelfth century or earlier. Surviving documents consist principally of the records of the kings, princes, and churches, which taxed, chartered, and granted privileges to organizations. Some evidence also exists in the records of notaries and courts, which recorded and enforced contracts between guild masters and outsiders, such as the parents of apprentices. Better records survive from the fourteenth and fifteenth centuries, including statute books and other documents describing the internal organization and operation of guilds.

TABLE 8.10. Time Line of Craft and Merchant Guilds and Jewish Moneylending in Europe, 850–1500

Year	Event
850–1250	Jews migrated to, from, and within the Muslim caliphates, the Byzantine Empire, and Europe as urban dwellers specialized in skilled crafts, trade, moneylending, and medicine.
From 1000	Jews in Europe began specializing and became prominent in moneylending. Jewish scholars issued many rulings to regulate moneylending during the eleventh and twelfth centuries.
1200–1350	Craft and merchant guilds began growing.
1350–1550	Guilds dominated manufacturing and commerce in many European towns.

Source: See text.

Only town residents could belong to the local craft and merchant guilds. Jews were excluded from membership, because in most locations they were considered foreigners under special protection of the rulers. The exclusion was irrelevant, however, because by the time the guilds became powerful, the Jews in western Europe had entered and then become specialized and prominent in moneylending for at least two centuries.

Another observation casts doubts on the hypothesis that the exclusion of Jews from craft and merchant guilds may have pushed them into moneylending. The Jews in the Byzantine Empire in the early Middle Ages neither specialized nor became prominent in moneylending, even though craft and merchant guilds excluded them and any other foreigner from engaging in the occupations under their regulation and control.[68]

Muslim and Christian Bans on Usury

In order for the other popular argument—that usury bans prevented Muslims and Christians from lending money at interest, a void the Jews filled—to be consistent with the historical evidence, three conditions must hold:

- The usury prohibitions on Muslims and Christians were enacted before the Jews entered and became specialized in moneylending.
- The bans were not mere legal norms but were enforced in practice.
- The Jews were de facto monopolists in lending money at interest.

[68] Holo (2009, chap. 6).

TABLE 8.11. Time Line of Usury Bans and Jewish Specialization in Moneylending in Europe, 300–1500

Year	Location	Event
325	Roman Empire	Church prohibited clergy from charging interest on loans.
500–1100	Europe	Church extended (but did not enforce) usury ban to the laity.
650–1250	Muslim caliphates	Koran prohibited Muslims from charging interest on loans.
750–900	Mesopotamia and Persia	Jews left farming, moved to urban centers, and entered nearly 450 occupations, including skilled crafts, trade, medicine, and moneylending.
850–1250	Muslim caliphates, Byzantine Empire, Europe	Jews migrated to, from, and within the Muslim caliphates, the Byzantine Empire, and Europe as urban dwellers specialized in skilled crafts, trade, moneylending, and medicine.
From 1000	Europe	Jews began specializing and became prominent in moneylending. Jewish scholars issued many rulings to regulate moneylending during the eleventh and twelfth centuries.
1200–1400	Europe	Church strictly enforced usury ban on Christians.

Source: See text.

The time line of the key events shown in table 8.11 reveals that none of these conditions was met in the Muslim caliphates or, later, in medieval Europe.

Given that moneylending is just one of the many skilled occupations that can be grouped into the category of "trade," the usury ban on Muslims may explain why *within* the occupations belonging to the category of trade the Jews further specialized in moneylending. Yet, moneylending was just one of the many (indeed hundreds, according to the documents of the Cairo Geniza) occupations from which the large Jewish community in the vast territory under Muslim rule earned its living (see chapters 6 and 7).

What about the usury bans imposed by the Catholic Church on Christians in medieval Europe? As the time line in tables 8.9 and 8.11 shows, from the ninth century onward, the Jews who immigrated to Europe from the Byzantine Empire and North Africa arrived as urban dwellers already specialized in myriad urban occupations, moneylending being one of them. The responsa and the rulings of leading rabbis and scholars in

Europe during the eleventh and twelfth centuries discussed and regulated lending money at interest. The fact that eminent Jewish scholars devoted much time to discussing and ruling on this matter indicates that Jews were already heavily involved in lending money at interest at that time.

At the Council of Nicaea in 325, the Church prohibited the taking of interest by the clergy—a rule that was extended to the laity in subsequent centuries (see table 8.9). Until the mid-twelfth century, however, the Church's attitude was to condemn rather than explicitly prohibit lending at interest. The anti-usury movement started to gain momentum in 1175 and reached its zenith in 1311–13, when Pope Clement V made the ban on usury absolute and declared all secular legislation in its favor null and void. Hence, usury bans on Christians in medieval Europe were enforced *at least two centuries after* the Jews in England, France, and Germany had entered and become specialized in moneylending.

Finally, as Toch forcefully argues, at almost no time did European Jewry hold a monopoly in moneylending.[69] As the wealth of microdata on Tuscan credit markets in the early Renaissance presented above shows, Jews supplied only a portion of the loans extended to Tuscan households. No Jews lived in England for almost four centuries after 1290 or in France from the late fourteenth century. They were expelled from, and called back to, many German and Italian towns during the fourteenth and fifteenth centuries. In the absence of the Jewish moneylenders, who provided consumption loans to farmers waiting for the next harvest? Who advanced the loans for the construction of bridges or churches or the financing of wars? Even when the usury bans on Christians were strictly enforced from the thirteenth to the fourteenth century, local merchants and foreign bankers (e.g., the Lombards and the Tuscan bankers) were the main competitors of the Jews in selling on credit and moneylending.

Persecutions and Portable Human Capital

The argument that Jews entered and specialized in moneylending because the persecutions to which they were subject (like other religious and ethnic minorities) made both mobility and the consequent investment in human capital important assets is faulty for three reasons.

First, as shown in chapter 5, the implementation of the Jewish religious norm requiring fathers to educate their sons occurred during the Talmud era (third to sixth century)—centuries *before* the Jews began migrating to, from, and within the Muslim caliphates, the Byzantine Empire, and Europe. The direction of causality thus runs from investment in literacy and education to entering crafts and trade and further entering and

[69]Toch (2005, p. 11; 2011, 2012).

specializing into the profession that most benefited from literacy and education (moneylending) to migrating in search of business opportunities—not the other way around.

Second, successful moneylenders need to reside in a local community on a continuous basis in order to understand the creditworthiness of the borrowers and to recover the loans. Moving is *not* an asset (while networking is) for being successful in moneylending.

Third, persecutions, temporary banishments, or expulsions of Jews came *later* as the outcome of their specialization in moneylending. The Jews were forced to stop lending money at interest when the local population or the rulers decided to repudiate their debts during periods of economic hardship. Hence, the direction of causality runs the other way—from moneylending to persecutions.

Involvement in the Wine Trade

The most recent argument—the hypothesis that Jewish laws concerning wine making and wine trading are the missing link that can explain the movement of German Jewry into moneylending—cannot be extended to other locations in Europe. Anglo and French Jews specialized in moneylending at least one or two centuries *before* German Jews did so. As wine was not a major trading or debt instrument for Anglo or French Jews, it cannot explain their entry and early prominence in moneylending.[70]

FROM MERCHANTS TO MONEYLENDERS: COMPARATIVE ADVANTAGE IN COMPLEX INTERMEDIATION

If the rise of craft and merchant guilds, usury bans on Muslims and Christians, persecutions inflicted on the Jews, and Jewish involvement in wine making and wine trading all fail to explain the entry and, later, specialization and prominence of Jews in moneylending in medieval Europe, what else can account for this distinctive feature of their history? We show that the entry and then specialization of the Jews in lending money at interest can be explained by their comparative advantage in the four assets that were (and still are) the pillars of financial intermediation: capital, networking, literacy and numeracy, and contract-enforcement institutions.

Our simple theory of occupational choice, based on Roy's model, presented in chapter 6, predicts that individuals choose an occupation based on their advantage in the skills required for that occupation and

---

[70] Non-Jewish sources include descriptions of Jews trading in grain, pepper, cattle, and sheep, but not wine.

the expected earnings in that occupation versus alternative occupations. Trade and moneylending (and financial intermediation in general) require more capital, more networking, more literacy and numeracy, and stronger contract-enforcement institutions than farming. An individual with these four assets has a comparative advantage in trade and moneylending—professions that are far more profitable than farming.

When applied to the history of the Jewish people, this theory of occupational choice predicts that in the absence of any legal restriction, people endowed with a comparative advantage for being moneylenders would prefer to be moneylenders. This is exactly what happened to European Jewry during the Middle Ages for several reasons.

First, many Jews had accumulated wealth as urban dwellers engaged in skilled crafts, local commerce, and long-distance trade in the Byzantine Empire and the Muslim Middle East and North Africa from the eighth to the tenth century. When, from the ninth century onward, Jewish craftsmen and traders began migrating from the Byzantine Empire and North Africa to the northern shores of the Mediterranean, they had the capital to become moneylenders and, later, prominent bankers and financiers. Growing business opportunities created by the rise of urbanization and the commercial revival of Europe fostered these Jewish migrations. With the expansion of trade, coupled with the widespread practice of selling on credit, artisans, shopkeepers, merchants, and traders needed higher and higher levels of initial capital that could be leveraged through the use of moneylending. Individuals, such as the Jews, who had accumulated wealth had a clear advantage over others in moneylending.[71]

Second, as documented by the travel itinerary of Benjamin of Tudela (c. 1165–73), during the Middle Ages, the Jews lived in myriad locations over a vast territory spanning from the Iberian Peninsula to India. Wherever they lived, they could rely on the rabbinic academies and courts, which used a common written language (Hebrew) and a common law (halakha), based on the Talmud. During the Middle Ages, the trading routes of Jewish merchants in Europe corresponded to the web of networking activities related to the rabbinic responsa. Some of these responsa document the numerous partnerships in trade and moneylending among Jews in different locations. One of the most extensive webs of business transactions and flows of information existed in England, where many Jewish moneylenders worked as agents for the extremely wealthy and very

[71] The inheritance laws laid down in the Talmud—according to which wealth passed from fathers to sons without being dispersed in tiny and rigid portions across many members of the extended family, as it was among Muslims—may have helped Jews accumulate capital and transmit it across generations.

prominent Aaron of Lincoln.[72] Because of the geographical scattering of the Jewish communities and the related flows of information generated by the activities of the academies and the rabbinic courts, Jews in distant locations could easily communicate and exchange information, including information on local market conditions, prices of commodities, demand for money and credit, interest rate ceilings, and so forth. Their networking ability enabled Jews to gain from arbitrage opportunities in trade and, later, moneylending.

Third, most Jews were highly literate and educated. In a medieval Europe populated largely by illiterate people—with the exception of merchants, traders, moneylenders, priests, and monks—the Jews had a comparative advantage in writing and reading contracts, business letters, and account books. As traders, they were already accustomed to conducting business through agreements in documents and letters. They also had the arithmetic skills that enabled them to calculate interest and exchanges rates.[73]

Fourth, Jewish moneylenders in medieval Europe could rely on two contract-enforcement institutions. The local rabbinic courts ensured that Talmudic laws pertaining to any aspect of economic life, including business partnerships and loans among Jews and from Jews to Christians, were enforced within the Jewish communities in all locations. In addition, Jewish moneylenders secured protection of their business activity and the enforcement of loan payment through the written charters granted by local rulers, as shown above in the description of Jewish moneylending in the countries of medieval Europe. Binding both parties for a period of one to twenty years, the charters regulated and provided legal enforcement for every detail of Jewish moneylending, including the type of collateral, the courts competent to settle disputes, and interest rate ceilings.

No legal or religious restriction prevented the Jews from lending money at interest to Gentiles in early medieval Europe; the potential religious ban on lending money at interest to Jews was partially resolved by Rabbenu Gershom in the early eleventh century and accepted by the eminent Rabbenu Tam in the mid-twelfth century, by which time Jews in England and France—and shortly later, Germany—were fully involved in lending money at interest. Their entry and then specialization in moneylending began well before the establishment of the craft and merchant guilds, and well before the strict enforcement by the Catholic Church of usury bans on Christians.

Where detailed microdata on credit markets and Jewish moneylending are available, such as in late medieval and early Renaissance Tuscany, they

[72] Goldin (1996).
[73] H. Ben-Sasson (1976, p. 398).

clearly show that Jews were competing with non-Jews and specializing in segments of the market in which they had a comparative advantage. Legal restrictions on land ownership for Jews in late medieval Europe were imposed to limit the type of collateral they could use and to prevent too much land and real estate from falling into their hands through the moneylending business. These legal restrictions were *not* the reason why the Jews entered and then specialized in moneylending and became successful in this profitable sector.

In medieval Europe, as today, financial intermediation required highly literate and skilled individuals and provided higher returns than other occupations. European Jews during the Middle Ages and their descendants worldwide have been leaders in this profession for more than a thousand years thanks to their comparative advantage in the four key assets required for success: capital, networking, literacy and numeracy, and contract-enforcement institutions.

ANNEX 8.A: THE CHARTER TO THE JEWS OF VIENNA

This is the text of the charter issued by Duke Frederick II of Austria to the Jews of Austria in 1244:[74]

> Frederick, by the grace of God Duke of Austria and Styria and lord of Carniola, offers greetings at all times to all who will read this letter in the future. Inasmuch as we desire that men of all classes dwelling in our land should share our favor and good will, we do therefore decree that these laws, devised for all Jews found in the land of Austria, shall be observed by them without violation.
>
> I. We decree, therefore, first, that in cases involving money, or immovable property, or a criminal complaint touching the person or property of a Jew, no Christian shall be admitted as a witness against a Jew unless there is a Jewish witness together with the Christian.
>
> II. Likewise, if a Christian should bring suit against a Jew, asserting that he had pawned his pledges with him and the Jew should deny this, and then if the Christian should not wish to accord any belief in the mere statement of the Jew, the Jew may prove his contention by taking an oath upon an object equivalent in value to that which was brought to him, and shall then go forth free.
>
> III. Likewise, if a Christian has deposited a pledge with a Jew, stating that he had left it with the Jew for a smaller sum than the Jew admits, the Jew shall then take an oath upon the pledge pawned with him, and the Christian must not refuse to pay the amount that the Jew has proved through his oath.

[74] Marcus (1938, pp. 31–35).

IV. Likewise, if a Jew says that he returned the Christian's pledge as a loan to the Christian, without, however, the presence of witnesses, and if the Christian deny this, then the Christian is able to clear himself in this matter through the oath of himself alone.

V. Likewise, a Jew is allowed to receive all things as pledges which may be pawned with him—no matter what they are called without making any investigation about them—except bloody and wet clothes which he shall under no circumstances accept.

VI. Likewise, if a Christian charges that the pledge which a Jew has, was taken from him by theft or robbery, the Jew must swear on that pledge that when he received it he did not know that it had been removed by theft or robbery. In this oath the amount for which the pledge was pawned to him shall also be included. Then, inasmuch as the Jew has brought his proof, the Christian shall pay him the capital and the interest that has accrued in the meantime.

VII. Likewise, if a Jew, through the accident of fire or through theft or violence, should lose his [own] goods, together with the pledges pawned with him, and this is established, yet the Christian who has pledged something with him nevertheless brings suit against him, the Jew may free himself merely by his own oath.

VIII. Likewise, if the Jews engage in quarreling or actually fight among themselves, the judge of our city shall claim no jurisdiction over them; only the Duke alone or the chief official of his land shall exercise jurisdiction. If, however, the accusation touches the person, this case shall be reserved for the Duke alone for judgment.

IX. Likewise, if a Christian should inflict any sort of a wound upon a Jew, the accused shall pay to the Duke twelve marks of gold which are to be turned in to the treasury. He must also pay, to the person who has been injured, twelve marks of silver and the expenses incurred for the medicine needed in his cure.

X. Likewise, if a Christian should kill a Jew he shall be punished with the proper sentence, death, and all his movable and immovable property shall pass into the power of the Duke.

XI. Likewise, if a Christian strikes a Jew, without, however, having spilt his blood, he shall pay to the Duke four marks of gold, and to the man he struck four marks of silver. If he has no money, he shall offer satisfaction for the crime committed by the loss of his hand.

XII. Likewise, wherever a Jew shall pass through our territory no one shall offer any hindrance to him or molest or trouble him. If, however, he should be carrying any goods or other things for which he must pay duty at all custom offices, he shall pay only the prescribed duty which a citizen of that town, in which the Jew is then dwelling, pays.

XIII. Likewise, if the Jews, as is their custom, should transport any of their dead either from city to city, or from province to province, or from one

Austrian land into another, we do not wish anything to be demanded of them by our customs officers. If, however, a customs officer should extort anything, then he is to be punished for *praedatio mortui*, which means, in common language, robbery of the dead.

XIV. Likewise, if a Christian, moved by insolence, shall break into the cemetery of the Jews, he shall die, as the court determines, and all his property, whatever it may be, shall be forfeited to the treasury of the Duke.

XV. Likewise, if any one wickedly throws something at the synagogues of the Jews we order that he pay two talents to the judge of the Jews.

XVI. Likewise, if a Jew be condemned by his judge to a money penalty, which is called *wandel* ("fine"), he shall pay only twelve dinars to him.

XVII. Likewise, if a Jew is summoned to court by order of his judge, but does not come the first or second time, he must pay the judge four dinars for each time. If he does not come at the third summons he shall pay thirty-six dinars to the judge mentioned.

XVIII. Likewise, if a Jew has wounded another Jew he may not refuse to pay a penalty of two talents, which is called wandel, to his judge.

XIX. Likewise, we decree that no Jew shall take an oath on the Torah unless he has been summoned to our [the Duke's] presence.

XX. Likewise, if a Jew was secretly murdered, and if through the testimony it cannot be determined by his friends who murdered him, yet if after an investigation has been made the Jews begin to suspect someone, we are willing to supply the Jews with a champion against this suspect.

XXI. Likewise, if a Christian raises his hand in violence against a Jewess, we order that the hand of that person be cut off.

XXXII. Likewise, the [Christian] judge of the Jews shall bring no case that has arisen among the Jews before his court, unless he is invited due to a complaint.

XXIII. Likewise, if a Christian has redeemed his pledge from a Jew but has not paid the interest, the interest due shall become compounded if it is not paid within a month.

XXIV. Likewise, we do not wish any one to seek quarters in a Jewish house.

XXV. Likewise, if a Jew has lent money to a magnate of the country on his possessions or on a note and proves this documentarily, we assign the pledged possessions to the Jew and defend them for him against violence.

XXVI. Likewise, if any man or woman should kidnap a Jewish child we wish that he be punished as a thief [by death].

XXVII. Likewise, if a Jew has held in his possession, for a year, a pledge received from a Christian, and if the value of the pledge does not exceed the money lent together with the interest, the Jew may show the pledge to his judge and shall then have the right to sell it. If any pledge shall remain for a "year and a day" with a Jew, he shall not have to account for it afterward to anyone.

XXVIII. Likewise, whatever Christian shall take his pledge away from a Jew by force or shall exercise violence in the Jew's home shall be severely punished as a plunderer of our treasury.

XXIX. Likewise, one shall in no place proceed in judgment against a Jew except in front of his synagogues, saving ourselves who have the power to summon them to our presence.

XXX. Likewise, we decree that Jews shall indeed receive only eight dinars a week interest on the talent. . . . [This was 173.33 per cent annual interest. Such a high rate was not unusual because of the insecurity of the times.]

Given at Starkenberg, in the year of the incarnation of the Lord, 1244, on the first of July.

CHAPTER 9

The Mongol Shock

CAN JUDAISM SURVIVE WHEN TRADE AND URBAN ECONOMIES COLLAPSE?

> Do not ask . . . what happened to your servant at the time
> when he arrived in this country, after he had been in danger
> from the Tatars three times. The last was that they arrived on
> the morning of the Fast, when we were in al-'Imrāniyya. They
> remained outside the town killing everybody who was on his
> way to or from the town, while we stayed in the synagogue
> waiting for what the enemy would do from hour to hour. . . .
> Finally we went down finding the country full of dead.
> —*Correspondence between a Jew in Mesopotamia*
> *and a Jew in Egypt, 1236*

OUR HISTORICAL JOURNEY LEAVES MEDIEVAL EUROPE AND BRINGS US
back to the Middle East and North Africa under Muslim rule circa
1170, at the time of Benjamin of Tudela's journey. The majority of world
Jewry was located in the enormous territory under Muslim rule stretching from Persia to Morocco, with communities in Samarkand, Isfahan,
Baghdad, Basra, Mosul, Kufa, Aden, Damascus, Cairo, and Alexandria.
Most of the Jews were engaged in crafts, local commerce, long-distance
trade, moneylending, court banking, medicine, and a wide array of urban
skilled occupations.

By the mid-tenth century, the Abbasid Empire had fragmented into
many autonomous provinces with almost completely independent rulers,
armies, and local taxes, and the central power of the caliph in Baghdad
had weakened. Both local and Persian rulers attempted to gain control of
Mesopotamia but the Abbasid dynasty succeeded in surviving and keeping Baghdad as the center of the fragmented empire. Islamic civilization
reached new heights, Islam expanded in Africa and Asia, and trade continued to thrive, thanks to relatively easy and safe mobility within the empire.
Similarly, Egypt and the Maghreb under the Fatimid caliphate during the
tenth and eleventh centuries and the Ayyubid sultanate during the late
twelfth and early thirteenth centuries were vibrant urban economies, the

crossroads of trading routes connecting the entire Mediterranean area all the way to the Indian Ocean.[1]

Conditions changed dramatically at the beginning of the thirteenth century. In 1206, Genghis Khan began the first of several waves of Mongol invasions that would ravage most of Asia and the Middle East in the following two centuries and establish one of the largest empires in history. Before he died in 1227, his empire included a vast territory stretching from northern China to the Caspian Sea and from northern Persia and Pakistan all the way to Poland.

One of the most important economic consequences of these invasions was the disruption of the trading routes from China and other parts of Asia to Europe. The decline in trade destabilized the economy throughout the entire Abbasid caliphate. The fear of the unstoppable Mongol troops, with their devastating impact, was well known to both the rulers and the populations of the Muslim caliphates in the 1220s. What was the impact of this geopolitical turmoil on the large and prosperous Jewish population of the Middle East and North Africa that was described in Benjamin of Tudela's travel itinerary only fifty years earlier?

THE MONGOL CONQUEST OF THE MUSLIM MIDDLE EAST

In 1219, after conquering most of Central Asia, Genghis Khan invaded northern Persia and Armenia. On his way to the Middle East, he sacked many cities including Samarkand, which was one of the largest and most commercial cities along the Silk Route from Europe to China, hosting a wealthy Jewish community. (In his travel itinerary, Benjamin of Tudela listed 50,000 Jews in Samarkand. Since he did not visit the city, he probably reported hearsay. Even if the number of Jews in Samarkand was not the one proposed by Benjamin of Tudela, other historical sources confirm that there were sizable Jewish communities in Central Asia along the Silk Route.) Genghis Khan used his large army both to invade new territories and to control his newly established empire. The basic military strategy of the Mongol rulers was to generate fear and terror, to loot and collect all valuables and food for their army and for Mongol civilian consumption, and to impose heavy taxes of many forms.[2] In consequence, urban centers

---

[1] Goitein (1967–88, vol. 1); Greif (1989); Lewis (2002); Gil (2004); Goitein and Friedman (2007); Kuran (2010b).

[2] Most of the information on the economic conditions of Persia and Mesopotamia during and after the Mongol Conquest reported in this section comes from Ashtor (1939, 1959a, 1959b, 1972, 1976), Baron (1952, vol. 17, chap. 73), Petrushevsky (1968), Bausani (1971), and Gil (2004, pp. 431–33), who studied many primary sources, including viziers' chronicles, state bureaucrats' compendia, and travelers' accounts, such as the ones by Ibn Battūta and Hamdullah Mustawfi bin Abu Bakr al-Qazwini.

collapsed, agricultural production fell sharply, and the population of the invaded territories declined dramatically as a result of massacres, epidemics, and famines.

Benjamin of Tudela and other medieval sources document that in the late twelfth century, sizable Jewish communities lived in almost all urban centers in northern Persia later conquered by the Mongol army. Neither medieval travel records nor the massive responsa literature nor the wealth of documents in the Cairo Geniza contain any evidence of mass migrations to Europe by Jews from Persia. Thus, when Genghis Khan's army began his conquest of Persia in 1219, Persian Jews were possibly as numerous and prominent as they had been fifty years earlier. It is unlikely that under the threat of the Mongol invasions, Persian Jews tried to escape to Europe, because the Mongol army controlled all the main roads to the west in order to prevent any potential threat from the Muslim army.

At the death of Genghis Khan, his son Ogedei continued the Mongol conquest of Persia and Mesopotamia. Some interesting evidence on this military campaign from the point of view of the Jewish communities in the Middle East comes from the documents of the Cairo Geniza. A letter written in December 1236 by a leading member of the large Jewish community in the city of Mosul (on the River Tigris in northern Mesopotamia)—excerpted in the epigraph to this chapter—provides a firsthand description of the devastation caused by the Mongols. The letter was dispatched to the *nasi*, the head of the Jewish community in Egypt, who at the time resided in Fustat (Cairo). The writer describes how he, together with a few other Jews, managed to escape from a Mongol attack while they were in the synagogue in the town of Imrania. This town was a large trading center located about 100 kilometers east of Mosul next to an important castle named Irbil, which is also mentioned in Benjamin of Tudela's travel itinerary. The Mongols did not attack the synagogue; during the night a group of several men climbed the mountain, hidden by the trees, and saw about fifty Mongol horsemen. They hid there for eight days; when they returned to the town, they found it full of dead bodies.[3]

This letter and other historical evidence shed light on the geopolitical situation and economic conditions in Persia and Mesopotamia under the threat of the Mongol invasions, highlighting in particular three important points. First, the Jews throughout the Middle East and North Africa were fully aware of the devastating consequences of the Mongols' invasion of Persia and the dismal prospects if the Mongols were to bring their military campaign to Mesopotamia. Second, the Mongol military tactics included sudden attacks to surprise and terrorize the rival army as well as the local population; as a result, few people could run away and survive once the Mongol army decided to conquer a town or village. Third, Mesopotamian

---

[3] Goitein (1956); Gil (2004, p. 432).

Jews did not have a plan to migrate to Europe, although they were aware of the potential threat the Mongols posed to the entire Abbasid Empire.

In the meantime, the Mongol threat began looming over Europe. In 1236, Ogedei extended his military campaign toward eastern Europe. His army gained control of Moscow in 1238 and of Kiev in December 1240. The Mongols ruled Russia until the middle of the fifteenth century. At the beginning of December 1241, after defeating the Hungarian and Polish armies in several battles, the Mongol troops marched toward Vienna, threatening to bring their devastating force to the rest of Europe. The death of Ogedei on December 11 forced the Mongol army to retreat and to give up the plan to invade western Europe. After several years of family disputes, Mongke, a grandson of Genghis Khan, became the Great Khan. During the early 1250s, European monarchs and the pope tried to negotiate agreements with the Mongols in order to prevent invasions of Europe and direct the Mongol military expansion toward the Muslim Middle East.

While these events were unfolding, Mesopotamian Jewry represented the largest Jewish community in the world. The possibility of a Mongol invasion of Mesopotamia posed a threat to the region's urban and commercial economy and to the many Jews who were involved in crafts, shopkeeping, trade, commerce, medicine, money changing, and moneylending.

In 1252, Mongke Khan put his brother Hulagu in command of the army with the task of conquering the Middle East and gaining full control of all of the territory under Muslim rule. The Mongol troops once again crossed into Persia, massacring the Muslim sect known in Europe as the Assassins (*Isma'ilis*) and opening their way to Baghdad, which they entered in February 1258. After the Abbasid caliph refused their ultimatum to surrender, the Mongols demolished the city, one of the world's largest. Many descriptions of this event indicate that almost all Sunni Muslims were butchered. In contrast, Christians, Jews, and Shia Muslims were mostly spared, because the Mongols viewed them as opposing the Abbasid regime.[4] Several hundred thousand inhabitants (some sources indicate 800,000) were massacred or died of starvation or disease. Baghdad lost its status as the religious and cultural capital of Islam, and its destruction ended the Abbasid caliphate.[5]

In 1259, Hulagu's troops entered Damascus, where the Christian population welcomed them as part of the European Christian attempt to establish a coalition with the Mongols against the Abbasid Empire. The Mongols then headed toward Egypt, leaving untouched the cities under the Crusaders' rule on the Mediterranean coast, such as Akko (Acre) in

---

[4]Christians may have been spared because of the diplomatic envoys sent by the pope and some western European rulers to the Mongol leaders in an attempt to stop the Mongol march to Europe.

[5]Baron (1952, vol. 17, chap. 73).

the Land of Israel, as well as Tyre and Tripoli in Lebanon. On September 3, 1260, the Mamluks ruling Egypt stopped the Mongol military campaign in the battle of Ain Jalut in the eastern Galilee.[6]

This battle was a watershed, because for the first time since the beginning of their westward expansion, the Mongols were decisively defeated and permanently gave up their attempts to conquer the Middle East, North Africa, and Europe. One of the reasons for this defeat was that Hulagu returned to Asia with most of his troops, planning to succeed Mongke Khan, who had died. The Mongol army left to face the Mamluks at Ain Jalut was nevertheless similar in size to the Mamluk army. Thanks to the tactics of the Mamluk generals, the invaders were forced to retreat; many Mongols were killed; and Hulagu's deputy, Ket Buqa Noyan, was captured and executed. On their way back to Mesopotamia, the Mongol troops who had survived the defeat by the Mamluks brought more devastation and massacres. Hulagu Khan moved the capital of the Ilkhanate from Baghdad to Tabriz, in northwestern Persia, reducing even further the prominent role Mesopotamia had played in the Abbasid era.

In 1291, the Mamluks returned to the Land of Israel and defeated the last Crusaders in the coastal ports. From the late 1290s until 1517, when the Ottoman Empire gained control of the area, the Mamluk sultanate, with its capital in Damascus, ruled over the Land of Israel, Syria, Lebanon, Egypt, and most of North Africa. During roughly the same period, the Mongol Ilkhanate controlled Persia, Mesopotamia, Armenia, and Asia Minor, marking almost the end of the once urban and commercially vibrant economy of the Middle East.

SOCIOECONOMIC CONDITIONS IN THE MIDDLE EAST UNDER THE MONGOLS

At the height of Muslim rule, from the early eighth to the late eleventh century, the Middle East and North Africa thrived economically. Scientific and technological advances, the growth of both agricultural productivity and manufacture, a bustling commercial economy with trade connecting the Iberian Peninsula to the Far East, and spectacular urbanization went hand in hand, placing Mesopotamia, Persia, Yemen, Syria, Lebanon, Egypt, the Maghreb, the Iberian Peninsula, and Sicily under the Umayyad, Abbasid, and Fatimid caliphates among the wealthiest, most urban, and

---

[6] See Ashtor and Amitai (2007). The Mamluks were enslaved children and young adults from Central Asia, who were educated as Muslims and trained as loyal soldiers by the Abbasid and Fatimid rulers during the tenth and eleventh centuries. During the twelfth and thirteenth centuries, they served as soldiers for the Ayyubid dynasty that ruled Egypt, Syria, Lebanon, and the Land of Israel. The Mamluks took control over Egypt in 1250, after the last sultan died. They then extended their power to Syria and other parts of the Middle East.

culturally prominent areas in world history. During this period, cities in the Middle East, North Africa, the Iberian Peninsula, and Sicily were much larger than urban centers in Europe (see table 1.4). Benjamin of Tudela and other travelers recorded with astonishment the wealth and high standards of living of Christians, Jews, and Muslims living in the cities, towns, and villages of these regions.

The Mongol invasions dramatically changed this picture. Mesopotamia and Persia underwent radical socioeconomic transformation and experienced a traumatic demographic and economic collapse. Large urban centers like Baghdad, Mosul, and Basra turned into much smaller towns. In the mid-fourteenth century, for example, the population of Baghdad numbered about 60,000 people—still a sizable figure compared with European cities of that time but much smaller than it had been in the ninth and tenth centuries, when it numbered 600,000–1,000,000 people.[7]

Until roughly the 1290s, the Mongol Khans imposed their nomadic way of living in the newly conquered areas. They also imposed heavy taxes and demanded substantial tributes. As the number of insolvent farmers grew, many became slaves of the soil—a position previously unheard of in the Islamic world, which regarded farmers and land laborers as freemen. Some 50–90 percent of the villages in the major provinces of Persia and Mesopotamia were abandoned, and, according to the detailed account in the chronicles of Rashiduddin Fazlullah, only a tenth of the soil in Persia remained cultivated.[8] The cultivated area in Mesopotamia shrank by 50 percent.

Tax revenues from all provinces in Persia and Mesopotamia decreased by nearly 90 percent between the late thirteenth century and the end of Mongol control of the area in the fourteenth century. Given that tax rates rose, the fact that tax revenues collapsed by roughly 90 percent indicates that taxable earnings must have shrunk by far more than 90 percent. Crafts and trade were not spared. Craftsmen and other urban workers toiled under semi-slavery conditions, with their wages and earnings paid in certain commodities set by decree by the Mongol rulers. Shopkeepers, traders, and merchants had to pay high taxes (30–70 percent of their sales). The combination of heavy taxes and demographic collapse dealt a devastating blow to the urban and commercial economy of Mesopotamia and Persia.

[7] Information in this section comes from Baron (1952, vol. 17, chap. 73); Ashtor (1959a, 1959b, 1972, 1976); Petrushevsky (1968); Bausani (1971); Lapidus (1981); Watson (1981); Gil (2004, pp. 431–33).

[8] One of the most important accounts of the Mongol invasions was written by Rashiduddin Fazlullah (also known as Rashid al-Din Fadhlullah Hamadani), the vizier of the Ilkhanate ruler Ghazan Khan. Written in Persian, his *Jami'u't-tawarikh* (*Compendium of Chronicles*) describes the history of the Turkish and Mongol peoples, the rise of Genghis Khan, and the Mongol conquests, as well as the histories of other nations, including the Persians, Arabs, Greeks, Chinese, Indians, and Franks (Europeans).

By the end of the thirteenth century, the collapse in tax revenues and the almost empty treasury of the Ilkhanate led the Mongol rulers to introduce paper money for trade transactions within Mesopotamia and Persia, as they had done earlier in China. In this way, all coins could be kept in the treasury. Paper banknotes were issued from the capital of the Ilkhanate, Tabriz. People were trying to avoid using the paper money due to the decrease of its value (inflation). However, the Ilkhanate regime forced them to accept and use the notes under the threat of death. The consequences of this move were disastrous for crafts and trade: bazaars and shops closed down, and households had hard times finding commodities and merchandise.

JEWISH DEMOGRAPHY UNDER MONGOL AND MAMLUK RULE: AN EXPERIMENT

Circa 1170, about 800,000 to one million Jews lived in Mesopotamia, Persia, and the Arabian Peninsula (mainly in Yemen) under the Abbasid caliphate, whereas about 70,000 dwelled in North Africa and about 55,000 in Syria and Lebanon under the Ayyubid sultanate (see table 1.7 and appendix, tables A.1 and A.2). When, in the early sixteenth century, the Ottoman sultans extended their rule over this vast area, there were only about 250,000–350,000 Jews in Mesopotamia and Persia, roughly 5,000 in Egypt and about 7,000 in Syria and Lebanon. This decrease in about 300 years represents one of the largest changes in Jewish demography. Most of the drop occurred in an even shorter time span, from the late thirteenth to the mid-fourteenth centuries. It was larger in percentage terms and occurred much more rapidly than the corresponding Jewish population decline during Talmudic times. In light of this, it is surprising that almost no major work on the history of the Jewish people tackles this question (exceptions are the work of Eliyahu Ashtor and Salo Baron).[9]

What happened to the large, urban, wealthy, and prominent Jewish communities in the Middle East and North Africa? Were the massacres, famines, and diseases that hit Mesopotamia and Persia during and after the Mongol conquests responsible for the striking Jewish population decline? Did mass migrations of Jews to Europe make the West the new center of world Jewry? Could the conversion of the Mongol Khans to Islam and their attempt to convert non-Muslim religious minorities account for the sharp reduction of the Jewish population in the Middle East and North Africa?[10] Or did voluntary conversions of Jews to Islam—

[9]Ashtor (1939, 1959a, 1959b, 1967, 1968, 1972, 1976); Baron (1952, vol. 17, chap. 73).

[10]The Mongols were a nomadic and tribal society without a well-established religion. When they invaded Mesopotamia and Persia, their goal was to overthrow the Abbasid

similar to the conversions of Jews to Christianity during Talmudic times described in chapter 5—explain a proportion of the huge drop in the number of Egyptian, Mesopotamian, Persian, and Syrian Jews during the late thirteenth and early fourteenth centuries?

Persia

As the Mesopotamian academies started losing prominence during the mid-eleventh and twelfth centuries, the Jewish population in Persia grew in both size and wealth. Based on Benjamin of Tudela's figures, circa 1170 it numbered about 250,000–350,000 people (see appendix, tables A.1 and A.2), considering his figures as the number of individuals for the towns he did not actually visit but he only heard of, and adding Jews to locations in which it is known they lived from other historical sources but which Benjamin either failed to mention or for which he provided no numbers although acknowledging their existence.

By the mid-1230s, the Mongols had completed their conquest of Persia, and the number of Persian Jews shrank significantly. The best estimate is that circa 1490, there were no more than 100,000–150,000 Jews in Persia.[11] Between 1170 and 1490, the total population of Persia (and Mesopotamia) decreased by about 35 percent (table 1.7), whereas the Jewish population in Persia shrank by about 58 percent.

What happened to the Persian Jews? Why was their demographic decline larger than that of the rest of the population? Famines and epidemics (including the Black Death of 1348 and subsequent bouts of plague during the late fourteenth and the fifteenth centuries) took a huge toll on the entire population of the Middle East, and the Jews were no exception. Yet, as mentioned earlier, the Mongol rulers spared the religious minorities (e.g., Christians and Jews) from the massacres that they inflicted on the local Sunni Muslim population; hence, from this point of view, the Jewish population decline should have been smaller than the general population decline.

There is also no evidence that Persian Jews fled to Baghdad or any other city in Mesopotamia or other locations west of Persia before 1260—probably because it was difficult to migrate to eastern Europe or the Balkans. Between 1230 and 1241, the Mongols were fighting Russian,

---

Empire, whose religious leadership was vested in the Sunni sect. To gain support against the Abbasid caliphate, they employed Shia Muslims as well as members of religious minorities, foremost Christians and Jews, as part of the new administration and state bureaucracy. The influence of the dominant culture and religion led the Ilkhanate ruler Ghazan to convert to Islam, in 1295.

[11] Ashtor (1939, 1959a, 1959b, 1976); Clark (1968); Baron (1952, vol. 17, chap. 73; 1971b); McEvedy and Jones (1978).

Polish, and Hungarian armies; in the northern parts of Persia, Armenia, and Anatolia, they had full control of the main routes from east to west. The historical record is also completely silent about huge migrations of Persian Jews to southern and western Europe (see chapter 7). Something else must account for the larger decline of the Jewish population of Persia compared to the rest of the population.

Although the Mongols spared the lives of Christians and Jews as well as Shia Muslims, they did much economic damage to these religious minorities. Given the high tax rates imposed by the Mongol Khans on all economic activities, it is likely that Persian Jews were subject to an economic fate that was bad—or even worse—in comparison with that of the local Muslim population. The reason is as follows. Before the Mongol invasions, most Jews were engaged in urban skilled occupations, including crafts, shopkeeping, and trade, which raised their average incomes above those of the rest of the population, who were engaged mainly in agriculture. With the economic setback caused by the Mongol Conquest, Persian Jews probably experienced a larger loss of earnings and a comparatively greater decline in their standards of living. Finding themselves living in a subsistence agrarian and pastoral economy, with few opportunities for trade or urban activities, the region's Jews entered a long period of assimilation and conversion to Islam, which can partly explain their demographic decline in Persia.[12]

Mesopotamia

As in Persia, between 1170 and 1490, the total population of Mesopotamia decreased by about 35 percent (table 1.7). At the time of Benjamin of Tudela's journey circa 1170, the Jewish population of Mesopotamia amounted to about 600,000 (see table 1.7 and appendix, tables A.1 and A.2), with Baghdad and its surrounding area hosting about 40,000 Jewish households, many synagogues, and ten academies of higher learning. By 1490, 100,000–150,000 Jews remained in Mesopotamia—a reduction of about 80 percent—with Baghdad probably hosting no more than 1,000–2,000 Jews.[13]

---

[12] Baron (1952, vol. 17, chap. 73, pp. 165, 181–83; 1971b) and Ashtor (1959a) document the voluntary conversion and assimilation process of the Jews in the Middle East after the Mongol Conquest.

[13] Ashtor (1939, 1959a, 1959b, 1976); Baron (1952, vol. 17, chap. 73; 1971b); Clark (1968); McEvedy and Jones (1978); Gil (2004, pp. 491–96). Given that Benjamin of Tudela visited and described in detail cities and towns in Mesopotamia circa 1170, we take his figures as the number of households in each location, and, hence, we multiply his figures by five, assuming that each household consisted, on average, of five people. See appendix for more details.

What happened to the once numerous and prominent Jewish population in Mesopotamia? Like their Persian co-religionists, Mesopotamian Jews seem to have been spared the carnage that hit mainly the Sunni Muslim population during the Mongol Conquest. Neither Jewish nor non-Jewish primary sources include references to mass massacres of Jews by the Mongol rulers. Some persecutions and organized attacks on Jews by Muslims occurred in 1285 and 1291, when the Muslims who had left Baghdad in the aftermath of the Mongol attacks returned to the city. Most synagogues were destroyed, and a local Jewish vizier who was a high official in the Ilkhanate administration was murdered.

Famines and epidemics (including the Black Death of 1348 and subsequent plagues) took a toll on the Jewish population, as they did on the rest of the population. Mesopotamian Jews migrated to North Africa and Syria but not in huge numbers. There is no record of mass migrations of Jews from Mesopotamia to eastern or western Europe in the two and a half centuries after the Mongol Conquest. Hence, wars, epidemics, or migrations alone cannot explain the precipitous decline of the once numerous Jewish population of Mesopotamia. Part of the decline probably reflects conversion to Islam by a large segment of Mesopotamian Jewry.[14]

These conversions occurred at a time when the economic conditions of the Jews in Mesopotamia declined. The economic collapse experienced by the region under the Ilkhanate—the reverse of the urban and economic growth during the Abbasid caliphate—hit Mesopotamian Jews, who had been engaged in the most urban and skilled occupations during the golden age of the Abbasid Empire, especially hard. In this declining economy, the urban structure of Jewish life based on synagogues, schools, and academies could not survive. The complete disappearance of the academies in Mesopotamia and of the wealthy Jewish leadership of the "house of David" still glorified by Benjamin of Tudela in 1170 is a tangible sign of the economic hardship of the Jews in Mesopotamia in the two and a half centuries after the Mongol Conquest.

Egypt and Syria

Between 1170 and 1490, the population of Egypt and the rest of North Africa decreased by about 6 percent, and that of Syria and Lebanon remained fairly stable (table 1.7). Circa 1170, Jews numbered about 40,000 in Egypt, about 30,000 in the rest of North Africa, and roughly 55,000 in Syria and Lebanon. Despite some migration of Jews from Mesopotamia

---

[14]Baron (1952, vol. 17, chap. 73, pp. 165, 181–83) and Ashtor (1959a, pp. 65–66) document the conversion and assimilation process to Islam of Jews in the Middle East after the Mongol Conquest.

and Persia to Syria and North Africa in the aftermath of the Mongol Conquest, by 1490 there were no more than about 5,000 Jews in Egypt and 7,000 in Syria.[15]

Why did Egyptian and Syrian Jewry decline much more than the rest of the population in these regions? There was a terrible plague and famine in Egypt in 1201–1202 that killed huge numbers. Repeated episodes of plague—beginning with the most famous of all, the Black Death of 1348—took a heavy toll on the populations of North Africa and the Levant, including the Jews, during the fourteenth and fifteenth centuries. In addition to these factors that account for both general and Jewish population decline, conversion can explain the larger drop in the size of the Jewish population in North Africa and Syria compared with the rest of the population. Rabbinic responsa produced by the descendants of Maimonides indicate that a proportion of Jews in North Africa and Syria assimilated or voluntarily converted to Islam, exactly as their co-religionists had done in Persia and Mesopotamia.[16]

WHY JUDAISM CANNOT SURVIVE WHEN TRADE AND URBAN ECONOMIES COLLAPSE

The conversion to Islam of a large proportion of Jews in the Middle East during the two centuries after the Mongol shock was not part of the conversion process of the entire population. The mass conversions, voluntary or forced, of the local populations to Islam had occurred much earlier, in the eighth through eleventh century.[17] In contrast, conversions of a proportion of Jews to Islam reflected the economic collapse of the Middle East.

Obeying the many laws and norms of the Jewish religion, including maintaining the synagogues and the schools, paying the teachers' salaries, purchasing the books for the children, and forgoing the earnings that sons could earn instead of going to school, was expensive for a significant

---

[15]Ashtor (1959a, 1967, 1968, 1976); Baron (1952, vol. 17, chap. 73; 1971b); Clark (1968); McEvedy and Jones (1978). The information on Jewish population and occupational structure in the late twelfth century comes from Benjamin of Tudela's figures compared with figures from other sources, such as Maimonides's accounts. For the late fifteenth century, the information is mostly based on the travelers' reports such as Joseph Montagna (c. 1480), Meshullam of Volterra (c. 1481), Obadiah de Bertinoro (c. 1488), and an anonymous student of de Bertinoro (c. 1495). See the appendix for a more detailed discussion of Benjamin of Tudela's Jewish population estimates.

[16]Baron (1952, vol. 17, chap. 73, pp. 165, 181–83) and Ashtor (1959a, pp. 65–66) document the conversion and assimilation process to Islam of Jews in Egypt and Syria.

[17]Bulliet (1979a, 1979b) gives estimates of the conversions to Islam in Persia, Mesopotamia, North Africa, Syria, Lebanon, the Land of Israel, and the Iberian Peninsula.

portion of the Jewish population in the poverty-stricken economies of Mesopotamia and Persia after the Mongol Conquest, and in North Africa and Syria under Mamluk rule. A large proportion of Jews may therefore have chosen not to send their sons to schools or synagogues to acquire Hebrew religious literacy, as required by the Jewish religion. Moreover, with crafts, trade, commerce, and moneylending severely hit by the economic collapse during the Mongol Ilkhanate and the Mamluk sultanate, many Jews found it difficult to find employment in occupations with high returns to their investment in literacy and education. They could engage only in farming or live in cities as poor wage laborers or shopkeepers, like the rest of the population.

Converting to Islam freed them of the religious requirement to educate their children—a costly investment with no financial return in economies that were no longer the urban and commercially bustling ones of the Umayyad, Abbasid, and Fatimid caliphates. Of course, conversion may occur for reasons that have little to do with the cost of educating one's children as required by Judaism. But it is interesting to note that the assimilation or conversion to Islam of a portion of the Jews in the Middle East, North Africa, and Syria did not occur when these regions were wealthy commercial economies. In contrast, a proportion of Jews converted when these regions once again became subsistence agrarian and pastoral societies, as they had been in the first half of the first millennium—the other period in Jewish history in which Jews converted (to Christianity).

These historical facts are consistent with our theory, outlined in chapter 4, which predicts that in each generation, a portion of Jews converts because the cost of remaining Jewish offsets the benefit. Judaism thrives in urban and commercial societies and is bound to disappear when trade and urban economies collapse.

SUMMARY

The Mongol Conquest brought traumatic demographic and economic consequences to the Middle East. By circa 1260, Persia and Mesopotamia under the Mongol Ilkhanate and North Africa and the Levant under Mamluk rule were no longer the populated, urban, and commercially thriving regions they had been at the height of the Umayyad, Abbasid, and Fatimid caliphates (eighth through eleventh century). Subsistence farming and nomadic pastoral activities became the source of income for most households, including Jewish households. Heavy taxation reduced both agricultural incomes and the earnings of town dwellers. The cultural and intellectual splendor that had characterized the cities and urban centers during the Muslim caliphates disappeared.

Most Jews in these regions, who found it harder to continue to work in urban skilled occupations and were unable to migrate to Europe, had to resort to farming or other low-income occupations. The investment in their children's literacy and education, as required by the Jewish religious norm, became too costly. As a result, many assimilated or converted to Islam, the dominant religion throughout the region, which enabled them to avoid both the head tax imposed on religious minorities and the need to invest in their children's religious literacy and education.

While conversions (in addition to epidemics and, to a smaller extent, the massacres ensuing from the Mongol invasions) caused the Jewish population in the Middle East, North Africa, and Syria to decrease in the two and a half centuries after the 1250s, those who chose to continue to practice Judaism kept investing in the religious and general literacy of their children and kept holding urban skilled occupations, consistent with the predictions of our theory described in chapter 6 and also with the descriptions of the Jewish communities in the Middle East and North Africa in the 1480s documented in the reports of the Jewish travelers, as shown in the next chapter.

CHAPTER 10

1492 to Today

OPEN QUESTIONS

> In the whole world there is no city as beautiful as Damas-
> cus . . . There are also in Damascus 450 Jewish households,
> rich and honored merchants all of them, their head is a wise,
> honored, and pious Jew, R. Joseph, the physician.
> —*Rabbi Meshullam ben R. Menahem, 1481*

> The modern age is the Jewish age, and the twentieth century,
> in particular, is the Jewish Century. Modernization is about
> everyone becoming urban, mobile, literate, articulate, intel-
> lectually intricate, physically fastidious, and occupationally
> flexible. It is about how to cultivate people and symbols, not
> fields and herd.
> —*Yuri Slezkine, The Jewish Century, 2004*

THE HISTORICAL JOURNEY IN THIS BOOK BEGAN IN 70 CE, WHEN THE
Second Temple in Jerusalem was burned and destroyed forever, and ended
in 1492 with the edict of expulsion of the Jews from Spain. Between these
two traumatic events, the history of the Jewish people has been marked
by some unique features that we explained through the lens of economic
theory. Before summarizing what we learned, we will let two well-known
Jewish travelers take us to the Jewish communities in Egypt and the
Levant in the 1480s to see how different these communities were from
their ancestors who lived in the same locations fifteen centuries earlier.

PORTRAIT OF WORLD JEWRY CIRCA 1492

On May 4, 1481, Rabbi Meshullam ben R. Menahem of Volterra, Italy
reached Rhodes on his way to Egypt, the Land of Israel, and Syria.[1] A

---

[1] Adler (1987, pp. 156–250) edited the letters and travel itineraries of Rabbi Meshullam
and Rabbi Obadiah summarized in this chapter.

month later, he arrived in Alexandria, where, he reported, sixty Jewish households dwelled. These families recalled that a few decades earlier, 4,000 Jewish households had lived in the city. After a relatively easy sail from Alexandria to Misr (Cairo) through Rosetta, Meshullam recounted that "in Misr there are 650 Jewish households, as well as 150 Karaite and 50 Samaritan households." Each community had its own quarter and synagogue. The rabbi met the Mamluk sultan, who "has placed over the Jews, the Karaites, and the Samaritans, a Jewish lord, rich and learned, and much honored." This was the *nagid*, who had power over all criminal and civil matters within the Jewish community. In Cairo, Meshullam knew a prominent Jewish dealer in precious stones, who twenty-two years earlier had visited his house in Florence. This contact and his own wealth made him a welcome and well-respected visitor of the Jewish community in Cairo.

From Cairo, Meshullam headed east, arriving in Gaza before traveling on to Hebron and Jerusalem. He described this part of his journey as so dangerous that he needed to hire guards and pay to escape several attempts by local Bedouins to hold him and his partners for ransom. From Jaffa he sailed to Beirut, from which he reached Damascus. Meshullam praised the beauty and richness of that city in comparison with Cairo or any other city in Italy. He completed his journey by returning to Venice in October 1481.

Seven years later, another prominent Jewish rabbi and commentator of the Mishna, Obadiah ben Abraham of Bertinoro (a town near Forlì in Italy), sailed to Jerusalem. Unlike Meshullam, who returned to Italy, Obadiah settled in Jerusalem, becoming the intellectual leader of the Jewish community there.

Both Meshullam and Obadiah needed the approval of the Mamluk sultan to travel to Egypt and from there to Jerusalem. Obadiah reported a smaller number of Jewish households (500) dwelling in Cairo, including a small group of Jews who had left the Iberian Peninsula to avoid forced conversion. He also described the communities of 150 Karaite and 50 Samaritan households. He recorded 60 Jewish households in Alexandria, 50 in Bilbeis, and 20 in al-Khanqa. Alexandria is described as being the size of Florence, with large buildings but many of them in ruins. At the end of the fifteenth century, as these travel diaries suggest, Egypt seems to have been home to no more than 5,000 Jews, mainly merchants and artisans, living in small communities in many cities.

Like Benjamin of Tudela three centuries earlier, Meshullam and Obadiah recorded the numbers of Jewish households in each location they visited and the names of the local Jewish leaders. Obadiah mentions the Jewish Ashkenazi rabbi of Gaza and the existence of a small Jewish community in Hebron. He confirms the information on the Jewish community in Damascus supplied by Meshullam, praising the community's wealth and beautiful houses and gardens.

The Jerusalem Obadiah describes was mostly in ruins, with no surrounding walls, and had a population of about 4,000 households, out of which only 70 were Jewish. The Jews were not persecuted, and they could freely practice their religion under the Mamluk ruler, who appointed a *nagid*, who was in charge of collecting the tax levied on all Jewish adults. The tiny community was divided into Ashkenazi and Sephardic groups, which had their own synagogues and intellectual milieus. Jews from Damascus, Cairo, and Yemen visited Jerusalem. Obadiah pointed out that the Sephardic Jews did not know the Talmud but adhered very closely to the works of Maimonides.

What do we learn from the reports of these late medieval Jewish travelers? First, Cairo and Damascus under the Mamluk sultanate were large and wealthy cities in comparison to cities and towns in Europe. The Jews living in Cairo and Damascus were urban dwellers, who enjoyed, on average, higher standards of living than the local population, which was engaged mainly in agriculture. Other cities were in ruins and small relative to earlier times.

Second, the Jewish communities in Egypt, the Land of Israel, and Syria were much smaller than those Benjamin of Tudela described three centuries earlier. Jewish communities dwelled only in cities; despite their small size, they had synagogues, schools, rabbinic courts, and other communal institutions.

Third, Jews from Asia Minor, the Balkans, Egypt, Germany, the Iberian Peninsula, Italy, Syria, and Yemen visited or settled in Jerusalem, but there is no mention in the letters of Meshullam or Obadiah of Jews from Mesopotamia and Persia doing so. A short letter by an Italian rabbi and traveler, Elijah of Ferrara, written from Jerusalem in 1438, mentions stories related to Jews in Ethiopia and India.

Fourth, the letters and travel accounts of late medieval Jewish rabbis fail to devote even a single line to the existence of large and wealthy Jewish communities in Mesopotamia and Persia. Silence seems to surround what Benjamin of Tudela and other sources had described as the largest and most prominent Jewish communities in the world at the end of the twelfth century.

The description of the local economies in the travel reports of Obadiah and Meshullam are consistent with the overall economic conditions in Egypt, the Land of Israel, Mesopotamia, Persia, and Syria described in chapter 9. Following the fall of the Abbasid Empire after the Mongol Conquest, there was a long period of deteriorating economic conditions, general population decline, and a substantial, disproportional decrease in the Jewish population. Trade declined with worsening safety in travel, and cities became smaller. Yet, the reports of the late medieval Jewish travelers document that the surviving small Jewish communities maintained their commitment to universal male education, as required by Judaism. There is no evidence of large academies in these locations, but the late medieval Jewish travelers emphasized that even in poor communities, such as in Rhodes, the Jews were literate. The communities reaped the benefits of their investment in literacy by selecting into urban skilled occupations. These facts are consistent with the predictions of our theory presented in chapter 6.

Jewish History, 70 CE–1492: Epilogue

This gallop across many centuries of Jewish history has raised some intriguing questions. Our book answers them—with a novel interpretation of the history of the Jewish people. The first set of questions were about the distinctive change in the occupational structure of the Jews that transformed them from a population of illiterate farmers in the first century CE into a twenty-first century population of highly literate and educated individuals engaged mainly in trade, banking, finance, law, and medicine. The second set of questions concerned why the Jews established a worldwide Diaspora of small urban communities from the ninth century onward. The third set of questions related to the demographic history of the Jewish people. We asked what were the factors behind the stunning demographic decline that hit world Jewry from the time of Jesus to the time of Muhammad, and later, after the Mongol Conquest in the late Middle Ages.

We showed that none of the existing theories can explain why the Jews left farming or became a Diaspora population. We then documented that the distinctive characteristics of the Jewish people were the outcome of a profound transformation of Judaism after the destruction of the Second Temple. This change shifted the religious leadership within the Jewish community and transformed Judaism from a cult based on sacrifices in the temple to a religion whose main norm required every Jewish man to read and to study the Torah in Hebrew and to send his sons to primary school or synagogue beginning at age six or seven to learn to do so. Evidence from the Talmud, the early Gaonic responsa, and archaeological remains of the synagogues suggests that during the Talmud era (third to sixth century), a growing proportion of Jewish farmers obeyed the new religious norm.

The increase in religious and general literacy among the predominantly rural Jewish population occurred at a time when world Jewry was declining. The demographic collapse of world Jewry partly as the outcome of voluntary conversions to Christianity in the agrarian economies of the Talmud period supports the prediction of our theory regarding the dynamics of the Jewish religion: in the long run, rabbinic Judaism cannot survive in subsistence farming societies, because the heavy costs imposed on Jewish families to obey the norms of their religion, including the costly norm requiring fathers to educate their sons and the lack of economic returns to this investment in literacy, will prompt a proportion of Jews to leave Judaism and embrace other religions that have less-demanding norms.

Yet the higher literacy of the Jewish people, coupled with a set of contract-enforcement institutions, gave the Jews a comparative advantage over non-Jews in skilled crafts, trade, commerce, and moneylending once the spectacular urbanization, the rise of manufacture, and the growth of local and long-distance trade in the newly established Abbasid caliphate during the eighth and ninth centuries created a huge demand for these occupations. Urbanization and commercial expansion also helped the Jewish population stabilize between the eighth and the twelfth centuries, because once Jews transitioned into literate and urban dwellers who engaged in myriad crafts and commercial activities that enjoyed contract-enforcement institutions as members of the same religious community, they had little incentive to voluntarily convert to other religions. The eighth to twelfth century also marked the intellectual golden age of the Jewish communities in the Middle East and the Mediterranean.

Once set in motion, this occupational and residential transition never reverted but rather became even stronger. From then on, the Jews became a small population of highly literate people, who continued to search for opportunities to reap returns from their investment in literacy and contract-enforcement institutions. We documented that the Jewish Diaspora in early medieval times had to do with the Jews' specialization in the most skilled urban occupations, such as crafts, trade, moneylending, and medicine. The demand for skilled occupations and the state of the local economies enhanced Jewish mobility and the need to migrate in search of locations that offered the possibility of profitably engaging in crafts, trade, and later, in the most skilled and profitable occupation—moneylending.

We showed that the rise of craft and merchant guilds, usury bans on Muslims and Christians, persecutions inflicted on the Jews, and Jewish involvement in wine making and wine trading all fail to explain the specialization and prominence of the Jews in moneylending in medieval Europe. We provided evidence that this specialization can be explained by the Jews' comparative advantages in the four assets that were, and still are, the pillars of financial intermediation: capital, networking, literacy and numeracy, and contract-enforcement institutions.

Last, we turned our attention to the history of the Jews in the Middle East and North Africa during and after the Mongol Conquest, which brought a traumatic geopolitical turmoil to these areas. The explanation we proposed for the Jewish demographic collapse during the Talmud era and the decline of the Jewish population in the Middle East and North Africa in the two and a half centuries after the Mongol invasions is the same. In subsistence rural economies, where literacy did not bring any economic return and where urban skilled jobs benefiting from literacy were almost absent, it became more expensive and less profitable for a significant proportion of the Jews to obey the norms of their religion, including the costly norm requiring fathers to educate their children. Hence, some of them converted.

One of the main lessons that the fifteen centuries of Jewish history surveyed here illustrate is that both rabbinic Judaism, with its unique religious norm requiring fathers to educate their sons, and the Jewish people who decided to obey this norm thrived in urban and commercial societies, and both were bound to disappear when trade and urban economies collapsed. To the growing literature that investigates the nexus between religion and economic outcomes, as well as to the literature that analyzes the interactions between cultural values, social norms, institutions, and economic outcomes (see the introduction), our book adds the insight that the salient and distinctive features of the demographic and economic history of the Jews from 70 CE to 1492 have been shaped by the social norms and contract-enforcement institutions that the Jewish religion fostered two millennia ago.

TRAJECTORY OF THE JEWISH PEOPLE OVER THE PAST 500 YEARS

Our books ends with the history of the Jews in 1492. The history of the Jewish people after 1500 will be the subject of our next journey of learning and our next book. In the next few pages we aim to highlight some puzzles and questions that the past 500 years of Jewish history raise. The following summary and analysis are neither detailed nor exhaustive. Nevertheless, we hope they can generate some curiosity and eagerness to learn about the history of the Jews in the early modern and modern periods.

By 1500, world Jewry had reached its lowest population level since the beginning of the first millennium. The once large and prominent communities in Mesopotamia, Persia, Egypt, and Syria, which during the golden age of Jewish history (ninth to twelfth centuries) had been the economic, religious, and intellectual hubs of Jewish life, were in decline, both numerically and economically. The small but wealthy communities of Jewish moneylenders had been expelled from England and France. German Jewry suffered from recurrent persecutions and temporary banishments from many towns and urban centers.

TABLE 10.1. Jewish Population by Geographical Area, c. 1490–1939 (millions)

Region	c. 1490	1939
Eastern Europe and Balkans	0.09	8.15
Americas	0	5.4
Middle East, Africa, and Asia	0.27–0.37	1.6
Western Europe	0.51	1.35
All locations	0.8–1	16.5

Sources: Data on Jewish population from Baron (1971b) and DellaPergola (2001, table 2).
Note: DellaPergola (2001, table 2) provides an estimate of 1.3 million Jews in 1490.
See appendix, note to tables 1.6 and 1.7, for the explanation of why our Jewish population
estimates for 1490 are lower than the ones provided by DellaPergola.

At the close of the fifteenth century, world Jewry consisted of fewer than one million people.[2] About half were Sephardic Jews, who lived mainly in Asia Minor, the Balkans, Egypt and the Maghreb, the Iberian Peninsula, Italy, the Land of Israel, Mesopotamia, Persia, Syria, and Yemen. The other half were Ashkenazi Jews, who lived in Austria, Germany, Hungary, Italy, the Netherlands, Poland, Romania, Russia, and Ukraine. There were no Jews in England, France, or Scandinavia. At this time, both Sephardic and Ashkenazi Jews were moneylenders, traders, merchants, shopkeepers, skilled craftsmen, physicians, and scholars, who lived in cities and urban centers. Overall, they enjoyed similar standards of living in all locations, as illustrated by the reports of the late medieval Jewish travelers.

How did the size and geographical distribution of Sephardic and Ashkenazi communities change in the following 500 years? By 1939, there were nearly 16.5 million Jews (table 10.1): 8.15 million in eastern Europe and the Balkans; 5.4 million in the Americas; 1.6 million in the Middle East, Africa, and Asia; and 1.35 million in western Europe. Of the total 16.5 million Jews, about 2.2 million were Sephardic, and about 14.3 were Ashkenazi. In the regions in which they lived, Jews represented about 1 percent of the population in 1490 and about 2 percent in 1939. The geographical distribution and total number of Jews in western and eastern Europe roughly coincide with that provided in the notorious Wannsee Protocol redacted by the Nazis in 1942.[3]

[2] Baron (1971b); DellaPergola (1992, 2001).
[3] The Wannsee Protocol, also known as "The Final Solution of the Jewish Question," was presented at a meeting in Berlin on January 20, 1942, attended by the top German military and political establishment.

Some 450 years after the expulsion of the Jews from the Iberian Peninsula in 1492–97, at which time there were roughly equal numbers of Sephardic and Ashkenazi Jews, there were seven times as many Ashkenazi Jews as Sephardic Jews. The change was spurred by the spectacular demographic growth of eastern European Jewry during the eighteenth and nineteenth centuries that increased the number of Jews living in Belarus, Czechoslovakia, Germany, Hungary, Poland, Romania, Russia, and Ukraine to more than eight million just before World War II.

What accounts for this change?[4] To answer this question, one must first carefully document the main trends in the demographic history of the Jewish people after 1500, as well as the key political, economic, and cultural events that marked the history of the many locales of the Jewish Diaspora in the past 500 years. In our next research project, we will investigate whether the economic theory with which we explained the demographic history of the Jews from 70 CE to 1492 can help unravel the demographic history of the Jews after 1500.

PERSISTENCE OF JEWISH OCCUPATIONAL STRUCTURE

Most of the Jewish craftsmen, traders, moneylenders, and physicians who left Spain after the edict of expulsion in 1492 went first to Portugal, where they remained only briefly before being expelled again, in 1496–97. Those who remained in the Iberian Peninsula and converted to Christianity but secretly kept their Jewish religious traditions became a distinct group

---

[4]Two recent books advance a similar hypothesis to explain this demographic puzzle. Sand (2008) maintains that the demographic growth of the Jewish population of eastern Europe is connected to the supposed conversion of the kingdom of Kuzaria—located between the Black and Caspian Seas, on the Silk Route from Europe to China—to Judaism between the seventh and eighth centuries. Brook (2006) argues that there were about 30,000 Jews in Kuzaria before the Mongol Conquest. Later, some of them migrated to the north, reaching Poland, Russia, and Ukraine. The presence of relatively large Jewish communities in this area was documented in Benjamin of Tudela's travel journal. There are at least two reasons for being skeptical about the above argument. First, in chapter 9 we show that the Mongols invaded this region in the 1220s, disrupting trade and killing a large portion of the local population. By the end of the fourteenth century, no more than a few thousand Jews likely remained in this area. It seems unlikely that this dwindling Jewish population could have spurred the spectacular demographic growth of the Jewish population in eastern Europe during the eighteenth and nineteenth centuries. Second, Jews in eastern Europe followed the Ashkenazi religious and cultural tradition and spoke Yiddish, whereas the Jews of Kuzaria were connected to Mesopotamian and Persian Jewry, which adhered to the Sephardic tradition. For example, Eckstein, Epstein, and Landau—common surnames of eastern European Jews—are cities and villages in Germany. These names were most likely given to Jewish immigrants to Poland and Ukraine based on their original location in Germany.

nicknamed Marranos.[5] Many of them and their descendants became leading traders and merchants all over the world from the sixteenth to the eighteenth century. Marrano traders imported spices, luxury goods, textiles,
and precious stones from the East Indies and the Americas which they
sold in Europe. Other Marrano merchants were involved in trading and
commercial activities in Africa, Brazil, and the West Indies. In addition
to the Iberian Peninsula, where the spice trade represented a very important share of Marrano business, the main European centers in which these
traders established their business in the sixteenth and early seventeenth
centuries were Amsterdam, Antwerp, Hamburg, Leghorn, and Venice.[6]

In the Ottoman Empire, Jews played a very important role in the silk,
spice, and jewel trade, connecting Europe to East and South Asia. Many
Jews who were expelled from Portugal in 1496–97 were expert producers
of arms, guns, and cannons—skills they brought to Constantinople.

In the second half of the seventeenth century and during the eighteenth
century, Amsterdam, London, Poland, and Lithuania became the main
centers of Jewish traders. The community of Portuguese Jews in Amsterdam was involved in colonial trade, as well as in speculative trade in commodities and company shares. Sephardic Jews in London were actively
involved in long-distance trade with West Africa and the West Indies.
Ashkenazi Jews in Poland and Lithuania connected trade in eastern and
western Europe with the rest of the world.

Among the various goods Jewish merchants and traders handled, diamonds occupy a special place. The Jews became dominant workers and
traders of diamonds from the early modern period through recent times.
Amsterdam first, then Hamburg, and later London became the headquar-
ters of Sephardic Jewish traders of Portuguese descent and later Ashkenazi Jews, who imported diamonds from India. The records and account
books of the British East India Company indicate that most merchants
involved in the diamond trade from India in the eighteenth century were
Jews. The dominance of Jewish traders in the diamond industry and
trade continued when Brazil in the mid-eighteenth century and South
Africa in the late nineteenth century became the main suppliers of uncut
diamonds.[7]

Ashkenazi Jews in eastern Europe gained prominence in forming and
running mints, especially in Hamburg and Prague. In the late seventeenth

[5]There is no scholarly consensus on the etymology of the name (see M. A. Cohen 2007).
[6]The very brief summary of the main stylized facts on the economic history of the Jews
in the early modern and modern periods presented in this section is based on Reich (1949);
Halpern (1960); Roth (1960a, 1960b); Baron, Kahan, and Gross (1975); Ettinger (1976); and
Trivellato (2009).
[7]Richman (2006).

and the eighteenth centuries, Jews in Bohemia, Galicia, Germany, Hungary, Moravia, Poland, and Russia produced and sold many goods and services to the local population. Among the sectors in which Jewish entrepreneurs and traders were most active in German and Russian towns were the mining and metal industries. The Jews were also the first to develop coal mines in eastern and central Europe and to export coal to England in the eighteenth and nineteenth centuries.[8]

Although many Ashkenazi Jews played leading roles in the economies of central and eastern Europe, the majority of the Jewish population in these areas was poor and scattered in small semi-urban locations in rural areas, including the shtetls. Both nineteenth- and twentieth-century writers, as well as census and tax records before 1939, describe a relatively poor Jewish population, engaged mainly in a large variety of trades. The occupational structure of world Jewry circa 1930 collected and analyzed by Kuznets show that the proportion of the Jewish labor force in central and eastern Europe engaged in agriculture was negligible (1–9 percent) (table 2.4).

The success story of many Jewish traders, financiers, scientists, and scholars after 1500 is epitomized by the history of their return to England in the seventeenth century, almost four centuries after their expulsion in 1290. About 1656, Oliver Cromwell, the Lord Protector of England, accepted the request by Rabbi Menasseh Ben Israel, one of the leaders of the Jewish community in Amsterdam, to readmit Jews to London under the promise of economic and religious freedom. Cromwell believed that with their connections and commercial networks to the New World, the Jews could make London as great a commercial center as Amsterdam. For their part, the Jewish traders and stockbrokers in Amsterdam forecast that England could become the leading center of international trade and finance. Among the most prominent Jews belonging to this new group of immigrants to England was David Ricardo, one of the pioneers of economics and the father of the theory of comparative advantage. Ricardo exemplifies the history of a minority of Jews who became intellectual and scientific leaders in the early modern and modern era.[9]

---

[8] Jews also held skilled and high-income occupations in nineteenth- and twentieth-century Ireland (Ó Gráda [2006]).

[9] Heertje (2004). Born in London in 1772, Ricardo came from a Jewish family that had moved to London after spending some years in Amsterdam. Ricardo's father was a stockbroker who had made a fortune on the London Stock Exchange. After attending school in London and spending a brief period in Amsterdam, Ricardo joined his father's business, at age fourteen. After working with his father, he established his own stockbroker business and in a few years acquired an astonishing fortune. At twenty-one, he married Priscilla Anne Wilkinson, a Quaker, and became a Unitarian.

Jews such as philosopher Baruch Spinoza (1632–77), economist David Ricardo (1772–1823), and statesman Benjamin Disraeli (1804–81) are the exception before the mid-nineteenth century. As Joel Mokyr documents, Jews contributed very little to the development of ideas, technologies, or institutions during the Scientific Revolution, the Enlightenment, or the Industrial Revolution.[10] The minor role in these fields is in striking contrast with the prominent role Jews played in the commercial and financial sectors during the seventeenth to nineteenth century. Only beginning in the second half of the nineteenth century did the Jews play a major role also in science, technology, philosophy, and literature.[11] Why?

The Jews' remarkable success in the United States epitomizes their historical trajectory.[12] Some 2,000 Jews—most of them of Sephardic origin—lived in the colonies in 1776. Most dwelled in the East Coast seaports as both shopkeepers and merchants, importing textiles, wine, tea, and hardware from Europe and exporting grain, furs, fish, and lumber. They were also engaged in international finance. With the movement west and the expansion of the frontier came many more opportunities for Jews to enter other branches of industry and trade, such as insurance, banking, mining, shipping, railroad investment and construction, and land development. During the mid-nineteenth century, German Jewish immigrants settled throughout the country. Often beginning as itinerant peddlers, they advanced to small businesses; some went on to create large-scale business in retail trade. In the late nineteenth century, some Jewish entrepreneurs were the founders of the most successful department stores in the United States. By 1880, German-Jewish immigrants and their descendants represented about 55 percent of the 250,000 Jews in the United States.

The largest wave of Jewish immigrants arrived between 1880 and 1920, when about 1.5 million Yiddish-speaking eastern European and Russian Jews settled in the United States. Almost all arrived without any capital, poor but literate, directly from the shtetls. These Jews are the ancestors of

---

[10] Mokyr (2011). Moses Mendelsohn, the German-Jewish philosopher, made significant contributions to the Enlightenment. Most Jews, however, objected to the philosophical and intellectual movement.

[11] Some numbers give an idea of the impressive achievements of contemporary Jews. In the United States, for example, Jews represent 2 percent of the population but account for 21 percent of Ivy League students, 26 percent of Kennedy Center honorees, 38 percent of leading philanthropists, and 51 percent of Pulitzer Prize winners for nonfiction (Pease [2009]; Brooks [2010]). Cochran, Hardy, and Harpending (2005) generated a lively debate on whether Jews, in particular Ashkenazi Jews, display higher average IQs than the rest of the population, and if so, why. See Murray (2007) for a discussion of this debate.

[12] B. Chiswick (2007, 2010) carefully documents the economic history, occupational structure, and earnings of American Jewry. The information in this section summarizes his main findings.

most American Jews today. Starting in commerce, crafts, and laborer jobs in small-scale manufacturing or retail trade in the northern and midwestern industrial cities, they rapidly advanced to middle- and upper-middle-class status.

Over the course of the twentieth century, their descendants made very impressive economic achievements. By 2000, 53 percent of Jewish men (compared with 20 percent of all white non-Jewish men) were in professional occupations. Among working women, 51 percent of Jews and 28 percent of non-Jewish whites held professional positions. Holding human capital determinants of earnings, including schooling, constant, American Jewish men earned about 16 percent more than other white men. Even when controlling for occupation, Jews earned about 8 percent more. When other variables, including schooling, are held constant, Jews have higher levels of wealth and higher rates of wealth accumulation than other groups.

No legal restriction ever prevented American Jews from becoming farmers. Yet they almost never engaged in farming. Their selection was into the same urban, high-skill, high-income occupations that Jews in the Middle East held 1,000 years earlier.

Can this persistence of Jewish occupational structure account for some puzzling features of their migrations in modern times? Did the Jewish occupational structure enable them to maintain standards of living that were higher than those of the local populations in the Americas, Poland, Russia, and Ukraine? How did their astonishing economic and intellectual success in the United States occur, given that most of the growth in Jewish population was among Ashkenazi Jews who came from repressive regimes in eastern Europe? Is the rapid growth in the Ashkenazi population in those parts of Europe until World War II consistent with the poverty and persecutions that characterized the lives of many European Jews?

Given the repressive regimes in which the Jews lived, they could have migrated to, and settled in, the Middle East, but they did so only at the time that migration to the Americas started, at the end of the nineteenth century. The Jewish communities in the Middle East and North Africa were growing, but not at the same rate as the ones in eastern Europe. Why?

Jewish migrations to the Americas greatly accelerated at the end of the nineteenth and the beginning of the twentieth century. These migrants came almost entirely from eastern Europe. Why did they begin migrating at that time and not earlier? Were repression and pogroms the reasons for these events, or did economic factors explain their migration? Given that literacy was relatively widespread in the United States when the Jews arrived, how one can explain their rapid economic success? Why was there almost no migration of Jews from the Middle East and North Africa to Canada, the United States, and South America?

More questions come from the comparison of Jews living in Israel with Jews living in the Diaspora today. About 40 percent of the thirteen million Jews in the world live in the United States, about 15 percent in Western Europe, and 5 percent in the rest of the world excluding Israel.[13] Diaspora Jews outside the United States have the same occupational structure (high-skill jobs) and earnings distribution (higher than the rest of the population) as those in the United States. In contrast, 5.8 million Jews live in Israel, where their occupational structure is similar to that of any small European country or that of the general population of the United States. About 80 percent of Jews in the United States are college educated; in Israel less than 40 percent have a college education. Can this gap persist? Is the occupational-choice theory consistent with the exceptional success of the recent Israeli hi-tech boom?

The many questions concerning the economic history of the Jewish people after 1500 require a deeper and more extensive study, which will be the subject of our next journey through Jewish history. In our next research project, we will investigate whether the economic theory with which we explained the economic history of the Jews from 70 CE to 1492 can help us understand the economic history of the Jews after 1500.

---

[13] DellaPergola (1992, 2001).

Appendix

THIS APPENDIX LISTS THE SECONDARY SOURCES THAT WE READ AND critically evaluated to build the numbers in tables 1.1, 1.2, 1.3, 1.5, 1.6, 1.7 and figure 1.1. It presents and discusses tables A.1 and A.2 with Benjamin of Tudela's Jewish population estimates circa 1170. Also, it clarifies how some estimates in some tables and figures have been calculated and why they diverge from the ones provided by other scholars when they differ.

CHAPTER 1

- Table 1.1 Jewish and Total Population, 65 CE–650, by Region

and

- Table 1.2 Effect of Wars on Jewish Population, 65 CE–650, by Region

Sources: For the LAND OF ISRAEL: Baron (1971b), Broshi (1979, 1982, 2001), Hamel (1990, pp. 137–40), Herr and Oppenheimer (1990, pp. 108–9), DellaPergola (1992, 2001), S. Schwartz (2001, pp. 10–11; 2006, pp. 23, 36). For MESOPOTAMIA AND PERSIA: Neusner (1965–70, vol. 1, pp. 14–15, vol. 2, pp. 246–48), Baron (1971b), Issawi (1981, pp. 376, 381), and DellaPergola (1992, 2001). For NORTH AFRICA: Baron (1971b), Issawi (1981, pp. 376, 381), Musallam (1981, p. 432), and DellaPergola (1992, 2001). For data on Jewish population in all locations: Engleman (1960), Baron (1971b), and DellaPergola (1992, 2001). For data on total population: Russell (1958), Clark (1968), Durand (1977, table 1), McEvedy and Jones (1978), Biraben (1979), and Kremer (1993).

Notes: Baron's estimate of 8 million Jews in the first century CE comes from the following addition: 2.5 million for the Land of Israel, 1 million for Mesopotamia and Persia, 1 million for Egypt, 1 million for Syria and Lebanon, 1 million for Asia Minor, and the remaining 1.5 million in western and southern Europe under Roman rule.

DellaPergola's estimate of 4.5 million Jews in the first century BCE comes from adding much smaller numbers for Syria, Asia Minor, and western Europe.

Broshi's, Hamel's, and Schwartz's estimates of 2.5 million Jews in the world before 70 CE (with the Land of Israel hosting no more than 1 million Jews and the remaining 1.5 million Jews being in the Diaspora) are based on the reasoning that given the area in the Land of Israel and the likely population density at that time, the 2.5 million Jews in the sole Land of Israel estimated by Baron would be completely unreasonable.

Our estimate of 5–5.5 million Jews on the eve of the first Jewish-Roman war is obtained by adding to the estimate of 4.5 million Jews in the first century BCE provided by DellaPergola an estimated 0.5–1 million Jews as the outcome of natural growth and the documented conversions of pagans to Judaism in the two centuries before the destruction of the Second Temple.

- Figure 1.1 Jewish and Total Population, c. 65, 650, 1170, and 1490

Sources: See sources for tables 1.1, 1.6, and 1.7 in this appendix.

- Table 1.3 Percentage of Jewish Labor Force Engaged in Farming and Skilled Occupations, 1 CE–650, by Region

Sources: For the LAND OF ISRAEL in 1 CE–400: Baron (1937, vol. 1; 1952, vols. 1 and 2; 1971a), Applebaum (1976a), S. Safrai (1976b), M. Stern (1976), Avi-Yonah (1984), Hamel (1990), L. Jacobs (1990), and Z. Safrai (1994). For MESOPOTAMIA AND PERSIA in 1 CE–400: Newman (1932), Baron (1937, vol. 1; 1952, vols. 1 and 2; 1971a), Neusner (1965–70, vol. 1, pp. 94–99; vol. 2, p. 14; vol. 3, pp. 24–25; 1990c; 1990e), M. Stern (1974), Applebaum (1976b), L. Jacobs (1990), and Goodblatt (2006b). For NORTH AFRICA IN 1 CE–400: Baron (1937, vol. 1; 1952, vols. 1 and 2; 1971a), Tcherikover (1945, 1961), M. Stern (1974), Applebaum (1976b), S. Safrai (1976b), and Kasher (1985). For the ROMAN EMPIRE IN 1 CE–400: Juster (1914), Baron (1937, vol. 1; 1952, vols. 1 and 2; and 1971a), Frank (1938), A. Jones (1964), M. Stern (1974), Applebaum (1976b), S. Safrai (1976b), and Goodman (1998). For the LAND OF ISRAEL IN 400–650: Baron (1971a), S. Safrai (1976b), Avi-Yonah (1984), Dan (1990), Herr and Oppenheimer (1990), and L. Jacobs (1990). For MESOPOTAMIA AND PERSIA in 400–650: Newman (1932), Neusner (1965–70, vol. 5), Baron (1971a), Beer (1974), S. Safrai (1976b), and L. Jacobs (1990). For the ROMAN AND BYZANTINE EMPIRES in 400–650: Juster (1912, 1914), Sharf (1966, 1971), Baron (1971a), and Jacoby (2011).

- Table 1.5 Percentage of Jewish Labor Force Engaged in Farming and Skilled Occupations, 400–1250, by Region

Sources: For the LAND OF ISRAEL in 400–650: Baron (1971a), S. Safrai (1976b), Avi-Yonah (1984), Dan (1990), Herr and Oppenheimer (1990), and L. Jacobs (1990). For MESOPOTAMIA AND PERSIA in 400–650: Newman (1932), Neusner (1965–70, vol. 5), Baron (1971a), Beer (1974), S. Safrai (1976b), and L. Jacobs (1990). For the ROMAN AND BYZANTINE EMPIRES in 400–650: Juster (1912, 1914), Sharf (1966, 1971), Baron (1971a), and Jacoby (2011). For the LAND OF ISRAEL, SYRIA AND LEBANON,

MESOPOTAMIA AND PERSIA, and NORTH AFRICA in 650–1250: Mann (1920–22), Baron (1952, vol. 3; 1971a), Goitein (1967–88, vol. 1), Ashtor (1976), H. Ben-Sasson (1976), Morony (1981), Udovitch (1981), Lewis (1984, 2002), Benjamin of Tudela ([1170] 1983), Raphael (1985), Gil (1992, 2004), M. R. Cohen (1994), Ashtor and Sagiv (2007), Ashtor, Yaari, and Cohen (2007), Assis and Beinart (2007), Ben-Yaacob et al. (2007), Corcos (2007), Fischel (2007), Fischel, Cohen, and Netzer (2007), and Haim (2007). For the BYZANTINE EMPIRE after 650: Jacoby (2008, 2011) and Holo (2009). For WESTERN EUROPE in 650–1250: Abrahams (1896, chaps. 11 and 12, and pp. 245–49), Agus (1965), Cantera Burgos (1966), Baron (1971a), Benjamin de Tudela ([1170] 1983), Baron, Kahan, and Gross (1975), Roth (1938, 1960a), and Toch (2003, 2005, 2008, 2011, 2012).

- Table 1.6 Jewish and Total Population, c. 650 and c. 1170, by Region

and

- Table 1.7 Jewish and Total Population, 1170–1490, by Region

Sources: For the LAND OF ISRAEL: Baron (1971b), Broshi (1979, 1982, 2001), Hamel (1990, pp. 137–40), Herr and Oppenheimer (1990, pp. 108–9), DellaPergola (1992, 2001), and S. Schwartz (2001, pp. 10–11; 2006, pp. 23, 36). For MESOPOTAMIA AND PERSIA: Neusner (1965–70, vol. 1, pp. 14–15; vol. 2, pp. 246–48), Baron (1971b), Issawi (1981, pp. 376–81), and DellaPergola (1992, 2001). For NORTH AFRICA: Ashtor (1959a; 1967; 1968, p. 13; 1976, chap. 7), Baron (1971b), Issawi (1981, pp. 376–81), Musallam (1981, p. 432), Dols (1981, p. 400–404), and DellaPergola (1992, 2001). For the BYZANTINE EMPIRE: Baron (1971b), Jacoby (2008, 2011) and Holo (2009). For EUROPE: Baron (1971b), DellaPergola (1992, 2001), and Toch (2005, 2012). For data on Jewish population in all locations: Ashtor (1959a; 1967; 1968; 1976, chap. 7), Roth (1960a), Engleman (1960), Baron (1971b), Dols (1981, pp. 400–404), and DellaPergola (1992, 2001). For data on total population: Russell (1958), Clark (1968), Durand (1977, table 1), McEvedy and Jones (1978), and Kremer (1993).

Notes: See table A.2 in this appendix for the complete list of the cities mentioned in Benjamin of Tudela's travel itinerary. Our Jewish population estimate for Mesopotamia, Persia, and the Arabian Peninsula circa 1170 differs from the one given by DellaPergola (2001, tables 1 and 2) for two reasons. First, we significantly reduce Benjamin of Tudela's figures for the Jews living in the Arabian Peninsula (mainly Yemen), given that he did not visit these places and his figures have been recognized by scholars as being vast exaggerations.

Second, we agree with Ashtor (1959a; 1967; 1968; 1976, chap. 6) and Gil (2004, pp. 491–532), who propose interpreting Benjamin's estimates as the numbers of *individuals* for those locations that Benjamin did not visit but only heard of (i.e., Persia, Central Asia, India, China, and some locations in Egypt), and as the numbers of *households* for the locations that he actually visited (i.e., Europe, the Balkans, Asia Minor, Lebanon, Syria, the Land of Israel, Mesopotamia, and some locations in Egypt). This argument is also supported by data from contemporary tax records in Mesopotamia and Egypt studied by Gil (e.g., Benjamin of Tudela reports 40,000 Jewish households for Baghdad and its surrounding area, and a tax census compiled a few decades later lists 36,000 Jewish taxpayers, that is, household heads). Hence, for those locations in which Benjamin's figures are to be considered as the number of households, we multiply his figures by five, under the assumption that each household consisted, on average, of five individuals.

CHAPTER 7

Here we explain how we interpreted Benjamin of Tudela's Jewish population estimates in order to build tables A.1 and A.2.

Historians and demographers have discussed the reliability of Benjamin's data. Two issues seem the most controversial: first, some of his numbers for locations he did not visit but only heard of seem vastly exaggerated (e.g., the number of Jews in Yemen), whereas he fails to mention Jewish communities that are known to have existed in some locations from other sources. Hence, in tables A.1 and A.2, we significantly reduced Benjamin's estimates for the locations in Yemen and other areas of the Arabian Peninsula he did not visit (in some instances, he even confused locations in Yemen with India, he said that Basra is in Yemen, or he provided the names of locations, such as Tilmas, which cannot be found in any other source including the contemporary records of the Cairo Geniza). We refer to the introduction by Marcus Nathan Adler to Benjamin's travel itinerary ([c. 1170] 1983), in which the problems related to identifying the locations in Yemen are discussed at length.

The second issue is whether Benjamin's figures should be interpreted as the number of individuals or households. After cross-checking population data from other sources (i.e., tax records), Ashtor (1967, 1968, 1976) and Gil (1992, 2004) maintain that for the better-documented areas— such as Europe, the Balkans, Asia Minor, Syria, Lebanon, the Land of Israel, Mesopotamia, and some locations in Egypt (e.g., Alexandria and Cairo)—his data should be taken as referring to *households*, and when multiplied by a factor of five persons per household, one would obtain total population figures in each location. For other areas that Benjamin did not visit but only heard of (Persia, the Arabian Peninsula including Yemen, Central Asia, India, China, and some locations in Egypt), the figures should be taken as the number of *individuals* (i.e., as total population figures).

We agree with Ashtor's and Gil's argument, and in tables A.1 and A.2 we adjusted Benjamin of Tudela's data by keeping all these caveats in mind. In particular:

- For table A.1: The population estimates are computed using the population figures in table A.2. The RAW FIGURES column lists Benjamin's figures as given in his travel itinerary. The ADJUSTED FIGURES column amends the raw figures as follows:

  o For MESOPOTAMIA, whose locations Benjamin visited and described in detail, we take his estimates as the number of households; hence, we multiply his figures by five assuming that each household had, on average, five people.

  o For PERSIA, which Benjamin did not visit, we take his figures as population estimates; hence, we leave his figures unchanged in column 3.

  o For PERSIA + MISSING CITIES, we add an estimated figure of about 100,000 Jews for locations in which large Jewish communities are known to have resided, even though Benjamin did not mention them in his travel itinerary.

  o For ARABIAN PENINSULA, we significantly reduce Benjamin's estimates (from 463,000 to 83,000) given that he did not visit Yemen or other regions in the peninsula.

  o For ARABIAN PENINSULA + MISSING CITIES, we add an estimate of 17,000–67,000 Jews (for a total of 100,000–150,000 Jews) to take into account the issue that Benjamin failed to mention, or did not provide population estimates for, locations in Yemen (e.g., Aden) in which Jews are known from many other sources to have dwelled.

- For table A.2: The RAW FIGURES column reports the figures as given in Benjamin's travel itinerary. The figures in the ADJUSTED FIGURES column are obtained as follows:

  o For all the cities and towns in Europe, the Balkans, Asia Minor, Lebanon, the Land of Israel, Syria, Mesopotamia, Cairo, and Alexandria, which Benjamin visited, we take his figures as the number of households and multiply them by five, assuming that each household consisted, on average, of five people.

  o For Persia, Central Asia, India, China, and the other towns in Egypt, which Benjamin did not visit but only heard of, we take his figures as the number of people and we leave them as they are listed.

  o For the locations in Yemen and the Arabian Peninsula, which Benjamin did not visit, or gave names that could not be found in any other sources (e.g., Tilmas), we reduced his figures while maintaining the relative size of the locations.

TABLE A.1. Jewish Population Estimates in the Middle East, Based on Benjamin of Tudela's Travel Itinerary, by Region, c. 1170

Region/country	Raw figures	Adjusted figures
Mesopotamia	120,420	592,100
Persia	245,000	245,000
Persia + missing cities	—	345,000
Arabian Peninsula	463,000	83,000
Arabian Peninsula + missing cities	—	100,000–150,000
Total = Mesopotamia + Persia + Arabian Peninsula	828,420	920,100
Total = Mesopotamia + (Persia + missing cities) + Arabian Peninsula	—	1,020,100
Total = Mesopotamia + (Persia + missing cities) + (Arabian Peninsula + missing cities)	—	1,037,100–1,087,100

Source: Benjamin of Tudela ([c. 1170] 1983).
— Not available.

TABLE A.2. List of Locations and Jewish Population Estimates in Benjamin of Tudela's Travel Itinerary, c. 1170

Region/country	City	Raw figures	Adjusted figures
Europe			
Spain	Tudela		
	Saragossa		
	Tortosa		
	Tarragona		
	Barcelona		
	Gerona		
France	Narbonne	300	1,500
	Beziers		
	Montpellier		
	Lunel	300	1,500
	Posquiers	40	200
	Bourg de St. Gilles	100	500
	Arles	200	1,000
	Marseilles	300	1,500
Italy	Genoa	2	10
	Pisa	20	100
	Lucca	40	200
	Rome	200	1,000
	Capua	300	1,500
	Pozzuoli		
	Naples	500	2,500
	Salerno	600	3,000
	Amalfi	20	100
	Benevento	200	1,000
	Melfi	200	1,000
	Ascoli	40	200
	Trani	200	1,000
	Bari	0	0
	Taranto	300	1,500
	Brindisi	10	50
	Otranto	500	2,500
Balkans	Corfu	1	5
	Larta	100	500
	Aphilon	30	150
	Anatolica		
	Patras	50	250
	Lepanto	100	500
	Crissa	200	1,000
	Corinth	300	1,500
	Thebes	2,000	10,000
	Egripo	200	1,000
	Jabustrisa	100	500
	Rabonica	100	500
	Sinon Potamo	50	250

TABLE A.2. (*continued*)

Region/country	City	Raw figures	Adjusted figures
Europe			
Balkans	Wallachia region		
	Gardiki		
Asia Minor	Armylo	400	2,000
	Vissena	100	500
	Salonica	500	2,500
	Demetrizi	50	250
	Drama	140	700
	Christopoli	20	100
	Abydos		
	Constantinople	2,500	12,500
	Rhaedestus	400	2,000
	Gallipoli	200	1,000
	Kales	50	250
	Mytilene		
	Chios	400	2,000
	Samos	300	1,500
	Rhodes	400	2,000
On the way back from the Middle East and North Africa			
Italy	Messina	200	1,000
	Palermo	1,500	7,500
	Syracuse		
	Marsala		
	Catania		
	Petralia		
	Trapani		
	Rome		
	Lucca		
Germany	Verdun		
	Cologne		
	Regensburg		
	Metz		
	Treves		
	Coblenz		
	Andernach		
	Bonn		
	Cologne		
	Bingen		
	Munster		
	Worms		
	Strassburg		
	Wurzburg		
	Mantern		
	Bamberg		

(*continued*)

TABLE A.2. (*continued*)

Region/country	City	Raw figures	Adjusted figures
On the way back from the Middle East and North Africa			
Germany	Freising		
	Regensburg		
Bohemia	Prague		
France	Auxerre		
	Paris		
Asia			
	Cyprus		
Armenia	Curicus		
Asia Minor	Malmistras		
	Antioch the Great	10	50
	Ladikya	100	500
Jordania	Gebal		
	Kadmus		
Lebanon	Tarabulus (Tripolis)		
	Gubail (Byblus)	150	750
	Beirut	50	250
	Sidon	20	100
	Area with Druses	0	0
	Sarepta		
	Tyre	500	2,500
Land of Israel	Acre	200	1000
	Haifa		
	Carmel		
	Capernaum		
	Caesarea	200	1,000
	Keilath	0	0
	Ludd	1	5
	Sebastiya	0	0
	Nablus	0	0
	Mount Gilboa		
	Unnamed village	0	0
	Gibeon the Great	0	0
	Jerusalem	200	1,000
	Bethlehem	2	10
	Hebron		
	Beit Jibrin	3	15
	Shiloh		
	Gibeah of Saul	0	0
	Nob	2	10
	Ramleh	300	1,500
	Jaffa	1	5
	Jabneh	0	0
	Ashdod	0	0
	Askelon	240	1,200

TABLE A.2. (*continued*)

Region/country	City	Raw figures	Adjusted figures
Asia			
Israel	Ludd (Lydda)		
	Jezreel	1	5
	Sepphoris		
	Tiberias	50	250
	Tymin		
	Meron		
	Almah	50	250
	Kades	0	0
	Banias		
Syria	Damascus	3,000	15,000
	Galid	60	300
	Salchah		
	Baalbec		
	Tadmor (Palmyra)	2,000	10,000
	Karjaten	1	5
	Emesa	20	100
	Hamath	70	350
	Sheizar		
	Dimin		
	Aleppo	5,000	25,000
	Balis	10	50
	Kalat Jabar	2,000	10,000
Mesopotamia	Rakka	700	3,500
	Harran	20	100
	Ras-el-Ain	200	1,000
	Nisibis	1,000	5,000
	Geziret Ibn Omar	4,000	20,000
	Mosul	7,000	35,000
	Nineveh		
	Arbela		
	Rahbah	2,000	10,000
	Karkisiya	500	2,500
	Pumbedita (El-Hanbar)	3,000	15,000
	Hadara	15,000	75,000
	Okbara	10,000	50,000
	Baghdad	40,000	200,000
	Gazigan	5,000	25,000
	Babylon	3,000	15,000
	Hillah	10,000	40,000
	Tower of Babel		
	Kaphri	200	1,000
	Synagogue of Ezechiel		
	Kotsonath	300	1,500
	Ain Siptha		
	Kefar Al-Keram		

(*continued*)

TABLE A.2. (*continued*)

Region/country	City	Raw figures	Adjusted figures
Asia			
Mesopotamia	Unnamed village		
	Unnamed village		
	Kufa	7,000	35,000
	Sura		
	Shafjathib		
	Pumbedita (El-Hanbar)		
Arabian Peninsula	Hillah		
	Kheibar	50,000	10,000
	Teima		
	Tilmas	100,000	20,000
	Tanai	300,000	50,000
	Location in al-Yemen	3,000	3,000
Mesopotamia	Basra	10,000	50,000
	Sepulchre of Ezra	1,500	7,500
Persia	Susa	7,000	7,000
	Sepulchre of Daniel		
	Rudbar	20,000	20,000
	Nihawand	4,000	4,000
	Land of Mulahid		
	Amadia	25,000	25,000
	Hamadan	30,000	30,000
	Tabaristan	4,000	4,000
	Isfahan	15,000	15,000
	Shiraz	10,000	10,000
	Ghaznah	80,000	80,000
	Samarkand	50,000	50,000
Central Asia	Tibet		
	Naisabur		
	Land of Khuzistan		
	Island of Kish	500	500
Arabia	Katifa	5,000	5,000
India	Khulam (Quilon)		
	Ibrig	3,000	3,000
China	China		
	Al-Gingaleh	1,000	1,000
	Chulan	0	0
Yemen	Zebid		
	Aden		
North Africa			
Egypt	Abyssinia		
	Assuan		
	Seba		
	Heluam	300	300

TABLE A.2. (*continued*)

Region/country	City	Raw figures	Adjusted figures
North Africa			
Egypt	Land of Zawilah		
	Desert of Sahara		
	Kutz	300	300
	Fayum	200	200
	Cairo	7,000	35,000
	Bilbais	300	300
	Ramses		
	Al-Bubzig	200	200
	Benha	60	60
	Munhe Sifte	500	500
	Samnu	200	200
	Damira	700	700
	Lammanah	500	500
	Alexandria	3,000	15,000
	Damietta	200	200
	Simasin	100	100
	Sunbat		
	Elim		
	Rephidim	0	0
	Mount Sinai		
	Tur Sinai		
	Damietta		
	Tanis	40	40

Source: Benjamin of Tudela ([c. 1170] 1983).

Note: The order in the table follows the order of the locations as listed in Benjamin of Tudela's travel itinerary. See the explanation above in this appendix for the interpretation of the figures in columns 3 and 4.

Bibliography

PRIMARY SOURCES

Cortona, Archivio Storico del Comune, Manuscript F.
Cortona, Biblioteca dell'Accademia Etrusca, *Codice Cortonese*, Manuscript 520, *Capitoli del Monte Pio.*
Florence, State Archives, *Catasto* 207, 208, 213, 214, 215, 216, 219, 233, 234, 235, 236, 248, 249, 252, 253, 254, 257, 258, 266, 269.
Florence, State Archives, *Statuti delle Comunitá Autonome e Soggette,* 201, fol. 482; 280, fol. 251; 501, fol. 158; 759, fol. 201.
Pisa, State Archives, *Archivio Fiumi e Fossi, Serie Catasto* 532, 533, 535, 552, 557, 558.

SECONDARY SOURCES

Aberbach, Moshe. *Jewish Education in the Mishna and Talmud.* Jerusalem: Reuven Mas, 1982 (in Hebrew).
Abrahams, Israel. *Jewish Life in the Middle Ages.* London: Macmillan, 1896.
Abramitsky, Ran. "The Limits of Equality: Insights from the Israeli Kibbutz." *Quarterly Journal of Economics* 123, no. 3 (2008): 1111–59.
———. "Lessons from the Kibbutz on the Equality-Incentives Trade-off." *Journal of Economic Perspectives* 25, no. 1 (2011a): 185–208.
———. "On the (Lack of) Stability of Communes: An Economic Perspective." In *Oxford Handbook of the Economics of Religion,* edited by Rachel McCleary, 169–89. Oxford: Oxford University Press, 2011b.
Abulafia, David. *The Western Mediterranean Kingdoms, 1200–1500: The Struggle for Dominion.* London: Longman, 1997.
———. *Mediterranean Encounters, Economic, Religious, Political, 1100–1550.* Burlington, VT: Ashgate, 2000.
———. "The Jews of Sicily and Southern Italy: Economic Activity." In *Wirtschaftsgeschichte der mittelalterlichen Juden. Fragen und Einschtzungen,* edited by Michael Toch, 49–62. Munich: Oldebourg, 2008.
Acemoglu, Daron, Tarek A. Hassan, and James A. Robinson. "Social Structure and Development: A Legacy of the Holocaust in Russia." *Quarterly Journal of Economics* 126, no. 2 (2011): 895–946.
Acemoglu, Daron, and Simon Johnson. "Unbundling Institutions." *Journal of Political Economy* 113, no. 5 (2005): 949–95.
Acemoglu, Daron, Simon Johnson, and James Robinson. "The Colonial Origins of Comparative Development: An Empirical Investigation." *American Economic Review* 91, no. 5 (2001): 1369–1401.

————. "Reversal of Fortune: Geography and Institutions in the Making of the Modern World Income Distribution." *Quarterly Journal of Economics* 117, no. 4 (2002): 1231–94.

————. "The Rise of Europe: Atlantic Trade, Institutional Change, and Economic Growth." *American Economic Review* 95, no. 3 (2005): 546–79.

Adler, Elkan Nathan. *Jewish Travellers in the Middle Ages: 19 Firsthand Accounts.* New York: Dover, 1987.

Agus, Irving A. *Urban Civilization in Pre-Crusade Europe: A Study of Organized Town-Life in Northwestern Europe during the Tenth and Eleventh Centuries Based on the Responsa Literature.* 2 vols. Leiden: Brill, 1965.

Aharoni, Yohanan, Michael Avi-Yonah, Anson F. Rainey, and Zeev Safrai. *The Carta Bible Atlas.* Jerusalem: Carta, 2002.

Alesina, Alberto, and Eliana La Ferrara. "Participation in Heterogeneous Communities." *Quarterly Journal of Economics* 115, no. 3 (2000): 847–904.

————. "Who Trusts Others?" *Journal of Public Economics* 85, no. 2 (2002): 207–34.

Allen, Robert C. "The Great Divergence in European Wages and Prices from the Middle Ages to the First World War." *Explorations in Economic History* 38, no. 4 (2001): 411–47.

————. "Real Wages in Europe and Asia: A First Look at the Long-Term Patterns." In *Living Standards in the Past: New Perspectives on Well-Being in Asia and Europe,* edited by Robert C. Allen, Tommy Bengtsson, and Martin Dribe, chap. 5. Oxford: Oxford University Press, 2005.

Alon, Gedaliah. *The Jews in their Land in the Talmudic Age (70–640 C.E.).* 2 vols. Jerusalem: Hebrew University Magnes Press, 1980–1984.

Applebaum, Shimon. "Economic Life in Palestine." In *The Jewish People in the First Century: Historical Geography, Political History, Social, Cultural, and Religious Life and Institutions,* edited by Shmuel Safrai and Menahem Stern, vol. 2, 631–700. Assen: Van Gorcum, 1976a.

————. "The Social and Economic Status of the Jews in the Diaspora." In *The Jewish People in the First Century: Historical Geography, Political History, Social, Cultural, and Religious Life and Institutions,* edited by Shmuel Safrai and Menahem Stern, vol. 2, 701–27. Assen: Van Gorcum, 1976b.

Armstrong, John A. "Mobilized and Proletarian Diasporas." *American Political Science Review* 70, no. 2 (1976): 393–408.

Ashtor, Eliyahu. "The Mongol Storm and the Jews: A Contribution to the History of Oriental Jewry from the Arabic Sources." *Zion* 4 (1939): 51–70.

————. "Documents Pertaining to the Study of the Economic and Social History of the Jews in the Near East." *Zion* 7 (1942): 140–55.

————. "Prolegomena to the Medieval History of Oriental Jewry." *Jewish Quarterly Review* 50, no. 1 (1959a): 55–68.

————. "Prolegomena to the Medieval History of Oriental Jewry." *Jewish Quarterly Review* 50, no. 2 (1959b): 147–66.

————. "The Number of Jews in Medieval Egypt." *Journal of Jewish Studies* 18 (1967): 9–42.

————. "The Number of Jews in Medieval Egypt." *Journal of Jewish Studies* 19 (1968): 1–22.

———. "Un mouvement migratoire au haut moyen âge: migrations de l'Irak vers les pays méditerranées." *Annales ESC* 27 (1972): 185–214.

———. *The Jews of Moslem Spain*. 3 vols. Philadelphia: Jewish Publication Society of America, 1973–1984.

———. *A Social and Economic History of the Near East*. Berkeley: University of California Press, 1976.

———. "Fatimids." In *Encyclopaedia Judaica*, edited by Michael Berenbaum and Fred Skolnik, 2nd ed., vol. 6, 723–24. Detroit: Macmillan Reference USA, 2007.

Ashtor, Eliyahu, and Reuven Amitai. "Mamluks." In *Encyclopaedia Judaica*, edited by Michael Berenbaum and Fred Skolnik, 2nd ed., vol. 13, 438–41. Detroit: Macmillan Reference USA, 2007.

Ashtor, Eliyahu, and David M. Sagiv. "Basra." In *Encyclopaedia Judaica*, edited by Michael Berenbaum and Fred Skolnik, 2nd ed., vol. 3, 205–6. Detroit: Macmillan Reference USA, 2007.

Ashtor, Eliyahu, Avraham Yaari, and Haim J. Cohen. "Cairo." In *Encyclopaedia Judaica*, edited by Michael Berenbaum and Fred Skolnik, 2nd ed., vol. 4, 342–46. Detroit: Macmillan Reference USA, 2007.

Ashtor, Eliyahu, Simon R. Schwarzfuchs, Jeonathan Prato, and Haim Avni. "Spain." In *Encyclopaedia Judaica*, edited by Michael Berenbaum and Fred Skolnik, 2nd ed., vol. 19, 67–83. Detroit: Macmillan Reference USA, 2007.

Assaf, Simha. *A Source Book for the History of Jewish Education from the Beginning of the Middle Ages to the Period of the Haskalah*, with added comments and supplements, edited by Shmuel Glick. 5 vols. New York: Jewish Theological Seminary of America, 2002–2006 (in Hebrew).

Assis, Yom Tov, and Haim Beinart. "Seville." In *Encyclopaedia Judaica*, edited by Michael Berenbaum and Fred Skolnik, 2nd ed., vol. 18, 325–29. Detroit: Macmillan Reference USA, 2007.

Avi-Yonah, Michael. *The Jews of Palestine. A Political History from the Bar Kokhba War to the Arab Conquest*. Oxford: Basil Blackwell, 1976.

———. *The Jews under Roman and Byzantine Rule*. 2nd ed. Jerusalem: Hebrew University Magnes Press, 1984.

Ayal, Eliezer B., and Barry R. Chiswick. "The Economics of the Diaspora Revisited." *Economic Development and Cultural Change* 31, no. 4 (1983): 861–75.

Bachrach, Bernard S. *Early Medieval Jewish Policy in Western Europe*. Minneapolis: University of Minnesota Press, 1977.

Baer, Yitzhak. *A History of the Jews in Christian Spain*. vol. 1. Philadelphia: Jewish Publication Society of America, 1961.

Bar, Doron. "Third-Century Crisis in the Roman Empire and Its Validity in Palestine." *Zion* 66, no. 2 (2001): 143–70.

———. "Was There a Third-Century Economic Crisis in Palestine?" In *The Roman and Byzantine Near East*: *Some Recent Archaeological Research*, vol. 3, 43–54. Journal of Roman Archaeology, Supplementary Series 49, edited by John H. Humphrey. Portsmouth, RI: Journal of Roman Archaeology, 2002.

———. "The Christianization of Rural Palestine during Late Antiquity." *Journal of Ecclesiastical History* 54, no. 3 (2003a): 401–21.

———. "Settlement and Economy in Late Roman and Byzantine Palestine." *Cathedra* 107 (2003b): 1–16.

Barclay, John M. G. *Jews in the Mediterranean Diaspora: From Alexander to Trajan (323 BCE–117 CE)*. Edinburgh: T&T Clark, 1996.

———. "Who Was Considered an Apostate in the Jewish Diaspora?" In *Tolerance and Intolerance in Early Judaism and Christianity*, edited by Graham N. Stanton and Guy G. Stroumsa, 80–98. Cambridge: Cambridge University Press, 1998.

Bareket, Elinoar. "Radhanites." In *Jewish Civilization: An Encyclopedia*, edited by Norman Roth, 558–61. London: Routledge, 2002.

Bar-Ilan, Meir. "Illiteracy in the Land of Israel in the First Centuries C.E." In *Essays in the Social Scientific Study of Judaism and Jewish Society*, edited by Simcha Fishbane, Stuart Schoenfeld, and Alain Goldschleger, vol. 2, 46–61. Hoboken, NJ: Ktav, 1992.

Baron, Salo Wittmayer. "Ghetto and Emancipation: Shall We Revise the Traditional View?" *Menorah Journal* 14 (1928): 515–26.

———. *A Social and Religious History of the Jews*, 1st ed. 3 vols. New York: Columbia University Press, 1937.

———. *A Social and Religious History of the Jews*, 2nd ed. 18 vols. New York: Columbia University Press, 1952.

———. "Economic History." In *Encyclopedia Judaica*, edited by Cecil Roth, vol. 6, 95–117. New York: Macmillan, 1971a.

———. "Population." In *Encyclopedia Judaica*, edited by Cecil Roth, vol. 13, 866–903. New York: Macmillan, 1971b.

Baron, Salo W., Arkadius Kahan, and Nachum Gross. *Economic History of the Jews*. Jerusalem: Keter, 1975.

Barro, Robert J., and Rachel M. McCleary. "Which Countries Have State Religions?" *Quarterly Journal of Economics* 120, no. 4 (2005): 1331–70.

———. "Religion and Political Economy in an International Panel." *Journal for the Scientific Study of Religion* 45, no. 2 (2006): 149–75.

Barzel, Yoram. "Confiscation by the Ruler: The Rise and Fall of Jewish Lending in the Middle Ages." *Journal of Law and Economics* 35, no. 1 (1992): 1–13.

Bashan, Eliezer, and Elinoar Bareket. "Nagid." In *Encyclopaedia Judaica*, edited by Michael Berenbaum and Fred Skolnik, 2nd ed., vol. 14, 729–33. Detroit: Macmillan Reference USA, 2007.

Bato, Yomtov Ludwig, Evelyn Adunka, and Israel O. Lehman. "Vienna." *Encyclopaedia Judaica*, edited by Michael Berenbaum and Fred Skolnik, 2nd ed., vol. 20, 518–23. Detroit: Macmillan Reference USA, 2007.

Baumgarten, Albert. *The Flourishing of Jewish Sects in the Maccabean Era: An Interpretation*. Leiden: Brill, 1997.

Bausani, Alessandro. *The Persians, from the Earliest Days to the Twentieth Century*. New York: St. Martin's, 1971.

Becker, Gary S., and H. Gregg Lewis. "On the Interaction between the Quantity and Quality of Children." *Journal of Political Economy* 81, no. S2 (1973): S279–88.

Becker, Sascha O., and Ludger Woessmann. "Was Weber Wrong? A Human Capital Theory of Protestant Economic History." *Quarterly Journal of Economics* 124, no. 2 (2009): 531–96.

Beek, Martin A. *Atlas of Mesopotamia: A Survey of the History and Civilisation of Mesopotamia from the Stone Age to the Fall of Babylon*. London: Nelson, 1962.

Beer, Moshe. *The Babylonian Amoraim: Aspects of Economic Life.* Ramat Gan: Bar Ilan University Press, 1974 (in Hebrew).

Bein, Alex. *The Jewish Question: Biography of a World Problem.* Translated by Harry Zohn. Rutherford, NJ: Fairleigh Dickinson University Press, 1990.

Beinart, Haim, ed. *The Sephardi Legacy.* 2 vols. Jerusalem: Hebrew University Magnes Press, 1992–1993.

———. "Order of the Expulsion from Spain: Antecedents, Causes, and Textual Analysis." In *Crisis and Creativity in the Sephardic World, 1391–1648,* edited by Benjamin Gampel, 79–94. New York: Columbia University Press, 1998.

———. "Córdoba." In *Encyclopaedia Judaica,* edited by Michael Berenbaum and Fred Skolnik, 2nd ed., vol. 5, 218–19. Detroit: Macmillan Reference USA, 2007a.

———. "Granada." In *Encyclopaedia Judaica,* edited by Michael Berenbaum and Fred Skolnik, 2nd ed., vol. 8, 32. Detroit: Macmillan Reference USA, 2007b.

Benbassa, Esther. *The Jews of France: A History from Antiquity to the Present.* Translated by M. B. DeBevoise. Princeton, NJ: Princeton University Press, 1999.

Benjamin of Tudela [c. 1170]. *The Itinerary of Benjamin of Tudela: Travels in the Middle Ages.* Critical text, translation, and commentary by Marcus Nathan Adler, with introductions by Michael A. Signer, Marcus Nathan Adler, and Adolf Asher. Malibu, CA: Joseph Simon, 1983.

Ben-Sasson, Haim Hillel. "The Middle Ages." In *A History of the Jewish People,* edited by Haim Hillel Ben-Sasson, 393–723. Cambridge, MA: Harvard University Press, 1976.

Ben-Sasson, Haim Hillel, Samuel Miklos Stern, Robert Weltsch, Michael Berenbaum, Jacob S. Levinger, and Chaim Yahil. "Germany." In *Encyclopaedia Judaica,* edited by Michael Berenbaum and Fred Skolnik, 2nd ed., vol. 7, 518–46. Detroit: Macmillan Reference USA, 2007.

Ben-Sasson, Menahem. *The Jews of Sicily, 825–1068: Documents and Sources.* Jerusalem: Ben Zvi Institute, 1991.

———. "The History of the Jews in Muslim Lands during the Middle Ages." In *A Historical Atlas of the Jewish People: From the Time of Patriarchs to the Present,* edited by Eli Barnavi, 74–75, 80–83, 86–93, 116–117. New York: Schocken Books, 1992.

———. *The Emergence of the Local Jewish Community in the Muslim World (Qayrawan, 800–1057).* Jerusalem: Hebrew University Magnes Press, 1996.

Ben-Yaacob, Abraham, Nissim Kazzaz, Hayyim J. Cohen, and Avraham Yaari. "Baghdad." In *Encyclopaedia Judaica,* edited by Michael Berenbaum and Fred Skolnik, 2nd ed., vol. 3, 55–59. Detroit: Macmillan Reference USA, 2007.

Berenbaum, Michael, and Alexander Carlebach. "Cologne." In *Encyclopaedia Judaica,* edited by Michael Berenbaum and Fred Skolnik, 2nd ed., vol. 5, 59–62. Detroit: Macmillan Reference USA, 2007.

Berman, Eli. "Sect, Subsidy and Sacrifice: An Economist's View of Ultra-Orthodox Jews." *Quarterly Journal of Economics* 115, no. 3 (2000): 905–53.

———. *Radical, Religious and Violent: The New Economics of Terrorism.* Cambridge, MA: MIT Press, 2009.

Biraben, Jean N. "Essai sur l'evolution du nombre des hommes." *Population* 34, no. 1 (1979): 13–25.

Blumenkranz, Bernhard. "Germany, 843–1096." In *The Dark Ages: Jews in Christian Europe, 711–1096*, edited by Cecil Roth and I. H. Levine, 162–74. New Brunswick, NJ: Rutgers University Press, 1966.

Blumenkranz, Bernhard, Lucien Steinberg, and Doris Bensimon-Donath. "Paris." In *Encyclopaedia Judaica*, edited by Michael Berenbaum and Fred Skolnik, 2nd ed., vol. 15, 642–47. Detroit: Macmillan Reference USA, 2007.

Blumenkranz, Bernhard, Simon R. Schwarzfuchs, Lucien Steinberg, David Weinberg, Doris Bensimon-Donath, and Nelly Hannson. "France." In *Encyclopaedia Judaica*, edited by Michael Berenbaum and Fred Skolnik, 2nd ed., vol. 7, 146–70. Detroit: Macmillan Reference USA, 2007.

Bonfil, Robert. *Jewish Life In Renaissance Italy*. Berkeley: University of California Press, 1994.

Bonfil, Robert, Oded Irshai, Guy G. Stroumsa, and Rina Talgam, eds. *Jews in Byzantium. Dialectics of Minority and Majority Cultures*. Leiden: Brill, 2011.

Bonné-Tamir, Batsheva, and Avinoam Adam, eds. *Genetic Diversity among Jews: Diseases and Markers at the DNA Level*. New York: Oxford University Press, 1992.

Bonné-Tamir, B., J. G. Bodmer, W. F. Bodmer, P. Pickbourne, C. Brautbar, E. Gazit, S. Nevo, and R. Zamir. "HLA Polymorphism in Israel: An Overall Analysis." *Tissue Antigens* 11 (1978): 235–50.

Bonné-Tamir, Batsheva, Avshalom Zoossman-Diskin, and Aharon Ticher. "Genetic Diversity among Jews Reexamined: Preliminary Analysis at the DNA Level." In *Genetic Diversity among Jews: Diseases and Markers at the DNA Level*, edited by Batsheva Bonné-Tamir and Avinoam Adam, 80–94. New York: Oxford University Press, 1992.

Boone, Marc, Karel Davids, and Paul Janssens, eds. *Urban Public Debts. Urban Government and the Market for Annuities in Western Europe (14th–18th Centuries)*. Turnhout: Brepols, 2003.

Botticini, Maristella. "New Evidence on Jewish Money Lending in Tuscany, 1310–1430: The 'Friends and Family Connection' Again." In *Zakhor: Rivista di storia degli ebrei in Italia* 1 (1997): 77–93.

———. "A Tale of 'Benevolent' Governments: Private Credit Markets, Public Finance, and the Role of Jewish Lenders in Medieval and Renaissance Italy." *Journal of Economic History* 60, no. 1 (2000): 165–89.

Botticini, Maristella, and Zvi Eckstein. "Jewish Occupational Selection: Education, Restrictions, or Minorities?" *Journal of Economic History* 65, no. 4 (2005): 922–48.

———. "From Farmers to Merchants, Conversions and Diaspora: Human Capital and Jewish History." *Journal of the European Economic Association* 5, no. 5 (2007): 885–926.

———. "Path Dependence and Occupations." In *The New Palgrave Dictionary of Economics*, edited by Steven N. Durlauf and Lawrence Blume. New York: Palgrave MacMillan, 2008.

———. "Religious Norms, Human Capital, and Money Lending in Jewish European History." In *Oxford Handbook of the Economics of Religion*, edited by Rachel McCleary, 57–80. New York: Oxford University Press, 2011.

Bowen, James. *A History of Western Education*. 3 vols. London: Methuen, 1972–81.

Brasalawsky, Joseph. "Jewish Trade between the Mediterranean and India in the Twelfth Century." *Zion* 7 (1942): 135–39.

Braudel, Fernand. *The Wheels of Commerce*. New York: Harper & Row, 1982.

Brawer, Abraham J. "Land of Israel: Geographical Survey." In *Encyclopaedia Judaica*, edited by Michael Berenbaum and Fred Skolnik, 2nd ed., vol. 10, 100–143. Detroit: Macmillan Reference USA, 2007.

Brenner, Reuven, and Nicholas M. Kiefer. "The Economics of the Diaspora: Discrimination and Occupational Structure." *Economic Development and Cultural Change* 29, no. 3 (1981): 517–34.

Breuer, Yochanan. "Aramaic in Late Antiquity." In *The Cambridge History of Judaism*. Vol. 4, *The Late Roman-Rabbinic Period*, edited by Steven T. Katz, 457–91. New York: Cambridge University Press, 2006.

Brice, William C. *An Historical Atlas of Islam*. Leiden: Brill, 1981.

Brody, Robert. *The Geonim of Babylonia and the Shaping of Medieval Jewish Culture*. New Haven, CT: Yale University Press, 1998.

Brook, Kevin A. *The Jews of Khazaria*. Northvale, NJ: Jason Aronson, 2006.

Brooks, David. "The Tel Aviv Cluster." *New York Times*, January 12, 2010.

Broshi, Magen. "The Population of Western Palestine in the Roman-Byzantine Period." *Bulletin of the American Schools of Oriental Research* 236 (1979): 1–10.

———. "The Population of the Land of Israel in the Roman Byzantine Period." In *Eretz Israel from the Destruction of the Second Temple to the Muslim Conquest*, edited by Zvi Baras, Shmuel Safrai, Yoram Tsafrir, and Menahem Stern, vol. 1, 442–55. Jerusalem: Yad Yitzhak Ben-Tzvi, 1982.

———. *Bread, Wine, Walls and Scrolls*. New York: Continuum International, 2001.

Brown, Peter. *The Rise of Western Christendom, A.D, 200–1000*. New York: Blackwell, 1996.

Bulliet, Richard W. "Conversion to Islam and the Emergence of a Muslim Society in Iran." In *Conversion to Islam*, edited by Nehemia Levtzion, 30–51. New York: Holmes & Meier, 1979a.

———. *Conversion to Islam in the Medieval Period: An Essay in Quantitative History*. Cambridge, MA: Harvard University Press, 1979b.

Buringh, Eltjo, and Jan Luiten van Zanden. "Charting the 'Rise of the West': Manuscripts and Printed Books in Europe, A Long-Term Perspective from the Sixth through Eighteenth Centuries." *Journal of Economic History* 69, no. 2 (2009): 409–45.

Cahill, Thomas. *The Gifts of the Jews: How a Tribe of Desert Nomads Changed the Way Everyone Thinks and Feels*. New York: Anchor Books, 1998.

Cantera Burgos, Francisco. "Christian Spain." In *The Dark Ages: Jews in Christian Europe, 711–1096*, edited by Cecil Roth and I. H. Levine, 357–81. New Brunswick, NJ: Rutgers University Press, 1966.

Cantoni, Davide. "The Economic Effects of the Protestant Reformation: Testing the Weber Hypothesis in the German Lands." Manuscript, December 2010.

Carlton, Dennis W., and Avi Weiss. "The Economics of Religion, Jewish Survival, and Jewish Attitudes toward Competition in Torah Education." *Journal of Legal Studies* 30, no. 1 (2001): 253–75.

Cassuto, Umberto. *Gli ebrei a Firenze nell'età del Rinascimento*. Florence: Leo S. Olschki Editore, 1918.

Cave, Roy C., and Herbert H. Coulson. *A Source Book for Medieval Economic History*. New York: Biblo & Tannen, 1965.

Chancey, Mark A. *The Myth of a Gentile Galilee*. Cambridge: Cambridge University Press, 2002.

Chazan, Robert. *The Jews of Medieval Western Christendom, 1000–1500*. New York: Cambridge University Press, 2006.

Chiswick, Barry R. "Differences in Education and Earnings Across Racial and Ethnic Groups: Tastes, Discrimination, and Investment in Child Quality." *Quarterly Journal of Economics* 103, no. 3 (1988): 571–97.

———. "The Occupational Attainment of American Jewry: 1990–2000." *Contemporary Jewry* 27, no. 1 (2007): 80–111.

———. "The Economic Progress of American Jewry: From 18th Century Merchants to 21st Century Professionals." In *The Oxford Handbook of Judaism and Economics*, edited by Aaron Levine, 625–45. New York: Oxford University Press, 2010.

Chiswick, Carmel Ullman. "The Economics of Jewish Continuity." *Contemporary Jewry* 20, no. 1 (1999): 30–56.

———. "An Economic Perspective on Religious Education: Complements and Substitutes in a Human Capital Portfolio." *Research in Labor Economics* 24 (2006): 429–67.

Cipolla, Carlo Maria. *Literacy and Development in the West*. Baltimore: Pelican, 1969.

———. *Before the Industrial Revolution: European Society and Economy, 1000–1700*. New York: Norton, 1976.

———. *The Monetary Policy of Fourteenth-Century Florence*. Berkeley: University of California Press, 1982.

Clark, Colin. *Population Growth and Land Use*. London: Macmillan, 1968.

Cochran, Gregory, Jason Hardy, and Henry Harpending. "Natural History of Ashkenazi Intelligence." *Journal of Biosocial Science* 38, no. 5 (2005): 659–93.

Cohen, Gerson D. "Judaism: Rabbinic Judaism." In *The New Encyclopaedia Britannica*, 15th ed. Chicago: New Encylopaedia Britannica, 2002.

Cohen, Mark R. *Jewish Self-Government in Medieval Egypt: The Origins of the Office of Head of the Jews, ca. 1065–1126*. Princeton, NJ: Princeton University Press, 1980.

———. *Under Crescent and Cross: The Jews in the Middle Ages*. Princeton, NJ: Princeton University Press, 1994.

———. "The Foreign Jewish Poor in Medieval Egypt." In *Poverty and Charity in Middle Eastern Contexts*, edited by Michael Bonner, Mone Ener, and Amy Singer, 53–72. Albany: State University of New York Press, 2003.

———. "Geniza for Islamicists, Islamic Geniza, and the 'New Cairo Geniza.'" *Harvard Middle Eastern and Islamic Review* 7 (2006): 129–45.

Cohen, Martin A. "Marrano." In *Encyclopaedia Judaica*, edited by Michael Berenbaum and Fred Skolnik, 2nd ed., vol. 13, 559. Detroit: Macmillan Reference USA, 2007.

Cohen, Shaye J. D. *From the Maccabees to the Mishna*. Philadelphia: Westminster Press, 1987.

———. *The Beginnings of Jewishness: Boundaries, Varieties, Uncertainties*. Berkeley: University of California Press, 1999.

Corcos, David. "Kairouan." In *Encyclopaedia Judaica*, edited by Michael Berenbaum and Fred Skolnik, 2nd ed., vol. 11, 726–28. Detroit: Macmillan Reference USA, 2007.

Cozzi, Gaetano, ed. *Gli ebrei e Venezia, secoli XIV–XVIII*. Atti del Convegno Internazionale organizzato dalla Fondazione G. Cini, Venezia, Isola di San Giorgio Maggiore, 5–10 giugno 1983. Milan: Edizioni Comunitá, 1987.

Crenshaw, James L. *Education in Ancient Israel: Across the Deadening Silence*. New York: Bantam Doubleday Publishing, 1998.

Crown, Alan D., ed. *The Samaritans*. Tübingen: Mohr Siebeck, 1989.

Crown, Alan D., Reinhard Pummer, and Abraham Tal, eds. *A Companion to Samaritan Studies*. Tübingen: Mohr Siebeck, 1993.

Dan, Yaron. "The Byzantine Rule (395–640 CE)." In *The History of Eretz Yisrael: The Roman-Byzantine Period, The Mishna and Talmud Period, and the Byzantine Rule (70–640)*, edited by Mosheh David Herr, 231–374. Jerusalem: Keter Publishing, 1990.

Danièlou, Jean. *The Theology of Jewish Christianity*. Chicago: The Henry Regnery Company, 1964.

Danièlou, Jean, and Henri I. Marrou. *The Christian Centuries*. Vol. 1, *The First Six Hundred Years*. New York: McGraw-Hill, 1964.

Daniels, Peter T. "The First Civilizations." In *The World's Writing Systems*, edited by Peter T. Daniels and William Bright, 21–32. Oxford: Oxford University Press, 1996.

Decker, Michael. "Plants and Progress: Rethinking the Islamic Agricultural Revolution." *Journal of World History* 20, no. 2 (2009): 187–206.

DellaPergola, Sergio. "Major Demographic Trends of World Jewry: The Last Hundred Years." In *Genetic Diversity among Jews: Diseases and Markers at the DNA Level*, edited by Batsheva Bonné-Tamir and Avinoam Adam, 3–30. New York: Oxford University Press, 1992.

———. "Some Fundamentals of Jewish Demographic History." In *Papers in Jewish Demography 1997, Jewish Population Studies* 29, edited by Sergio DellaPergola and Judith Even, 11–33. Jerusalem: Hebrew University Press, 2001.

DeLong, J. Bradford, and Andrei Shleifer. "Princes and Merchants: European City Growth Before the Industrial Revolution." *Journal of Law and Economics* 36, no. 2 (1993): 671–702.

Demsky, Aaron. "Literacy." In *Oxford Encyclopedia of Archeology in the Near East*, vol. 3, 362–69. Oxford: Oxford University Press, 1997.

Demsky, Aaron, Yehuda Moriel, Elijah Bortniker, Fred Skolnik, Chaim S. Kazdan, and Gil Graff. "Education, Jewish." In *Encyclopaedia Judaica*, edited by Michael Berenbaum and Fred Skolnik, 2nd ed., vol. 6, 162–214. Detroit: Macmillan Reference USA, 2007.

De Roover, Raymond. *Money, Banking, and Credit in Medieval Bruges: Italian Merchant-Bankers, Lombards, and Money Changers: A Study in the Origins of Banking*. Cambridge, MA: Mediaeval Academy of America, 1948.

———. *The Rise and Decline of the Medici Bank: 1397–1494*. New York: Norton, 1966.

Doepke, Matthias, and Fabrizio Zilibotti. "Occupational Choice and the Spirit of Capitalism." *Quarterly Journal of Economics* 123, no. 2 (2008): 747–93.

Dols, Michael. "The General Mortality of the Black Death in the Mamluk Empire." In *The Islamic Middle East, 700–1900. Studies in Economic and Social History*, edited by Abraham L. Udovitch, 397–428. Princeton, NJ: Darwin Press, 1981.

Drazin, Nathan. *History of Jewish Education from 515 BCE to 220 CE*. Baltimore: Johns Hopkins University Press, 1940.

Duby, George. *Rural Economy and Country Life in the Medieval West*. Columbia: University of South Carolina Press, 1968.

Durand, John D. "Historical Estimates of World Population: An Evaluation." *Population and Development Review* 3, no. 3 (1977): 253–96.

Ebner, Eliezer. *Elementary Education in Ancient Israel during the Tannaic Period (10–220 CE)*. New York: Bloch, 1956.

Ekelund, Robert B., Robert F. Hebert, Robert D. Tollison, Gary M. Anderson, and Audrey B. Davidson. *Sacred Trust: The Medieval Church as an Economic Firm*. New York: Oxford University Press, 1996.

Elman, Peter. "The Economic Causes of the Expulsion of the Jews in 1290." *Economic History Review* 7, no. 2 (1937): 145–54.

Elon, Menachem. *Jewish Law: History, Sources, Principles*. Translated from the Hebrew by Bernard Auerbach and Melvin J. Sykes. 4 vols. Philadelphia: Jewish Publication Society, 1994.

Engel, David. "Crisis and Lachrymosity: On Salo Baron, Neobaronianism, and the Study of Modern European Jewish History." *Jewish History* 20, no. 3–4 (2006): 243–64.

Engleman, Uriah Zevi. "Sources of Jewish Statistics." In *The Jews: Their History, Culture and Religion*, edited by Louis Finkelstein, 1510–35. Philadelphia: Harper and Brothers, 1960.

Epstein, Stephan R. "Craft Guilds, Apprenticeships, and Technological Change in Pre-Industrial Europe." *Journal of Economic History* 58, no. 3 (1998): 684–713.

Epstein, Steven A. *Wage and Labor Guilds in Medieval Europe*. Chapel Hill: University of North Carolina Press, 1991.

———. *Genoa and the Genoese, 958–1528*. Chapel Hill: University of North Carolina Press, 1996.

Ettinger, Shmuel. "The Modern Period." In *A History of the Jewish People*, edited by Haim Hillel Ben-Sasson, 727–1096. Cambridge, MA: Harvard University Press, 1976.

Feldman, Louis H. *Jew and Gentile in the Ancient World: Attitudes and Interactions from Alexander to Justinian*. Princeton, NJ: Princeton University Press, 1993.

———. "Diaspora Synagogues: New Light from Inscriptions and Papyri." In *Sacred Realm: The Emergence of the Synagogue in the Ancient World*, edited by Steven Fine, 48–66. New York: Oxford University Press, 1996a.

———. *Studies in Hellenistic Judaism*. Leiden: Brill, 1996b.

Feldman, Louis H., and Meyer Reinhold. *Jewish Life and Thought among Greeks and Romans: Primary Readings*. Minneapolis: Augsburg Fortress, 1996.

Ferguson, Everett. *Backgrounds of Early Christianity*. 3rd ed. Grand Rapids, MI: William B. Eerdmans, 2003.

Ferguson, Niall. *The Ascent of Money: A Financial History of the World*. New York: Penguin Press, 2008.

Fernández, Raquel, and Alessandra Fogli. "Fertility: The Role of Culture and Family Experience." *Journal of the European Economic Association* 4, no. 2–3 (2006): 552–61.

———. "Culture: An Empirical Investigation of Beliefs, Work and Fertility." *American Economic Journal: Macroeconomics* 1, no. 1 (2009): 146–77.

Fernández, Raquel, Alessandra Fogli, and Claudia Olivetti. "Mothers and Sons: Preference Transmission and Female Labor Force Dynamics." *Quarterly Journal of Economics* 119, no. 4 (2004): 1249–99.

Fine, Steven, ed. *Sacred Realm: The Emergence of the Synagogue in the Ancient World.* New York: Oxford University Press, 1996.

———. *Jews, Christians, and Polytheists in the Ancient Synagogue; Cultural Interaction During the Greco-Roman Period.* London: Routledge, 1999.

Finkelstein, Israel, and Neil Asher Silberman. *The Bible Unearthed: Archaeology's New Vision of Ancient Israel and the Origin of Its Sacred Texts.* New York: Free Press, 2001.

———. *David and Solomon: In Search of the Bible's Sacred Kings and the Roots of the Western Tradition.* New York: Free Press, 2006.

Fischel, Walter Joseph. "Nishapur." In *Encyclopaedia Judaica*, edited by Michael Berenbaum and Fred Skolnik, 2nd ed., vol. 15, 275. Detroit: Macmillan Reference USA, 2007.

Fischel, Walter Joseph, Hayyim J. Cohen, and Amnon Netzer. "Isfahan." In *Encyclopaedia Judaica*, edited by Michael Berenbaum and Fred Skolnik, 2nd ed., vol. 10, 79–80. Detroit: Macmillan Reference USA, 2007.

Flavius, Josephus. *Josephus: The Complete Works.* Translated by William Whiston. Nashville, TN: T. Nelson, 1998.

Flesher, Paul V. M. "Palestinian Synagogues before 70 C.E.: A Review of the Evidence." In *Ancient Synagogues: Historical Analysis and Archaeological Discovery*, edited by Dan Urman and Paul V. M. Flesher, vol. 1, 27–39. Leiden: Brill, 1998.

Flusser, David. *Judaism and the Origins of Christianity.* Jerusalem: Hebrew University Magnes Press, 1988.

Fornasari, Marco. *Il "Thesoro" della città: Il Monte di Pietá e l'economia bolognese nei secoli XV e XVI.* Bologna: Il Mulino, 1993.

Fossier, Robert. *Peasant Life in the Medieval West.* New York: Blackwell, 1988.

Fox, Robin Lane. *Pagans and Christians.* New York: Knopf, 1987.

Frank, Tenney. *Economic Survey of Ancient Rome.* Baltimore: Johns Hopkins University Press, 1938.

Frend, William H. C. *The Archaeology of Early Christianity: A History.* Minneapolis: Fortress Press, 1996.

Friedman, Richard E. *Who Wrote the Bible?* New York: HarperCollins, 1997.

Fuchs, Daniel, and Harold A. Sevener. *From Bondage to Freedom: A Survey of Jewish History from the Babylonian Captivity to the Coming of the Messiah.* Neptune, NJ: Loizeaux, 1995.

Fuss, Abraham M. "Inter-Jewish Loans in Pre-Expulsion England." *Jewish Quarterly Review* 65, no. 4 (1975): 229–45.

Gafni, Isaiah. *Jews of Babylonia in the Talmudic Era.* Jerusalem: Zalman Shazar Center for Jewish History, 1990 (in Hebrew).

———. "Synagogues in Babylonia in the Talmudic Period." In *Ancient Synagogues: Historical Analysis and Archaeological Discovery*, edited by Dan Urman and Paul V. M. Flesher, vol. 1, 221–31. Leiden: Brill, 1998.

Galor, Oded, and Omer Moav. "Natural Selection and the Origin of Economic Growth." *Quarterly Journal of Economics* 117, no. 4 (2002): 1133–91.

Gampel, Benjamin. *The Last Jews on Iberian Soil*. Berkeley: University of California Press, 1989.

———, ed. *Crisis and Creativity in the Sephardic World, 1391–1648*. New York: Columbia University Press, 1998.

Georgi, Dieter. "The Early Church: Internal Jewish Migration or New Religion?" *Harvard Theological Review* 88, no. 1 (1995): 35–68.

Ghosh, Amitav. *In an Antique Land*. New York: Vintage, 1992.

Gil, Moshe. "The Radhanite Merchants and the Land of Radhan." *Journal of the Economic and Social History of the Orient* 17, no. 3 (1976): 299–328.

———. *A History of Palestine, 634–1099*. Cambridge: Cambridge University Press, 1992.

———. *Jews in Islamic Countries in the Middle Ages*. Translated by David Strassler. Leiden: Brill, 2004.

———. *And the Roman Was Then in the Land*. Tel Aviv: Hakibutz Ha-meukhad, 2008.

Gilat, Yitzhak Dov. "Kallah, Months of." In *Encyclopaedia Judaica*, edited by Michael Berenbaum and Fred Skolnik, 2nd ed., vol. 11, 741–42. Detroit: Macmillan Reference USA, 2007.

Ginzberg, Louis. *Students, Scholars, and Saints*. 2nd ed. Philadelphia: The Jewish Publication Society of America, 1943.

Glaeser, Edward L., and José A. Scheinkman. "Neither a Borrower nor a Lender Be: An Economic Analysis of Interest Restrictions and Usury Laws." *Journal of Law and Economics* 41, no. 1 (1998): 1–36.

Glick, Leonard B. *Abraham's Heirs: Jews and Christians in Medieval Europe*. Syracuse, NY: Syracuse University Press, 1999.

Glick, Thomas F. "On Converso and Marrano Ethnicity." In *Crisis and Creativity in the Sephardic World, 1391–1648*, edited by Benjamin Gampel, 59–76. New York: Columbia University Press, 1998.

Goitein, Shelomo Dov. *Jews and Arabs: Their Contact through the Ages*. New York: Schocken Books, 1955.

———. "Glimpses from the Cairo Geniza on Naval Warfare in the Mediterranean and on the Mongol Invasion." In *Studi Orientalistici in onore di Giorgio Levi Della Vida*, 393–408. Rome: Istituto per l'Oriente, 1956.

———. *Jewish Education in Muslim Countries during the Geonim and the Rambam: New Sources from the Cairo Geniza*. Jerusalem: Yad Yitzhak Ben-Zvi Institute, 1962 (in Hebrew).

———. *A Mediterranean Society: The Jewish Communities of the Arab World as Portrayed in the Documents of the Cairo Geniza*. 5 vols. Los Angeles: University of California Press, 1967–1988.

———. *Letters of Medieval Jewish Traders*. Translated from the Arabic with introductions and notes by Shelomo Dov Goitein. Princeton, NJ: Princeton University Press, 1973.

Goitein, Shelomo Dov, and Mordechai Akiva Friedman. *India Traders of the Middle Ages. Documents from the Cairo Geniza "India Book."* Leiden: Brill, 2007.

Goldin, Simha. "Companies of Disciples and Companies of Colleagues: Communication in Jewish Intellectual Circles." In *Communication in the Jewish Diaspora: The Pre-Modern World,* edited by Sophia Menache, 127–39. Leiden: Brill, 1996.

Goldthwaite, Richard A. *Banks, Palaces, and Entrepreneurs in Renaissance Florence.* Aldershot, UK: Ashgate, 1995.

Goodblatt, David. *Rabbinic Instruction in Sasanian Babylonia.* Leiden: Brill, 1974.

———. "The Talmudic Sources on the Origins of Organized Jewish Education." In *Studies in the History of the Jewish People and the Land of Israel* 5 (1980): 83–103.

———. "The History of the Babylonian Academies." In *The Cambridge History of Judaism.* Vol. 4, *The Late Roman-Rabbinic Period,* edited by Steven T. Katz, 821–39. New York: Cambridge University Press, 2006a.

———. "The Jews in Babylonia 66–235 CE." In *The Cambridge History of Judaism.* Vol. 4, *The Late Roman-Rabbinic Period,* edited by Steven T. Katz, 82–90. New York: Cambridge University Press, 2006b.

———. "The Political and Social History of the Jewish Community in the Land of Israel, c. 235–638." In *The Cambridge History of Judaism.* Vol. 4, *The Late Roman-Rabbinic Period,* edited by Steven T. Katz, 404–30. New York: Cambridge University Press, 2006c.

Goodman, Martin. *The Ruling Class of Judaea: The Origins of the Jewish Revolt against Rome, AD 66–70.* Cambridge: Cambridge University Press, 1987.

———. *Mission and Conversion: Proselytizing in the Religious History of the Roman Empire.* Oxford: Clarendon Press, 1994.

———, ed. *Jews in a Graeco-Roman World.* Oxford: Clarendon Press, 1998.

———. "Trajan and the Origins of Roman Hostility to the Jews." *Past and Present* 182 (2004): 3–31.

———. *Rome and Jerusalem: The Clash of Ancient Civilizations.* London: Penguin, 2008.

Grabbe, Lester L. "Synagogues in Pre-70 Palestine: A Re-assessment." In *Ancient Synagogues: Historical Analysis and Archaeological Discovery,* edited by Dan Urman and Paul V. M. Flesher, vol. 1, 17–26. Leiden: Brill, 1998.

Greenberg, Moshe, and Haim Hermann Cohn. "Ḥerem." In *Encyclopaedia Judaica,* edited by Michael Berenbaum and Fred Skolnik, 2nd ed., vol. 9, 10–16. Detroit: Macmillan Reference USA, 2007.

Greenberg, Simon. "Jewish Educational Institutions." In *The Jews, Their History, Culture, and Religion,* edited by Louis Finkelstein, vol. 2, 1254–87. Philadelphia: Harper and Brothers, 1960.

Greif, Avner. "Reputation and Coalitions in Medieval Trade: Evidence on the Maghribi Traders." *Journal of Economic History* 49, no. 4 (1989): 857–82.

———. "Contract Enforceability and Economic Institutions in Early Trade: The Maghribi Traders' Coalition." *American Economic Review* 83, no. 3 (1993): 525–48.

———. "Cultural Beliefs and the Organization of Society: A Historical and Theoretical Reflection on Collectivist and Individualist Societies." *Journal of Political Economy* 102, no. 5 (1994): 912–50.

———. *Institutions and the Path to the Modern Economy: Lessons from Medieval Trade.* Cambridge: Cambridge University Press, 2006.

Griffin, Miriam T. *Nero: The End of a Dynasty.* New Haven, CT: Yale University Press, 1984.

Griffiths, J. Gwyn. "Egypt and the Rise of the Synagogue." In *Ancient Synagogues: Historical Analysis and Archaeological Discovery*, edited by Dan Urman and Paul V. M. Flesher, vol. 1, 3–16. Leiden: Brill, 1998.

Grintz, Yehoshua M., and Raphael Posner. "Jew." In *Encyclopedia Judaica*, edited by Michael Berenbaum and Fred Skolnik, 2nd ed., vol. 11, 253–55. Detroit: Macmillan Reference USA, 2007.

Grossman, Avraham. "Relations between Spanish and Ashkenazi Jewry in the Middle Ages." In *The Sephardi Legacy*, edited by Haim Beinart, vol. 1, 220–39. Jerusalem: Hebrew University Magnes Press, 1992.

———. "The Yeshivot in Babylonia, Germany, and France from the Ninth to the Eleventh Centuries." In *Education and History*, edited by Immanuel Etkes, 79–99. Jerusalem: Zalman Shazar Center, 1999 (in Hebrew).

Guinnane, Timothy W. "Cooperatives as Information Machines: German Rural Credit Cooperatives, 1883–1914." *Journal of Economic History* 61, no. 2 (2001): 366–89.

Guiso, Luigi, Paola Sapienza, and Luigi Zingales (2003). "People's Opium? Religion and Economic Attitudes." *Journal of Monetary Economics* 50 (2003): 225–82.

———. "Does Culture Affect Economic Outcomes?" *Journal of Economic Perspectives* 20, no. 2 (2006): 23–48.

Gustafsson, Bo. "The Rise and Economic Behavior of Medieval Craft Guilds: An Economic-Theoretical Interpretation." *Scandinavian Journal of Economics* 35, no. 1 (1987): 1–40.

Haas, Peter. "The Am Ha-aretz as Literary Character." In *From Ancient Israel to Modern Judaism: Intellect in Quest of Understanding; Essays in Honor of Marvin Fox*, edited by Jacob Neusner, vol. 2, 139–53. Atlanta: Scholars Press, 1989.

Hachlili, Rachel. *Ancient Jewish Art and Archeology in the Land of Israel.* Leiden: Brill, 1988.

———, ed. *Ancient Synagogues in Israel: Third–Seventh Century C.E.* Oxford: BAR, 1989.

Haim, Abraham. "Kufa." In *Encyclopaedia Judaica*, edited by Michael Berenbaum and Fred Skolnik, 2nd ed., vol. 12, 379. Detroit: Macmillan Reference USA, 2007.

Halpern, Israel. "The Jews in Eastern Europe (From Ancient Times until the Partitions of Poland, 1772–1775)." In *The Jews: Their History, Culture, and Religion*, edited by Louis Finkelstein, vol. 1, 287–321. Philadelphia: Harper and Brothers, 1960.

Hamel, Gildas. *Poverty and Charity in Roman Palestine, First Three Centuries C.E.* Berkeley: University of California Press, 1990.

Hammer, M. F., A. J. Redd, E. T. Wood, M. R. Bonner, H. Jarjanazi, T. Karafet, S. Santachiara-Benerecetti, A. Oppenheim, M.A. Jobling, T. Jenkins, H. Ostrer, and B. Bonnè-Tamir. "Jewish and Middle Eastern non-Jewish Populations Share a Common Pool of Y-Chromosome Biallelic Haplotypes." *Proceedings of the National Academy of Sciences* (2000): 1–6.

Harnack, Adolf von. *The Mission and Expansion of Christianity in the First Three Centuries.* 2 vols. London: Williams and Norgate; New York, G. P. Putnam, 1908.

Harris, William V. *Ancient Literacy.* Cambridge, MA: Harvard University Press, 1991.

Heertje, Arnold. "The Dutch and Portuguese-Jewish Background of David Ricardo." In *European Journal History of Economic Thought* 11, no. 2 (2004): 281–94.

Herr, Mosheh David, and Aharon Oppenheimer. "Social-Economic and Cultural-Religious History from the Destruction of the Second Temple to the Division of the Empire (70–395 CE)." In *The History of Eretz Yisrael: The Roman-Byzantine Period, the Mishna and Talmud Period, and the Byzantine Rule (70–640)*, edited by Mosheh David Herr, 107–229. Jerusalem: Keter, 1990 (in Hebrew).

Hertzberg, Arthur, and Fred Skolnik. "Jewish Identity." In *Encyclopedia Judaica*, edited by Michael Berenbaum and Fred Skolnik, 2nd ed., vol. 11, 292–99. Detroit: Macmillan Reference USA, 2007.

Hezser, Catherine. *Jewish Literacy in Roman Palestine.* Tübingen: Mohr Siebeck, 2001.

Hodges, Richard. *Towns and Trade in the Age of Charlemagne.* London: Duckworth, 2000.

Holo, Joshua. *Byzantine Jewry in the Mediterranean Economy.* Cambridge: Cambridge University Press, 2009.

Hunt, Edwin. *The Medieval Super-Companies: A Study of the Peruzzi Company of Florence.* Cambridge: Cambridge University Press, 1994.

Iannaccone, Laurence R. "Sacrifices and Stigma: Reducing the Free-Riding in Cults, Communes and Other Collectives." *Journal of Political Economy* 100, no. 2 (1992): 271–91.

———. "Introduction to the Economics of Religion." *Journal of Economic Literature* 36, no. 3 (1998): 1465–95.

Iannaccone, Laurence R., Rodney Stark, and Roger Finke. "Rationality and the 'Religious Mind.'" *Economic Inquiry* 36, no. 3 (1998): 373–89.

Ilan, Zvi. "The Synagogue and House of Study at Meroth." In *Ancient Synagogues: Historical and Archaeological Study*, edited by Dan Urman and Paul V. M. Flesher, vol. 1, 256–87. Leiden: Brill, 1998.

Isaac, Benjamin. "Jews, Christians and Others in Palestine: The Evidence from Eusebius." In *Jews in a Graeco-Roman World*, edited by Martin Goodman, 65–74. Oxford: Clarendon Press, 1998.

Issawi, Charles. "The Area and Population of the Arab Empire: an Essay in Speculation." In *The Islamic Middle East, 700–1900:. Studies in Economic and Social History*, edited by Abraham L. Udovitch, 375–96. Princeton, NJ: Darwin Press, 1981.

Jacobs, Joseph. "When Did the Jews First Settle in England?" *Jewish Quarterly Review* 1 (1889): 286–88.

———. "Notes on the Jews of England under the Angevin Kings." *Jewish Quarterly Review* 4 (1892): 628–55.

———. *The Jews of Angevin England. Documents and Records, from Latin and Hebrew Sources.* London: D. Nutt, 1893.

———. "The Typical Character of Anglo-Jewish History." *Jewish Quarterly Review* 10 (1898): 217–37.

Jacobs, Louis. "The Economic Conditions of the Jews in Babylon in Talmudic Times Compared with Palestine." In *History of the Jews in the Second through Seventh Centuries of the Common Era. Origins of Judaism*, edited by Jacob Neusner, vol. 8, pt. 1, 333–43. New York: Garland, 1990.

Jacoby, David. "The Jews in Byzantium and the Eastern Mediterranean: Economic Activities from the Thirteenth to the Mid-Fifteenth Century." In *Wirtschaftsgeschichte der mittelalterlichen Juden. Fragen und Einschtzungen*, edited by Michael Toch, 25–48. Munich: Oldebourg, 2008.

———. "The Jews in the Byzantine Economy, Seventh to Mid-Fifteenth Century." In *Jews in Byzantium. Dialectics of Minority and Majority Cultures*, edited by Robert Bonfil, Oded Irshai, Guy G. Stroumsa, Rina Talgam. Leiden: Brill, 2011.

Jones, Arnold H. M. *The Later Roman Empire 284–602: A Social, Economic, and Administrative Survey*. 2 vols. Oxford: Blackwell, 1964.

Jones, F. Stanley. *An Ancient Jewish Christian Source on the History of Christianity: Pseudo-Clementine Recognitions 1.27–71*. Texts and Translations 37. Christian Apocrypha Series 2. Atlanta: Scholars Press, 1995.

Jones, Lindsay, ed. *Encyclopedia of Religion*. 2nd ed. 15 vols. New York: Macmillan Reference, 2004.

Juster, Jean. *La condition legale des juifs sous les rois visigoths*. Paris: Paul Geuthner, 1912.

———. *Les Juifs dans l'Empire Romain: leur condition juridique, économique et sociale*. 2 vols. Paris: Paul Geuthner, 1914.

Kalmin, Richard. *The Sage in Jewish Society of Late Antiquity*. London: Routledge Press, 1999.

Kanarfogel, Ephraim. *Jewish Education and Society in the High Middle Ages*. Detroit: Wayne State University Press, 1992.

Karlin, Samuel, Ron Kennet, and Batsheva Bonné-Tamir. "Analysis of Biochemical Genetic Data of Jewish Populations." *American Journal of Human Genetics* 31 (1979): 341–65.

Kasher, Aryeh. *The Jews in Hellenistic and Roman Egypt: The Struggle for Equal Rights*. Tübingen: Mohr Siebeck, 1985.

———. "Synagogues as Houses of Prayer and Holy Places in the Jewish Communities of Hellenistic and Roman Egypt." In *Ancient Synagogues: Historical Analysis and Archaeological Discovery*, edited by Dan Urman and Paul V. M. Flesher, vol. 1, 205–20. Leiden: Brill, 1998.

Kasher, Aryeh, Aharon Oppenheimer, and Uriel Rappaport, eds. *Synagogues in Antiquity*. Jerusalem: Yad Yitzhak Ben-Tzvi, 1987 (in Hebrew).

Katz, Jacob. *Exclusiveness and Tolerance: Studies in Jewish-Gentile Relations in Medieval and Modern Times*. Oxford: Oxford University Press, 1961.

———. "Considerations on the Relationship between Religion and the Economy." In *Religion and Economy: Connection and Interaction*, edited by Menahem Ben-Sasson, 33–46. Jerusalem: Zalman Shazar Center, 1995.

Katz, Solomon. *The Jews in the Visigothic and Frankish Kingdoms of Spain and Gaul*. Cambridge, MA: Mediaeval Academy of America, 1937.

Kessel, Reuben. "Price Discrimination in Medicine." *Journal of Law and Economics* 1 (1958): 20–53.

Kestenberg-Gladstein, R. "The Early Jewish Settlement in Central and Eastern Europe: Bohemia." In *The Dark Ages: Jews in Christian Europe, 711–1096*, edited by Cecil Roth and I. H. Levine, 309–12. New Brunswick, NJ: Rutgers University Press, 1966.

Kirshner, Julius. "The Moral Problem of Discounting Genoese Paghe, 1450–1550." *Archivum Fratrum Praedicatorum* 47 (1977): 109–67.

———. "Encumbering Private Claims to Public Debt in Renaissance Florence." In *The Growth of the Bank as Institution and the Development of Money-Business Law*, edited by Vito Piergiovanni, 19–76. Berlin: Duncker & Humblot, 1993.

Kremer, Michael. "Population Growth and Technological Change: One Million B.C. to 1990." *Quarterly Journal of Economics* 108, no. 4 (1993): 681–716.

Kuran, Timur. "The Economic Ascent of the Middle East's Religious Minorities: The Role of Islamic Legal Pluralism." *Journal of Legal Studies* 33, no. 2 (2004): 475–515.

———. "Economic Development in the Middle East: The Historical Roles of Culture, Institutions, and Religion." In *Culture and Development*, edited by Jean-Philippe Platteau, 87–102. New York: Routledge, 2010a.

———. *The Long Divergence: How Islamic Law Held Back the Middle East*. Princeton, NJ: Princeton University Press, 2010b.

———. "The Scale of Entrepreneurship in Middle Eastern History: Inhibitive Roles of Islamic Institutions." In *The Invention of Enterprise: Entrepreneurship from Ancient Mesopotamia to Modern Times*, edited by William J. Baumol, David S. Landes, and Joel Mokyr, 62–87. Princeton, NJ: Princeton University Press, 2010c.

Kuznets, Simon. "Economic Structure and Life of the Jews." In *The Jews: Their History, Culture, and Religion*, edited by Louis Finkelstein, 1597–1666. Philadelphia: Harper and Brothers, 1960.

———. *Economic Structure of U.S. Jewry: Recent Trends*. Jerusalem: Institute of Contemporary Jewry, Hebrew University of Jerusalem, 1972.

Lambton, Ann K. S. *Continuity and Change in Medieval Persia: Aspects of Administrative, Economic, and Social History, 11th–14th Century*. Albany, NY: Bibliotheca Persica, 1988.

Lane, Frederic C., and Reinhold C. Mueller. *Money and Banking in Medieval and Renaissance Venice: Coins and Moneys of Account*. Baltimore: Johns Hopkins University Press, 1985.

Lapidus, Ira M. "Arab Settlement and Economic Development of Iraq and Iran in the Age of the Umayyad and the Early Abbasid Caliphs." In *The Islamic Middle East, 700–1900: Studies in Economic and Social History*, edited by Abraham L. Udovitch, 177–208. Princeton, NJ: Darwin Press, 1981.

Latourette, Kenneth S. *A History of Christianity*. Vol. 1, *To A.D. 1500*. New York: Harper & Row, 1975.

Le Goff, Jacques. *Medieval Civilization*. London: Blackwell, 1988.

Leibner, Uzi. "Settlement and Demography in Late Roman and Byzantine Eastern Galilee." In *Settlements and Demography in the Near East in Late Antiquity*, edited by Ariel S. Lewin and Pietrina Pellegrini, vol. 2, 105–30. Pisa: Istituti Editoriali e Poligrafici Internazionali, 2006.

——. *Settlement and History in Hellenistic, Roman, and Byzantine Galilee: An Archaeological Survey of the Eastern Galilee.* Tübingen: Mohr Siebeck, 2009.

Levine, Lee I., ed. *Ancient Synagogues Revealed.* Detroit: Wayne State University Press, 1982.

——. "The Synagogue in the Time of the Second Temple—Its Character and Development." In *Synagogues in Antiquity*, edited by Aryeh Kasher, Aaron Oppenheimer, and Uriel Rappaport, 11–30. Jerusalem: Yad Yitzhak Ben-Tzvi, 1987.

——. "The Hellenistic-Roman Diaspora, 70–235 C.E.: The Archaeological Evidence." In *The Cambridge History of Judaism*, vol. 3, 991–1024. Cambridge: Cambridge University Press, 1999.

——. *The Ancient Synagogue: The First Thousand Years.* 2nd ed. New Haven, CT: Yale University Press, 2005.

Levy, Tony. "Hebrew Mathematics in the Middle Ages: An Assessment." In *Tradition, Transmission, Transformation*, edited by F. Jamil Ragep and Sally P. Rajep with Steven Livesey, 71–88. Leiden: Brill, 1996.

Lewis, Bernard. *Studies in Classical and Ottoman Islam, 7th–16th Centuries.* London: Variorum, 1976.

——. *The Jews of Islam.* Princeton, NJ: Princeton University Press, 1984.

——. *The Arabs in History.* 6th ed. New York: Oxford University Press, 2002.

Limor, Ora. "Resemblance and Difference." In *Jews and Christians in Western Europe: Encounter between Cultures in the Middle Ages and the Renaissance*, edited by Ora Limor, vol. 2, 156–286. Tel Aviv: Open University Press, 1993.

Limor, Ora, and Amnon Raz-Krakotzkin. "Majority and Minority." In *Jews and Christians in Western Europe: Encounter between Cultures in the Middle Ages and the Renaissance*, edited by Ora Limor, vol. 2, 1–145. Tel Aviv: Open University Press, 1993.

Linder, Amnon. *The Jews in Roman Imperial Legislation.* Jerusalem: Israel Academy of Sciences and Humanities, 1987.

——. *The Jews in the Legal Sources of the Early Middle Ages.* Jerusalem: Israel Academy of Sciences and Humanities, 1997.

Lopez, Robert. *The Commercial Revolution of the Middle Ages, 950–1350.* Cambridge: Cambridge University Press, 1976.

Louth, Andrew. "The Byzantine Empire in the Seventh Century." In *The New Cambridge Medieval History*, edited by Paul Fouracre, vol. 1, chap. 11. Cambridge: Cambridge University Press, 2005.

Lucas, Robert E. "Life Earnings and Rural-Urban Migration." *Journal of Political Economy* 112, no. S1 (2004): S29–S59.

Lüdemann, Gerd. *Opposition to Paul in Jewish Christianity.* Minneapolis: Fortress Press, 1989.

Luzzati, Michele. "I legami tra i banchi ebraici toscani e i banchi veneti e dell'Italia settentrionale." In *Gli ebrei e Venezia, secoli XIV–XVIII*, edited by Gaetano Cozzi, 571–94. Milan: Edizioni Comunitá, 1987.

——. "Banchi e insediamenti ebraici nell'Italia centro-settentrionale fra tardo medioevo e inizi dell'etá moderna." In *Storia d'Italia: Annali 11, Gli ebrei in Italia*, edited by Corrado Vivanti, 175–238. Turin: Einaudi Editore, 1996.

Luzzati, Michele, and Alessandra Veronese. *Banche e banchieri a Volterra nel Medioevo e nel Rinascimento*. Pisa: Pacini Editore, 1993.

Luzzatto, Gino. *I banchieri ebrei in Urbino nell'età ducale: Appunti di storia economica con appendice di documenti*. Bologna: Fomi Editore, 1902.

Lynch, Joseph. *The Medieval Church: A Brief History*. London: Longman, 1992.

MacMullen, Ramsay. *Christianizing the Roman Empire (A.D. 100–400)*. New Haven, CT: Yale University Press, 1984.

Malanima, Paolo. "Urbanisation and the Italian Economy during the Last Millennium." *European Review of Economic History* 9, no. 1 (2005): 97–122.

———. "Wages, Productivity and Working Time in Italy 1300–1913." *Journal of European Economic History* 36, no. 1 (2007): 127–74.

Maller, Julius B. "The Role of Education in Jewish History." In *The Jews: Their History, Culture, and Religion*, edited by Louis Finkelstein, vol. 2, 1234–53. Philadelphia: Harper and Brothers, 1960.

Mann, Jacob. *The Responsa of the Babylonian Geonim as a Source of Jewish History*. Philadelphia: Dropsie College for Hebrew and Cognate Learning, 1917–1921.

———. *The Jews in Egypt and in Palestine under the Fatimid Caliphs*. London: Oxford University Press, 1920–1922.

Mansoor, Menahem. "Pharisees." In *Encyclopaedia Judaica*, edited by Michael Berenbaum and Fred Skolnik, 2nd ed., vol. 16, 30–32. Detroit: Macmillan Reference USA, 2007a.

———. "Sadducees." In *Encyclopaedia Judaica*, edited by Michael Berenbaum and Fred Skolnik, 2nd ed., vol. 17, 654–55. Detroit: Macmillan Reference USA, 2007b.

Marcus, David, Haïm Z'ew Hirschberg, and Abraham Ben-Yaacob. "Ezra." In *Encyclopaedia Judaica*, edited by Michael Berenbaum and Fred Skolnik, 2nd ed., vol. 6, 652–54. Detroit: Macmillan Reference USA, 2007.

Marcus, Jacob. *The Jew in the Medieval World: A Sourcebook, 315–1791*. Cincinnati: Sinai Press, 1938.

Marrou, Henri I. *A History of Education in Antiquity*. Madison: University of Wisconsin Press, 1982.

Marx, Karl. "Zur Judenfrage [On the Jewish Question]." In *Deutsch-Französische Jahrbücher* (February 1844). Reprinted in Karl Marx and Friedrich Engels, *Werke*, 16th ed., vol. 1, 347–77. Berlin: Dietz Verlag, 2007.

McCleary, Rachel M., ed. *The Oxford Encyclopedia of the Economics of Religion*. Oxford: Oxford University Press, 2011.

McCleary, Rachel M., and Robert J. Barro. "Religion and Economic Growth across Countries." *American Sociological Review* 68, no. 5 (2003): 760–81.

———. "Religion and Economy." *Journal of Economic Perspectives* 20, no. 2 (2006): 49–72.

McEvedy, Colin, and Richard Jones. *Atlas of World Population History*. New York: Penguin, 1978.

Meeks, Wayne A. *The First Urban Christians: The Social World of the Apostle Paul*. New Haven, CT: Yale University Press, 1983.

Menning, Carolyn B. *Charity and State in Late Renaissance Italy: The Monte di Pietà of Florence*. Ithaca: Cornell University Press, 1993.

Milano, Attilio. "Considerazion sulla lotta dei Monti di Pietá contro il prestito ebraico." In *Scritti in onore di Sally Mayer*, edited by Umberto Nahon, 199–221. Jerusalem: Israel Academy of Sciences and Humanities, 1956.

———. *Storia degli ebrei in Italia*. Turin: Einaudi Editore, 1963.

Milano, Attilio, Daniel Carpi, Sergio Itzhak Minerbi, Sergio DellaPergola, Lisa Palmieri-Billig, and Yohanan Meroz. "Italy." In *Encyclopaedia Judaica*, edited by Michael Berenbaum and Fred Skolnik, 2nd ed., vol. 10, 795–816. Detroit: Macmillan Reference USA, 2007.

Millard, Alan R. *Reading and Writing in the Time of Jesus*. Sheffield: Sheffield Academic Press, 2000.

Mokyr, Joel. *The Lever of Riches. Technological Creativity and Economic Progress*. New York: Oxford University Press, 1990.

———. *The Gifts of Athena: Historical Origins of the Knowledge Economy*. Princeton, NJ: Princeton University Press, 2002.

———. "Long-Term Economic Growth and the History of Technology." In *Handbook of Economic Growth*, vol. 1b, edited by Philippe Aghion and Steven N. Durlauf, 1113–80. Amsterdam: North-Holland, 2005.

———. "The Institutional Origins of the Industrial Revolution." In *Institutions and Economic Performance*, edited by Elhanan Helpman, 64–119. Cambridge, MA: Harvard University Press, 2008.

———. "Intellectual Property Rights, the Industrial Revolution, and the Beginnings of Modern Economic Growth." *American Economic Review Papers and Proceedings* 99, no. 2 (2009): 349–55.

———. "The Economics of Being Jewish." *Critical Review* 23, no. 1–2 (2011): 195–206.

Mokyr, Joel, and Joachim Voth. "Understanding Growth in Europe, 1700–1870: Theory and Evidence." In *Cambridge Economic History of Modern Europe, Volume 1: 1700–1870*, edited by Stephen Broadberry and Kevin H. O'Rourke, 7–42. Cambridge: Cambridge University Press, 2010.

Molho, Anthony. *Florentine Public Finances in the Early Renaissance, 1400–1433*. Cambridge, MA: Harvard University Press, 1971.

———. "The State and Public Finance: A Hypothesis Based on the History of Late Medieval Florence." In *The Origins of the State in Italy, 1300–1600*, edited by Julius Kirshner, 97–135. Chicago: University of Chicago Press, 1995.

Montgomery, James A. *The Samaritan:. The Earliest Jewish Sect; Their History, Theology, and Literature*. New York: Ktav, 1968.

Morgan, Gwyn. *69 AD: The Year of Four Emperors*. Oxford: Oxford University Press, 2006.

Morony, Michael G. "Religious Communities in Late Sasanian and Early Muslim Iraq." *Journal of the Economic and Social History of the Orient* 17, no. 2 (1974): 113–135.

———. "Landholding in Seventh-Century Iraq: Late Sasanian and Early Islamic Patterns." In *The Islamic Middle East, 700–1900: Studies in Economic and Social History*, edited by Abraham L. Udovitch, 135–76. Princeton, NJ: Darwin Press, 1981.

Morris, Nathan. *A History of Jewish Education from the Earliest Times to the Sixteenth Century*. 2 vols. Jerusalem: Rubin Mas, 1977 (in Hebrew).

Mueller, Reinhold C. "Charitable Institutions, the Jewish Community, and Venetian Society. A Discussion of the Recent Volume of Brian Pullan." *Studi Veneziani* 14, no. 1 (1972): 37–82.

———. "Pratiques économiques et groupes sociaux." *Annales* 30, no. 5 (1975): 1277–1302.

———. *The Venetian Money Market: Banks, Panics and the Public Debt, 1200–1500.* Vol. 2 of *Money and Banking in Medieval and Renaissance Venice.* Baltimore: Johns Hopkins University Press, 1997.

———. "The Status and Economic Activity of Jews in the Venetian Dominions during the Fifteenth Century." In *Wirtschaftsgeschichte der mittelalterlichen Juden: Fragen und Einschtzungen,* edited by Michael Toch, 63–92. Munich: Oldebourg, 2008.

Mullen, Roderic L. *The Expansion of Christianity: A Gazetteer of Its First Three Centuries.* Leiden: Brill, 2004.

Muller, Jerry Z. *Capitalism and the Jews.* Princeton, NJ: Princeton University Press, 2010.

Mundill, Robin R. "Lumbard and Son: The Businesses and Debtors of Two Jewish Moneylenders in Late Thirteenth-Century England." *Jewish Quarterly Review* 82, no. 1–2 (1991): 137–70.

———. *The King's Jews: Money, Massacre, and Exodus in Medieval England.* London: Continuum, 2010.

Munro, John H. "The Medieval Origins of the Financial Revolution: Usury, Rentes, and Negotiability." *International History Review* 25, no. 3 (2003): 505–62.

Murray, Charles. "Jewish Genius." *Commentary* (2007): 29–35.

Musallam, Basim. "Birth Control and Middle Eastern History: Evidence and Hypotheses." In *The Islamic Middle East, 700–1900: Studies in Economic and Social History,* edited by Abraham L. Udovitch, 429–69. Princeton, NJ: Darwin Press, 1981.

Muzzarelli, Maria Giuseppina. *Ebrei e città d'Italia in etá di transizione: Il caso di Cesena dal XIV al XVI secolo.* Bologna: CLUEB, 1984.

———, ed. *Banchi ebraici a Bologna nel quindicesimo secolo.* Bologna: Il Mulino, 1994.

Nakosteen, Mehdi Khan. *History of Islamic Origins of Western Education, A.D. 800–1350.* Boulder: University of Colorado Press, 1964.

Nelson, Benjamin. *The Idea of Usury: From Tribal Brotherhood to Universal Otherhood.* Chicago: University of Chicago Press, 1969.

Neusner, Jacob. *A History of the Jews in Babylonia.* 5 vols. Leiden: Brill, 1965–1970.

———. *Talmudic Judaism in Sasanian Babylonia: Essays and Studies.* Leiden: Brill, 1976.

———. *School, Court, Public Administration: Judaism and Its Institutions in Talmudic Babylonia.* Atlanta: Scholars Press, 1987.

———, ed. *Judaism and Christianity in the First Century.* New York: Garland, 1990a.

———. *Judaism, Christianity, and Zoroastrianism in Talmudic Babylonia.* Atlanta: Scholars Press, 1990b.

———. "New Perspectives on Babylonian Jewry in the Tannaitic Age." In *History of the Jews in the Second through Seventh Centuries of the Common Era: Origins of Judaism,* edited by Jacob Neusner, vol. 8, pt. 1, 430–56. New York: Garland, 1990c.

———, ed. *The Pharisees and Other Sects*. New York: Garland, 1990d.

———. "Some Aspects of the Economic and Political Life of Babylonian Jewry, ca. 160–220 C.E." In *History of the Jews in the Second Century of the Common Era: Origins of Judaism*, edited by Jacob Neusner, vol. 7, 165–96. New York: Garland, 1990e.

———. *Judaism in the Matrix of Christianity*. Atlanta: Scholars Press, 1991.

———. *The Economics of the Mishna*. Atlanta: Scholars Press, 1998.

Newman, Julius. *The Agricultural Life of the Jews in Babylonia between the Years 200 C.E. and 500 C.E.* London: Oxford University Press, 1932.

Nock, Arthur D. *Conversion: The Old and the New in Religion from Alexander the Great to Augustine of Hippo*. London: Oxford University Press, 1969.

Noonan, John T. *The Scholastic Analysis of Usury*. Cambridge, MA: Harvard University Press, 1957.

North, Douglass C. *Institutions, Institutional Change, and Economic Performance*. Cambridge: Cambridge University Press, 1990.

O'Connor, Michael P. "Epigraphic Semitic Scripts." In *The World's Writing Systems*, edited by Peter T. Daniels and William Bright, 88–107. Oxford: Oxford University Press, 1996.

Ó Gráda, Cormac. *Jewish Ireland in the Age of Joyce: A Socioeconomic History*. Princeton, NJ: Princeton University Press, 2006.

Olson, Birger, and Magnus Zetterholm, eds. *The Ancient Synagogue from Its Origins until 200 C.E.* Stockholm: Almqvist & Wiksell International, 2003.

Oppenheimer, Aharon. *The am ha-aretz: A Study in the Social History of the Jewish People in the Hellenistic-Roman Period*. Leiden: Brill, 1977.

———. "The Uniqueness of the House of Study." *Cathedra* 18 (1981): 45–48.

———. "Babylonian Synagogues with Historical Associations." In *Ancient Synagogues: Historical Analysis and Archaeological Discovery*, edited by Dan Urman and Paul V. M. Flesher, vol. 1, 40–48. Leiden: Brill, 1998.

———. *Between Rome and Babylon*. Texts and Studies in Ancient Judaism, 108. Tübingen: Mohr Siebeck, 2005.

———. "Terumot and Ma'aserot." In *Encyclopaedia Judaica*, edited by Michael Berenbaum and Fred Skolnik, 2nd ed., vol. 19, 652–54. Detroit: Macmillan Reference USA, 2007.

Ovadiah, Asher. "Ancient Synagogues in Asia-Minor." In *Proceedings of the 10th International Congress of Classical Archaeology*, edited by Ekrem Akurgal, 857–66. Ankara: Turk Tarih Kurumu, 1978.

Ovrut, Barnett D. "Edward I and the Expulsion of the Jews." *Jewish Quarterly Review* 67, no. 4 (1977): 224–35.

Pakter, Walter. *Medieval Canon Law and the Jews*. Ebelsbach: Verlag Rolf Gremer, 1988.

Parkes, James W. *The Conflict of the Church and the Synagogue: A Study in the Origins of Antisemitism*. New York: Jewish Publication Society, 1934.

———. *The Jew in the Medieval Community: A Study of His Political and Economic Situation*. London: Soncino Press, 1938.

Pease, Steven L. *The Golden Age of Jewish Achievement*. Sonoma: Deucalion, 2009.

Perlow, Towa. *L'Education et l'Enseignement chez les Juifs a l'epoque talmudique*. Paris: E. Leroux, 1931.

Petrushevsky, Ilyia Pavlovich. "The Socio-Economic Condition of Iran under the Il-Khans." In *The Cambridge History of Iran*, vol. 5, *The Saljuq and Mongol Periods*, edited by J. A. Boyle, 483–537. Cambridge: Cambridge University Press, 1968.

Pezzolo, Luciano. "Government Debts and Credit Markets in Renaissance Italy." Manuscript, University of Venice, 2007.

Philippon, Thomas, and Ariell Reshef. "Wages and Human Capital in the U.S. Financial Industry: 1909–2006." NBER Working Paper No. 14644, 2009.

Philo. "On the Embassy to Gaius." In *Philo: Volume X*, translated by Francis H. Colson. Loeb Classical Library 379. Cambridge, MA: Harvard University Press, 1962.

Pini, Antonio Ivan. "Famiglie, insediamenti e banchi ebraici a Bologna e nel bolognese nella seconda metá del Trecento." *Quaderni Storici* 54, no. 3 (1983): 783–814.

Pirenne, Henry. *Mohammed and Charlemagne*. London: George Allen & Unwin, 1954.

Pisa, Franco. "Sulle attivitá bancarie locali nell'Italia dei secoli XIV–XVI." *Zakhor Rivista di storia degli ebrei in Italia* 1 (1997): 113–49.

Pullan, Brian. *Rich and Poor in Renaissance Venice: The Social Institutions of a Catholic State, to 1620*. Cambridge, MA: Harvard University Press, 1971.

———. "Jewish Moneylending in Venice: From Private Enterprise to Public Service." In *Gli ebrei e Venezia, secoli XIV–XVIII*, edited by Gaetano Cozzi, 671–86. Milan: Edizioni Comunitá, 1987.

Raphael, Chaim. *The Road from Babylon. The Story of Sephardi and Oriental Jews*. New York: Harper and Row, 1985.

Rapoport, Hillel, and Avi Weiss. "In-group Cooperation in a Hostile Environment: An Economic Perspective on Some Aspects of Jewish Life in (Premodern) Diaspora." In *Jewish Society and Culture: An Economic Perspective*, edited by Carmel Chiswick, Tikva Lecker, and Nava Kahana, 103–28. Ramat Gan: Bar-Ilan University Press, 2007.

Reed, Clyde G., and Cliff T. Bekar. "Religious Prohibitions against Usury." *Explorations in Economic History* 40, no. 4 (2003): 347–68.

Reich, Nathan. "The Economic Structure of Modern Jewry." In *The Jews: Their History, Culture, and Religion*, edited by Louis Finkelstein, 1239–67. Philadelphia: Harper and Brothers, 1949.

Reif, Stefan C. *A Jewish Archive from Old Cairo: The History of Cambridge University's Genizah Collection*. Richmond, UK: Curzon Press, 2000.

Reinhart, Carmen M., and Kenneth S. Rogoff. *This Time Is Different: Eight Centuries of Financial Folly*. Princeton, NJ: Princeton University Press, 2009.

Reis, Jaime. "Economic Growth, Human Capital Formation and Consumption in Western Europe Before 1800." In *Living Standards in the Past: New Perspectives on Well-Being in Asia and Europe*, edited by Robert C. Allen, Tommy Bengtsson, and Martin Dribe, 195–225. Oxford: Oxford University Press, 2004.

Richardson, Gary. "Guilds, Laws, and Markets for Manufactured Merchandise in Late-Medieval England." *Explorations in Economic History* 41, no. 1 (2004): 1–25.

Richman, Barak D. "How Community Institutions Create Economic Advantage: Jewish Diamond Merchants in New York." *Law and Social Inquiry* 31, no. 2 (2006): 383–420.

Ritte, U., E. Neufeld, M. Broit, D. Shavit, and U. Motra. "The Differences among Jewish Communities—Maternal and Paternal Contributions." *Journal of Molecular Evolution* 37, no. 4 (1993a): 435–40.

Ritte, U., E. Neufeld, M. Prager, M. Gross, I. Hakim, A. Khatib, and B. Bonné-Tamir. "Mitochondrial DNA Affinity of Several Jewish Communities." *Human Biology* 65, no. 3 (1993b): 359–85.

Roth, Cecil. *The Jewish Contribution to Civilization.* London: Macmillan, 1938.

———. *The History of the Jews of Italy.* Philadelphia: Jewish Publication Society of America, 1946.

———. "The European Age in Jewish History." In *The Jews: Their History, Culture, and Religion,* edited by Louis Finkelstein, 216–49. Philadelphia: Harper and Brothers, 1960a.

———. "The Jews of Western Europe (from 1648)." In *The Jews: Their History, Culture, and Religion,* edited by Louis Finkelstein, 250–86. Philadelphia: Harper and Brothers, 1960b.

———. *A History of the Jews in England.* Oxford: Clarendon Press, 1964.

———. "Economic Life and Population Movements." In *The Dark Ages: Jews in Christian Europe, 711–1096,* edited by Cecil Roth and I. H. Levine, 13–48. New Brunswick, NJ: Rutgers University Press, 1966a.

———. "Italy." In *The Dark Ages: Jews in Christian Europe, 711–1096,* edited by Cecil Roth and I. H. Levine, 100–121. New Brunswick, NJ: Rutgers University Press, 1966b.

———. "Benjamin (ben Jonah) of Tudela." In *Encyclopaedia Judaica,* edited by Michael Berenbaum and Fred Skolnik, 2nd ed., vol. 3, 362–64. Detroit: Macmillan Reference USA, 2007.

Roth, Cecil, Ernest Krausz, David Cesarani, Arthur Lourie, Vivian David Lipman, and David Ceserani. "England." In *Encyclopaedia Judaica,* edited by Michael Berenbaum and Fred Skolnik, 2nd ed., vol. 6, 410–32. Detroit: Macmillan Reference USA, 2007.

Rothkoff, Aaron, Avraham Grossman, Menahem Zevi Kaddari, Jona Fraenkel, Israel Moses Ta-Shma, and Judith R. Baskin. "Rashi." In *Encyclopaedia Judaica,* edited by Michael Berenbaum and Fred Skolnik, 2nd ed., vol. 17, 101–6. Detroit: Macmillan Reference USA, 2007.

Roy, A. D. "Some Thoughts on the Distribution of Earnings." *Oxford Economic Papers* 3 (1951): 135–46.

Ruderman, David B. *The World of a Renaissance Jew: The Life and Thought of Abraham b. Mordecai Farissol.* Cincinnati: Hebrew Union College Press, 1981.

Russell, Josiah C. "Late Ancient and Medieval Population." *Transactions of the American Philosophical Society* 48, no. 3 (1958): 1–152.

Rutgers, Leonard V. "Diaspora Synagogues: Synagogue Archaeology in the Greco-Roman World." In *Sacred Realm: The Emergence of the Synagogue in the Ancient World,* edited by Steven Fine, 67–95. New York: Oxford University Press, 1996.

Safrai, Shmuel. "Elementary Education: Its Religious and Social Significance in the Talmudic Period." *Cahiers d'Histoire Mondiale* 11, no. 1–2 (1968): 148–69.

———. "Education and the Study of the Torah." In *The Jewish People in the First Century: Historical Geography, Political History, Social, Cultural, and Religious Life and Institutions*, edited by Shmuel Safrai and Menahem Stern, vol. 2, 945–70. Assen: Van Gorcum, 1976a.

———. "The Era of the Mishna and Talmud." In *A History of the Jewish People*, edited by Haim Hillel Ben-Sasson, 307–82. Cambridge, MA: Harvard University Press, 1976b.

———. "Bet Hillel and Bet Shammai." In *Encyclopaedia Judaica*, edited by Michael Berenbaum and Fred Skolnik, 2nd ed., vol. 3, 530–33. Detroit: Macmillan Reference USA, 2007.

Safrai, Zeev. "Financing Synagogue Construction in the Period of the Mishna and the Talmud." In *Synagogues in Antiquity*, edited by Aryeh Kasher, Aharon Oppenheimer, and Uriel Rappaport, 77–96. Jerusalem: Yad Yitzhak Ben-Tzvi, 1987.

———. "Ancient Field Structures in Israel in the Roman Period." *Cathedra* 89 (1989): 7–40.

———. *The Economy of Roman Palestine*. London: Routledge, 1994.

———. "The Communal Functions of the Synagogue in the Land of Israel in the Rabbinic Period." In *Ancient Synagogues: Historical Analysis and Archaeological Discovery*, edited by Dan Urman and Paul V. M. Flesher, vol. 1, 181–204. Leiden: Brill, 1998.

Sand, Shlomo. *When and How Were the Jewish People Invented?* Tel Aviv: Resling, 2008.

Sanders, Ed P. *Paul and Palestinian Judaism: A Comparison of Patterns of Religion*. Philadelphia: Fortress Press, 1977.

———, ed. *Jewish and Christian Self-Definition*. Vol. 1, *The Shaping of Christianity in the Second and Third Centuries*. Philadelphia: Fortress Press, 1980.

———. *Judaism: Practice and Belief, 63 B.C.E.–66 C.E.* Philadelphia: Trinity Press International, 1992.

Sanders, Jack T. "Did Early Christianity Succeed because of Jewish Conversions?" *Social Compass* 46, no. 4 (1999): 493–505.

———. *Charisma, Converts, Competitors: Societal and Sociological Factors in the Success of Early Christianity*. London: SCM Press, 2000.

Sapir Abulafia, Anna. *Christian-Jewish Relations, 1000–1300: Jews in the Service of Medieval Christendom*. Harlow, UK: Pearson, 2011.

Sargent, Thomas J., and François R. Velde. *The Big Problem of Small Change*. Princeton, NJ: Princeton University Press, 2002.

Scheiber, Alexander. "The Early Jewish Settlement in Central and Eastern Europe: Hungary." In *The Dark Ages: Jews in Christian Europe, 711–1096*, edited by Cecil Roth and I. H. Levine, 313–18. New Brunswick: Rutgers University Press, 1966.

Schiffman, Lawrence H. *Who Was a Jew? Rabbinic and Halakhic Perspectives on the Jewish Christian Schism*. Hoboken, NJ: Ktav, 1985.

———. "The Early History of Public Reading of the Torah." In *Jews, Christians, and Polytheists in the Ancient Synagogue; Cultural Interaction During the Greco-Roman Period*, edited by Steven Fine, 44–56. London: Routledge, 1999.

———. *Understanding Second Temple and Rabbinic Judaism*. Jersey City, NJ: Ktav, 2003.

Schoeps, Hans-Joachim. *Jewish Christianity: Factional Disputes in the Early Church*. Philadelphia: Fortress Press, 1969.

Schulman, Alan Richard, Sharon Keller, Evasio de Marcellis, Eliyahu Ashtor, Hayyim J. Cohen, and Jacob M. Landau. "Egypt." In *Encyclopaedia Judaica*, edited by Michael Berenbaum and Fred Skolnik, 2nd ed., vol. 6, 222–36. Detroit: Macmillan Reference USA, 2007.

Schwartz, Daniel R. *Studies in the Jewish Background of Christianity*. Tübingen: Mohr Siebeck, 1992.

Schwartz, Joshua. "The Material Realities of Jewish Life in the Land of Israel, c. 235–638." In *The Cambridge History of Judaism*. Vol. 4, *The Late Roman-Rabbinic Period*, edited by Steven T. Katz, 431–56. New York: Cambridge University Press, 2006.

Schwartz, Seth. *Josephus and Judean Politics*. Leiden: Brill, 1990.

———. *Imperialism and Jewish Society, 200 B.C.E. to 640 C.E.* Princeton, NJ: Princeton University Press, 2001.

———. "Political, Social, and Economic Life in the Land of Israel, 66–c. 235." In *The Cambridge History of Judaism*. Vol. 4, *The Late Roman-Rabbinic Period*, edited by Steven T. Katz, 23–52. New York: Cambridge University Press, 2006.

Schwarzfuchs, Simon. "France and Germany under the Carolingians." In *The Dark Ages: Jews in Christian Europe, 711–1096*, edited by Cecil Roth and I. H. Levine, 122–42. New Brunswick, NJ: Rutgers University Press, 1966a.

———. "France under the Early Capets." In *The Dark Ages: Jews in Christian Europe, 711–1096*, edited by Cecil Roth and I. H. Levine, 143–61. New Brunswick, NJ: Rutgers University Press, 1966b.

Segal, Eli. "Talmud." In *New Twentieth Century Encyclopedia of Religious Knowledge*, edited by James D. Douglas, 807–8. 2nd ed. Grand Rapids: Baker Book House, 1991.

Segre, Renata, ed. *The Jews in Piedmont, 1297–1798*. Jerusalem: Israel Academy of Sciences and Humanities, 1986–1990.

Sharf, Andrew. "The Jews in Byzantium." In *The Dark Ages: Jews in Christian Europe, 711–1096*, edited by Cecil Roth and I. H. Levine, 49–68. New Brunswick, NJ: Rutgers University Press, 1966.

———. *Byzantine Jewry: From Justinian to the Fourth Crusade*. London: Routledge & K. Paul, 1971.

Shatzmiller, Joseph. *Shylock Reconsidered: Jews, Moneylending, and Medieval Society*. Berkeley: University of California Press, 1990.

Shmueli, Efraim. "The 'Pariah-People' and Its 'Charismatic Leadership': A Revaluation of Max Weber's 'Ancient Judaism.'" *Proceedings of the American Academy for Jewish Research* 36 (1968): 167–247.

Simonsohn, Shlomo. *History of the Jews in the Duchy of Mantua*, 2 vols. Jerusalem: National Academy of Sciences, 1977.

———. *The Jews in the Duchy of Milan*, 4 vols. Jerusalem: National Academy of Sciences, 1982–1986.

———. *The Apostolic See and the Jews*. 8 vols. Toronto: Pontifical Institute of Mediaeval Studies, 1988–1991.

———. *The Jews in Sicily*. 18 vols. Leiden: Brill, 1997–2010.

———. *Between Scylla and Charybdis: The Jews in Sicily*. Leiden: Brill, 2011.

Singer, Sholom A. "The Expulsion of the Jews from England in 1290." *Jewish Quarterly Review* 55, no. 2 (1964): 117–36.

Slezkine, Yuri. *The Jewish Century*. Princeton, NJ: Princeton University Press, 2004.

Smallwood, E. Mary. *The Jews under Roman Rule: From Pompey to Diocletian; A Study in Political Relations*. Leiden: Brill, 1981.

Soloveitchik, Haym. *Pawnbroking: A Study in the Inter-Relationship between Halakhah, Economic Activity, and Communal Self Image*. Jerusalem: Hebrew University, 1985 (in Hebrew).

———. *Principles and Pressures: Jewish Trade in Gentile Wine in the Middle Ages*. Tel Aviv: Am Oved, 2003 (in Hebrew).

———. "The Jewish Attitude in the High and Late Middle Ages." In *Credito e usura fra teologia, diritto e amministrazione: Linguaggi a confronto, sec. XII–XVI*, edited by Diego Quaglioni, Giacomo Todeschini, and Gian Maria Varanini, 115–27. Rome: École française de Rome, 2005.

Sombart, Werner. *The Jews and Modern Capitalism*. London: T. F. Unwin, 1913 (first edition 1911 in German).

Sperber, Daniel. "Costs of Living in Roman Palestine." *Journal of the Economic and Social History of the Orient* 8, no. 3 (1965): 248–71.

———. "Costs of Living in Roman Palestine." *Journal of the Economic and Social History of the Orient* 9, no. 3 (1966): 182–211.

———. "Costs of Living in Roman Palestine." *Journal of the Economic and Social History of the Orient* 11, no. 1–3 (1968): 233–74.

———. "Costs of Living in Roman Palestine." *Journal of the Economic and Social History of the Orient* 13, no. 1–3 (1970): 1–15.

———. *Roman Palestine, 200–400: The Land; Crisis and Change in Agrarian Society as Reflected in Rabbinic Sources*. Ramat-Gan: Bar-Ilan University, 1978.

Spufford, Peter. *Money and Its Use in Medieval Europe*. New York: Cambridge University Press, 1988.

Stark, Rodney. "Jewish Conversion and the Rise of Christianity: Rethinking the Received Wisdom." In *Society of Biblical Literature Seminar Papers*, edited by Kent Harold Richards, 314–29. Atlanta: Scholars Press, 1986.

———. *The Rise of Christianity: A Sociologist Reconsiders History*. Princeton, NJ: Princeton University Press, 1996.

Stein, Siegfried. "The Development of the Jewish Law of Interest from the Biblical Period to the Expulsion from England." *Historia Judaica* 17 (1955): 3–40.

———. "Moneylending." In *Encyclopaedia Judaica*, edited by Michael Berenbaum and Fred Skolnik, 2nd ed., vol. 14, 436–43. Detroit: Macmillan Reference USA, 2007.

Stemberger, Günter. *Jews and Christians in the Holy Land: Palestine in the Fourth Century*. Translated by Ruth Tuschling. Edinburgh: T. & T. Clark, 2000.

Stern, Ephraim, ed. *The New Encyclopedia of Archaeological Excavations in the Holy Land*. 4 vols. New York: Simon & Schuster, 1993.

Stern, Menahem. "The Jewish Diaspora." In *The Jewish People in the First Century: Historical Geography, Political History, Social, Cultural, and Religious Life and Institutions*, edited by Shmuel Safrai and Menahem Stern, vol. 1, 117–83. Assen: Van Gorcum, 1974.

———. "The Period of the Second Temple." In *A History of the Jewish People*, edited by Haim Hillel Ben-Sasson, 185–303. Cambridge, MA: Harvard University Press, 1976.

Stevenson, James. *A New Eusebius: Documents Illustrative of the History of the Church to A.D. 337*. Revised edition with additional documents by William H. C. Frend. London: Society for Promoting Christian Knowledge, 1987.

Stigler, George J., and Gary S. Becker. "De Gustibus Non Est Disputandum." *American Economic Review* 67, no. 2 (1977): 76–90.

Stiglitz, Joseph E. "Information and the Change in the Paradigm in Economics." *American Economic Review* 92, no. 3 (2002): 460–501.

Stillman, Norman A. "The Jews in the Medieval Islamic City." In *The Jews of Medieval Islam. Community, Society, and Identity*, edited by Daniel Frank, 3–13. Leiden: Brill, 1995.

Stow, Kenneth R. "Papal and Royal Attitudes toward Jewish Lending in the Thirteenth Century." *Association for Jewish Studies Review* 6 (1981): 161–84.

———. *Alienated Minority: The Jews of Medieval Latin Europe*. Cambridge, MA: Harvard University Press, 1992.

———. *The Jews in Rome*. 2 vols. Leiden: Brill, 1995–1997.

———. "The Church and the Jews: St. Paul to Pius IX." In *Popes, Church, and Jews in the Middle Ages*, edited by Kenneth R. Stow, 1–69. Burlington, VT: Ashgate, 2007.

Stroumsa, Sarah. *Maimonides in His World: Portrait of a Mediterranean Thinker*. Princeton, NJ: Princeton University Press, 2009.

Swift, Fletcher H. *Education in Ancient Israel from Earliest Times to 70 CE*. London: Open Court, 1919.

Tabellini, Guido. "Institutions and Culture." *Journal of the European Economic Association* 6, no. 2–3 (2008): 255–94.

———. "Culture and Institutions: Economic Development in the Regions of Europe." *Journal of the European Economic Association* 8, no. 4 (2010): 677–716.

Tadmor, Hayim. "The Period of the First Temple, the Babylonian Exile and the Restoration." In *A History of the Jewish People*, edited by Haim Hillel Ben-Sasson, 91–182. Cambridge, MA: Harvard University Press, 1976.

Taitz, Emily. *The Jews of Medieval France: The Community of Champagne*. Westport, CT: Greenwood Press, 1994.

Tcherikover, Victor. *The Jews in Egypt in the Hellenistic-Roman Age in the Light of the Papyri*. Jerusalem: Hebrew University Press, 1945.

———. *Hellenistic Civilization and the Jews*. Philadelphia: Jewish Publication Society of America, 1961.

Temin, Peter. "Is It Kosher to Talk about Culture?" *Journal of Economic History* 57, no. 2 (1997): 267–87.

Theissen, Gerd. *Social Reality and the Early Christians: Theology, Ethics, and the World of the New Testament*. Minneapolis: Fortress Press, 1992.

Tirole, Jean. "Illiquidity and All Its Friends." *Journal of Economic Literature* 49, no. 2 (2011): 287–325.

Toaff, Ariel. *Gli ebrei a Perugia*. Perugia: Deputazione di Storia Patria, 1975.

———. *The Jews in Umbria*. 3 vols. Leiden: Brill, 1992–1994.

Toch, Michael. "The Economic Activity of German Jews in the 10th–12th Centuries: Between Historiography and History." In *Facing the Cross: The Persecutions of 1096 in History and Historiography*, edited by Yom Tov Assis, Jeremy Cohen, Aaron Kedar, Ora Limor, and Michael Toch, 32–54. Jerusalem: Hebrew University Magnes Press, 2000a (in Hebrew).

———. "Jews and Commerce: Modern Fancies and Medieval Realities." In *Il ruolo economico delle minoranze in Europa, Secc. XIII–XVIII (Atti della XXXI Settimana di Studi, Istituto Francesco Datini, Prato)*, edited by Simonetta Cavaciocchi, 43–58. Florence: Le Monnier, 2000b.

———. *Peasants and Jews in Medieval Germany: Studies in Cultural, Social and Economic History*. Burlington, VT: Ashgate, 2003.

———. "The Jews in Europe, 500–1050." In *The New Cambridge Medieval History*, edited by Paul Fouracre, vol. 1, 547–70, 872–78. Cambridge: Cambridge University Press, 2005.

———. "Economic Activities of German Jews in the Middle Ages." In *Wirtschaftsgeschichte der mittelalterlichen Juden: Fragen und Einschtzungen*, edited by Michael Toch, 181–210. Munich: Oldebourg, 2008.

———. "Jewish Peasants in the Middle Ages? Agriculture and Jewish Landownership in 8th to 12th Century Europe." *Zion* 75 (2010): 291–312.

———. "Commerce: Medieval and Early Modern Europe." In *The Cambridge Dictionary of Judaism and Jewish Culture*, edited by Judith R. Baskin, 110–11. Cambridge: Cambridge University Press, 2011.

———. *The Economic History of Medieval European Jews*. Vol. 1, *Late Antiquity and Early Middle Ages*. Leiden: Brill, 2012.

Todeschini, Giacomo. *La ricchezza degli ebrei: Merci e denaro nella riflessione ebraica e nella definizione cristiana dell'usura alla fine del Medioevo*. Spoleto: Centro italiano di studi sull'Alto Medioevo, 1989.

———. "Christian Perceptions of Jewish Economic Activity in the Middle Ages." In *Wirtschaftsgeschichte der mittelalterlichen Juden: Fragen und Einschtzungen*, edited by Michael Toch, 1–16. Munich: Oldenbourg, 2008.

Trivellato, Francesca. *The Familiarity of Strangers: The Sephardic Diaspora, Livorno, and Cross-Cultural Trade in the Early Modern Period*. New Haven, CT: Yale University Press, 2009.

Udovitch, Abraham L., ed. *The Islamic Middle East, 700–1900: Studies in Economic and Social History*. Princeton, NJ: Darwin Press, 1981.

Urman, Dan. "The Synagogue and the House of Study (Beth ha-Midrash)—Are They One and the Same?" In *Ancient Synagogues: Historical Analysis and Archaeological Discovery*, edited by Dan Urman and Paul V. M. Flesher, vol. 1, 232–55. Leiden: Brill, 1998.

Urman, Dan, and Paul V. M. Flesher, eds. *Ancient Synagogues: Historical Analysis and Archaeological Discovery*. 2 vols. Leiden: Brill, 1998.

van Zanden, Jan Luiten. "The Skill Premium and the 'Great Divergence.'" *European Review of Economic History* 13, no. 1 (2009): 121–53.

Veblen, Thorstein. "The Intellectual Pre-Eminence of Jews in Modern Europe." *Political Science Quarterly* 34, no. 1 (1919): 33–42.

Wald, Stephen G. "Judah HaNasi." In *Encyclopaedia Judaica*, edited by Michael Berenbaum and Fred Skolnik, 2nd ed., vol. 11, 501–5. Detroit: Macmillan Reference USA, 2007a.

———. "Tosefta." In *Encyclopaedia Judaica*, edited by Michael Berenbaum and Fred Skolnik, 2nd ed., vol. 20, 70–72. Detroit: Macmillan Reference USA, 2007b.

Watson, Andrew M. "The Arab Agricultural Revolution and Its Diffusion, 700–1100." *Journal of Economic History* 34, no. 1 (1974): 8–35.

————. "A Medieval Green Revolution: New Crops and Farming Techniques in the Early Islamic World." In *The Islamic Middle East, 700–1900: Studies in Economic and Social History*, edited by Abraham L. Udovitch, 29–58. Princeton, NJ: Darwin Press, 1981.

Weber, Max. *The Protestant Ethic and the Spirit of Capitalism*. Translated by Talcott Parsons. New York: Scribner, 1930 (first edition 1904–1905 in German).

————. *Ancient Judaism*. Translated and edited by Hans H. Gerth and Don Martindale. Glencoe, IL: Free Press, 1952 (first edition 1917 in German).

————. *Essays in Sociology*. Translated, edited, and with an introduction by Hans Heinrich Gerth and Charles Wright Mills. New York: Oxford University Press, 1980 (first edition 1915 in German).

White, K. D. *Roman Farming*. Ithaca, NY: Cornell University Press, 1970.

Wolfson, Harry A. *Philo: Foundations of Religious Philosophy in Judaism, Christianity, and Islam*. 2 vols. Cambridge, MA: Harvard University Press, 1947.

Zeitlin, Solomon. *The Rise and Fall of the Judaean State: A Political, Social, and Religious History of the Second Commonwealth (66 CE –120 CE)*, vol. 3. Philadelphia: Jewish Publication Society of America, 1978.

Zetterholm, Magnus. *The Formation of Christianity in Antioch: A Social-Scientific Approach to the Separation between Judaism and Christianity*. London: Routledge, 2003.

Index

The letter *n* following a page number indicates a note on that page. The figure following the *n* indicates the number of the note if there is more than one on the page. Italic type indicates a figure, map, or table on that page.

THE PRINCETON ECONOMIC HISTORY
OF THE WESTERN WORLD

Joel Mokyr, Series Editor

CPSIA information can be obtained
at www.ICGtesting.com
Printed in the USA
BVHW040916101022
649064BV00010B/306